Communication of Social Support

Communication of Social Support

Messages, Interactions, Relationships, and Community

edited by

Brant R. Burleson
Terrance L. Albrecht
Irwin G. Sarason

SAGE Publications
International Educational and Professional Publisher
Thousand Oaks   London   New Delhi

For information address:

 SAGE Publications, Inc.
2455 Teller Road
Thousand Oaks, California 91320

SAGE Publications Ltd.
6 Bonhill Street
London EC2A 4PU
United Kingdom

SAGE Publications India Pvt. Ltd.
M-32 Market
Greater Kailash I
New Delhi 110 048 India

Printed in the United States of America

Library of Congress Cataloging-in-Publication Data

Main entry under title:

Communication of social support: messages, interactions,
    relationships, and community / edited by Brant R. Burleson, Terrance L.
Albrecht, Irwin G. Sarason.
        p. cm.
    Includes bibliographical references and index.
    ISBN 0-8039-4350-4. — ISBN 0-8039-4351-2 (pbk.)
    1. Social networks. 2. Social interaction. 3. Interpersonal
communication. 4. Interpersonal relations. I. Burleson, Brant
Raney, 1952-   . II. Albrecht, Terrance L. III. Sarason, Irwin G.
HM131.C74283 1994
    302—dc20   93-40639
94 95 96 97 10 9 8 7 6 5 4 3 2 1

Sage Production Editor: Diane S. Foster

Contents

Part II: Characteristics of Supportive Interactions

Part III: Characteristics of Supportive Relationships

Preface

This book represents an interdisciplinary effort to provide a close examination of the communication of social support. The editors of this book come from the disciplines of communication (Burleson, Albrecht) and psychology (Sarason), and the contributors represent several branches of both of these disciplines (interpersonal communication, health communication, organizational communication, social psychology, clinical psychology, community psychology). Regardless of disciplinary backgrounds and affiliations, all share an interest in illuminating "the communication of social support"—a phrase referencing both the activities through which support is communicated and the substance of supportive communications. We believe the mix of contributors and perspectives results in uniquely insightful explorations of both the process and content of supportive communication, as conveyed both verbally and nonverbally, in a diversity of social relationships (friends, coworkers, spouses, parents-children) and contexts (home, work, school).

This book had its genesis in the development of a special issue on communication and social support that the three of us guest-edited for *Communication Research* (vol. 19, April 1992). Several of the chapters in this book began as shorter articles appearing in that issue, and several of the contributors to this volume served as referees for submissions to that special issue. We are indebted to Peter Monge, then editor of *CR*, for his scholarly vision, his strong support of the special issue, and his encouragement to pursue this book as a second stage of the project. We also want to thank the contributors to this volume for their excellent work, their tenacity, and their patience. Finally, Brant Burleson would like to acknowledge Daena Goldsmith and Sandra Metts for contributing in especially important ways to his understanding of communication and social support, and Kathy Rowan for her many communications supporting his work on this project.

BRANT R. BURLESON
TERRANCE L. ALBRECHT
IRWIN G. SARASON

Introduction

The Communication of Social Support

BRANT R. BURLESON

TERRANCE L. ALBRECHT

DAENA J. GOLDSMITH

IRWIN G. SARASON

In the state of nature, nobody cares about other people. Fortunately, we do not live in this dismal state. (Elster, 1990, p. 44)

Elster's comment probably would be more appropriate if it were worded: "It is *usually* fortunate *when* we do not live in this dismal state." The presence of caring relationships and the experience of social support indisputably contribute to the quality of a person's life. People know this to be true intuitively. And for the last 20 years, scientists have been exploring in fascinating empirical detail the effects of caring, helping, and social support on individual well-being. Supportive, prosocial behavior received from friends, kin, acquaintances, work associates, and even strangers has remarkable effects, both direct and indirect, on physiology, cognition, and emotion. Paradoxically, "supportive" behaviors can also have negative effects on the health and well-being of both their providers and their recipients.

Social support has been defined in multiple ways. Most early definitions referred to an emotional caring dimension. For example, Moss (1973) defined support as "the subjective feeling of belonging, of being accepted or being loved, of being needed all for oneself and for what one can do" (p. 237). Cobb (1976) equated the term with being esteemed and valued, of belonging "to a network of communication and mutual obligation" (p. 300). Increasingly, scholars have come to conceptualize the process of supporting others as an interactional or communicative process occurring between people.

In this "Introduction," we attempt to further the case for examining social support as a form of interaction or communication. We do so by first reviewing some of the powerful social and theoretical concerns that motivate the study of supportive actions. Next, we sketch some of the major approaches that have informed the study of social support, describing how the conception of support as communication has emerged in recent years. Finally, we overview the chapters in this book, showing how the study of supportive messages, interactions, and relationships helps illuminate the fine structure of this interesting and complex behavior.

Imperatives for the Study of Social Support

The study of social support received its initial impetus from epidemiological studies (e.g., Cassel, 1976) suggesting that social ties had significant effects on health and well-being. However, we see at least three major reasons or imperatives that currently motivate the study of social support. These include practical reasons or a *pragmatic imperative*, scientific reasons or a *theoretical imperative*, and ethical reasons or a *moral imperative*.

THE PRAGMATIC IMPERATIVE

A massive body of research findings has accumulated over the past two decades on the role of social support in health and well-being. The empirically demonstrated link between social support and health constitutes a compelling justification for continued efforts in this area of study.

Many studies have shown direct and indirect links between support behaviors and perceptions and emotional and physical health (see the reviews by Cohen & Wills, 1985; Hobfoll & Stephens, 1990). Among other relevant findings, research has found causal and correlational ties between indices of support and (a) disease etiology, life expectancy, and immune system functioning (Kennedy, Kiecolt-Glaser, & Glaser, 1990; Wortman, 1984); (b) recovery from illness and the ability to adjust and cope with extreme stress and loss (e.g., Hobfoll & Stephens, 1990); (c) effective role and life transition (Hirsch, 1980); (d) job performance, work innovation, and trust levels between persons in mixed status relationships (e.g., Albrecht & Hall, 1991); and (e) improved performance on academic tasks and exams (Goldsmith & Albrecht, 1993; I. Sarason & Sarason, 1986).

Yet, the negative effects of supportive encounters are also a reality and thus demand study. There is evidence that some forms of support can create dependencies that delay recovery from strokes (McLeroy, DeVellis, DeVellis, Kaplan, & Toole, 1984). Support from certain individuals or groups can exacerbate health problems (Kaplan & Toshima, 1990) and reinforce negative self-images (Swann & Brown, 1990). Well-intended supportive messages can, at times, intensify feelings of uncertainty (Goldsmith, 1992; Peters-Golden, 1982), and some supportive interactions drain providers of important personal resources (Belle, 1982; Hobfoll & Stephens, 1990).

In short, supportive communication can contribute (positively and negatively) to how well people recover from illness, cope with loss or transition, manage chronic health conditions, deal with everyday upsets and disruptions, perform on a variety of tasks, and generally feel about themselves and their quality of life. Clearly, there is ample pragmatic warrant for the continued study of social support, particularly how it is transacted and how these transactions produce health-related outcomes.

THE THEORETICAL IMPERATIVE

Regardless of its health-related outcomes, social support is a fundamental form of human interaction, as basic and pervasive as interactions intended to influence or inform (Burleson, Albrecht, & Goldsmith, 1993). As such, social support plays a crucial role in the formation and development of interpersonal relationships. Research primarily concerned with how supportive interactions contribute to the formation and maintenance of relationships reflects what we term a *theoretical imperative* for the study of support.

The interest in how social support contributes to the formation and development of relationships has emerged relatively recently with current research focusing on how relationships, especially important personal relationships, are the *product or outgrowth* of supportive interactions (e.g., Barbee, 1990; Burleson, 1990). For example, supportive interactions lie at the heart of healthy family life (Eggert, 1987; Malson, 1983). Indeed, it is the lack of supportive interactions (or the presence of support pathologies) tends to mark a family as abusive or dysfunctional (see Hansson, Jones, & Fletcher, 1990).

Our most important voluntary relationships (friendships, romantic relationships) are often the direct outgrowth of supportive interactions (Adelman, Parks, & Albrecht, 1987; Argyle & Henderson, 1985; Rawlins, 1992). Supportive actions indicate liking, caring, and concern for their recipient; signal interest; and tacitly send a message that the provider regards the recipient as special and important. Feelings of warmth, gratitude, and affection often result from supportive actions; these become powerful forces driving relationship development (Goldsmith & Parks, 1990). Further, there is growing appreciation that supportive interactions play a critical role in the formation of amicable and productive work relationships (Albrecht & Hall, 1991; Ray, 1987, 1993).

In sum, research flowing from a theoretical imperative is chiefly interested in providing systematic accounts for fundamental social processes associated with interpersonal relationships. Supportive interactions are a basic form of human behavior and thus have profound implications for the formation and development of social and personal relationships.

THE MORAL IMPERATIVE

If supportive actions are viewed as flowing from altruistic impulses (Barbee, 1990; Elster, 1990), then social support clearly has moral foundation. Supportive actions frequently display the highest expressions of the human spirit: altruism, charity, help, caring, rescuing, kindness, comfort, and love. Even "supportive" actions stemming from nonaltruistic motives—those performed out of obligation or in an effort to foster dependency—have moral and ethical overtones. Thus, a final reason for studying social support stems from a *moral imperative*: Social support is moral (or morally relevant) conduct, and by studying it we better acquaint ourselves with the nature and practice of virtue. When we study supportive acts—whether it is a child giving a cookie to a distressed friend or an adult risking his or her life to rescue a persecuted stranger—we learn something about the nature (and limits) of human goodness. The study of social support can edify and uplift. It can furnish moral instruction.

The moral imperative is unabashedly nonscientific. The aim here is not to understand social support so as to improve health or explain patterns of relationship formation and development. Rather, the aim is to explore the character of moral action, to develop notions about right conduct, and to gain a better sense of community and the good life. The study of moral conduct needs no pragmatic or theoretical justification. If the practice of virtue is its own reward, then so, surely, is its study.

Approaches to the Study of Social Support

Three general approaches have informed much of the empirical work on social support completed in the last 20 years. These include *sociological* or social network approaches, *psychological* or perceptual approaches, and *communicative* or interactional approaches. These three approaches have emerged sequentially, with the sociological perspective being the earliest and the communicative the most recent. Thus the current call for research on the processes through which social support is conveyed or communicated in face-to-face interactions represents an evolution of interest in the community of social support researchers.

SOCIAL NETWORK APPROACHES

Early research on social support and health was dominated by social network methods (e.g., Berkman & Smye, 1979; Hirsch, 1980; House, Robbins, & Metzner, 1982). These methods were viewed as appropriate since research initially seemed to suggest that it was the mere existence of social ties, or the existence of ties of a certain sort, that resulted in improved or protected health. Thus research focused on how the size, density, multiplexity, and other features of an individual's social network correlated with varied indices of health and well-being (see Gottlieb, 1981). The research thus tended to exhibit a sociological focus, concentrating on how the existence of objective social ties influenced health-related outcomes.

Network studies of social support have been subjected to several significant criticisms. First, there is increasing evidence that structural characteristics of social networks are only weakly associated both with the availability or adequacy of support and with health-related outcomes (Sarason, Sarason, & Pierce, 1990; Seeman & Berkman, 1988). Second, researchers have increasingly recognized that not all social ties are health promoting. Many social ties are source of stress, while others are sources of both stress and support (Rook, 1984; Rook & Pietromonaco, 1987; Sandler & Barrera, 1984). This recognition highlights the need to consider the *quality* and *meaning* of social relationships, in addition to their quantity and structure. Third, several studies (e.g., Antonucci & Israel, 1986; Sarason, Shearin, Pierce, & Sarason, 1987; Wethington & Kessler, 1986) have concluded that health outcomes are best predicted by an individual's perceptions of the quality and availability of support, not structural features of social networks. These latter findings served as an impetus for psychological approaches to the study of social support.

PSYCHOLOGICAL APPROACHES

The psychological perspective emphasizes the individual's *subjective sense of being supported* or perceptions of support availability and satisfaction (see Sarason, Pierce, & Sarason, 1990). Initially, research stemming from the psychological perspective focused on how the quality of the individual's social relationships influenced his or her sense of support and, subsequently, indices of health and well-being (e.g., Sandler & Lakey, 1982; Wethington & Kessler, 1986). More recently, the sense of support has been conceptualized as a relatively stable personality characteristic, having its genesis in attachment experiences early in life (Sarason et al., 1990). Increasing evidence indicates that this stable sense of support is an important buffer against stress and health problems (see Pierce, Sarason, & Sarason, 1990).

Although the psychological perspective has contributed a great deal to our understanding of social support and its effects, there are limits to this approach. Several theorists (Dunkel-Schetter & Bennett, 1990; Kessler, Price, & Wortman, 1985) have pointed out that relationships themselves are not directly supportive (or unsupportive). Rather, it is specific *actions* that relationship partners carry out on behalf of each other that provide support (see Burleson, 1990; Thoits, 1985). This highlights an important shortcoming of the psychological perspective, for as Gottlieb (1985) argues, this perspective does not "gauge actual or experienced support that is expressed in ongoing social interactions," but rather taps a "cognitive representation of the phenomenon whose correspondence with social reality is uncertain" (p. 356). Thus, as Hobfoll and Stokes (1988) suggest, research is needed that focuses attention on "the actual building of supportive ties, seeking and obtaining aid, and behavioral, cognitive, and emotional reactions to that aid, as well as thoughts, emotions, and behaviors that mediate such reactions" (pp. 497-498). In other words, what's needed is research providing detailed examinations of the communicative and interactional processes through which social support is solicited and conveyed.

COMMUNICATION AND
INTERACTIONAL APPROACHES

In the last half-dozen years, an increasing number of scholars have initiated programs of research focused on examining social support as interactions or exchanges that frequently occur in the context of enduring relationships (Albrecht & Adelman, 1987; Albrecht, Burleson, & Sarason, 1992; Duck with Silver, 1990; Sarason, Sarason, & Pierce, 1990). A central interest of this research has been with understanding how and why "a 'provider' attempts to proffer support and a 'recipient' may be helped or benefited by the attempt" (Dunkel-Schetter & Skokan, 1990, p. 437). Conceptualizing social support as communication can advance this interest by providing heuristics for developing and organizing questions about inputs into, the occurrence of, and outcomes of supportive interactions (see Burleson et al., 1993). There are also several more specific advantages to viewing social support as a form of communication.

First, although some approaches to social support do not directly feature communication, communication remains a central (if implicit) mechanism through which support is conveyed. For example, although communication is not directly examined in sociological or network approaches to social support, it is assumed in several ways: the relationships examined in this research are created through communication, they must be maintained through communication, and most explanations of why extensive social ties contribute to health assume that information is transmitted through the medium of communication.

Second, regardless of whether the "subjective sense of support" featured by the psychological perspective is viewed as an enduring personality characteristic or a situationally specific state, communication processes contribute to its development. If the sense of support is viewed as an individual-difference variable taking shape early in life, inquiry may focus on patterns of nurturant parental communication that contribute to (or undermine) stable, secure attachment (e.g., Applegate, Burleson, & Delia, 1992; Sarason, Pierce, Shearin, Sarason, Waltz, & Poppe, 1991). And if the sense of support is viewed as situationally specific, then it is especially important to examine how this context-specific state is created by messages and interactional behaviors occurring over the course of a social episode (Cutrona & Suhr, 1992; Dunkel-Schetter & Bennett, 1990).

Third, studying how support is communicated will help generate a basis for advising people about how to be more supportive. The pragmatic benefits of social support warrant developing prescriptive knowledge about how support can be enacted most effectively. Because much support is accomplished through interaction, how support is communicated must be studied if researchers are to provide useful instruction to those interested in behaving more supportively.

In sum, social support should be studied as communication because it is ultimately conveyed through messages directed by one individual to another in the context of a relationship that is created and sustained through interaction. What does it mean to study support as communication? For us, it means studying the *messages* through which people both seek and express support; studying the *interactions* in which supportive messages are produced and interpreted; and studying the *relationships* that are created by and contextualize the supportive interactions in which people engage. We next overview how the contributions to this book examine supportive messages, interactions, and relationships.

Communicating Social Support
Through Messages, Interactions, and Relationships

CHARACTERISTICS OF SUPPORTIVE MESSAGES

The chapters composing Part I provide a detailed look at the messages people produce when seeking to provide social support. Thus far, only limited research has examined specific features of the messages through which people attempt to express different forms of support. Significantly, several studies (e.g., Dakof & Taylor, 1990; Wortman & Lehman, 1985) indicate that not all efforts to provide support are equally successful. Moreover, the intention to provide support does not always result in a sophisticated, sensitive message being produced (e.g., Lehman, Ellard, & Wortman, 1986; Lehman & Hemphill, 1990). These findings highlight the need for theories of message design and message effects that explain the characteristics and impacts of different messages. They also emphasize the need for detailed descriptions of the verbal and nonverbal behaviors comprising more and less supportive messages. Conceptualizing social support as communication may advance our understanding of supportive and unsupportive messages by providing tools for message description and analysis.

The chapter by Burleson examines features and effects of the messages people use when attempting to comfort others experiencing emotional upsets arising from the hassles and disappointments of everyday life. Drawing from sociolinguistic and cognitive-developmental theories, Burleson describes a framework for distinguishing among more and less *sophisticated* comforting message strategies. Specifically, he suggests that sophisticated comforting strategies are those which acknowledge, elaborate, legitimize, and contextualize the feelings and perspective of a distressed other. Burleson also proposes a multidimensional approach to assessing message outcomes that emphasizes immediate and long-term message effects, as well as instrumental and interpersonal effects. Research is reviewed showing that more sophisticated comforting messages generally result in more desirable outcomes.

In Chapter 2, Goldsmith employs the politeness theory of Brown and Levinson (1987) as a framework for distinguishing among more and less competent support messages. Several writers (Albrecht & Adelman, 1987; Coyne, Ellard, & Smith, 1990; Goldsmith & Parks, 1990) have commented that producing supportive messages is a challenging and difficult task fraught with paradoxes and dilemmas. Supportive messages frequently address personal, emotional, and potentially stigmatizing topics that may engender discomfort for both parties. Goldsmith suggests that the desires for acceptance and autonomy inherent in all social interaction become especially salient in supportive interactions. Recipients of support risk looking weak to others, may have embarrassing information become known, and may incur feelings of obligation and debt. Providers risk appearing incompetent or uncaring if they proffer inappropriate or ineffective support. These threats to individual "face" introduce multiple goals in supportive interactions: Individuals must provide an appropriate form of support while also conveying acceptance and respect for one another. Goldsmith reports preliminary evidence showing that messages managing face concerns while providing support are perceived as more helpful and accepting.

In Chapter 3, Zimmermann and Applegate detail how aspects of Burleson's work on comforting, Goldsmith's research on facework, and ethnographic studies of storytelling can be elaborated to develop message-centered approaches to studying supportive communication in organizations. Most research on social support in formal organizations has employed either social network or self-report methods. Although valuable insights can be gleaned from these approaches, they do not permit fine-grained examinations of the messages and processes through which support gets communicated. In contrast, message-centered approaches provide particulars concerning what constitutes support for organization members, how support is communicated, and why supportive communication plays a role in organizational outcomes. Zimmermann and Applegate illustrate these claims with examples drawn from their study of comforting communication among coworkers in a stressful organizational environment, the hospice.

Much of the research on supportive communication has focused on messages people use when providing emotional support to an intimate. Balancing this emphasis, the chapter by Tardy reports a series of studies examining how messages expressing instrumental and/or emotional support affect performance on a stressful problem-solving task. Tardy reports that brief messages offering instrumental support significantly enhance performance on a cognitive task. Moreover, messages offering instrumental support are perceived not only as providing more help and assistance, but also as conveying as much concern as experimental messages designed to convey emotional support. These intriguing findings suggest that what counts as emotional support may vary as a function of the context. Clearly, the effects of a message depend not only on the elements composing it, but on the interactional context in which it is produced and interpreted—a point addressed in detail by several of the chapters in Part II.

CHARACTERISTICS OF
SUPPORTIVE INTERACTIONS

Isolated messages do not, of course, comprise the whole of social support. Rather, messages intended to provide support are produced in complex social episodes. Varied features of the support episode powerfully shape whether, how, and from whom support is solicited. Aspects of the episode also influence the kinds of support provided, the form and content of messages generated, and the effects of provided supports on both the recipient and the recipient-provider relationship.

The chapters in Part II explore multiple facets of supportive interactions and the contexts in which they occur. In Chapter 5, Sarason, Sarason, and Pierce overview an interactional-cognitive perspective to the study of support. This approach maintains that the understanding of supportive interactions requires descriptions of the situations in which support occurs (or fails to occur), assessment of how individuals interpret and provide support, and specification of the social relationship between the provider and recipient. Producing such descriptions demands a detailed analysis of situational, intrapersonal, and interpersonal factors in support episodes and how these factors interact with one another (see Pierce et al., 1990). In the current chapter, Sarason et al. extend their prior work by suggesting that both a *global* sense of support (beliefs about the general forthcomingness of the social environment) and the sense of support individuals get from particular relationships (*relationship-specific support*) contribute to health and well-being.

The notion that features of the context shape supportive interactions and the kinds of aid provided in those interactions has been a mainstay of social support theories for nearly 20 years (e.g., Cohen & McKay, 1984; Weiss, 1974). The idea that the type of support provided needs to be appropriate to the context and type of stress experienced has been most fully developed by Cutrona and her coworkers in their *optimal matching model* (Cutrona & Russell, 1990; Cutrona & Suhr, 1992; Cutrona, Suhr, & MacFarlane, 1990). Early versions of this model maintained that the victim's capacity to control the stressor determined the kind of support helpers should provide: Stressors under victim control call for action-facilitating support (informational support and tangible aid), which equip the victim to manage the stressor, whereas stressors beyond victim control call for nurturant support (emotional and network support), which facilitate adjustment to the stressful situation. In Chapter 6, Cutrona and Suhr present a revised version of the optimal matching model, which maintains that characteristics of the *relationship* between the stress victim and the support provider must be considered (in addition to characteristics of the stressor) when attempting to identify the most beneficial type of social support. Cutrona and Suhr describe two studies that, although providing some evidence for the revised optimal matching model, suggest still further revisions in the model are needed to account more adequately for the effect of contextual factors. For example, Cutrona and Suhr found some interesting, but unexpected, gender differences in patterns of supportive behavior.

The effects of gender on social support is an important but understudied area. In Chapter 7, Derlega, Barbee, and Winstead suggest that gender-role expectations promulgated by our culture about appropriate behavior influence how and when men and women seek, obtain, and enact supportive behaviors in stressful situations. But the effects of gender on support do not always follow cultural stereotypes. Indeed, Derlega et al. show that the effects of gender on the provision and outcome of social support are complex, varying as a function of relationship (friend vs. stranger), outcome (feelings of confidence vs. feelings of depression), stressor (cognitive vs. emotional problem), and several other factors. These findings serve to remind us that seeking and providing social support are complicated behaviors contingent on numerous contextual variables, and will not be explained by coarse, stereotypical generalizations.

Substantive features of supportive episodes are only one feature of the context deserving of examination. Understanding how support gets communicated also requires comprehending social support as a dynamic, interactive process that unfolds in a distinctive manner. Several researchers have recently suggested that supportive interactions may exhibit a characteristic sequential structure. Pearlin and McCall (1990), for example, propose a four-stage model for supportive interactions: recognition or disclosure of the need for support, assessment of the recipient's deservingness of support, the actual expression of support, and evaluation of the impact or helpfulness of supportive acts.

In Chapter 8, Steinberg and Gottlieb report an intensive study of the final stage identified by Pearlin and McCall, the evaluation of support efforts. Steinberg and Gottlieb present a detailed analysis of wives' evaluations of husbands' support behaviors generated in response to work-family conflicts. Qualitative analysis of the wives' descriptions of supportive episodes indicates that the way the support process unfolds— how support gets mobilized and provided—along with multiple contextual and relationship factors influence the meaning the support effort comes to have for each spouse, the perceived effectiveness of that support effort, and the consequences of the support episode on the quality of the marital relationship. This latter finding anticipates the focus of Part III, how *relationships* both affect and are affected by supportive interactions.

CHARACTERISTICS OF
SUPPORTIVE RELATIONSHIPS

Although not denying the significance of specific messages or interactions in the support process, the chapters in Part III describe several different ways in which personal relationships communicate support. For example, most researchers have viewed social support as a distinct class of behaviors (e.g., providing comfort, reassurance, information, tangible aid) solicited and produced in response to special, stressful circumstances. In contrast, Barnes and Duck suggest in Chapter 9 that social support is a basic, ongoing process in many social relationships: Support is the *norm* rather than the *exception*. Barnes and Duck describe how social support emerges in multiple ways from the everyday behaviors that make up relationships, demonstrating how the mere existence of relationships—or, more properly, their enactment—is supportive. Barnes and Duck urge researchers to give this expanded concept of support greater attention, especially how a variety of support functions are realized through everyday talk. They also describe several innovative methodologies for conducting research on the supportive functions of relationships in everyday life.

Although many personal relationships provide support, not all do so, at least to desired levels. When available personal relationships consistently fail to provide desired levels of support, dissatisfactions such as loneliness occur. In Chapter 10, Samter suggests that the discrepancy between what lonely individuals want from their relationships and what they get may lie in the inability of network members to provide meaningful social support. Although lonely individuals may suffer from skill deficiencies, a primary reason for their feelings of loneliness may stem from members of their social network also having skill deficiencies, especially with respect to the motivation and ability to provide those varied forms of social support usually obtained from intimates. Samter summarizes a study providing some confirmation of these notions: The members of the lonely person's social network are themselves likely to be lonely, view supportive communication skills as less important in intimate relationships, and are less skilled at supportive forms of communication. These are disturbing findings, for they suggest that lonely people maintain associations with people for whom "friendship" means something quite different than it does to the nonlonely. Improving the lot of such individuals may require not only teaching them social skills, but altering their *meanings* for social relationships.

The meanings people associate with supportive relationships and messages are scrutinized by Miller and Ray in Chapter 11. Minimal work has focused on the specific messages that generate perceptions of support and the meanings people co-construct in supportive interactions. Nor has much research explored how the *intentions* of support providers get inferred and aligned or reconciled with recipient perceptions. This is significant since abundant evidence (e.g., Dakof & Taylor, 1990; Lehman et al., 1986) indicates that behaviors intended by a provider to be supportive are often perceived by recipients to be interfering, manipulative, or insensitive. To facilitate more meaning-centered research, Miller and Ray describe two approaches for studying supportive messages and relationships: the study of *memorable messages* (where participants describe specific messages recalled as providing significant support), and the study of *semantic networks* (wherein network linkages are based, not on formal roles or interaction patterns, but on shared meanings and interpretations). The analysis of such meaning structures may contribute to explaining why, for example, support from coworkers more effectively manages work-related stresses than support from family members (see Constable & Russell, 1986; Ray, 1987).

In Chapter 12, Metts, Geist, and Gray directly explore the contributions of support received from work and family relationships to the management of job-related stressors. Metts et al. argue that individuals' conceptions of and expectations for varied relationships constitute orienting interpretive frameworks within which supportive messages are understood and experienced. These researchers thus suggest a dialectic between support behaviors and personal relationships: Supportive actions contribute to development and definition of a relationship, but once formulated, definitions of the relationship constrain the interpretation of actions occurring within its confines. To illustrate one moment of the support/ relationship dialectic, Metts et al. report a study showing that the effectiveness of specific types of supports (emotional, informational) varies significantly as a function of type and quality of the relationship the recipient has with the provider. Thus it is not only objective features of the stressor or message that determine the appropriateness and impact of supportive actions; rather, outcomes are also significantly influenced by how actions are contextualized and interpreted within the frame of specific provider-recipient relationships.

Metts et al. emphasize the effects that *type* of relationship can have on the provision and effects of support. In Chapter 13, Pierce systematically explores how support processes are influenced by the *quality* of the relationship between provider and recipient. Pierce notes that an expanding body of studies have examined the contributions of specific relationships (e.g., marriage, the parent-child relationship) to the health and well-being of the individual. Further, the quality of the relationship (e.g., the presence or absence of conflict) contextualizes the occurrence and effects of supportive actions (see Coyne & DeLongis, 1986). Unfortunately, research addressing how relationship quality influences social support processes has been hampered by the lack of appropriate methodologies. To address this methodological gap, Pierce presents the *Quality of Relationships Inventory* (QRI), a convenient, self-report instrument assessing perceptions of the degree of support, conflict, and depth associated with a particular relationship. He summarizes an impressive program of research already completed with the QRI, including cross-sectional, longitudinal, observational, and experimental studies conducted with college students and their parents, siblings, and peers.

Conclusion: The Communication of Social Support and the Creation of Supportive Communities

The contributions to this book thus detail a variety of ways in which support is communicated. Messages can convey support through the acknowledgment, elaboration, and legitimation of an emotionally distressed other's feelings; through careful facework that attends sensitively to the other's needs for positive evaluation and autonomy; or through offering specific forms of assistance to those facing stressful task demands. Supportive interactions appear to exhibit a characteristic sequential structure defined by the appraisals and actions of both providers and recipients. The content and outcome of supportive interactions are influenced by a multitude of variables, but interactions generally appear most effective at conveying support when the type of aid offered matches the specific needs imposed by stressor on the recipient and is appropriate within the context of the provider-recipient relationship. Finally, personal relationships convey support in numerous ways: they provide subtle, often implicit messages of acceptance, confirmation, and liking during the course of routine interactions; they may furnish socially skilled partners who value the provision of support in close relationships; and they supply others who share common experiential backgrounds and therefore understand the stresses affecting an individual and know what to do about them.

One of the most potent, if unexplored, consequences of the communication of social support may be the creation of culturally shared value systems that promote supportive, prosocial conduct on a communitywide scale. In the Epilogue, Albrecht explores the dynamic relations among supportive behaviors, moral codes, and community actions as these were played out in the Danes' heroic rescue of their Jewish neighbors during the Nazi occupation. Albrecht argues that supportive messages, interactions, and relationships are manifestations of the overarching community in which they are embedded. Demonstrating the value of historical methods for social support research, Albrecht shows how the wholesale rescue by Danish citizens of their Jewish brethren from the Nazi pogrom grew out of a culturally shared moral code and networks of interaction. Clearly, the moral codes of a culture play a crucial role in motivating public acts of heroism and private acts of compassion—both of which serve essential functions in sustaining communities, enhancing the quality of life for individuals, and perpetuating desirable values.

Albrecht's study thus reminds us of the theoretical, pragmatic, and moral imperatives motivating research on social support and how it gets communicated: Understanding what social support is and how it functions should help us better comprehend how human relationships are created and maintained, how these relationships contribute to the health and well-being of individuals, and what it means to be a good and caring person.

References

Adelman, M. B., Parks, M. R., & Albrecht, T. L. (1987). Supporting friends in need. In T. L. Albrecht & M. B. Adelman (Eds.), *Communicating social support* (pp. 105-125). Newbury Park, CA: Sage.

Albrecht, T. L., & Adelman, M. B. (Eds.). (1987a). *Communicating social support*. Newbury Park, CA: Sage.

Albrecht, T. L., & Adelman, M. B. (1987b). Rethinking the relationship between communication and social support: An introduction. In T. L. Albrecht & M. B. Adelman (Eds.), *Communicating social support* (pp. 13-17). Newbury Park, CA: Sage.

Albrecht, T. L., Burleson, B. R., & Sarason, I. (1992). Meaning and method in the study of social support: An introduction. *Communication Research, 19,* 149-153.

Albrecht, T. L., & Hall, B. J. (1991). The role of personal relationships in organizational innovation. *Communication Monographs, 58,* 273-288.

Antonucci, T. C., & Israel, B. (1986). Veridicality of social support: A comparison of principal and network members responses. *Journal of Consulting and Clinical Psychology, 54,* 1-25.

Applegate, J. L., Burleson, B. R., & Delia, J. G. (1992). Reflection-enhancing parenting as antecedent to children's social-cognitive and communicative development. In I. E. Sigel, A. V. McGillicuddy-Delisi, & J. J. Goodnow (Eds.), *Parental belief systems: The psychological consequences for children* (2nd ed., pp. 3-39). Hillsdale, NJ: Lawrence Erlbaum.

Argyle, M., & Henderson, M. (1985). *The anatomy of relationships*. London: Heinemann.

Barbee, A. P. (1990). Interactive coping: The cheering-up process in close relationships. In S. Duck with R. Silver (Eds.), *Personal relationships and social support* (pp. 46-65). London: Sage.

Belle, D. (1982). The stress of caring: Women as providers of social support. In L. Goldberger & S. Bresnitz (Eds.), *Handbook of stress: Theoretical and clinical aspects* (pp. 496-505). New York: Free Press.

Berkman, L. F., & Smye, S. L. (1979). Social networks, host resistance, and mortality: A nine-year follow-up of Alameda County residents. *American Journal of Epidemiology, 109,* 186-204.

Brown, P., & Levinson, S. (1987). *Politeness: Some universals in language usage*. New York: Cambridge University Press.

Burleson, B. R. (1990). Comforting as social support: Relational consequences of supportive messages. In S. Duck with R. Silver (Eds.), *Personal relationships and social support* (pp. 66-82). London: Sage.

Burleson, B. R., Albrecht, T. L., & Goldsmith, D. (1993). Social support and communication: New directions for theory, research, and practice. *ISSPR Bulletin, 9* (2), 5-9.

Cassel, J. (1976). The contributions of the environment to host resistance. *American Journal of Epidemiology, 104,* 107-123.

Cobb, S. (1976). Social support as a moderator of life stress. *Psychosomatic Medicine, 38,* 300-314.

Cohen, S., & McKay, G. (1984). Social support, stress, and the buffering hypothesis: A theoretical analysis. In A. Baum, J. E. Singer, Y. S. E. Taylor (Eds.), *Handbook of psychology and health* (pp. 253-267). Hillsdale, NJ: Lawrence Erlbaum.

Cohen, S., & Wills, T. A. (1985). Stress, social support, and the buffering hypothesis. *Psychological Bulletin, 98,* 310-357.

Constable, J. F., & Russell, D. (1986). The effect of social support and the work environment upon burnout among nurses. *Journal of Human Stress, 12,* 20-26.

Coyne, J. C., & DeLongis, A. (1986). Going beyond social support: The role of social relationships in adaptation. *Journal of Consulting and Clinical Psychology, 54,* 454-460.

Coyne, J. C., Ellard, J. H., & Smith, D. A. F. (1990). Social support, interdependence, and the dilemmas of helping. In B. R. Sarason, I. G. Sarason, & G. R. Pierce (Eds.), *Social support: An interactional view* (pp. 129-149). New York: John Wiley.

Cutrona, C. E., & Russell, D. W. (1990). Types of social support and specific stress: Toward a theory of optimal matching. In B. R. Sarason, I. G. Sarason, & G. R. Pierce (Eds.), *Social support: An interactional view* (pp. 319-366). New York: John Wiley.

Cutrona, C. E., & Suhr, J. A. (1992). Controllability of stressful events and satisfaction with spouse support behaviors. *Communication Research, 19,* 154-174.

Cutrona, C. E., Suhr, J. A., & MacFarlane, R. (1990). Interpersonal transactions and the psychological sense of support. In S. Duck with R. Silver (Eds.), *Personal relationships and social support* (pp. 30-45). London: Sage.

Dakof, G. A., & Taylor, S. E. (1990). Victims' perceptions of support attempts: What is helpful from whom? *Journal of Personality and Social Psychology, 58,* 80-89.

Duck, S., with Silver, R. (Eds.). (1990). *Personal relationships and social support*. London: Sage.

Dunkel-Schetter, C., & Bennett, T. L. (1990). Differentiating the cognitive and behavioral aspects of social support. In B. R. Sarason, I. G. Sarason, & G. R. Pierce (Eds.), *Social support: An interactional view* (pp. 267-296). New York: John Wiley.

Dunkel-Schetter, C., & Skokan, L. A. (1990). Determinants of social support in personal relationships. *Journal of Personal and Social Relationships, 7*, 437-450.

Eggert, L. L. (1987). Support in family ties: Stress, coping, and adaptation. In T. L. Albrecht & M. B. Adelman (Eds.), *Communicating social support* (pp. 80-104). Newbury Park, CA: Sage.

Elster, J. (1990). Selfishness and altruism. In J. J. Mansbridge (Ed.), *Beyond self-interest* (pp. 44-53). Chicago: University of Chicago Press.

Goldsmith, D. (1992). Managing conflicting goals in supportive interaction: An integrative theoretical framework. *Communication Research, 19*, 264-286.

Goldsmith, D., & Albrecht, T. L. (1993). The impact of supportive communication networks on test anxiety and performance. *Communication Education, 42*, 142-158.

Goldsmith, D., & Parks, M. (1990). Communicative strategies for managing the risks of seeking social support. In S. Duck with R. Silver (Eds.), *Personal relationships and social support* (pp. 104-121). London: Sage.

Gottlieb, B. H. (1981). *Social networks and social support*. Beverly Hills, CA: Sage.

Gottlieb, B. H. (1985). Social support and the study of close relationships. *Journal of Social and Personal Relationships, 2*, 351-375.

Hansson, R. O., Jones, W. H., & Fletcher, W. L. (1990). Troubled relationships in later life: Implications for support. *Journal of Social and Personal Relationships, 7*, 451-464.

Hirsch, B. J. (1980). Natural support systems and coping with major life changes. *American Journal of Community Psychology, 8*, 159-172.

Hobfoll, S. E., & Stephens, M. A. P. (1990). Social support during extreme stress: Consequences and intervention. In B. R. Sarason, I. G. Sarason, & G. R. Pierce (Eds.), *Social support: An interactional view* (pp. 454-481). New York: John Wiley.

Hobfoll, S. E., & Stokes, J. P. (1988). The process and mechanics of social support. In S. Duck (Ed.), *Handbook of personal relationships* (pp. 497-519). London: John Wiley.

House, J. S., Robbins, C., & Metzner, H. C. (1982). The association of social relationships and activities with mortality: Prospective evidence from the Tecumseh community health study. *American Journal of Epidemiology, 116*, 123-140.

Kaplan, R. M., & Toshima, M. T. (1990). The functional effects of social relationships on chronic illness and disability. In B. R. Sarason, I. G. Sarason, & G. R. Pierce (Eds.), *Social support: An interactional view* (pp. 427-453). New York: John Wiley.

Kennedy, S., Kiecolt-Glaser, J. K., & Glaser, R. (1990). Social support, stress, and the immune system. In B. R. Sarason, I. G. Sarason, & G. R. Pierce (Eds.), *Social support: An interactional view* (pp. 253-266). New York: John Wiley.

Kessler, R. C., Price, R. H., & Wortman, C. B. (1985). Social factors in psychopathology: Stress, social support, and coping processes. *Annual Review of Psychology, 36*, 531-572.

Lehman, D. R., Ellard, J. H., & Wortman, C. B. (1986). Social support for the bereaved: Recipients' and providers' perspectives on what is helpful. *Journal of Consulting and Clinical Psychology, 54*, 438-446.

Lehman, D. R., & Hemphill, K. J. (1990). Recipients' perceptions of support attempts and attributions for support attempts that fail. *Journal of Social and Personal Relationships, 7*, 563-574.

Malson, M. (1983). The social support systems of black families. *Marriage and Family Review, 5,* 35-57.

McLeroy, K. R., DeVellis, R., DeVellis, B., Kaplan, B., & Toole, J. (1984). Social support and physical recovery in a stroke population. *Journal of Social and Personal Relationships, 1,* 395-413.

Moss, G. E. (1973). *Illness, immunity, and social interaction.* New York: John Wiley.

Pearlin, L. I., & McCall, M. E. (1990). Occupational stress and marital support: A description of microprocesses. In J. Eckenrode & S. Gore (Eds.), *Stress between work and family* (pp. 39-60). New York: Plenum.

Peters-Golden, H. (1982). Breast cancer: Varied perceptions of social support in the illness experience. *Social Science and Medicine, 16,* 483-491.

Pierce, G., Sarason, I., & Sarason, B. (1990). Integrating social support perspectives: Working models, personal relationships, and situational factors. In S. Duck with R. Silver (Eds.), *Personal relationships and social support* (pp. 173-189). London: Sage.

Rawlins, W. K. (1992). *Friendship matters: Communication, dialectics, and the life course.* New York: Aldine de Gruyter.

Ray, E. B. (1987). Supportive relationships and occupational stress in the workplace. In T. L. Albrecht & M. B. Adelman (Eds.), *Communicating social support* (pp. 172-191). Newbury Park, CA: Sage.

Ray, E. B. (1993). When the links become chains: Considering dysfunctions of supportive communication in the workplace. *Communication Monographs, 60,* 106-111.

Rook, K. S. (1984). The negative side of social interaction: Impact on psychological well-being. *Journal of Personality and Social Psychology, 46,* 1097-1108.

Rook, K. S., & Pietromonaco, P. (1987). Close relationships: Ties that heal or ties that bind? In W. H. Jones & D. Perlman (Eds.), *Advances in personal relationships* (vol. 1, pp. 1-35). Greenwich, CT: JAI Press.

Sandler, I. N., & Barrera, M., Jr. (1984). Toward a multimethod approach to addressing the effects of social support. *American Journal of Community Psychology, 12,* 37-52.

Sandler, I. N., & Lakey, B. (1982). Locus of control as a stress moderator: The role of control perceptions and social support. *American Journal of Community Psychology, 10,* 65-80.

Sarason, B. R., Pierce, G. R., & Sarason, I. G. (1990). Social support: The sense of acceptance and the role of relationships. In B. R. Sarason, I. G. Sarason, & G. R. Pierce (Eds.), *Social support: An interactional view* (pp. 97-128). New York: John Wiley.

Sarason, B. R., Pierce, G. R., Shearin, E. N., Sarason, I. G., & Waltz, J. A., & Poppe, L. (1991). Perceived social support and working models of self and actual others. *Journal of Personality and Social Psychology, 60,* 273-287.

Sarason, B. R., Sarason, I. G., & Pierce, G. R. (Eds.). (1990). *Social support: An interactional view.* New York: John John Wiley.

Sarason, B. R., Shearin, E. N., Pierce, G. R., & Sarason, I. G. (1987). Interrelationships among social support measures: Theoretical and practical implications. *Journal of Personality and Social Psychology, 52,* 813-832.

Sarason, I. G., & Sarason, B. R. (1986). Experimentally provided social support. *Journal of Personality and Social Psychology, 50,* 1222-1225.

Seeman, T. E., & Berkman, L. F. (1988). Structural characteristics of social networks and their relationship with social support in the elderly: Who provides support. *Social Science and Medicine, 26,* 737-749.

Swann, W. B., Jr., & Brown, J. D. (1990). From self to health: Self-verification and identity disruption. In B. R. Sarason, I. G. Sarason, & G. R. Pierce (Eds.), *Social support: An interactional view* (pp. 150-172). New York: John Wiley.

Thoits, P. A. (1985). Social support and psychological well-being: Theoretical possibilities. In I. G. Sarason & B. R. Sarason (Eds.), *Social support: Theory, research, and applications* (pp. 51-72). Dordrecht, The Netherlands: Martinus Nijhoff.

Weiss, R. S. (1974). The provisions of social relationships. In Z. Rubin (Ed.), *Doing unto others* (pp. 17-26). Englewood Cliffs, NJ: Prentice Hall.

Wethington, E., & Kessler, R. C. (1986). Perceived support, received support, and adjustment to stressful life events. *Journal of Health and Social Behavior, 27,* 78-89.

Wortman, C. B. (1984). Social support and the cancer patient: Conceptual and methodological issues. *Cancer, 53,* 2339-2360.

Wortman, C. B., & Lehman, D. R. (1985). Reactions to victims of life crises: Support attempts that fail. In I. G. Sarason & B. R. Sarason (Eds.), *Social support: Theory, research, and applications* (pp. 463-489). Dordrecht, The Netherlands: Martinus Nijhoff.

PART I

Characteristics
of Supportive Messages

1

Comforting Messages

Significance, Approaches, and Effects

BRANT R. BURLESON

As many of the contributors to this volume observe, scholars of social support have become increasingly interested in the processes and behaviors through which support is elicited and provided. One form of support that has received a good deal of descriptive research is emotional support, the provision of aid and security during times of stress that leads a person to feel he or she is cared for by others (Cutrona & Russell, 1990, p. 322). Within the broad category of emotional support, one behavior of particular interest has been the strategies that people use in the effort to comfort those experiencing emotional distress. Elsewhere, I have defined comforting behaviors as messages having the goal of alleviating or lessening the emotional distresses experienced by others (Burleson, 1985).

The development of the competence to engage in comforting and related forms of emotional support have received considerable attention from researchers studying communication (see the reviews by Burleson, 1984a, 1985) and prosocial behavior (Eisenberg, 1989; Olweus, Block, & Radke-Yarrow, 1986). This research has increased our understanding of factors associated with both the ability to provide comfort and the motivation to engage in such acts. Thus far, however, only limited research has focused on the *outcomes* of different comforting messages. Clearly, understanding the effects of different comforting messages would be of interest to social support scholars given their historical interest in social behaviors that facilitate health and well being: Knowing which messages generally do the best job of relieving emotional distress would have significant implications for improving the efficacy of everyday helping efforts, as well as for practice in therapy, counseling, and other helping professions. Unfortunately, assessing the effects of comforting messages is no simple task. Indeed, what "effectiveness" or "success" means in the context of comforting turns out to be a complex matter.

The current chapter synthesizes and integrates much of the current literature on the effects of comforting messages. It begins by discussing the significance of comforting behavior in everyday life. Next, the chapter overviews several distinct approaches to the collection of comforting messages and the evaluation of their effects. Then, utilizing a multidimensional framework for the assessment of message effects, the core of the chapter reviews studies examining how people perceive and are affected by different comforting messages. Messages are evaluated for both their effectiveness in reducing emotional distress and their consequences for the interpersonal relationship between provider and recipient.

Significance and
Functions of Everyday Comforting

EVERYDAY STRESSORS AND EMOTIONAL SUPPORT

A growing body of evidence shows that the minor hassles, disappointments, and hurts people routinely experience are major determinants of moods and psychological well-being. Not surprisingly, studies (e.g., Stone, 1981) routinely find associations between depression or negative mood states and the frequency with which unpleasant events are experienced. More importantly, other research (Eckenrode, 1984; Kanner, Coyne, Schaefer, & Lazarus, 1981) has found that stress resulting from everyday hassles and disappointments is a better predictor of mood and psychological well-being than stress resulting from major life events (e.g., death of a spouse) or chronic conditions (e.g., living in poverty). Some work (DeLongis, Coyne, Dakof, Folkman, & Lazarus, 1982) also shows that the stress resulting from daily upsets may even be a better predictor of physical health than the stress resulting from major life events. Thus the ordinary distresses and upsets addressed in routine acts of comforting are major determinants of mood, psychological well-being, and even physical health.

The emotional support provided through the comforting activities of social network members affords substantial help as people attempt to manage the upsets and stresses associated with everyday hurts and disappointments. Supportive actions that express concern and solidarity, prompt the articulation of feelings, display sympathy and understanding, and provide new information or alternative perspectives on a distressful situation significantly contribute to feelings of well-being, acceptance, and control over events (e.g., Elliott, 1985; Wortman, 1984). These feelings, in turn, are important predictors of functional modes of coping with stress and several indices of physical and emotional health (see Albrecht & Adelman, 1987; Thoits, 1985). For example, emotional support has been found to buffer the effects of financial strain (Krause, 1987), anxiety and depression (Frankel & Turner, 1983), minor crimes (Krause, 1986), family stress (Hirsch & Reischl, 1985), work stress (Constable & Russell, 1986), and a variety of other upsets (see the review by Cutrona & Russell, 1990).

The comfort and emotional support people receive from others thus helps them to feel better, relieves hurt and stress, and improves life quality. If everyday comforting did nothing more, there would still be good reason for valuing this activity and those who do it well. But comforting *does* do more—much more. Comforting acts signal care, commitment, and interest. They also may express compassion and love. Comforting and other emotionally supportive actions are thus relationally significant behaviors.

EMOTIONAL SUPPORT AND
RELATIONSHIP DEVELOPMENT

People see the provision of emotional support as one of the central functions intimate relationships are expected to serve (Burleson, 1990; Burleson & Samter, in press). Across the life span, people look to friends and romantic partners as primary providers of emotional support (Barbee & Yankeelov, 1992; Berndt & Perry, 1986; Davis & Todd, 1985; see the review by Tesch, 1983). Because comforting acts signal interest, caring, liking, and concern, these acts play a central role in the formation and development of intimate relationships (see Barbee, Druen, Gulley, Yankeelov, & Cunningham, in press; Burleson & Samter, in press). In several recent studies, my colleagues and I have found that people value the activity of comforting and tend to like and develop relationships with those who value comforting and do it well.

To assess the value people placed on comforting activity in comparison to other activities in which intimates engage, we developed an instrument called the *Communicative Functions Questionnaire* (CFQ) (Burleson & Samter, 1990). This instrument has subjects evaluate the importance of eight different communication skills for a specified relationship (e.g., same sex friendship, opposite-sex dating partner). The eight skills include: comforting ability, ego-support skill, referential ability, narrative ability, conversational skill, regulative skill, conflict management ability, and persuasive skill. Several studies employing the CFQ (Burleson, Kunkel, & Birch, 1993; Burleson & Samter, 1990; Burleson, Werking, Samter, and Holloway, 1988) have found that young adults have a strong appreciation for the significance of comforting activity, rating this skill as among the most important in both friendships and romantic relationships.

Because people value comforting skill, it is likely that they will like those who view comforting as important and display talent at this activity. Consistent with this prediction, Samter and Burleson (1990a) found that fraternity and sorority members who placed a relatively high value on comforting skill were more preferred by housemates as social companions, reported lower levels of loneliness on the UCLA loneliness scale, and were less likely to be rejected by housemates than those placing less value on this skill. In a related study, Samter (1992) found that individuals whose friends placed a relatively low value on comforting skill were more lonely than persons whose friends place a high value on this skill. Several other studies (reviewed below) indicate that individuals with good comforting skills are perceived as more attractive social companions and are more likely to be accepted by peers.

In sum, people certainly seem to value the comfort and emotional support they receive from friends, family, and coworkers. They should: Research shows these activities play important roles in the development and maintenance of interpersonal relationships and help individuals cope with a variety of common stresses and upsets. Thus comforting and emotional support serve several significant functions in everyday life. The messages through which people provide emotional comfort to one another clearly warrant study.

Approaches to the
Study of Comforting Messages

It is possible to identify at least three major approaches to the study of comforting messages: an inductive-descriptive approach typical in the social support literature, a deductive-prescriptive approach characteristic in the clinical and counseling literatures, and functional-hierarchic approach taken in the communication literature.[1] The following sections describe each of these approaches and weigh their strengths and limitations. First, however, some special problems associated with the study of comforting behavior are noted.

PECULIARITIES IN ASSESSING THE PROPERTIES
AND EFFECTS OF COMFORTING MESSAGES

Research assessing the qualities and effects of different comforting messages faces problems not encountered by work on other forms of social support or other communicative goals. For example, studies assessing the effects of informative or persuasive messages can randomly assign subjects to different message treatments; the effects of message variables can then be assessed by looking at differences in knowledge or attitudes. However, both ethical and practical problems complicate the use of such experimental methods in studies of comforting.

Assessing experimentally the effectiveness of comforting messages requires samples of emotionally distressed persons. Some would insist on ethical grounds that researchers should never do anything to create such samples. Others argue that mild distress can be temporarily created in subjects with very minimal risks or harm to them. For example, Barbee (1990) has had participants repeat a series of depressing statements or watch clips from sad movies to induce mild states of sadness. Obviously, though, great care must be exercised if distress or depression is experimentally induced.

Another ethical problem involves the researcher's responsibilities to emotionally distressed individuals, regardless of whether distressed states are "natural" or experimentally induced. Some might argue that whenever confronted with persons experiencing emotional distress there is an ethical obligation to do all one can to help. Randomly assigning distressed people to different message treatments might be viewed as ethically suspect, especially if it is possible that some message treatments might exacerbate, rather than relieve, the distressed condition.

Further, there are limited options available for objectively determining the degree of emotional distress experienced by people. This makes it difficult to assess levels of emotional distress either before or after exposure to comforting messages. These practical and ethical concerns have led to the use of alternative research designs in the study of comforting.

AN INDUCTIVE-DESCRIPTIVE PERSPECTIVE ON COMFORTING

Some researchers interested in the effects of social support on health have approached the study of comforting behavior by asking people to provide retrospective self reports about the messages they have received when attempting to manage various stressors. Because of the focal interest in health outcomes, many of the stressors examined in these studies have been diseases or physical ailments such as multiple sclerosis (Lehman & Hemphill, 1990) and cancer (Dakof & Taylor, 1990; Dunkel-Schetter, 1984; Peters-Golden, 1982; Wortman, 1984). Researchers have also asked the bereaved (e.g., adults who lost a spouse or a child in an automobile accident) to report the comforting strategies others used with them (see Lehman, Ellard, & Wortman, 1986). Participants have often been asked to describe not only messages they perceived as helpful, but also messages that were ineffective or even counterproductive (i.e., those that may have made them feel worse).

After collection, researchers typically develop classification schemes to organize and describe the corpus of messages. For the most part, the categories composing these schemes have been derived from a careful inspection of the data, i.e., they have been induced. For example, Lehman and Hemphill (1990) describe the following set of categories for instances of emotional support: expressing love, concern, or understanding; providing encouragement; listening; praising abilities; including in social activities; and presence ("being there"). Dakof and Taylor (1990) developed the following subcategories for the general class of "helpful esteem/ emotional supports": physical presence; expressed concern, empathy, or affection; calmly accepted the patient's disease; expressed a special understanding because of being a similar other; was pleasant and kind. Because these studies focus on describing the messages people recollect as having been used, inducing categories of messages from the data, I term this approach the *inductive-descriptive perspective.*

Several advantages inhere in the inductive-descriptive perspective. This method is simple to use and is comparatively economical. Moreover, it can be used with a wide array of stressors. Indeed, this is probably the only method that can be used to study the messages generated in reaction to certain stressors (death of a close family member, cancer, etc.). Most important, this approach yields very rich data. Applications of the inductive-descriptive method have yielded the important finding that comforters frequently produce messages that, while well intended, are clumsy, insensitive, and likely to exacerbate distress (Dakof & Taylor, 1990; Lehman et al., 1986; Lehman & Hemphill, 1990).

There are, however, some important limitations to the inductive-descriptive approach. First, people often do not describe specific messages or things that others have said to them, but instead describe the goals or abstract actions of others. Research on memory for conversations (Stafford, Burggraf, & Sharkey, 1987; Stafford & Daly; 1984; Stafford, Waldron, & Infield, 1989) indicates that the behaviors of others tend to be coded and recalled in terms of intentions and abstract actions rather than in terms of specific statements. Thus retrospective reports about the specifics of what others say are of doubtful reliability, and this is an important limitation if the interest is in the detailed features of supportive messages.

Second, as Goldsmith (1992) indicates, many of the categories used to characterize recalled support efforts represent classifications of the recipient's *interpretation of behaviors* or *evaluation of their outcomes*, not features of the *messages* producing the interpretation or outcome. This is problematic because different messages can yield similar outcomes. Conversely, messages with similar features can result in different outcomes in different situations. Understanding message-outcome relationships thus requires detailed specification of message features, situational factors, and particular outcomes and interpretations. Such detailed information is required both for building theory and developing sound advice about how to provide comfort under varying circumstances.

An additional problem with most of the schemes used to classify support efforts is their lack of internal coherence. No single principle, or group of principles, inform the categories appearing in these typologies. The lack of coherence in the systems used to classify support efforts compounds the problem of providing a systematic theoretical representation of effective comforting messages.

Fourth, the reliance on frequency counts in some research stemming from this perspective (e.g., Cutrona & Suhr, 1992; Cutrona, Suhr, & MacFarlane, 1990) carries the assumption that "more is better"; i.e., that more instances of a certain behavior are more comforting, provide more emotional support, or result in more desirable outcomes. Clearly, though, more is not always better. More instances of a crude comforting strategy are probably not as desirable as a single instance of a highly sophisticated strategy.

In sum, the inductive-descriptive perspective provides rich information about the comforting efforts to which people recall being exposed. Researchers using this method must, however, be concerned about the accuracy and detail with which comforting efforts are recalled. More problematic, this method doesn't give any guidance about the features of comforting messages to which researchers should attend, nor does it facilitate developing theoretical representations of comforting messages or the comforting process.

A DEDUCTIVE-PRESCRIPTIVE
PERSPECTIVE ON COMFORTING

While the inductive-descriptive approach characteristic in the social support literature attempts to derive the features of effective comforting messages from the self reports of many individuals, the approach reflected in much of the counseling literature is deductive and prescriptive. That is, properties of "good" comforting messages are deduced, a priori, from theory. Theory also becomes a basis for prescribing what helpers should say to produce effective comforting messages.

Comforting is an activity in which counselors and psychotherapists regularly engage, so it is not surprising that several different representations of comforting appear in the counseling literature. One of the most popular analyses of comforting behavior has been forwarded by Rogers (1957, 1975) and his associates (Carkhuff & Berenson, 1977; Truax & Carkhuff, 1967). Rogers (1957) maintained that for a counselor to bring about improvement in a client, it was necessary and sufficient that the counselor express empathy, nonpossessive warmth (or unconditional positive regard), and genuineness (or congruence). *Empathy* refers to the degree to which therapists are successful in communicating their awareness and understanding of the client's feelings in language that is attuned to the client. *Respect* or *nonpossessive warmth* refers to the extent to which the therapist communicates nonevaluative caring and positive regard for the client, respecting the client as a person. *Genuineness* is the extent to which therapists are nondefensive, real, and authentic in their interactions with clients; whatever the therapist expresses is a real and significant part of himself or herself.

Empathy, warmth, and genuineness (often referred to collectively as the "therapeutic conditions") supposedly bring about improvement because the climate fostered by these conditions maximizes the individual's self-exploration, self-understanding, and development of appropriate plans of action (see Carkhuff & Berenson, 1977). Emotional hurt often stems from the invalidation of the self, either directly (e.g., rejection by a valued other) or indirectly (e.g., failing at something connected to one's self concept). The therapeutic conditions convey to distressed others that their feelings are recognized and appreciated, that they are valued as persons, and that they are accepted by another (the helper) in the context of an honest relationship.

Studies conducted by Rogers' students (see the summaries in Carkhuff & Berenson, 1977; Truax & Carkhuff, 1967; Truax & Mitchell, 1971) supported the notion that high levels of empathy, genuineness, and warmth bring about relatively great improvement in distressed others. However, much of this research has been the target of trenchant criticism (see the reviews by Lambert, DeJulio, & Stein, 1978; Mitchell, Bozarth, & Krauft, 1977; Parloff, Waskow, & Wolfe, 1978). In particular, studies have been indicted for vague and ambiguous conceptual definitions of the skills examined, reliance on instruments of dubious reliability and validity, and numerous technical problems (e.g., small sample sizes, interpretation of marginally significant results, lack of randomization, failure to use control groups, use of raters not blind to experimental treatments, etc.). Moreover, later studies employing more rigorous designs did not consistently support the claim that high levels of the therapeutic conditions ease emotional distresses associated with everyday hurts and disappointments (see Burleson, 1994).

Particularly noteworthy is the failure of research to (a) differentiate between characteristics of the communicator and the message, (b) distinguish between the verbal and nonverbal features of message behavior and (c) identify the specific features constituting and defining messages exhibiting high levels of the therapeutic conditions. The latter problem is particularly serious: Without precise and unambiguous specification of the "effective ingredients" of empathic, warm, and genuine messages (i.e., specification of the components giving these messages their distinctive character and power), it is impossible to design and conduct studies assessing whether such messages help people more than alternatives. In sum, although the deductive-prescriptive perspective contributes a general analysis of how the comforting process should work, this perspective exhibits insufficient precision and detail in its representation of effective comforting messages.

A FUNCTIONAL-HIERARCHICAL
APPROACH TO COMFORTING

A third approach to the analysis of comforting messages has been developed in the field of communication over the last decade by my colleagues and me (Applegate, 1980; Burleson, 1984a, 1985; Samter & Burleson, 1984). Drawing from the cognitive-developmental theory of Werner (1957) and the sociolinguistic work of Bernstein (1975), this approach provides a hierarchical scaling of comforting messages for the extent to which the feelings and perspective of a distressed other are explicitly acknowledged, elaborated, and granted legitimacy (see Burleson, 1984a, 1994). A coding system composed of nine hierarchically organized categories is used to evaluate messages (see Burleson, 1982, 1984b; Samter & Burleson, 1984). This coding system is composed of three major levels with three sublevels within each major level. Messages scored within the lowest major level of the hierarchy either implicitly or explicitly deny the feelings and perspective of the distressed other (e.g., "You shouldn't be so upset about losing your boyfriend. After all, there are a lot of fish in the sea. So forget him and go catch yourself another one"). Messages providing an implicit recognition of the feelings and perspective of the distressed other are scored within the second major level of the hierarchy (e.g., "Gee, I'm sorry you guys broke up. I guess things like this happen though. Breaking up just seems to be a part of relationships"). Messages providing an explicit acknowledgment and elaboration of the other's feelings and perspective are scored within the highest major level of the hierarchy (e.g., "I know it must hurt. I know you're feeling a lot of pain and anger right now. And that's OK, 'cause I know you were really involved; you guys were together a long time and you expected things to work out differently").

The hierarchically ordered categories of this system generally reflect the extent to which the feelings and perspective of a distressed other receive explicit acknowledgment, elaboration, and legitimation. However, there are several more specific ways in which highly sophisticated comforting strategies (as defined by this system) differ from less sophisticated strategies.

First, sophisticated comforting strategies project a greater degree of involvement with distressed others and their problems. Such strategies are more listener-centered (i.e., discover and explicate the *other's* feelings and perspective) whereas less sophisticated strategies are more speaker-centered (i.e., tell the other what the speaker thinks about the situation or how the speaker thinks the other should feel or act). Second, sophisticated comforting strategies are evaluatively neutral. That is, these strategies generally *describe* and explicate feelings and the situations producing these feelings. Less sophisticated strategies often contain direct evaluations of feelings, persons, and actions connected with the distressful situation. Third, sophisticated comforting strategies are more feeling centered. Sophisticated strategies tend to focus on the proximate causes of another's distressed state (i.e., the psychological and affective *reactions* to certain events) whereas less sophisticated strategies focus more on the distal causes of distress (i.e., the events themselves). Fourth, sophisticated comforting strategies are generally more accepting of the distressed other. These strategies legitimize the feelings and point of view of the other rather than imposing the speaker's point of view. Fifth, sophisticated strategies often contain a cognitively oriented explanation of the feelings being experienced by a distressed other. Due to the intensity and immediacy of their feelings, distressed persons may lack understanding of these feelings. The sensitive explication of these feelings may lead to insight and understanding by the distressed other, and thereby contribute to the other gaining distance from and a perspective on his or her feelings.

Comforting messages scored in the higher levels of the hierarchy are regarded as structurally and developmentally more sophisticated forms of behavior because explicitly acknowledging, elaborating, and legitimizing the other's feelings requires advanced cognitive abilities through which the other's perspective can be recognized, internally represented, coordinated with other relevant perspectives, and integrated with the speaker's own understanding of the situation (O'Keefe & Delia, 1982; Samter, Burleson, & Basden, 1989). In other words, messages scored in the higher levels of the hierarchy are regarded as more sophisticated and advanced because they reflect greater complexity in thinking about people, feelings, social situations, and the process of communication. However, viewing higher-level comforting strategies as more sophisticated is not equivalent to showing that these strategies are more *effective*. That is, additional evidence is needed to demonstrate that *formally* "better" strategies (i.e., cognitively more sophisticated forms of behavior) also are *functionally* better strategies (i.e, more effective at achieving their intended objective). The next section of the chapter reviews such evidence.

Research on the Effects of Comforting Messages

Burleson (1994) identifies four different outcomes or effects with which scholars of the comforting process should be concerned. Too often, studies of comforting have been limited by a unidimensional conception of message effect, with researchers focused exclusively on the outcome of obtaining relief from emotional distress in the immediate context. In addition to (a) the *immediate, instrumental effects* of a message (i.e., how well the message reduces emotional distress in the here and now), researchers should also be concerned with (b) *long-term instrumental effects* (the extent to which a message helps someone develop coping strategies that enhance the individual's long-term ability to manage emotional distress), (c) *immediate, relational and identity effects* (how a recipient will think about and feel toward the producer of a message, and how the producer might think about and feel toward himself or herself), and (d) *long-term relational effects* (how the consistent use of certain message forms affects the quality of a helper's relationships with others). Research with respect to each of these outcomes is examined below; a more extensive review of this literature appears elsewhere (Burleson, 1994).

THE IMMEDIATE, INSTRUMENTAL EFFECTS
OF SOPHISTICATED COMFORTING STRATEGIES

Do messages defined as "sophisticated" by the functional-hierarchical approach do a better job of relieving emotional distress? To address this question, Burleson and Samter (1985a, Study 1) employed confederates who feigned emotional distress and then evaluated the sensitivity of subjects' responses to their distress cues. The interactions were videotaped and all comforting efforts were coded using a modified form of hierarchical system described above. Ratings of participants' involvement, concern, responsiveness, sympathy, and support were positively related to the number of comforting acts exhibited by participants. More important, rated sensitivity of the participant's behavior was strongly associated with the proportion of highly sophisticated comforting acts produced by the participant, but unassociated with the proportion of unsophisticated comforting acts (i.e., those scored in the lowest major level of the hierarchy).

A second study (Burleson & Samter, 1985a, Study 2) had participants read several hypothetical situations depicting a friend experiencing some form of emotional distress. For each situation, participants rated nine experimenter-supplied messages (one corresponding to each category in the hierarchy) for effectiveness and sensitivity. In addition, participants ranked the nine messages for overall quality. Mean effectiveness ratings, mean sensitivity ratings, and mean quality rankings of the messages were found to correspond exactly with the hierarchical ordering defined by the coding system. These findings were subsequently replicated in three other investigations (Allen et al., 1992; Samter, Burleson, & Murphy, 1987, Studies 1 and 2). Finally, two studies (Burleson & Samter, 1985b; Samter et al., 1987) have found that evaluations of the sensitivity and effectiveness of comforting messages tend not to vary as a function of situational and individual differences. The available evidence thus indicates that the theoretically based ordering represented in our hierarchical coding system closely corresponds with people's everyday intuitions about the content of effective and sensitive comforting messages. There appear to be consensual notions (at least within the populations examined) about what constitutes "good" comforting messages, and these notions seem well captured by the analysis of message sophistication embedded in the hierarchical coding system.

Recent research by Elliott (1985) in clinical contexts substantiates the findings pertaining to the perceived effectiveness of sophisticated comforting strategies. Elliott had college students discuss a problem of their choosing with counselors. A tape of these interactions was played back for the students and they identified the four most helpful and least helpful comments made by the counselors. Analyses of the helpful comments identified both "task" and "interpersonal" clusters of comments. Within the task cluster, students perceived as most helpful those comments aiding them in getting a new perspective on their problem. Within the interpersonal cluster, the most helpful comments were perceived as those displaying appreciation of feelings and sympathy about the situation. Further, objective coders classified the comments students perceived most helpful as "interpretations," "reflections," or "reassurances,"—all types of statements in which the helper articulates and legitimizes the other's feelings (see Elliott, Barker, Caskey, & Pistrang, 1982; Elliott, Stiles, Shiffman, Barker, Burstein, & Goodman, 1982; Goodman & Dooley, 1976). Elliott's (1985) results were subsequently replicated with both clinical and non-clinical populations (see Barkham & Shapiro, 1986; Elliott, James, Reimschuessel, Cislo, & Sack, 1985). These findings support the notion that "sophisticated" comforting strategies represent effective means of handling emotional upsets. Moreover, these findings are particularly significant since they provide insight about the utterances people *subjectively* experience as helpful (also see Barbee, 1990).

The findings obtained by Elliot (1985) in a clinical context are remarkably similar to those obtained by Wortman (1984) in an interview study with cancer patients. Wortman had her participants describe comforting strategies they found both helpful and unhelpful. She concluded that "verbalizing personal concerns during a time of stress can help to clarify feelings, develop strategies for managing them more effectively, and begin active problem-solving" (Wortman, 1984, p. 2343). Messages from peers that encouraged them to engage in such verbalizations were perceived by patients as the most helpful. Several other studies confirm the value of encouraging distressed others to ventilate and reflect on their feelings (see Albrecht & Adelman, 1987, p. 33).

Other research from the inductive-descriptive perspective suggests that people view "sophisticated" comforting strategies as doing a good job of relieving emotional distress. For example, Dakof and Taylor (1990), Lehman and Hemphill (1990), and Lehman et al. (1986) all found that utterances acknowledging the legitimacy of the distressed other's feelings were viewed as "helpful." Equally important, inductive-descriptive studies have found that people report as ineffective those messages the functional-hierarchical perspective identifies as "unsophisticated" (see the review by Goldsmith, 1992). For example, a directive advising the individual how he or she *should* feel about an emotionally charged situation is almost always seen as unhelpful—and is frequently resented.

Research on the immediate, instrumental effects of comforting messages thus shows that people generally perceive theoretically "sophisticated" strategies as the most effective and sensitive means of responding to another's distress. Moreover, these perceptions do not vary as a function of several individual-difference and situational variables. Further, recent research informed by the deductive-prescriptive perspective (Elliot, 1985), the inductive-descriptive perspective (Dakof & Taylor, 1990; Lehman et al., 1986; Wortman, 1984), and other frameworks (e.g., Barbee, 1990), suggests that messages similar in structure to those regarded here as "sophisticated" are *experienced* by distressed others as particularly helpful.[2]

THE LONG-TERM, INSTRUMENTAL EFFECTS
OF SOPHISTICATED COMFORTING STRATEGIES

There are several ways in which regular exposure to sophisticated comforting strategies might help recipients develop the resources necessary for the self-management of distressful situations. Thoits (1984) suggests that individuals draw from an analysis of their personal methods for coping with stress in formulating comforting messages directed at helping others. However, the reverse could also be true: Message recipients might derive rules for the functional management of their emotions by analyzing comforting strategies to which they have been exposed. Such analyses could yield several rules for managing emotional distress, including: (a) don't suppress or ignore feelings, but rather work to explore, recognize, and articulate them, (b) view feelings as responses to specific situations (rather than as chronic conditions), (c) try to understand how particular features of situations, and their effects on hopes and goals, cause particular feelings, and (d) view distressful situations in the context of broader goals, ambitions, and hopes. If such rules are internalized, practiced, and used, they may help people manage the disappointments and hurts they are sure to encounter. Hochschild's (1979) research on the sociology of emotion demonstrates that people routinely engage in such "emotion work," and further shows that people acquire coping strategies interactively, i.e., from the comforting messages to which they have been exposed.

Socialization studies (e.g., Applegate, Burleson, & Delia, 1992) suggest that regular exposure to sophisticated comforting strategies enhances the social-cognitive development of message recipients. This may equip them with refined cognitive tools for understanding themselves, others, and affectively charged situations. Social-cognitive development is one important factor underlying the ability to produce sophisticated comforting strategies (see the reviews by Burleson, 1985, 1987). It is possible, then, that persons with advanced levels of social-cognitive development may also engage in more effective "self comforting."

In sum, regular exposure to sophisticated comforting strategies may facilitate the ability to self-manage emotional distress. Two mechanisms through which exposure to sophisticated comforting messages might influence the ability to self-manage distress have received some attention. As yet, however, no empirical evidence has conclusively shown that persons regularly exposed to sophisticated comforting strategies either derive rules for the functional management of affect from these strategies or develop advanced social-cognitive abilities. Future studies should examine more directly the extent to which these mechanisms contribute to the individual's capacity to cope with emotional upsets.

THE IMMEDIATE, RELATIONAL EFFECTS
OF SOPHISTICATED COMFORTING STRATEGIES

Several recent studies suggest that the users of sophisticated comforting strategies are perceived more positively than the users of less sophisticated strategies. Burleson and Samter (1985a, Study 1) found that confederates feigning emotional distress in the presence of experimental participants better liked those participants employing a high proportion of sophisticated comforting strategies. Samter et al. (1987) report that participants reading conversations containing sophisticated comforting strategies rated the fictional source of the messages more positively than subjects reading conversations containing less sophisticated strategies. If sophisticated comforting strategies are more effective at reducing emotional distress than their less sophisticated counterparts, then it makes sense to find that people like those who make them feel good (or, at least, make them feel less bad). Further, the evaluations of uninvolved observers (such as those in the Samter et al. [1987] investigation) suggest that people use comforting behavior they observe as a basis for judging the social competence and likability of message producers.

While comforting is an important activity, it is often difficult and demanding. Indeed, several recent studies document the difficulty of improving the affective state of a depressed other and suggest that a lack of success may lead to hostility toward and withdrawal from the other (see Coyne, Wortman, & Lehman, 1988; Gottlieb & Beatty, 1985). However, tendency to feel negatively toward those experiencing distress may be qualified by the comforting skill of the provider and the sophistication of the messages employed. Consistent with this view, Notarius and Herrick (1988) found that the users of sophisticated comforting strategies felt better about *themselves* than the users of less sensitive strategies. Participants interacted with a confederate who feigned distress about having been "dumped" by her boyfriend. Mood of the participants was assessed both before and after interacting with the confederate. Those using unsophisticated strategies were more anxious and depressed following the interaction than those using sophisticated strategies. In addition, users of less sophisticated strategies were more rejecting of the confederate following the episode than users of sophisticated strategies.

Those who produce ineffective, unsophisticated strategies may recognize their messages lack efficacy, and thus become frustrated with both their lack of success and the person they ineffectually seek to help (see DePaulo, 1982; Wortman & Lehman, 1985). Indeed there is some evidence that those less able to comfort others effectively engage in *victimization*, the tendency to blame and derogate the distressed other for the stressful situation (see Dunkel-Schetter & Bennett, 1990). If unskilled comforters are unsuccessful at helping others and tend to engage in victimization, they may come to ignore or avoid comforting situations (thereby, of course, eliminating the possibility of improving their comforting skills). In contrast, users of sophisticated strategies may experience a sense of accomplishment and receive appreciation from those they help. These positive experiences could lead users of sophisticated strategies to seek out situations in which they can practice and further develop their comforting skills.

THE LONG-TERM RELATIONAL CONSEQUENCES OF SOPHISTICATED COMFORTING STRATEGIES

Recent research (e.g., Burleson & Samter, 1990) indicates that people place a relatively high value on the comforting skills of significant relationship partners. This suggests that the regular use of sophisticated comforting strategies may contribute to the development of stable, satisfying interpersonal relationships (Burleson & Samter, in press). More specifically, those capable of producing sensitive and sophisticated comforting messages may be more effective in interpersonal relationships, and may thus come to be better liked and more valued as a social companion. Several studies have recently evaluated this hypothesis, examining the extent to which comforting skills contribute to an individual's long-term success in interpersonal relationships.

Three studies have assessed how individual differences in children's comforting skills influence the quality of peer relationships. Burleson, Applegate, Burke, Clark, Delia, and Kline (1986) had grade-school children complete a battery of six communication skills assessments, including the ability to produce sophisticated comforting messages. Sociometric methods were employed to classify the participants into groups of popular, average, neglected, and rejected children. It was found that among the six communication abilities, comforting skill best discriminated among the groups of children, with those in the rejected group having significantly poorer comforting skills than children in any of the other groups. Burleson and Waltman (1987) attempted to replicate the results of Burleson et al. (1986) with a group of preadolescents. Unfortunately, the task used by Burleson and Waltman to assess comforting skill failed to yield a meaningful range of scores; thus, no relationship was found between comforting skill and peer acceptance. However, Burleson, Delia, and Applegate (1992) found that children's comforting skills were both positively associated with their acceptance by peers and negatively associated with peer rejection.

The association between comforting skill and peer acceptance in adult populations was examined by Samter and Burleson (1990b). These researchers had college students living in fraternities and sororities complete a battery of communication skill assessments and provide both positive and negative sociometric nominations for all members of their houses. A significant negative association was found between comforting skill and the number of negative nominations received by an individual, indicating that persons with poor comforting skills were disliked by house members. Although these correlational findings are open to several interpretations, they replicate Burleson et al.'s (1986) results with children, and are consistent with the hypothesis that poor comforting skills contribute to peer rejection. In a related study, Samter (1992) found that individuals whose friends possessed poor comforting skills were significantly more lonely than those whose friends had good comforting skills.

In sum, a growing body of evidence suggests that the ability to provide sensitive, sophisticated comfort may have long-term effects on the quality of people's interpersonal relationships. Obviously the long-term relational effects of comforting styles need more extensive investigation. For example, recent studies indicate that interpersonal attraction and friendship patterns may be more a function of *similarity* in partners' levels of comforting skills rather than the absolute level of individuals' skill (see Burleson & Samter, in press). Still, the available evidence is consistent with the notion that skill in comforting has important consequences for interpersonal relationships, with those capable of generating highly sophisticated strategies more successful in personal relationships than those with less ability.

Conclusion

Comforting is an important activity in the world of everyday life. Even comparatively minor upsets and distresses can negatively affect health and well being. Fortunately research shows that sensitive comfort from family, friends, and coworkers can help individuals cope with the stressors they routinely encounter. Such aid has been found to improve the physical, emotional, and psychological well being of its recipients. Consistent with these findings, people view comforting as a significant behavior and place high value on the comforting skills of their friends. Moreover, comforting and related forms of emotional support play critical roles in the formation, development, and maintenance of close interpersonal relationships. Comforting interactions may help transform a casual relationship into a close one. And in close relationships, comforting interactions help reinforce intimacy by signaling care, interest, and commitment.

The study of comforting activity presents special challenges to researchers. Both ethical and practical considerations limit the techniques and designs that can be used to study the comforting process. Still, several different approaches have been used successfully in the study of comforting behavior, including experimentation, the observation of interactions between friends in the laboratory, the use of confederates feigning emotional distress, interviews with clients seeking support from professional counselors, and retrospective self reports. These methods generate different information about comforting messages and their effects. However, because comforting is a complex process with many nuances and contours, its study is enhanced by a diverse methodological arsenal. Moreover, the triangulation achieved through the use of multiple methods enables researchers to reach conclusions in which they have greater confidence.

One conclusion supported by research stemming from diverse theoretical and methodological roots is that comforting messages designated "sophisticated" by the functional-hierarchic perspective represent relatively effective ways of managing another's distress. Sophisticated messages are those which acknowledge, elaborate, legitimize, and contextualize the feelings and perspective of a distressed other. Some research has found that sophisticated messages are perceived as more effective than unsophisticated strategies, while other evidence suggests that these strategies do a better job of relieving emotional hurts. Moreover, regular exposure to sophisticated comforting messages may help recipients develop skills for the self-management of potentially distressful situations. Compared to persons using less sophisticated comforting strategies, users of sophisticated strategies are better liked and more positively evaluated by both message recipients and observers. Further, users of sophisticated comforting strategies report feeling better both about themselves and those they try to help. Also, evidence suggests that persons able to produce sophisticated comforting strategies have better relationships with peers than those less able to produce such strategies. In sum, the use of sophisticated comforting messages appears associated with several desirable outcomes.

Although existing findings about the effects of sophisticated comforting messages are encouraging, many gaps in our knowledge about these messages remain to be filled. One goal for future research should be improving our understanding about *how* comforting messages affect the emotional states of others (see Thoits, 1984). Considerable research influenced by the work of Lazarus (1968, 1991) views emotional states as resulting from the individual's *appraisal* of an event, the cognitive process of categorizing an event with respect to its significance for well being (see Parkinson & Manstead, 1992; Smith & Pope, 1992). For example, theorists writing from the perspective of attribution theory (e.g., Abramson, Seligman, & Teasdale, 1978; Brickman, Rabinowitz, Karuza, Coates, Cohn, & Kidder, 1982; Garber & Seligman, 1980) suggest appraisals about the controllability of events can lead to experiences of depression or loss. This implies that comforting messages may bring relief to others by getting them to reappraise the situation and modify their attributions (see Valins & Nisbett, 1972). Indeed, some research indicates that emotions such as fear (e.g., Ross, Rodin, & Zimbardo, 1969) and anxiety (e.g., Wilson & Linville, 1982) can be modified through messages directed at modifying the attributions of recipients. Other researchers (see Albrecht & Adelman, 1987, pp. 30-34) suggest that effective comforting messages encourage catharsis or the venting of pent-up emotions.

Appraisal theory thus offers a comprehensive framework explaining both the origin and modification of emotional states. Much more research is needed examining how the features of sophisticated comforting messages can facilitate the functional reappraisal of events. Such research promises to enhance our understanding not only of the comforting process, but also of our nature as emotional beings.

Notes

1. A fourth approach to the study of comforting messages might also be described: an experimental approach exhibited in the social psychology literature. In such research, comforting messages are elicited in the laboratory by having subjects respond to varied experimental tasks. A common task is to have a subject respond to a friend or stranger within whom mild emotional distress has been induced through some experimental procedure (e.g., giving a public speech, contemplating having to handle a large spider, watching a sad movie, repeating words indexing sad and depressed emotional states, etc.). Messages generated in response to such tasks are typically categorized within a nominal-level coding system (see Barbee, 1990). The effects of different messages are frequently inferred from subjects' performances on subsequent laboratory tasks. Evaluations of the quality of different messages have also been obtained from the participants in whom distress was induced. Additional features and applications of this approach are described by Derlega, Barbee, and Winstead in their chapter in this volume.

2. Although it appears that "sophisticated" comforting strategies are useful ways of managing the distressed states of others, it should not be assumed that such strategies are invariably the best or most effective responses. As Cutrona, Cohen, and Igram (1990) have shown, in developing a specific comforting response, helpers need to consider individual characteristics of the distressed other, the relationship shared with the other, features of the social situation, and the cultural milieu in which comforting occurs. It is quite conceivable that relatively unsophisticated strategies might do the best job of comforting another in a specific situation. Presumably, the advanced cognitive processes of those able to produce sophisticated strategies enable them to determine the specific strategy most likely to comfort another in a particular situation. This, however, is a hypothesis that remains to be tested. Clearly, giving useful advice about the provision of comfort in specific situations will require more research on the factors leading to different forms of emotional distress and how a variety of contextual variables influence the interpretation and, hence, effects of comforting efforts. In particular, research needs to examine systematically how aspects of the distressful event, features of the setting in which comforting occurs, and the character of the relationship between the helper and helpee influence the reception, processing, and effects of comforting messages.

References

Abramson, L. Y., Seligman, M.E.P., & Teasdale, J. D. (1978). Learned helplessness in humans: Critique and reformulation. *Journal of Abnormal Psychology, 87,* 49-74.

Albrecht, T. L., & Adelman, M. B. (Eds.). (1987). *Communicating social support.* Newbury Park, CA: Sage.

Allen, M., et al. (1992, November). *Comparing social, expert, and target ratings of comforting messages.* Paper presented at the annual meeting of the Speech Communication Association, Chicago, IL.

Applegate, J. L. (1980). Adaptive communication in educational contexts. *Communication Education, 29,* 158-170.

Applegate, J. L., Burleson, B. R., & Delia, J. G. (1992). Reflection-enhancing parenting as antecedent to children's social-cognitive and communicative development. In I. E. Sigel,

A. V. McGillicuddy-Delisi, & J. J. Goodnow (Eds.), *Parental belief systems: The psychological consequences for children* (2nd ed., pp. 3-39). Hillsdale, NJ: Lawrence Erlbaum.

Barbee, A. P. (1990). Interactive coping: The cheering-up process in close relationships. In S. Duck with R. Silver (Eds.), *Personal relationships and social support* (pp. 46-65). London: Sage.

Barbee, A. P., Druen, P. B., Gulley, M. R., Yankeelov, P. A., & Cunningham, M. R. (in press). Social support as a mechanism for the maintenance of close relationships. *Journal of Social and Personal Relationships.*

Barbee, A. P., & Yankeelov, P. A. (1992, July). *Social support as a mechanism for relationship maintenance.* Paper presented at the meeting of the International Society for the Study of Personal Relationships, Orono, ME.

Barkham, M., & Shapiro, D. A. (1986). Counselor verbal response modes and experienced empathy. *Journal of Counseling Psychology, 33,* 3-10.

Berndt, T. J., & Perry, T. B. (1986). Children's perceptions of friendships as supportive relationships. *Developmental Psychology, 22,* 640-648.

Bernstein, B. (1975). *Class, codes, and control: Theoretical studies towards a sociology of language* (rev. ed.). New York: Schocken Books.

Brickman, P., Rabinowitz, V. C., Karuza, J., Jr., Coates, D., Cohn, E., & Kidder, L. (1982). Models of helping and coping. *American Psychologist, 37,* 368-384.

Burleson, B. R. (1982). The development of comforting communication skills in childhood and adolescence. *Child Development, 53,* 1578-1588.

Burleson, B. R. (1984a). Comforting communication. In H. E. Sypher & J. L. Applegate (Eds.), *Communication by children and adults: Social cognitive and strategic processes* (pp. 63-104). Beverly Hills, CA: Sage.

Burleson, B. R. (1984b). Age, social-cognitive development, and the use of comforting strategies. *Communication Monographs, 51,* 140-153.

Burleson, B. R. (1985). The production of comforting messages: Social-cognitive foundations. *Journal of Language and Social Psychology, 4,* 253-273.

Burleson, B. R. (1987). Cognitive complexity. In J. C. McCroskey & J. A. Daly (Eds.), *Personality and interpersonal communication* (pp. 305-349). Newbury Park, CA: Sage.

Burleson, B. R. (1990). Comforting as everyday social support: Relational consequences of supportive behaviors. In S. Duck (Ed.), *Personal relationships and social support* (pp. 66-82). London: Sage.

Burleson, B. R. (1994). Comforting messages: Features, functions, and outcomes. In J. A. Daly & J. M. Wiemann (Eds.), *Strategic interpersonal communication* (pp. 135-161). Hillsdale, NJ: Lawrence Erlbaum.

Burleson, B. R., Applegate, J. L., Burke, J. A., Clark, R. A., Delia, J. G., & Kline, S. L. (1986). Communicative correlates of peer acceptance in childhood. *Communication Education, 35,* 349-361.

Burleson, B. R., Delia, J. G., & Applegate, J. L. (1992). Effects of maternal communication and children's social-cognitive and communication skills on children's acceptance by the peer group. *Family Relations, 41,* 264-272.

Burleson, B. R., Kunkel, A. W., & Birch, J. (1993). *Evaluations of communication skills by dating couples.* Unpublished data, Department of Communication, Purdue University, West Lafayette, IN.

Burleson, B. R., & Samter, W. (1985a). Consistencies in theoretical and naive evaluations of comforting messages. *Communication Monographs, 52,* 103-123.

Burleson, B. R., & Samter, W. (1985b). Individual differences in the perception of comforting messages: An exploratory investigation. *Central States Speech Journal, 36*, 39-50.

Burleson, B. R., & Samter, W. (1990). Effects of cognitive complexity on the perceived importance of communication skills in friends. *Communication Research, 17*, 165-182.

Burleson, B. R., & Samter, W. (in press). A social skills approach to relationship maintenance: How individual differences in communication skills affect the achievement of relationship functions. In D. J. Canary & L. Stafford (Eds.), *Communication and relational maintenance*. Orlando, FL: Academic Press.

Burleson, B. R., & Waltman, P. A. (1987). Popular, rejected, and supportive preadolescents: Social-cognitive and communicative characteristics. In M. L. McLaughlin (Ed.), *Communication yearbook* (Vol. 10, pp. 533-552). Newbury Park, CA: Sage.

Burleson, B. R., Werking, K. J., Samter, W., & Holloway, R. (1988, November). *Person-centered communication skills and friendship in young adults: Which skills matter most?* Paper presented at the Speech Communication Association convention, New Orleans.

Carkhuff, R. R., & Berenson, B. G. (1977). *Beyond counseling and therapy* (2nd ed.). New York: Holt, Rinehart, & Winston.

Constable, J. F., & Russell, D. W. (1986). The effect of social support and the work environment upon burnout among nurses. *Journal of Human Stress, 12*, 20-26.

Coyne,, J. C., Wortman, C. B., & Lehman, D. R. (1988). The other side of social support: Emotional overinvolvement and miscarried helping. In B. Gottlieb (Ed.), *Marshalling social support: Formats, processes, and effects* (pp. 305-330). Newbury Park, CA: Sage.

Cutrona, C. E., Cohen, B. B., & Igram, S. (1990). Contextual determinants of the perceived helpfulness of helping behaviors. *Journal of Social and Personal Relationships, 7*, 553-562.

Cutrona, C. E., & Russell, D. W. (1990). Types of social support and specific stress: Toward a theory of optimal matching. In B. R. Sarason, I. G. Sarason, & G. R. Pierce (Eds.), *Social support: An interactional view* (pp. 319-366). New York: John Wiley.

Cutrona, C. E., & Suhr, J. A. (1992). Controllability of stressful events and satisfaction with spouse support behaviors. *Communication Research, 19*, 154-174.

Cutrona, C. E., Suhr, J. A., & MacFarlane, R. (1990). Interpersonal transactions and the psychological sense of support. In S. Duck with R. Silver (Eds.), *Personal relationships and social support* (pp. 30-45). London: Sage.

Dakof, G. A., & Taylor, S. E. (1990). Victims' perceptions of support attempts: What is helpful from whom? *Journal of Personality and Social Psychology, 58*, 80-89.

Davis, K. E., & Todd, M. J. (1985). Assessing friendship: Prototypes, paradigm cases, and relationship description. In S. Duck & D. Perlman (Eds.), *Understanding personal relationships: An interdisciplinary approach* (pp. 17-38). London: Sage.

DeLongis, A., Coyne, J. C., Dakof, G., Folkman, S., & Lazarus, R. S. (1982). Relation of daily hassles, uplifts, and major life events to health status. *Health Psychology, 1*, 119-136.

DePaulo, B. M. (1982). Social-psychological processes in informal help seeking. In T. A. Willis (Ed.), *Basic processes in helping relationships* (pp. 255-279). New York: Academic Press.

Dunkel-Schetter, C. (1984). Social support and cancer: Findings based on patient interviews and their implications. *Journal of Social Issues, 40*, 77-98.

Dunkel-Schetter C., & Bennett, T. L. (1990). Differentiating the cognitive and behavioral aspects of social support. In B. R. Sarason, I. G. Sarason, & G. R. Pierce (Eds.), *Social support: An interactional view* (pp. 267-296). New York: John Wiley.

Eckenrode, J. (1984). Impact of chronic and acute stressors on daily reports of mood. *Journal of Personality and Social Psychology, 46*, 907-918.

Eisenberg, N. (1989). *The roots of prosocial behavior in children.* New York: Cambridge University Press.

Elliott, R. (1985). Helpful and nonhelpful events in brief counseling interviews: An empirical taxonomy. *Journal of Counseling Psychology, 32*, 307-322.

Elliott, R., Barker, C. B., Caskey, N., & Pistrang, N. (1982). Differential helpfulness of counselor verbal response modes. *Journal of Counseling Psychology, 29*, 354-361.

Elliott, R., James, E., Reimschuessel, C., Cislo, D., & Sack, N. (1985). Significant events and the analysis of immediate therapeutic impacts. *Psychotherapy, 22*, 620-630.

Elliott, R., Stiles, W. B., Shiffman, S., Barker, C. B., Burstine, B., & Goodman, G. (1982). The empirical analysis of help-intended communications: Conceptual framework and recent research. In T. A. Wills (Ed.), *Basic processes in helping relationships* (pp. 333-356). New York: Academic Press.

Frankel, B. G., & Turner, R. J. (1983). Psychological adjustment in chronic disability: The role of social support in the case of the hearing impaired. *Canadian Journal of Sociology, 8*, 273-291.

Garber, J., & Seligman, M. E. P. (1980). *Human helplessness: Theory and applications.* New York: Academic Press.

Goldsmith, D. (1992). Managing conflicting goals in supportive interaction: An integrative theoretical framework. *Communication Research, 19*, 264-286.

Goodman, G., & Dooley, D. (1976). A framework for help-intended communication. *Psychotherapy: Theory, Research, and Practice, 13*, 106-117.

Gottlieb, B. H., & Beatty, E. (1985). Negative responses to depression: The role of attributional style. *Cognitive Therapy Research, 9*, 91-103.

Hirsch, B. J., & Reischl, T. M. (1985). Social networks and developmental psychopathology: A comparison of adolescent children of depressed, arthritic, or normal parents. *Journal of Abnormal Psychology, 94*, 272-281.

Hochschild, A. (1979). Emotion work, feeling rules, and social structure. *American Journal of Sociology, 85*, 551-575.

Kanner, A. D., Coyne, J. C., Schaefer, C., & Lazarus, R. S. (1981). Comparison of two modes of stress measurement: Daily hassles and uplifts versus major life events. *Journal of Behavioral Medicine, 4*, 1-39.

Krause, N. (1986). Social support, stress, and well-being among older adults. *Journal of Gerontology, 41*, 512-519.

Krause, N. (1987). Chronic financial strain, social support, and depressive symptoms among older adults. *Psychology and Aging, 2*, 185-192.

Lambert, M. J., DeJulio, S. S., & Stein, D. M. (1978). Therapist interpersonal skills: Process, outcome, methodological considerations, and recommendations for future research. *Psychological Bulletin, 85*, 467-489.

Lazarus, R. S. (1968). Emotions and adaptation. In W. J. Arnold (Ed.), *Nebraska Symposium on Motivation* (vol. 16, pp. 175-265). Lincoln, NE: University of Nebraska Press.

Lazarus, R. S. (1991). *Emotion and adaptation.* New York: Oxford University Press.

Lehman, D. R., Ellard, J. H., & Wortman, C. B. (1986). Social support for the bereaved: Recipients' and providers' perspectives on what is helpful. *Journal of Consulting and Clinical Psychology, 54*, 438-446.

Lehman, D. R., & Hemphill, K. J. (1990). Recipients' perceptions of support attempts and attributions for support attempts that fail. *Journal of Social and Personal Relationships, 7*, 563-574.

Marcus, R. F. (1980). Empathy and popularity of preschool children. *Child Study Journal, 10*, 133-145.

Mitchell, K. M., Bozarth, J. D., & Krauft, C. C. (1977). A reappraisal of the therapeutic effectiveness of accurate empathy, non-possessive warmth, and genuineness. In A. S. Gurman & A. M. Razin (Eds.), *Effective psychotherapy: A handbook of research* (pp. 482-502). New York: Pergamon Press.

Notarius, C. I., & Herrick, L. R. (1988). Listener response strategies to a distressed other. *Journal of Social and Personal Relationships, 5*, 97-108.

O'Keefe, B. J., & Delia, J. G. (1982). Impression formation and message production. In M. E. Roloff & C. R. Berger (Eds.), *Social cognition and communication* (pp. 33-72). Beverly Hills, CA: Sage.

Olweus, D., Block, J., & Radke-Yarrow, M. (Eds.) (1986). *Development of antisocial and prosocial behavior: Research, theories, and issues.* Orlando, FL: Academic Press.

Parkinson, B., & Manstead, A. S. R. (1992). Appraisal as a cause of emotion. In M. S. Clark (Ed.), *Emotion* (pp. 122-149). Newbury Park, CA: Sage.

Parloff, M. B., Waskow, I., & Wolfe, B. (1978). Research on therapist variables in relation to process and outcome. In S. L. Garfield & A. E. Bergin (Eds.), *Handbook of psychotherapy and behavior change: An empirical analysis* (2nd ed., pp. 233-282). New York: John Wiley.

Peters-Golden, H. (1982). Breast cancer: Varied perceptions of social support in the illness experience. *Social Science and Medicine, 16*, 483-491.

Rogers, C. R. (1957). The necessary and sufficient conditions of therapeutic personality change. *Journal of Consulting Psychology, 21*, 95-103.

Rogers, C. R. (1975). Empathic: An unappreciated way of being. *Counseling Psychologist, 5*, 2-10.

Ross, L., Rodin, J., & Zimbardo, P. G. (1969). The reduction of fear through induced cognitive-emotional misattribution. *Journal of Personality and Social Psychology, 12*, 279-288.

Samter, W. (1992). Communicative characteristics of the lonely person's friendship circle. *Communication Research, 19*, 212-239.

Samter, W., & Burleson, B. R. (1984). Cognitive and motivational influences on spontaneous comforting behavior. *Human Communication Research, 11*, 231-260.

Samter, W., & Burleson, B. R. (1990a). Evaluations of communication skills as predictors of peer acceptance in a group living situation. *Communication Studies, 41*, 311-326.

Samter, W., & Burleson, B. R. (1990b, June). *The role of affectively oriented communication skills in the friendships of young adults: A sociometric study.* Paper presented at the International Communication Association convention, Dublin.

Samter, W., Burleson, B. R., & Basden, L. (1989). Behavioral complexity is in the eye of the beholder: Effects of cognitive complexity and message complexity on impressions of the source of comforting messages. *Human Communication Research, 15*, 612-629.

Samter, W., Burleson, B. R., & Murphy, L. (1987). Comforting conversations: Effects of strategy type on evaluations of messages and message producers. *Southern Speech Communication Journal, 52*, 263-284.

Smith, C. A., & Pope, L. K. (1992). Appraisal and emotion: The interactional contribution of dispositional and situational factors. In M. S. Clark (Ed.), *Emotion and social behavior* (pp. 32-62). Newbury Park, CA: Sage.

Stafford, L., Burggraf, C. S., & Sharkey, W. F. (1987). Conversational memory: The effects of time, recall mode, and memory expectancies on remembrances of natural conversations. *Human Communication Research, 14*, 203-229.

Stafford, L., & Daly, J. A. (1984). Conversational memory: The effects of recall mode and memory expectancies on remembrances of natural conversations. *Human Communication Research, 10*, 379-402.

Stafford, L., Waldron, V. R., & Infield, L. L. (1989). Actor-observer differences in conversational memory. *Human Communication Research, 15*, 590-611.

Stone, A. A. (1981). The association between perceptions of daily experiences and self- and spouse-rated mood. *Journal of Research in Personality, 15*, 510-522.

Tesch, S. A. (1983). Review of friendship development across the life span. *Human Development, 26*, 266-276.

Thoits, P. A. (1984). Coping, social support, and psychological outcomes. In P. Shaver (Ed.), *Review of personality and social psychology* (vol 5., pp. 219-238). Beverly Hills, CA: Sage.

Thoits, P. A. (1985). Social support and psychological well-being: Theoretical possibilities. In I. G. Sarason & B. R. Sarason (Eds.), *Social support: Theory, research, and applications* (pp. 51-72). Dordrecht, The Netherlands: Martinus Nijhoff.

Truax, C. B., & Carkhuff, R. R. (1967). *Toward effective counseling and psychotherapy.* Chicago: Aldine.

Truax, C. B., & Mitchell, K. (1971). Research on certain therapist characteristics. In A. Bergin & S. Garfield (Eds.), *Handbook of psychotherapy and behavior change.* New York: John Wiley.

Valins, S., & Nisbett, R. E. (1972). Attribution processes in the development and treatment of emotional disorders. In E. E. Jones, D. E. Kanouse, H. H. Kelley, R. E. Nisbett, S. Valins, & B. Weiner (Eds.), *Attribution: Perceiving the causes of behavior.* Morristown, NJ: General Learning Press.

Werner, H. (1957). The concept of development from a comparative and organismic point of view. In D. B. Harris (Ed.), *The concept of development* (pp. 125-146). Minneapolis, MN: University of Minnesota Press.

Wilson, T. D., & Linville, P. W. (1982). Improving the academic performance of college freshman: Attribution therapy revisited. *Journal of Personality and Social Psychology, 42*, 367-376.

Wortman, C. B. (1984). Social support and the cancer patient: Conceptual and methodological issues. *Cancer, 53*, 2339-2360.

Wortman, C. B., & Lehman, D. R. (1985). Reactions to victims of life crises: Support attempts that fail. In G. Sarason & B. R. Sarason (Eds.), *Social support: Theory, research, and application* (pp. 463-489). Dordrecht, The Netherlands: Martinus Nijhoff.

2

The Role of Facework
in Supportive Communication

DAENA J. GOLDSMITH

I recently saw a "get well" card that simply said "It's difficult to know what to say but I want you to know I am thinking of you." Greeting card companies may be on to something that researchers in social support have too often overlooked: It can be difficult to know what to say to someone experiencing distress and the particular type of support we decide to give and the manner in which we give it are important. Is giving advice helpful or is it better to listen empathically? How forceful should one be in offering advice? Is saying "I know exactly how you feel!" a helpful display of sympathy and solidarity or an insensitive way of turning the conversation to one's own problems? Does that depend on how one says it? Well-intentioned messages may not provide what a distressed person wants and even messages that are responsive to a person's needs can still burden a relationship, imply criticism, or create feelings of dependence and obligation.

In fact, there is evidence that "saying the right thing" doesn't always come easily. First, the communication behaviors we recognize as intended to convey support may not, in fact, be helpful (see Albrecht & Adelman, 1987 for a review) and the effects of negative interactions often have a greater impact than the effects of positive interactions (see Rook & Pietromonaco, 1987 for a review). Second, measures of the number of supportive behaviors a person has received are unevenly correlated with a recipient's perception of behaviors as supportive or with positive psychological and physical outcomes for the recipient (see Dunkel-Schetter & Bennett, 1990 for a review).

This chapter begins from the assumptions that "saying the right thing" involves selecting a message that is appropriate and that the impact of what we say is integrally related to how we say it. "Facework" strategies are an important aspect of how we convey a supportive message and a theory of facework provides an integrative explanatory framework for viewing previous research on support dilemmas and unhelpful messages. The theory also provides a starting point for identifying message features that affect the perceived helpfulness of a message. Finally, the approach to social interaction implicit in politeness theory suggests a useful way of conceptualizing supportive acts and supportive outcomes and suggests various directions for further research.

Politeness Theory

Researchers in micro-sociology, pragmatic linguistics, and speech communication have theorized that concerns for acceptance, autonomy, and self-presentation are intrinsic to all social interactions. This position has been most systematically developed in Brown and Levinson's (1987) theory of "politeness," where "politeness" is understood as the linguistic embellishment of messages beyond what mere efficiency in a message would require in order that interactants' self-images are preserved.

Brown and Levinson claim all persons want others to show acceptance of the self-image they project in interaction (positive face) and regard for their freedom of action and freedom from imposition (negative face). Because these are public claims, face is granted or not granted by others and this produces an ever present motivation in interactions to cooperatively show regard for one anothers' face.

Many of the other goals we might pursue in an interaction can threaten positive or negative face. For example, requests and offers impose on freedom of action, criticism challenges acceptance, giving advice may both impose and imply lack of acceptance. Brown and Levinson claim the face threat of an act may be mitigated or aggravated by social distance between speaker and hearer (e.g., a reprimand may be less threatening when it comes from a friend than a stranger) and power discrepancy between speaker and hearer (e.g., a request from inferior to superior is a greater imposition than a request between equals or from superior to inferior). In addition, interactants in a culture typically share some ideas

about the relative degree of threat intrinsic in certain acts (e.g., a "sugges-
tion" is less imposing than "advice").

Committing a face-threatening act may result in repair (e.g., apologies,
excuses) but more often, we design our messages to avoid offending
others' face. Five broad categories of options have been elaborated both
in Brown and Levinson's theory and in subsequent research; my purpose
here is to illustrate the types of options open to speakers rather than to
give a comprehensive treatment of the many ways of executing these
strategies.

Imagine an individual giving advice to a friend. The advice may provide
helpful information; however, giving advice could threaten the recipient's
positive face by suggesting he or she has handled a situation incorrectly
or is unable to act effectively. Giving advice threatens the recipient's
negative face if he or she feels obligated to follow the advice or resents
being told what to do. A would-be support provider may employ five
different types of strategies for giving advice and protecting face.

One option is simply to give the advice regardless of the consequences
for face. Brown and Levinson call this strategy "bald on record." Another
option is to commit the potentially face-threatening act (in this example,
giving advice) and add redress to positive face. For example, the support
giver might preface advice with an affirmation that the recipient has been
doing an able job of managing the situation or the support giver might
emphasize his or her similarity to the recipient to highlight acceptance. A
third option is to commit the face-threatening act and add redress for
negative face: phrases such as "I don't mean to tell you what to do" or "I
don't know if this would work but maybe you could try" soften the degree
to which the advice tells the recipient what to do or the degree to which
the recipient feels obligated to follow the advice. A fourth option is to
commit the face-threatening act "off-the-record": sharing a similar experience without explicitly suggesting the recipient do likewise can indirectly suggest a course of action without going on record as telling the
recipient what to do or saying the recipient has done it wrong. A final
option is to not give the advice and avoid threat to the other person's face
all together.

Bald-on-record is the clearest and most efficient way to give advice or
perform some other kind of supportive act. When a speaker departs from
the most efficient way of conveying a message by adding redress or
conveying the message indirectly, a hearer infers the speaker is trying to
convey something else as well: concern for positive or negative face. It
might appear that the safest, most supportive option would be to always

choose indirect strategies, since these mask the face threat. However, doing so may make the support offered less clear and effective. It may also lead a hearer to infer a greater threat to his or her face than need be: Is the speaker "beating around the bush" because he or she thinks my problem reveals an embarrassing weakness? Because he or she thinks I am too fragile to handle it? Consequently, a speaker's choice of a strategy must be adapted to multiple goals of conveying support, showing regard for face, and managing the inferences the hearer draws from the speaker's selection of one strategy rather than another.

Casting New Light on Extant Research

DILEMMAS OF SUPPORT

Support recipients experience threats to their positive face when they worry about the impression others will have of them. Receiving support may make the recipient look weak (Wills, 1983; Chapman & Pancoast, 1985) or undesirable information may become known in the interaction (Goldsmith, 1988). Seeking support for a problem may lead to stigmatization by others (Chesler & Barbarin, 1984; Wortman & Dunkel-Schetter, 1979) as well as negative self-evaluations. Recipients may feel less competent and in control and may feel a reduced sense of achievement as a result of having to seek help (DePaulo, 1982; Fisher, Nadler & Whitcher-Alagna, 1982).

Support can threaten a recipient's negative face by constraining freedom of action. Unwanted aid can be an intrusion and desired aid can still invade an individual's privacy (Chesler & Barbarin, 1984). Receiving aid may require disclosure of personal information or involvement in personal areas (Goldsmith, 1988). Support can also threaten autonomy by making the receiver feel obligated to accept help or follow the course of action others advise (Tripathi, Caplan & Naidu, 1986). Others may also impose their interpretations and beliefs on the recipient.

If many dilemmas of support arise from threats to face, facework strategies might minimize these risks of support. We know perceptions of supportive actions and beliefs about acceptance and personal mastery have an impact on well-being; facework strategies are a key way we communicate and negotiate our perceptions of support, self, and relationship.

HELPFUL AND UNHELPFUL BEHAVIORS

The literature on dilemmas of support concerns what effect supportive interactions have on perceptions of self and other. We know less about the interactive dynamics that could produce or prevent these interpretations. Some researchers have begun to develop typologies of helpful and unhelpful behaviors based on interviews with cancer patients (Dakof & Taylor, 1990; Dunkel-Schetter, 1984), individuals with multiple sclerosis (Lehman & Hemphill, 1990), individuals who have suffered the death of a spouse or child (Lehman, Ellard & Wortman, 1986), and subjects in an experiment who were about to undergo a fear-inducing experience (Costanza, Derlega & Winstead, 1988).[1]

Although the helpful and unhelpful behaviors reported in these studies provide little detail about message characteristics, themes of positive and negative face do appear. Many of the helpful behaviors can reasonably be interpreted as conveying acceptance: for example, all populations except experiment subjects said "expressions of love and concern" were helpful, cancer patients and MS patients reported "understanding," and MS patients responded favorably to "praising abilities." Behaviors such as "being treated normally" (reported by MS patients) and "talking about other topics" (reported by experimental subjects) could show respect for autonomy and privacy. Many of the behaviors that are perceived as unhelpful appear to pose threats to positive face, including "rude remarks" (reported by all populations except experimental subjects), "critical of patient's response," "too little concern," and "medical care without emotion" (all reported by cancer patients). Other unhelpful behaviors threaten negative face: "interference" (reported by the bereaved), "advice" (reported by cancer patients, MS patients, and the bereaved), and overconcern or overprotection (reported by cancer patients and MS patients).

The global categories of "helpful" and "unhelpful" behaviors in these studies represent recipients' interpretations of behaviors or evaluations of their outcomes. This is useful but we don't know what characteristics of the message produced the interpretations and evaluations. For example, "express concern" is perceived as helpful by cancer patients, but we don't know the messages and behaviors that produce this interpretation. This is particularly important because cancer patients report "overly concerned" or "showing too little concern" as unhelpful behaviors. What do supporters who "express concern" say or do that is different from supporters who are "overly concerned" or not concerned enough?

These studies also contain contradictory evaluations of the same supportive act by the same population. For example, some bereaved individuals found advice helpful, though the majority said it was unhelpful. "Practical assistance" is helpful for cancer patients but "unwanted practical assistance" is not (Dakof & Taylor, 1990). "Encouraging recovery" and "providing philosophical perspective" appear in both the helpful and unhelpful categories reported by the bereaved.

Cutrona and her colleagues (1990; Cutrona & Russell, 1990; Cutrona & Suhr, 1992) suggest different behaviors are perceived as helpful in coping with different kinds of stresses. Unless strategies are matched to stresses, support attempts will be unhelpful. Similarly, Dakof & Taylor (1990) suggest information and advice are helpful from experts (e.g., medical care experts) but not helpful from nonexperts (e.g., family and friends). Matching type of support to type of problem and type of supporter is a necessary but not sufficient condition for helpful messages. The binds and contradictions between what is helpful and unhelpful occur within studies of individuals with similar stresses, as well as in comparisons across stresses. So, for example, even if we assume that "bereavement" represents a particular kind of stress that calls for "emotional support," there are still more and less appropriate and skillful ways of actually "showing concern." There are more and less effective ways for experts to give information and advice, and more and less sensitive ways in which family and friends could convey other kinds of support. In fact, cancer patients complained about "medical care without emotion" (Dunkel-Schetter, 1984), indicating that matching the provider to the kind of support is not all that is required to be helpful.

In sum, studies and explanations of helpful and unhelpful messages fall short of specifying what people are doing when they "give information" or provide "practical assistance" and what ways of doing so are most useful to those with various kinds of needs. Theories of message characteristics are a necessary next step.

Research on "comforting strategies" is one example of such a theory of message characteristics (e.g., Burleson & Samter, 1985a, 1985b; Samter, Burleson & Murphy, 1987). Although proceeding from a different theoretical base, these findings may be interpreted through the lens of politeness theory as well.

"Comforting strategies" seek to alleviate the emotional distress of individuals experiencing daily hassles and disappointments. Burleson and Samter's hierarchical coding system rates messages as more or less sophisticated, depending on the degree to which messages are "person-centered." Messages tailored to the psychological experiences of the hearer are more sophisticated than messages that don't adapt to others at all or adapt to others only in a global, role-centered way. The rankings obtained with this theoretically derived hierarchy are similar to subjects' ratings of both written hypothetical comforting messages and experimentally induced comforting interactions.

The parallels between person-centered messages and polite messages suggest facework may be an important component distinguishing more from less effective comforting messages. Burleson (1990, p. 70) suggests messages that are perceived more favorably "project a greater degree of involvement with the distressed other, are more neutral evaluatively, are more feeling centered, are more accepting of the other, and contain more cognitively oriented explanations of the feelings experienced by the other." In general, messages that "project a greater degree of involvement" and "are more accepting of the other" are likely to be performing positive facework, while messages that "are more neutral evaluatively" are likely to pose lesser threats to both positive and negative face. Cognitively oriented explanations may work in part because they redress potential threats to one's belief in personal mastery and autonomy. Effective comforting messages are not only "person-centered" with reference to the unique, individual person; they are also person-centered with reference to the social person, to the common face wants we all claim by virtue of participating in interactions.

Explaining Effective Supportive Communication

The possibility that acts intended to convey support may not be supportive in their effects suggests a need to clarify the way in which we conceptualize "supportive communication." The oxymoronic label "unhelpful supportive communication" glosses two ways of describing communicative acts: "supportive" refers to the conventionally recognized purpose or intention of some acts while "unhelpful" refers to an evaluation of the outcome. Distinguishing these two senses of the term "supportive" is not simply a matter of terminological aesthetics: Thoits (1983) has discussed the tautology that results when we define social support in terms of the very outcomes we claim it causes.

One way out of the tautology is to let the term "supportive communication" refer to a category of speech acts and events that are culturally recognized as intending to convey assistance.[2] For example, the Inventory of Socially Supportive Behaviors (Barrera & Ainlay, 1983) provides a list of "supportive behaviors" derived from previous theory and research. Such measures assume respondents and researchers have shared ideas about what "giving advice" or "expressing concern" look like. Existing measures and typologies provide clues about what some supportive acts might be but fall short of specifying the underlying dimensions that enable providers and receivers to recognize an act as intending to communicate "support." Making explicit this shared cultural knowledge gives us a way to define "supportive communication" with reference to formal properties of discourse in a context: persons who share a culture recognize certain kinds of messages in certain contexts as constituting "giving advice" or "expressing concern."

Shared cultural knowledge is also involved in our evaluations of the helpfulness of supportive acts. First, we have knowledge about what kinds of support are appropriate in various situations. For example, whether or not "advice" is helpful may depend on the knowledge and experience of the provider, the needs of the receiver, and the type of stressor (e.g., Cutrona & Suhr, 1992). Second, we have criteria for competent execution of supportive acts. For example, effective information-giving probably requires that the information be relevant and accurate. Effective expressions of concern should appear sincere. Finally, we have shared knowledge of what kinds of acts threaten face, what kinds of relationships mitigate face threats, and what kinds of facework strategies are available for minimizing threats to face.

The importance of facework in this explanatory framework should not be underestimated. Threats to positive and negative face are pervasive cross-situational themes in the research on support dilemmas and helpful and unhelpful support behaviors. No matter who the supporter, no matter what the need, no matter what kind of support act is performed, face threats and face wants are a pervasive feature of supportive interactions because they are a pervasive feature of social life.

In addition, threats to face are not merely unwanted side-effects in the support process; they threaten the very outcomes that are believed to link supportive interactions to physical and psychological well-being. Some authors claim that feelings of acceptance are at the core of the social support construct (e.g., B. Sarason, Shearin, Pierce & I. Sarason, 1987); others emphasize the implications of support for personal control (e.g., Albrecht & Adelman, 1987) or self-esteem (e.g., Thoits, 1983). Positive and negative face strategies are one of the ways in which messages about both acceptance and personal control are manifested in interaction. Attention to facework may enable us to understand how communicating support is linked to the enduring perceptions of self (e.g., B. Sarason et al., 1987) and relationship (e.g., Coyne, Ellard & Smith, 1990) that are linked to health outcomes.

Politeness theory also provides a set of categories for identifying and classifying message features, including a much broader array of linguistic features than has previously been examined in support research (Brown & Levinson, 1987, pp. 91-227). Much of our present research on support behaviors relies on self-reports or coder judgments of the presence or absence of a communication act and not how it was enacted. Even studies that have examined actual messages focus strictly on the content of the message and overlook other verbal and nonverbal features (Burleson & Samter, 1985a; Cutrona & Suhr, 1992; Cutrona et al., 1990; Samter et al., 1987). In contrast, the study of politeness has been marked by fine-grained analysis of multiple message features, including syntax, intonation, emphasis, modifiers, qualifiers, in-group language, slang, repetition, hedging, verb form and tense, joking, laughter, "honorifics," pronouns, and terms of address.

This increased attention to message features is a needed compliment in social support research. Our failure to consider shared cultural knowledge about defining and evaluating support may explain why the social support literature has given less attention to messages and supportive communication than to perceptions and psychological dispositions. If we assume that the definition of an act as "supportive" or the perception that an act is "helpful" are individualized judgments, we end up focusing on the judge and the judgment and we may neglect the message. However, if we can discover shared cultural knowledge about what acts are supportive and what features are helpful in various situations, then we can and should devote further study to the actual messages.

A Preliminary Study

There is much to be done in examining how providers and receivers define and evaluate supportive communication and in discovering the facework strategies providers of support use. However, before undertaking this detailed work it would be useful to demonstrate that the selection of supportive acts and facework strategies does, in fact, make a difference in the perceived helpfulness of a message. Toward this end, I conducted a pilot study that examined reactions to various types of support and facework in different situations. The results were encouraging and are reported here despite their preliminary nature because they illustrate one approach to examining facework and provide evidence that facework is related to the perceived helpfulness of messages.

I asked 29 students to read 12 different messages a person might say in one of two situations: "upon hearing that a close friend has failed an important exam in his or her major and is very upset" or "if a close friend called to tell you he or she has just been dumped by his or her girlfriend or boyfriend." The 12 messages are given in Appendix 2.1; they represent three types of supportive acts with the four different kinds of facework.

Advice, offers, and expressions of concern represent a range of the kinds of acts typically included in measures of enacted support and also represent different degrees of face threat. Advice tells the hearer what to do and can imply criticism. An offer could impose on negative face by compelling the hearer to either accept or reject the offer; however, by definition an offer mitigates negative face threat by giving the hearer the option of accepting or rejecting. Like advice, an offer might imply the hearer is unable to act alone; yet unlike advice, offers also convey solidarity and liking by the willingness to do something with or for the hearer. Expressions of concern probably pose little threat to either kind of face unless they tell the hearer how to feel; on the other hand, concern may convey regard for positive face by emphasizing caring for the hearer.

For each kind of act, I created a bald-on-record version of the act and then manipulated this kernel message to include various facework strategies described in Brown and Levinson's theory. Positive politeness strategies included exaggerating interest and approval (e.g., "I know you can do better"), claiming common knowledge (e.g., "I know you work hard"), empathy (e.g., "I know how you feel because it's happened to me before too"), and indicating the speaker knows the hearer's wants (e.g., "it must be really hard"). Negative facework strategies included hedging, (e.g., "I don't know about you but . . ."), making statements in question form (e.g., "I guess you're kind of upset about this right now?"), depersonalizing the threatening act (e.g., "Maybe it would be best" instead of "I think" or "you should"), stating the threatening act as a general rule (e.g., "you know what they say"), and minimizing the imposition (e.g., "just study a little harder"). Off-the record facework strategies included giving hints (e.g., "How much time did you spend studying?"), using metaphors (e.g., "when you fall off of a horse you have to just get right back on again"), and being vague or ambiguous (e.g., "This is kind of weird because just the other day this guy/girl I know asked me if you were going out with anyone."").

Each student was randomly assigned to read one set of twelve messages for one of the situations and to sort the messages from most to least helpful. Students placed a mark for each message on a 15 centimeter line that said at one end "not at all helpful" and at the other end "very helpful" (ratings of perceived helpfulness were measured in centimeters). For the messages they identified as most and least helpful, students also explained why they rated the message that way.

Next, students completed additional tasks designed to see if they interpreted the types of acts and facework strategies as I had intended. Students completed a second and third sorting and line-marking procedure to indicate the extent to which messages "would make your friend feel liked and accepted" (positive face) and "would make your friend feel as if he or she is being told what to do or how to feel" (negative face). Finally, students indicated whether they perceived each message as advice, offer, or concern. I will provide a brief summary of my results here; a full description of my repeated measures analyses of variance and results is available on request.

As expected, the degree to which a message threatened face depended on the type of act and the type of facework. Advice posed the greatest threat to both positive face ($M = 9.95$, $SD = 1.47$) and negative face ($M = 10.57$, $SD = 1.97$). Offers posed the least threat to positive face ($M = 5.77$, $SD = 2.12$) and expressions of concern posed the least threat to negative face ($M = 4.80$, $SD = 2.95$). Messages with positive face strategies showed less threat to positive face ($M = 4.95$) than bald-on-record ($M = 8.81$, $SD = 1.76$), negative face ($M = 8.72$, $SD = 2.12$), or off-the-record strategies ($M = 7.33$, $SD = 1.87$). The negative face implications of facework strategies were less clearly differentiated but consistent with expectations. Negative face is less threatened by off-the-record ($M = 6.69$, $SD = 1.79$) and negative face strategies ($M = 7.62$, $SD = 2.33$) than by positive face ($M = 8.14$, $SD = 2.39$) or bald-on-record ($M = 8.55$, $SD = 1.76$) strategies.

The results also provide evidence of the importance of act type and facework to the perceived helpfulness of messages. Table 2.1 provides the mean helpfulness rating of each message, each act type, and each facework strategy across situations. The most helpful act type varied by situation ($F = 14.84$; 2, 54 df; $p < .0001$). In the relational break-up situation, expressions of concern ($M = 9.79$, $SD = 3.41$) were more helpful than offers to introduce the friend to someone else ($M = 4.60$, $SD = 2.51$; $t = 3.27$, 4, 26 df, $p < .05$). Advice about dating others fell in between

TABLE 2.1 Means and Standard Deviations for Helpfulness Ratings
of Messages

	Advice	Offer	Concern	Mean for Type of Facework
Bald-on-Record	5.08	5.68	7.35	6.04
	(3. 85)	(4. 48)	(5. 37)	
Positive Face	11.12	9.04	9.08	9.75
	(3.27)	(3.94)	(4.06)	
Negative Face	8.39	6.22	6.98	7.20
	(4.03)	(4.14)	(4.40)	
Off-the-Record	8.09	6.71	6.90	7.20
	(4.30)	(4.25)	(5.30)	
Mean for Type of Act	8.17	6.91	7.58	

NOTE: Entries enclosed in parentheses are standard deviations.

($M = 7.20$, $SD = 1.72$). In contrast, when the friend had failed an exam
advice about studying and seeing the professor ($M = 9.07$, $SD = 3.19$) and
offers to assist with these acts ($M = 9.07$, $SD = 2.79$) were both perceived
to be more helpful than expressions of concern about the friend's feelings
($M = 5.51$, $SD = 3.04$; $t = 2.10$, 4, 28 df, $p < .05$).[3]

In both situations facework strategies influenced the perceived helpfulness of messages ($F = 16.24$; 3, 81 df; $p < .00001$) and the messages without facework (bald-on-record) had the lowest mean helpfulness rating.
Positive face strategies were the most effective, significantly more effective than bald-on-record strategies ($t = 3.89$, 4, 81 df; $p < .05$), with
off-the-record and negative face strategies falling in between.

The combination of act type and facework also affect perceived helpfulness ($F = 3.64$; 6, 162 df; $p < .002$). Advice with positive facework was
significantly more helpful than the other kinds of advice ($t_{bor} = 10.49$; t_{neg}
$= 4.74$; $t_{otr} = 5.26$; all have 4, 135 df and $p < .01$). Advice with negative
facework and off-the-record advice were significantly more helpful than
bald-on-record advice ($t_{neg} = 5.75$, $p < .01$; $t_{otr} = 5.23$, $p < .01$). Positive
facework offers were significantly more helpful than bald-on-record offers ($t = 5.84$, $p < .01$) or negative facework offers ($t = 4.90$, $p < .01$). This
is consistent with my earlier analysis of how an offer has the potential to
both threaten and mitigate negative face threat. Perhaps a bald-on-record

offer is too threatening but negative facework makes the offer appear uncertain and insincere. There were no significant differences in facework strategies for expressing concern, probably because expressions of concern pose the least threat to positive and negative face.

These results suggest face threatening and face mitigating message features are related to respondents' assessments of message helpfulness. Evidence that respondents actually use these dimensions in evaluating messages comes from their open-ended explanations for the messages they rated as most and least helpful.

Twenty of the 28 respondents gave face-related reasons for selecting the message they rated as most helpful. Positive face rationales referred to how the message conveyed liking, caring, solidarity, and/or acceptance. Negative face rationales mentioned respecting privacy, giving options, and not telling the friend what to do. An additional four respondents gave rationales that explicitly mentioned the selection of an appropriate act or the competence of executing the act (e.g., "good" advice).

Fewer respondents gave face-related explanations for the message they rated least helpful. Only 6 of 28 respondents gave positive face related reasons (lack of solidarity, disliking, lack of acceptance) or negative face related reasons (tells them what to do). This appears to undermine the claim that threats to face provide an explanation for support dilemmas and unhelpful messages; however, 9 of 12 messages DID include facework (only bald-on-record messages did not). So, when positive face, negative face, or off-the-record messages in this study were rated unhelpful, we would expect it to be for reasons other than threats to face.[4] Consistent with this interpretation, 5 of the 6 face-related rationales were given when a bald-on-record act was selected as least helpful. Many of the other reasons for least helpful messages are relevant to the broader framework developed in this chapter: 13 rationales said the least helpful act was inappropriate or irrelevant in the situation, one said the message was poorly phrased, and one said the advice given was bad advice.

The rationales respondents gave for their perceptions of helpfulness indicate selecting the appropriate supportive act, executing it skillfully, and showing regard for face do make a difference. However, these open-ended data also suggested a more complex role for facework than discussed in this chapter. Confessing to academic failure or interpersonal rejection presents a face that is potentially unlikable, unacceptable and dissimilar and is not autonomous and private. Some face-sensitive features of messages seem not only to redress the threat posed by the support provider's message; facework also reconstructs an image of the friend as likeable and accepted following a breach in face created by the support seeker's disclosure of a failure or rejection. This multifunctional and interactional aspect of facework suggests an expansion of Brown and Levinson's theory when it is applied to supportive communication.

In sum, the results of the pilot study are consistent with the perspective on support and the role of facework proposed in this chapter. We do have shared notions about what kinds of messages count as various kinds of acts and about how different kinds of supportive acts pose different kinds of threats to face. Our perceptions of the helpfulness of an act are influenced by judgments about the appropriateness of the act, skill in execution, and the use of facework to mitigate face threats.

From Messages
to Situated Performances

Focusing on facework and face threats in a single message and then predicting helpfulness oversimplifies the communication process. Such a narrow focus is useful as a starting point. It shows the role of facework is worth further study and further work of this type would be useful to correct the limitations of this preliminary attempt.[5] In addition, our research should move from messages to situated performances, expanding our view of supportive communication in at least two ways.

First, we should expand the scope of phenomena considered, examining sequences of messages in an interaction, the way in which facework redresses threats in seeking as well as giving support, and possible threats to speaker's as well as hearer's face (e.g., Goldsmith, 1992; Penman, 1990; Tracy, 1990).

Second, the difference between predicting message evaluation and understanding situated performances involves expanding the means and ends of our research on supportive communication. I have proposed we discover the shared principles and dimensions by which receivers and providers of support recognize and evaluate messages intended to convey support. This emphasis on culturally shared knowledge may suggest that the fruits of our research would be a set of rules we could use to predict and control supportive outcomes. Yet, I started this chapter by claiming that in our everyday lives, it is often difficult to know what to say to someone in need of help. If we do in fact have shared cultural knowledge about supportive messages, why is it still difficult for well-socialized adults to know what to say to someone in distress?

One answer to this question lies in the distinction between having knowledge of what might be appropriate and having the ability to produce it. However, even if we could give support givers both knowledge of appropriate messages and the ability to produce them, we would be overlooking a creative and negotiated aspect of supportive communication. Cultural knowledge provides an outline or frame for knowing what acts count as what, for knowing how to signal regard for face, for recognizing what features of a situation are relevant to selecting acts and face strategies, and for winnowing out wildly inappropriate messages. As such there is some predictive utility in predicting perceptions and outcomes consistent with culturally shared definitions, rules, and criteria for supportive communication.

However, the most effective supporters are probably those who use this knowledge creatively (e.g., O'Keefe, 1991) and the most effective supportive interactions are probably those in which provider and receiver use cultural resources to collaboratively construct a sense of support and mutual respect for face. For example, controllability of a problem or the closeness of a relationship may influence what kind of act and face strategies are appropriate; but relationships and situations aren't always precisely pre-defined and supportive messages can include attempts to define and re-define situations and relationships. Similarly, a support provider's story about a similar experience with a problem could end up as an on-record offer or on-record advice as subsequent turns in the interaction reveal how giver and receiver see the point of telling the story and as they test the waters to be sure they aren't intruding or imposing on one another.

It is probably unrealistic and undesirable to strive for "support by the numbers" but it is feasible and useful to discover the systematic shared principles that guide our creation, interpretation, and evaluation of supportive interactions. Politeness theory provides a rich "descriptive account of the anatomy of face work phenomena" rather than a "formalized, hierarchical model of social interaction" (Aronsson & Rundström, 1989, p. 485). The study of facework can help us move beyond examining "independent variables feeding probabilities into a speech-output generating mechanism," to illuminate a broad range of message features that are "negotiated in interaction, against a multiply layered backcloth of identities, beliefs, orientations, intents, and evaluations" (Coupland, Grainger, & Coupland, 1988, p. 257). In this sense, the "role of facework in supportive communication" is two-fold: to draw our attention to both overlooked aspects of supportive communication and to alternative approaches and assumptions for understanding these phenomena.

Notes

1. A table summarizing the helpful and unhelpful behaviors in all five studies appears in Goldsmith, 1992.

2. This claim may seem to fly in the face of evidence that providers and receivers of support don't always agree that support was provided (e.g., Antonucci & Israel, 1986). However, the measures used in studies comparing provider and receiver reports typically measure perceptions of outcomes over some period of time (i.e., the act was in fact supportive) rather than intentions in a particular message (i.e., the act counts as "advice" or an "offer" or an "expression of concern" or some other act in the category of acts that represent attempts to help). Shared knowledge helps us understand that someone is trying to help; whether in fact they are helpful depends on other features of the message and the situation.

3. Although the act by situation interaction is highly significant, t-tests of the differences between acts within situations are not significant. This may be because situation is a between- ¿ ibjects factor, so tests on acts within situations are based on a smaller N. This reduces the power of the tests. In addition, the use of Tukey's honestly significant difference technique in the follow-up t-tests controls family-wise error rates with a conservative test.

4. This is a limitation in the design of this study, since the absence of face-related reasons for unhelpful messages could also occur because face is not relevant.

5. This pilot study is limited in several ways. Short, isolated, written sentences in response to hypothetical situations may elicit more stereotyped and consensual responses than natural messages in natural settings. Respondents' brief open-ended explanations provide only a glimpse of the rules and rationales they employ. We should be cautious in generalizing from this study's particular instantiations of advice, offers, concern, and facework strategies to the general types of acts and facework strategies. For example, when students indicate that offers weren't particularly helpful to a friend who had just been dumped, we can't be sure if that is because no type of offer is appropriate in that situation or whether they are reacting to the particular offer to introduce the friend to other people (Jackson, 1992).

References

Albrecht, T., & Adelman, A. (1987). *Communicating social support.* Beverly Hills, CA: Sage.

Antonucci, T. C., & Israel, B. A. (1986). Veridicality of social support: A comparison of principal and network members' responses. *Journal of Consulting and Clinical Psychology, 54,* 432-437.

Aronsson, K., & Rundström, B. (1989). Cats, dogs, and sweets in the clinical negotiation of reality: On politeness and coherence in pediatric discourse. *Language in Society, 18,* 483-504.

Barrera, M., Jr., & Ainlay, S. L. (1983). The structure of social support: A conceptual and empirical analysis. *Journal of Community Psychology, 11,* 133-143.

Brown, P., & Levinson, S. (1987). *Politeness: Some universals in language usage.* New York: Cambridge University Press.

Burleson, B. (1990). Comforting as social support: Relational consequences of supportive behaviors. In S. Duck (Ed.) with R. Cohen-Silver, *Personal relationships and social support* (pp. 66-82). London: Sage.

Burleson, B., & Samter, W. (1985a). Consistencies in theoretical and naive evaluations of comforting messages. *Communication Monographs, 52,* 103-123.

Burleson, B., & Samter, W. (1985b). Individual differences in the perception of comforting messages: An exploratory investigation. *Central States Speech Journal, 36,* 39-50.

Chapman, N. J., & Pancoast, D. L. (1985). Working with the informal help networks of the elderly: The experiences of three programs. *Journal of Social Issues, 41,* 47-63.

Chesler, M. A., & Barbarin, O. A. (1984). Dilemmas of providing help in a crisis: The role of friends with parents with cancer. *Journal of Social Issues, 41,* 47-63.

Costanza, R., Derlega, V. J., & Winstead, B. A. (1988). Positive and negative forms of social support: Effects of conversational topics on coping with stress among same-sex friends. *Journal of Experimental Social Psychology, 24,* 182-193.

Coupland, N., Grainger, K., & Coupland, J. (1988). Politeness in context: Intergenerational issues. *Language in Society, 17,* 253-262.

Coyne, J., Ellard, J., & Smith, D. (1990). Social support, interdependence, and the dilemmas of helping. In B. Sarason, I. Sarason, & G. Pierce (Eds.), *Social support: An interactional view* (pp. 129-149). New York: John Wiley.

Cutrona, C. E. (1990). Stress and social support: In search of optimal matching. *Journal of Social and Clinical Psychology, 9,* 3-14.

Cutrona, C. E., & Russell, D. W. (1990). Type of social support and specific stress: Toward a theory of optimal matching. In B. Sarason, I. Sarason, & G. Pierce (Eds.), *Social support: An interactional view* (pp. 319-366). New York: John Wiley.

Cutrona, C. E., & Suhr, J. A. (1992). Controllability of stressful events and satisfaction with spouse support behaviors. *Communication Research, 19,* 154-174.

Cutrona, C. E., Suhr, J., & MacFarlane, R. (1990). Interpersonal transactions and the psychological sense of support. In S. Duck (Ed.), with R. Cohen-Silver, *Personal relationships and social support* (pp. 30-45). London: Sage.

Dakof, G. A., & Taylor, S. A. (1990). Victim's perceptions of social support: What is helpful from whom? *Journal of Personality and Social Psychology, 58,* 80-89.

DePaulo, B. M. (1982). Social psychological processes in informal help seeking. In T. A. Wills (Ed.), *Basic processes in helping relationships* (pp. 255-279). New York: Academic Press.

Dunkel-Schetter, C. (1984). Social support and cancer: Findings based on patient interviews and their implications. *Journal of Social Issues, 40,* 77-98.

Dunkel-Schetter, C., & Bennett, T. L. (1990). Differentiating the cognitive and behavioral aspects of social support. In B. Sarason, I. Sarason, & G. Pierce (Eds.), *Social support: An interactional view* (pp. 267-296). New York: John Wiley.

Fisher, J. D., Nadler, A., & Whitcher-Alagna, S. (1982). Recipient reactions to aid. *Psychological Bulletin, 91,* 27-54.

Goldsmith, D. (1988). *To talk or not to talk: The flow of information between romantic dyads and members of their communication networks.* Unpublished masters thesis. University of Washington, Seattle, WA.

Goldsmith, D. (1992). Managing conflicting goals in supportive interaction. *Communication Research, 19,* 264-286.

Jackson, S. (1992). *Message effects research.* New York: Guilford.

Lehman, D., Ellard, J. H., & Wortman, C. B. (1986). Social support for the bereaved: Recipients' and providers' perspectives on what is helpful. *Journal of Consulting and Clinical Psychology, 54,* 438-446.

Lehman, D., & Hemphill, K. (1990). Recipients' perceptions of support attempts and attributions for support attempts that fail. *Journal of Social and Personal Relationships, 7*, 563-574.

O'Keefe, B. J. (1991). Message design logic and the management of multiple goals. In K. Tracy (Ed.), *Understanding face-to-face interaction: Issues linking goals and discourse* (pp. 131-150). Hillsdale, NJ: Lawrence Erlbaum.

Penman, R. (1990). Face work and politeness: Multiple goals in courtroom discourse. *Journal of Language and Social Psychology, 9*, 15-38.

Rook, K. S., & Pietromonaco, P. (1987). Close relationships: Ties that heal or ties that bind? In W. Jones & D. Perlman (Eds.), *Advances in personal relationships* (vol. 1, pp. 1-35). Greenwich, CT: JAI Press.

Samter, W., Burleson, B., & Murphy, L. B. (1987). Comforting conversations: The effects of strategy type on evaluations of messages and message producers. *The Southern Speech Communication Journal, 52*, 263-284.

Sarason, B., Shearin, E., Pierce, G., & Sarason, I. (1987). Interrelationships among social support measures: Theoretical and practical implications. *Journal of Personality and Social Psychology, 52*, 813-832.

Thoits, P. (1983). Social support and psychological well-being: Theoretical possibilities. In I. G. Sarason & B. R. Sarason (Eds.), *Social support: Theory, research, and applications* (pp. 51-72). Dordrecht, The Netherlands: Martinus Nijhoff.

Tracy, K. (1990). The many faces of facework. In H. Giles & W. P. Robinson (Eds.), *Handbook of language and social psychology* (pp. 209-226). New York: John Wiley.

Tripathi, R., Caplan, R., & Naidu, R. (1986). Accepting advice: A modifier of social support's effect on well-being. *Journal of Social and Personal Relationships, 3*, 213-228.

Wills, T. A. (1983). Social comparison in coping and help-seeking. In B. M. DePaulo, A. Nadler, & J. D. Fisher (Eds.), *New directions in helping, Volume 2: Help-seeking* (pp. 109-141). New York: Academic Press.

Wortman, C. B., & Dunkel-Schetter, C. (1979). Interpersonal relationships and cancer: A theoretical analysis. *Journal of Social Issues, 35*, 120-155.

Appendix 2.1

Messages in Pilot Study

Situation 1: Relational Breakup

ADVICE

BALD-ON-RECORD: You should just forget him/her and date other people.

POSITIVE FACE: Instead of focusing on him/her, think about all you have to offer someone. You're fun to be with and you're good-looking. There are lots of other people who would like to go out with you and who would appreciate you.

NEGATIVE FACE: Maybe it would be best to just try to think about it less. It might help to date other people—you know what they say "there are a lot of fish in the sea. "

OFF-THE-RECORD: It's like my mom always used to say, when you fall off a horse you have to just get right back on again.

OFFER

BALD-ON-RECORD: I'll set you up with this guy/girl I know who would be perfect for you.

POSITIVE FACE: You're such a great person! I'll introduce you to this good friend of mine who's really nice and really good looking. You deserve someone great and the two of you will be perfect for each other.

NEGATIVE FACE: If you want, maybe I could introduce you to this friend of mine, if you think that might help.

OFF-THE-RECORD: This is kind of weird because just the other day this guy/girl I know asked me if you were going out with anyone.

CONCERN

BALD-ON-RECORD: I'm sorry you guys broke up and I feel bad that you're upset about it.

POSITIVE FACE: This must be really hard on you! I know how you feel because it's happened to me before too. It happens to everyone sometime.

NEGATIVE FACE: I guess you're kind of upset about this right now. I don't know about you but when things like this happen to me I feel really bad.

OFF-THE-RECORD: You know your friends care about you.

Situation 2: Failed Exam

ADVICE

BALD-ON-RECORD: You should go talk to the professor right away and then study harder next time.

POSITIVE FACE: I know you usually do well in classes so I think you should see your instructor and find out what went wrong. I know you work hard and if you study even harder, I know you can do better next time.

NEGATIVE FACE: I don't know if this would help, but if I were you I'd just find out what questions you missed and maybe get some help from the professor and just study a little harder for the next exam.

OFF-THE-RECORD: A lot of times professors can help you figure out what you did wrong and help you do better in the future. How much time did you spend studying?

OFFER

BALD-ON-RECORD: I'm here for you to talk and I'll help you study for the next exam.

POSITIVE FACE: I'm sure you can do better next time—you're a good student. You know you can talk to me about this and we can even study together for the next exam.

NEGATIVE FACE: Maybe it will help for you to just talk this out. You know, get it out of your system? And then if you want, maybe I could help you study for the next exam.

OFF-THE-RECORD: I've found it really helps to just get your frustration out. And before exams it's also good to go to the library or someplace quiet with a friend—even if you're not in the same class you can encourage each other and take breaks together. I'm going to try to do that before the next exam.

CONCERN

BALD-ON-RECORD: I'm sorry you failed the exam and I feel bad that you're upset about it.

POSITIVE FACE: You're such a good student, it must be really hard. I know how you feel because it's happened to me before too.

NEGATIVE FACE: I guess you're kind of upset about this right now? I don't know about you but I always feel really bad when I don't do as well as I want on exams.

OFF-THE-RECORD: You know your friends care about you.

3

Communicating Social Support
in Organizations

A Message-Centered Approach

STEPHANIE ZIMMERMANN

JAMES L. APPLEGATE

Mainstream research in organizational behavior, communication, and management has historically focused on task accomplishment and bottom-line organizational outcomes. The instrumental focus of organizational research is particularly neglectful of the role of communication in defining the identities of and personal relationships between organizational members. Yet it is a truism that communication, wherever it occurs, is a multi-functional activity with outcomes dependent on the simultaneous management of multiple goals.

Clark and Delia (1979) specifically outline instrumental, identity, and relational goals as the three primary goals defining all communication. Voices in the wilderness have long called for greater attention to the identity and relational dimensions of communication in the workplace (e.g., Berger, 1974; Howton, 1969) both by those within the workplace itself and by those who study it. To the extent that identity or relational dimensions of communication have been seriously considered in mainstream research on organizations the dominant focus has been on narrowly task relevant features of superior-subordinate relationships. One other exception to the neglect of the human side of work is research on social support in the workplace, particularly as a mediator of work-related stress (e.g., Paine, 1982; Riley & Zaccaro, 1987).

Only relatively recently have communication researchers particularly focused attention on the multiple functions of communication in the organization and the need to treat those functions as parts of a process that defines the social reality within which the organization functions (e.g., Deetz, 1988; Pilotta, Widman, & Jasko, 1988; B. Sypher, Applegate, & H. Sypher, 1985). Also even more recently in the popular organizational literature we see explicit calls for greater attention to identity and relational issues in workplace communication. Issues of "the heart," the importance of trust and compassion in relationships, and the communication of positive regard are now making headlines in the management literature (e.g., Bracey, Rosenblum, Sanford, & Trueblood, 1990).

Our goal in this chapter is to contribute to current efforts to take identity and relational goals and strategies seriously in the study of organizational communication. We offer an approach for understanding how social support is communicated in the workplace, the functions it serves for the individuals and organizations involved, and its relation to important outcomes at both levels. Our approach to social support in organizations is grounded in a more general "constructivist" theory of communication (Applegate, 1990; Delia, O'Keefe, & O'Keefe, 1982). Our approach is message-centered. We see both what counts as social support and the explanation of its functions and effects as defined in the communication practices within which it is accomplished.

The first section of the chapter provides a framework for examining social support in the workplace from a message-centered approach. Second, we discuss applications of this approach to supportive communication. Finally, issues and future directions for the study of supportive communication in organizations are suggested.

A Message-Centered Approach to Social Support in Organizations

Based on a message-centered view of communication, social support in the workplace must be studied in terms of organization members' multiple communicative goals, strategies or lines of actions chosen in accomplishing those goals, the ways in which communicators negotiate definitions of supportive situations, and individual social-cognitive differences. This view is in contrast to other conceptualizations of social support in the workplace which have, for example, examined social support within a network analytic framework (e.g., Anderson & Gray-Toft, 1982; Ray, 1991), or in terms of a target individual's perceptions of supportive behavior received from others (e.g., Etzion, 1984; Seers, McGee, Serey, & Graen, 1983). Previous research concerned with social support has made a valuable contribution in linking workplace phenomena with health care issues. Social support has been established as a coping mechanism or as a buffer of workplace stress and burnout (e.g., Miller, Ellis, Zook, & Lyles, 1990; Ray, 1991; Ray & Miller, 1991). In addition, social support has been linked with increased job satisfaction (Argyle, 1992; LaRocco & Jones, 1978), satisfaction with the organization (LaRocco & Jones, 1978), and personal accomplishment (Miller et al., 1990); reduced job tedium (Albrecht, Irey, & Mundy, 1982), workplace role ambiguity (Ray & Miller, 1991), and job strain (Blau, 1981); and improvement in coping with job demands (House & Cottington, 1986).

Adoption of any message-centered approach to the study of social support requires a move away from perceptual data to data that actually display the strategic and interactive content of supportive messages. Several conceptual perspectives might guide a message-centered study of how social support is defined, communicated, and exerts effects in organizations. Dramaturgical, semiotic, and symbolic interactionist perspectives are approaches worth consideration. These approaches embrace at least two generic commitments that in our view define a message focus. First, *social support is an interactional accomplishment.* The conditions calling for support efforts, the structure and substance of what counts as support, and its effects are studied in a way that gives prominence to communication as the process that defines support and the world in which support occurs. Perceptions of support, affect, cognitive organization, traits, and attitudes are approached as products or at least correlates of communicative behavior rather than as antecedents to supportive communication.

This first commitment is a radical departure from the starting points of most traditional research on social support and communication generally. Social support is not simply there to study. Support and its cognitive and affective correlates are accomplished in talk. The need for social support is a problem that people develop communicative practices to solve. Moreover, the very definition of the problem and its recognition as a relevant feature of situations is a communicative outcome.

Hence, if we are to understand what support literally "is:" how it is signified in Garfinkel's terms (i.e., what is this thing people keep referring to on self-report perceptual scales) or why it comes to be interpreted as having a certain effect, we must make a second message-centered commitment. Our observations must be *focused on the ways support is strategically signified in the practice of language.* Whether focused on the strategic productions of individuals or interaction itself, this focus reveals the relevance to support efforts of public and situated realizations of cultural/organizational macro-structures, such as how the use of organizational language helps define appropriate contexts and topics for support. Also, we must understand how cognitive and affective micro-structures are similarly created and defined in supportive communication, as with how individuals come to say that a particular behavior was "helpful" and that they now "feel better," and what that means in terms of the world they strategically and discursively have created. In short, *a message-centered study of support must focus on actual supportive strategies and practices produced by people.* Ultimately, these supportive topoi must be situated within discourse to understand if and how they function supportively and why they are interpreted as effective/ineffective, relevant/irrelevant, appropriate/inappropriate, or attended to/ignored.

How do these two commitments, viewing social support as an interactional accomplishment and focusing on how it is strategically created in talk, make a difference in research on social support? First, they point to the gaps in our understanding sustained by current research practices. Much of this research treats support as a given commodity that is transmitted in varying quantities through differentially complicated networks. More constructively, these commitments can produce research that provides ethnographies of the problem of social support that define under what conditions (when) in particular organizations (where) the provision of support (what) is seen as appropriate (why). Also encouraged is research that explains: (a) individual differences in abilities to produce different types of strategic responses to the need for social support (see our discussion of constructivist communication research below), (b) the ways in which the language of organizational cultures simultaneously provide constraints and resources for the situated accomplishment of support, (c) the stasis factors that emerge in discourse blocking the effectiveness of efforts at support, and (d) the dynamics of the discursive "accounting" process that in large part defines the cognitive and affective consequences of supportive communication (e.g., how through talk we define what the supporter did and how the receiver of support now feels). This list of research foci for a message-centered approach to social support in the workplace is only meant to be suggestive.

Applications of a Message-Centered Approach
to Supportive Communication in Organizations

STORYTELLING AND OTHER
FORMS OF ORGANIZATIONAL TALK

A message-centered approach to supportive communication in organizations suggests a recognition of social support as a communicative phenomenon manifested in organization member interaction. This attention to actual supportive interaction and associated cultural/contextual constraints is in line with interpretive approaches to studying organizational phenomena. As Putnam (1983) argues, interpretive research "centers on the study of meanings, that is, the way individuals make sense of their world through their communicative behaviors" (p. 31). Communication is not contained in organizations, but rather, is the way in which organizational life is accomplished. Similarly, social support is not a commodity that organizations and their members give and receive; providing social support is a communicative goal that organization members attempt to achieve with varying degrees of success. Further, "the true promise of interpretive research in organizations is to explicate multiple senses of reality . . . and to reveal the multiple . . . voices which assign meaning to these senses of reality" (Trujillo, 1992, p. 366). Thus an interpretive view of social support would lead researchers to examine, for example, differences in the ways in which organization members define what support "is" and what it "does."

Much interpretive research in organizations has focused on stories (e.g., Brown, 1985; Martin, Feldman, Hatch, & Sitkin, 1983; Zimmermann, Seibert, Billings, & Hougland, 1990). "Stories, myths, rituals, and language use are not simply reflections of organizational meanings; they are the ongoing processes that constitute organizational life" (Putnam, 1983, p. 40). Martin et al.'s (1983) research suggests that organizational stories provide members with information concerning expectations of support from upper management. Recent work on organization member storytelling has moved away from simply identifying types of stories to uncovering the functions stories serve (Brown, 1990; Seibert, 1989). Brown (1990) proposes three main functions organizational stories fulfill: reducing organization member uncertainty, managing meaning through the implicit or explicit presentation of organizational values, and enhancing organization member bonding and identification with the organization. Employing participant observation to gather stories and interviews to identify story functions from both speaker and hearer perspectives, Seibert (1989) found that stories were told as a way to explain a point, for humor, and to share emotions. Examining supportive communication in organizations by focusing on organization member storytelling may reveal how interactants define social support, communicate social support through stories, and interpret the supportive attempts of others. As Faules (1982) notes, "participants use stories to determine what organizational events and activities mean" (p. 151). Thus researching organizational stories provides a way to focus on how social support is defined, communicated, and interpreted in interaction, fulfilling the first commitment to a message-centered approach. Examination of organizational storytelling practices also addresses the second commitment associated with a message-centered approach. Storytelling highlights the role of organizational culture in the communication of social support and may reveal the processes through which organization members come to define particular communicative acts as varying in degrees of "supportiveness."

SOCIAL SUPPORT AND FACEWORK

Goldsmith's (1992; this volume) link between supportive communication and facework provides one approach for identifying multiple goals in supportive interaction. Based on her application of politeness and facework theories to social support, Goldsmith (1992) defines supportive communication as "a category of speech acts and events that are culturally recognized as intending to convey various kinds of assistance" (p. 276). Further, Goldsmith (1992) argues that for a speaker to communicate support effectively, she or he must choose the appropriate strategy given the constraints of the situation, perform the selected acts competently, and fulfill the face wants of the hearer and speaker, as well as achieving the goal of helping the other. For example, an individual may notice that a coworker seems emotionally distressed after receiving her or his 6-month performance evaluation from the supervisor. The support provider must first decide what kind of assistance is appropriate given this situation (seemingly a poor job performance appraisal) and work relationships (e.g., the support provider may be the supervisor's golf partner and in the coworker's Thursday night bowling league). The support provider may identify comforting, advising, informing or offering assistance as the most appropriate strategy. Second, the speaker must perform the strategy (or strategies) chosen competently. For example, we would expect comfort to be expressed in a caring and nonjudgmental manner and an offer of assistance to be substantive and sincere. Finally, the support provider must comfort (or advise, inform, offer assistance, etc.) the other while not threatening her or his own face or the face of the coworker.

SOCIAL SUPPORT AND COMFORTING

We have found the application of constructivist theory particularly useful in the effort of communication researchers to focus on message production and interpretation. The theory has been applied successfully in explaining a variety of communicative behaviors including analysis of a specific form of social support (e.g., Burleson, 1990). Consistent with Clark and Delia's (1979) identification of the three primary goals of all communication *we define social support as those messages that contribute to the task, relational, or identity goals of others.* Such communication may contribute to more than one goal and may have subsidiary effects not all of which are positive. This definition underscores the multi-functional nature of supportive communication and the notion that supportive communication is defined in interaction. For example, Tardy (1992) found that in problem-solving situations, instrumental support both facilitated performance and was interpreted as more sensitive than emotional support. Further, the nature of the problem may influence the helpfulness of supportive communication (Cutrona & Suhr, 1992).

We recognize that our definition of support begs the question of whose point of view is privileged in defining social support. Should the analyst's conceptually-grounded reading of the interaction behavior as "supportive" of particular goals be the focus? Or should the actors' own reading of the events be privileged in a reading that focuses on what they see as the identity, relational, or task goals and behaviors supportive of those goals? This is a methodological question important to much more than social support research, probably not resolvable in any absolute sense, and certainly not resolvable within the confines of this chapter. (For a more detailed analysis of this general issue see Surra and Ridley, 1991.) For our purposes, we see utility in both readings of supportive strategies and interactions and, to date, have positioned our work in the former, analyst-privileging framework.

From a constructivist perspective, human action is intentional and goal-directed, although communicators' goals may vary in their degree of explicitness (Delia et al., 1982). Constructivists argue that interpretive schemes produce beliefs and intentions relevant to particular contexts that guide, but do not govern, choices of action (Delia et al., 1982). Because strategic choices are based on the individual's interpretive schemes employed in a particular context, constructivists see human action as situated (O'Keefe, Delia, & O'Keefe, 1980). Thus the functions and outcomes of support must be examined within the context in which support is communicated. When individuals interact, their lines of action are organized in relation to some purpose in the form of strategies (O'Keefe et al., 1980). Strategies are the ways in which individuals choose to act on an intention. Actors may use multiple strategies in achieving a single goal or a single strategy may fulfill multiple goals (O'Keefe & Delia, 1984). However, individuals may not be consciously aware of their strategic choices. Thus communicators' goals may be explicit and communicative strategies chosen consciously, as with union and management representatives negotiating a new contract, or goals may be more implicit and strategies chosen in a less conscious manner, as with an informal conversation between two coworkers on their lunch break. Within this general conception of communicative contexts, goals and behaviors, constructivist research focuses on individual differences in ability to manage more complex situations in which routine or ritualized behavior is less likely to be effective. Studies have tied communicative ability to individual development of more complex, abstract, and integrative cognitive schema for interpretation (e.g., see reviews of Applegate, 1990; Burleson, 1987).

Waltman (1989) correctly argues that "[t]he actual provision of social support is a specific communicative goal that needs further attention" (p. 10) within the context of this type of research which examines how "messages do things" (Sypher & Applegate, 1984, p. 323). This approach to communication emphasizes that social support as a communicative goal must be studied as it is realized in specific types of message behaviors. Such an approach is particularly applicable to studying the communication of social support for a number of reasons.

First, typically, situations where social support is called for are interpersonally complicated. Actors must provide support while minimizing threat to the face wants of others, accommodating to organizational norms for expression of emotion, issues of organizational power and status, and so on. Second, goal attainment is facilitated by the ability to organize contextual information to coordinate lines of action in pursuit of goals. For example, in the specific instance of comforting communication, Burleson's research demonstrates the importance of skill in "affect recognition, impression formation and organization, and perspective taking" (Burleson, 1984, p. 96) that requires the integration and restructuring of the meaning of messages. Last, contexts requiring supportive communication encourage more conscious awareness of goals by actors and require knowledge of the various linguistic and rhetorical resources through which alternative supportive strategies can be constructed. Differences in the competency of support providers to engage in more complex person-centered communication is one useful way to characterize differences in the quality and outcomes of attempts to communicate social support.

One example of applying this approach to social support in the organizational context is offered by Zimmermann and Applegate (1992). These authors examined person-centered comforting communication among members of five hospice interdisciplinary teams, identifying both sophistication of comfort-intended messages and perceptions of comforting communication in the team setting. Employing focus group interviews to generate situations in which team members would most likely comfort an emotionally distressed other, the researchers developed two hypothetical comforting situations salient to hospice team members. Team members then provided written responses to each situation. In addition, study participants were asked to assess the quality of comforting communication expressed by team members. Thus this study focused both on the actual production of comfort-intended messages by organization members and perceptions of these types of messages. Further, this study placed supportive communication within the team context by assessing the relationship of comforting communication to perceptions of satisfaction with the team's communication and assessments of the team's ability to accomplish its tasks.

Given the nature of hospice, it is not surprising that Zimmermann and Applegate (1992) found that members of hospice interdisciplinary teams produced fairly sophisticated messages when comforting each other. That is, participants' messages generally explicitly recognized and elaborated on the target person's perspective. What was surprising, however, was that training in hospice was negatively associated with person-centered message strategies. The researchers suggest that this could be due to the nature of hospice training, which focuses almost exclusively on patient and family care with little attention to developing skills in team interaction. In addition, perceptions of the quality of comforting communication from other team members were positively related to satisfaction with team communication and assessment of the team's ability to accomplish its task. This would suggest that supportive communication not only serves to achieve the relational goal of managing another's emotional distress, but task-related goals as well.

SUMMARY

A message-centered approach to supportive communication in organizations requires two commitments. The first recognizes social support as a communicative phenomenon accomplished in organization member interaction. The second is concerned with micro-structures, individual social-cognitive differences in message interpretation and production, and macro-structures, the organizational and cultural environments in which supportive talk is situated.

Issues and Future Directions for the Study of Supportive Communication in Organizations

Although many researchers have recognized the importance of social support in the workplace, we know little about how social support is communicated or how supportive events are interpreted, defined and negotiated by organization members. Because of the ways in which social support has been operationalized and studied, we are left with few convincing claims about why social support exerts the effects it does. As one example of the direction of current social support research, Miller et al. (1990) provide a useful model of communication, stress, burnout, and social support that underscores the complexity of the relationships among these variables. However, the how and the why of supportive communication are not addressed. An examination of Miller et al.'s (1990) questionnaire items reveals that they do not directly tap perceptions of *supportive communication* (e.g., "My coworkers go out of their way to make my like easier for me" and "My supervisor can be relied on when things get tough at work" [p. 313]). Therefore we are confined to drawing tentative conclusions about the relationship of *perceived supportive communication* and outcomes for organizational members. Studies such as this inform us about how perceptions of researchers' definitions of social support are related to workplace stress and burnout. However, we do not know *how* that support is communicated, *what* constitutes support for organization members, or *why* supportive communication plays a role in organizational outcomes. Not until we study the communication practices that define what counts as social support and the multiple functions and goals supportive communication serves, will we really be able to explain, for example, why the communication of social support exerts positive, and perhaps negative, effects on identities, relationships, and instrumental goals of organizations and organization members. In this last section of the chapter, we address issues and future directions for researching supportive communication in the organizational context.

OUTCOME ISSUES IN THE
COMMUNICATION OF SOCIAL SUPPORT

Organizational Outcomes
of Supportive Communication

One recent development in management theory has been the promotion of a "kinder, gentler" corporation and manager. "It's not that managers need to care more, but that they need to learn to make their care more evident and express it more effectively" (Bracey et al., 1990, p. ix). Horton and Reid (1991) suggest that for an organization to succeed in the 1990s, it must "commi[t] itself to doing things that will close the trust gap [between middle management and top administration]" (p. 213). The strategies these authors list for achieving this include recognizing managers' accomplishments, helping managers develop and broaden career-related skills, and facilitating managerial creativity and risk taking. Organizations should be more supportive of their employees and managers are to be more supportive of their subordinates. This supportive posture will increase employee productivity and efficiency (Bracey et al., 1990) and may be essential for organizational survival (Horton & Reid, 1991).

The notion that social support can influence organizational outcomes seems to be tied to the 1980s' trend of building strong corporate cultures (e.g., Deal & Kennedy, 1982; Peters & Waterman, 1982) and the recent emphasis on organizational ethics (e.g., Nash, 1990). For example, Harrington (1991) discusses managerial training programs in organizations that have been designed to develop more ethical corporate cultures. "Often the goal [of ethics training] is to avoid illegal or unethical corporate behavior leading to adverse governmental or societal reactions. . . . Codes of conduct and ethics training may be offered to avoid such reactions and impact to the bottom line" (Harrington, 1991, p. 21).

In order to survive, organizations must attend to ethical issues and develop organizational cultures that facilitate and support managerial and staff ethical behavior (Harrington, 1991; Horton & Reid, 1991; Nash, 1990). Nash (1990) directly links social support and ethical corporate behavior, arguing that ethical organizational decision making involves an other orientation, "a perception and acceptance of the validity of other people's needs and points of view" (p. 97, emphasis omitted). Pragmatically, this other orientation translates to "charitable giving, public-private partnerships, educational assistance, or compliance with environmental legislation" on the part of organizations (Nash, 1990, p. 102). For managers, business becomes "a series of enabling relationships rather than a set of efficiency measures" (Nash, 1990, p. 93, emphasis omitted). An other-directed attitude, along with integrating ethics and profit-making and facilitating competition, is essential "not just in terms of [organizational] productivity, . . . but also in terms of vitality" (Nash, 1990, p. 21). Providing assistance or support leads to more ethical organizational behavior which is necessary to corporate survival.

When organizations communicate support to employees, this may serve to manage employee stress (Horton & Reid, 1991). Reducing organization member stress is important to organizational survival in that "[b]urned-out, alienated managers are not going to help the organization meet its global competition. The best of them will leave for what they hope are greener pastures. And those who stay will be a drag on the organization's ability to be innovative and productive" (Horton & Reid, 1991, p. 189). Horton and Reid (1991) thus suggest "developing a corporate culture that encourages and enables employees to succeed," "giving middle managers recognition for their accomplishments," and "encouraging creativity and risk taking, without fear of punishment for failing" (p. 214). By communicating support to its members, organizations reduce employee turnover, enhance productivity, and increase the likelihood of achieving organizational goals. Further, Allen's (1992) recent study of information sources, perceived support, and organizational commitment suggests that perceptions of organizational support are both directly and indirectly tied to organization member commitment.

Although we have conceived of social support in fairly broad terms in examining its link to organizational outcomes, it seems that the current trend to a more supportive organizational environment merits attention. As with the study of individual outcomes of supportive communication in organizations, a greater focus on the messages organizations employ to communicate support to members and those outside the organization is necessary. That is, we need a more concrete link between the message strategies organizations employ in providing support and the outcomes of those strategies. As Allen (1992) notes, "researchers should investigate what is being said—especially in terms of actual message strength and strategies that influence feelings of perceived organizational support" (p. 364).

Negative Effects of Social Support

Particularly in the organizational setting, social support may produce costs as well as rewards. For example, Kessler, McLeod, and Wethington's (1985) research on the impact of social network crisis on individuals suggest that "time and energy demands placed on a supporter can themselves lead to distress, particularly when they come on top of an already demanding set of role responsibilities" (p. 499). And if Horton and Reid's (1991) assessment that today's organizations are characterized by "pushing managers harder in a struggle to keep up with global competition" and "managers who must shoulder the burden of work that was done by other managers who are no longer around" (p. 198), then managers, as well as their subordinates, may find that providing support in itself produces stress. One cost of providing support, then, may be an increase in providers' feelings of distress.

Providing support may also negatively impact the relationship between the provider and receiver. As La Gaipa (1990) notes, "[o]ffers of support may be misinterpreted or ineffectual" (p. 125). This can be especially problematic in the organizational context. For example, a subordinate offering advice to a supervisor may be perceived as attempting to "one-up" the supervisor. A supervisor who offers advice to a subordinate may be perceived as not having confidence in the receiver's abilities. Provisions of support may be interpreted as a negative comment on the receiver's competence, thus influencing how the receiver will subsequently interact with the provider and how the receiver will define her or his relationship with the provider.

Accepting support from others may have direct negative consequences for the receiver. For example, in the mentoring process, mentees may be viewed as receiving special favors from mentors, and therefore become the target of other organization members. Further, "[r]eliance on the advice of a more powerful person or one with higher status may also reduce a person's autonomy and personal decision making" (La Gaipa, 1990, p. 129). For an organization member, receiving advice from others may hinder her/his own ability to problem solve and identify alternative solutions. Moreover, the receiver may be perceived as simply a follower, lacking in important leadership skills.

Supportive communication may also have negative impacts on the larger organization. For example, organization members may focus on providing support to the neglect of the task at hand. Subordinates may come to rely on a supervisor who continually supports them and later have problems functioning independently. Organization members who consistently provide comforting to emotionally-distressed coworkers may be facilitating organizational norms, which encourage the unburdening of personal problems to such an extent that it interferes with accomplishing the job and achieving the organization's goals.

THE ISSUE OF POWER IN SUPPORTIVE COMMUNICATION

In defining organizational power, Pfeffer (1982) argues that it is not a static property of the organization, individuals within the organization, or subunits of the organization. Rather, "power is context or relationship specific" (Pfeffer, 1982, p. 3) and may change over time, issues, contexts and relationships. As a social phenomenon, power is a force that gives one social actor the ability to influence another to take an action which would not be taken without that motivating force. Power is a result of organizational structure, but also shapes that structure (Pfeffer, 1978). In addition, power is a function of the expertise and activities of individuals within the organization. Further, Deetz and Mumby (1990) argue that in organizations "discourse and power are integral to each other and thus interdependent" (p. 41). Supportive communication, as one form of organizational discourse, can clearly be linked with organizational power.

In a recent article reporting techniques used by managers to successfully influence other organizational members, Keys and Case (1990) found that communicating support was a useful source of power. "Only one tactic from our lateral influence study was noted significantly more often in successful influence attempts with peers—that of 'developing and showing support of others'" (Keys & Case, 1990, p. 42). And although "presenting a rational explanation" was ranked as the top tactic for successfully influencing a superior, "developing and showing support of others" was ranked fifth out of ten possible tactics. The researchers also found that "[f]requently they [managers] showed confidence, encouragement, or support when trying to win subordinates over" (Keys & Case, 1990, p. 42, emphasis omitted). The reliance on these tactics to influence other organization members clearly suggests that supportive communication may function primarily as a method for exercising power, and secondarily as advice, encouragement, or emotional comfort. Although these researchers relied on a researcher-generated list which respondents rank-ordered, the findings highlight the need to examine the actual supportive strategies employed by organization members, how those strategies are interpreted, and the functions supportive communication serves.

TAKING CULTURE SERIOUSLY
IN EXAMINING SOCIAL SUPPORT

Perhaps because of the lack of attention to the realization of social support in communicative messages and because of the rather homogenous populations studied, researchers have given little attention to how the social support process is influenced by culture. We understand little about the role of culture in providing constraints and resources influencing (a) definition of contextual conditions suggesting social support as an appropriate social goal, (b) definition of forms of behavior that might "count" as social support, (c) differences in the quality of support strategies employed, and (d) how such strategies are integrated within the goal structure of the communicative event (e.g., how support is ranked as a goal in relation to other identity, relational, and task goals). Given the increasingly multicultural and international quality of participants in all forms of organizational life researchers must attend to cultural differences in communicative practices relevant to the effective communication of social support across cultural boundaries.

For example, Chang and Holt (1991) recently outlined important differences in the way Chinese and Western peoples approach the causes for success and failure of interpersonal relationships that have direct implications for whether and how supportive communication would be expected in the face of relationship termination. Chinese use the concept of *yuan* to signify the multiple causes and contextual subtleties on which relationship development is dependent. Relationships are or are not "meant to be" in a very significant way. Westerners are much more likely to see relationships as standing or falling on the outcomes of specific events and individual initiatives. The implications for the form and effects of social support strategies in the face of relational difficulties are various. Support strategies designed to help a partner "think through" the specific reasons for relational problems and develop strategies to "resolve" or redefine sources of distress, while useful in a Western setting, may be unnecessary or even nonsensical in certain Chinese relational contexts.

Also suggestive of the importance of culture as a resource and frame for communicating social support is Kochman's (1981) and subsequent analyses of differences in the way emotion is displayed in the communication of African and European Americans. European Americans often see African Americans as more emotionally "upset" than they see themselves, largely because the latter group are more comfortable with the expression of emotion in the course of conflict or simply stating ideas. For African Americans, emotional involvement signals honest ownership of one's ideas and position. European Americans are more likely to see the same display of emotion as a sign of distress or losing control. Is someone "upset" or "in distress"? Is social support called for or would it be seen as inappropriate or even offensive? Answers to these questions must be grounded in research that takes culture's role in communication practices seriously.

Studies of the impact of collectivist versus individualist cultural values on communication, cultural differences in attention to face and face threats, and norms for self-disclosure and reciprocity are but a few other areas of main stream cross-cultural communication research that should be integrated with studies of social support: studies of when it is needed, the form it takes, the abilities it requires, and the outcomes its various realizations produce. A message-centered focus for research in multicultural contexts will make it difficult if not impossible to ignore these questions as we study the process of providing support.

THE NEED FOR METHODOLOGICAL CREATIVITY IN RESEARCHING SUPPORTIVE COMMUNICATION

The message-centered approach to examining the communication of social support in organizations we are advocating raises methodological as well as conceptual issues. For example, it is clear that we need to develop methods that tap into organization members' interpretive processes in supportive events. While our suggestions for employing more creative methodological strategies in examining social support in the workplace may seem difficult to accomplish, we believe that they are essential to discovering how supportive communication is accomplished in organizations.

One strategy for identifying supportive episodes in the organizational context has been the use of focus groups. For example, in a study of comforting communication within the hospice interdisciplinary team, Zimmermann and Applegate (1992) asked team members during focus group interviews to describe situations in which they would likely comfort a distressed coworker. The participants' responses were then used to develop hypothetical situations specific to the organization and organization members to which team members later responded. The use of hypothetical situations to generate comforting messages is then a valid one, assuming that the situation is one in which respondents can reasonably place themselves (Burleson, 1987). Conducting focus group interviews with members of the population to be studied is a useful method in developing meaningful hypothetical comforting situations.

While a few studies have shown that there is a correspondence between naturally-occurring message strategies and those produced using hypothetical situations, greater attention to "real world" message production is needed. One difficulty, however, in attempting to observe supportive episodes as they naturally occur in organizations, involves the social and organizational conventions associated with expressing emotions and subsequent attempts to comfort the distressed other. Duck (1991) suggests a diary method, either the Iowa Communication Record (Duck & Rutt, 1988) or the Rochester Interaction Record (Wheeler & Nezlek, 1977), which may be useful in studying supportive communication in organizations. Participants are asked to keep an interaction log which is somewhat structured by the researcher in that attention is focused on "specific sorts of social interaction or interpersonal behavior" (Duck, 1991, p. 142). The Rochester Interaction Record asks subjects to record types of interaction in which they participate, including who, where, when, and an evaluation of the interaction. The Iowa Communication Record requires more details as to what is discussed in the interaction episode, how it is discussed, and the participant's assessments of the impact of the interaction on the future of the relationship. This provides more qualitative data than the Rochester method, and may be a way to tap into actual messages used to provide support. In applying this diary method to supportive communication, organization members could be asked to describe supportive episodes in which they participated, including the setting (date, time and location), participants (typically initials to preserve anonymity), what was said (verbal messages) and done (nonverbal messages), and the recorders' reactions to the episode. While this method is labor intensive for both participants and researchers, it can yield a richness not possible with more quantitative methods, such as survey instruments. Duck (1991) does note that there are problems with the diary method, including participants not recording episodes and difficulty in recalling what occurred. In addition, asking organization members to keep a daily interaction log can introduce too much self consciousness into everyday interactions. However, it is representationally valid in that it captures organization members' interpretations and the way in which supportive episodes unfold in the organizational encounter. The validity of the diary method is linked with whose point of view is privileged, which we discussed earlier. If we are truly interested in delving into the multifunctional nature of communicating of social support in increasingly multicultural organizations, this method is indeed a valid and useful one.

Conclusion

As the workweek becomes longer, the commute to work farther, leisure time shorter, and family/friendship networks more fragmented, organizations increasingly serve as a primary site for supportive relationships. Management journals and texts calling for a more caring, other-centered, compassionate manager further suggest the need to more fully examine supportive communication in the workplace. Taking a message-centered, multiple-goals approach to the study of supportive communication in the organizational context requires a commitment to developing creative methodological strategies for examining the process of social support, how supportive communication functions in the workplace, and how the communication of social support affects organizational members and the organization. By recognizing the ways in which organization members manage multiple goals in supportive situations, negotiate definitions of supportive communication, and interpret supportive attempts, we can better understand the relationships, for example, among power, facework, and individual and organizational outcomes, in the support episodes. We can also identify negative as well as positive consequences in communicating social support in the organization context and delineate the role of culture in the social support process. And although we are less concerned with organizational task issues and the bottom-line than other researchers and practitioners may be, enhancing our understanding of supportive communication in the workplace can serve to improve organizational functioning as well as the quality of organizational life.

References

Albrecht, T., Irey, K., & Mundy, A. (1982). Integration in a communication network as a mediator of stress. *Social Work, 27*, 229-234.

Allen, M. W. (1992). Communication and organizational commitment: Perceived organizational support as a mediating factor. *Communication Quarterly, 40*, 357-367.

Anderson, J., & Gray-Toft, P. (1982, August). *Stress and burnout among nurses: A social network approach.* Paper presented at the annual conference of the International Sociological Association, Mexico City.

Applegate, J. (1990). Constructs and communication: A pragmatic integration. In R. Neimeyer & G. Neimeyer (Eds.), *Advances in personal construct psychology* (vol. 1, pp. 203-230). Greenwich, CT: JAI Press.

Argyle, M. (1992). Benefits produced by supportive social relationships. In H. Veiel & U. Baumann (Eds.), *The meaning and measurement of social support* (pp. 13-32). New York: Hemisphere.

Berger, P. (1974). *The homeless mind: Modernization and consciousness.* New York: Vintage.

Blau, G. (1981). An empirical investigation of job stress, social support, service length, and job strain. *Organizational Behavior and Human Performance, 27*, 279-302.

Bracey, H., Rosenblum, J., Sanford, A., & Trueblood, R. (1990). *Managing from the heart.* New York: Delacorte Press.

Brown, M. (1985). That reminds me of a story: Speech action in organizational socialization. *Western Journal of Speech Communication, 49*, 27-42.

Brown, M. (1990). Defining stories in organizations: Characteristics and functions. In J. Anderson (Ed.), *Communication yearbook 13* (pp. 162-190). Newbury Park, CA: Sage.

Burleson, B. (1984). Comforting communication. In H. Sypher & J. Applegate (Eds.), *Communication by children and adults: Social cognitive and strategic processes* (pp. 63-104). Beverly Hills, CA: Sage.

Burleson, B. (1987). Cognitive complexity. In. J. McCroskey & J. Daly (Eds.), *Personality and interpersonal communication* (pp. 305-349). Beverly Hills, CA: Sage.

Burleson, B. (1990). Comforting communication as everyday social support: Relational consequences of supportive behaviors. In S. Duck (Ed.), *Personal relationships and social support* (pp. 66-82). London: Sage.

Chang, H., & Holt, G. R. (1991). The concept of Yuan and Chinese interpersonal relationships. In S. Ting-Toomey & Felipe Korzenny (Eds.), *Cross-cultural interpersonal communication research* (pp. 28-57). Newbury Park, CA: Sage.

Clark, R., & Delia, J. (1979). Topoi and rhetorical competence. *Quarterly Journal of Speech, 65*, 187-206.

Cutrona, C., & Suhr, J. (1992). Controllability of stressful events and satisfaction with spouse support behaviors. *Communication Research, 19*, 154-174.

Deal, T., & Kennedy, J. (1982). *Corporate cultures.* New York: Addison-Wesley.

Deetz, S. (1988). Cultural studies: Studying meaning and action in organizations. In J. Andersen (Ed.), *Communication yearbook 11* (pp. 335-345). Newbury Park, CA: Sage.

Deetz, S., & Mumby, D. (1990). Power, discourse, and the workplace: Reclaiming the critical tradition. In J. Anderson (Ed.), *Communication yearbook 13* (pp. 18-47). Newbury Park, CA: Sage.

Delia, J., O'Keefe, B., & O'Keefe, D. (1982). The constructivist approach to communication. In F. Dance (Ed.), *Human communication theory* (pp. 147-191). New York: Harper & Row.

Duck, S. (1991). Diaries and logs. In B. Montgomery & S. Duck (Eds.), *Studying interpersonal interaction* (pp. 141-161). New York: Guilford.

Duck, S., & Rutt, D. (1988, November). *The experience of everyday relational conversations.* Paper presented at the annual convention of the Speech Communication Association, New Orleans, LA.

Etzion, D. (1984). Moderating effect of social support on the stress-burnout relationship. *Journal of Applied Psychology, 69*, 615-622.

Faules, D. (1982). The use of multi-methods in the organizational setting. *Western Journal of Speech Communication, 46*, 150-161.

Goldsmith, D. (1992). Managing conflicting goals in supportive interaction: An integrative theoretical framework. *Communication Research, 19*, 264-286.

Harrington, S. (1991). What corporate America is teaching about ethics. *The Academy of Management Executive, 5*(1), 21-30.

Horton, T., & Reid, P. (1991). *Beyond the trust gap: Forging a new partnership between managers and their employers.* Homewood, IL: Business One Irwin.

House, J., & Cottington, E. (1986). Health and the workplace. In L. Aiken & D. Mechanic (Eds.), *Applications of social science to clinical medicine and health policy* (pp. 392-416). New Brunswick, NJ: Rutgers University Press.

Howton, F. (1969). *Functionaries.* Chicago: Quadrangle Books.

Kessler, R., McLeod, J., & Wethington, E. (1985). The costs of caring: A perspective on the relationship between sex and psychological distress. In I. Sarason & B. Sarason (Eds.), *Social support: Theory, research and applications* (pp. 491-506). Dordrecht, The Netherlands: Martinus Nijhoff.

Keys, J., & Case, T. (1990). How to become an influential manager. *Academy of Management Executive, 4*(4), 38-51.

Kochman, T. (1981). *Black and white: Styles in conflict.* Chicago: University of Chicago Press.

La Gaipa, J. (1990). The negative effects of informal support systems. In S. Duck (Ed.), *Personal relationships and social support* (pp. 122-139). London: Sage.

LaRocco, J., & Jones, A. (1978). Co-worker and leader support as moderators of stress-strain relationships in work situations. *Journal of Applied Psychology, 63*, 629-634.

Martin, J., Feldman, M., Hatch, J., & Sitkin, S. (1983). The uniqueness paradox in organizational stories. *Administrative Science Quarterly, 28*, 438-453.

Miller, K., Ellis, B., Zook, E., & Lyles, J. (1990). An integrated model of communication, stress, and burnout in the workplace. *Communication Research, 17*, 300-326.

Nash, L. (1990). *Good intentions aside: A manager's guide to resolving ethical problems.* Boston, MA: Harvard Business School Press.

O'Keefe, B., & Delia, J. (1984). Psychological and interactional dimensions of communicative development. In H. Giles & R. St. Clair (Eds.), *Recent advances in language, communication, and social psychology* (pp. 41-85). London: Lawrence Erlbaum.

O'Keefe, B., Delia, J., & O'Keefe, D. (1980). Interaction analysis and the organization of interaction. In N. Denzin (Ed.), *Studies in symbolic interaction* (vol. 3, pp. 25-57). Greenwich, CT: JAI Press.

Paine, W. (Ed.). (1982). *Job stress and burnout*. Newbury Park, CA: Sage.

Peters, T., & Waterman, P. (1982). *In search of excellence*. New York: Harper and Row.

Pfeffer, J. (1978). *Organizational design*. Arlington Heights, IL: AHM Publishing.

Pfeffer, J. (1982). *Organizations and organization theory*. Boston, MA: Pitman.

Pilotta, J., Widman, T., & Jasko, S. (1988). Meaning and action in the organizational setting: An interpretive approach. In J. Andersen (Ed.), *Communication yearbook 11* (pp. 310-334). Beverly Hills, CA: Sage.

Putnam, L. (1983). The interpretive perspective: An alternative to functionalism. In L. Putnam & M. Pacanowsky (Eds.), *Communication and organizations: An interpretive approach* (pp. 31-53). Beverly Hills, CA: Sage.

Ray, E. (1991). The relationship among communication network roles, job stress, and burnout in educational organizations. *Communication Quarterly, 39*, 91-102.

Ray, E., & Miller, K. (1991). The influence of communication structure and social support on job stress and burnout. *Management Communication Quarterly, 4*, 506-527.

Riley, A.W., & Zaccaro, S. J. (1987). *Occupational stress and organizational effectiveness*. New York: Praeger.

Seers, A., McGee, G., Serey, T., & Graen, G. (1983). The interaction of job stress and social support: A strong inference investigation. *Academy of Management Journal, 26*, 273-284.

Seibert, J. (1989, April). *Organizational stories as language behaviors: What people say about why they tell them*. Paper presented at the annual meeting of the Southern Speech Communication Association, Louisville, KY.

Surra, C.A., & Ridley, C.A. (1991). Multiple perspectives on interaction: Participants, peers, and observers. In B. Montgomery & S. Duck (Eds.), *Studying interpersonal interaction* (pp. 35-57). New York: Guilford.

Sypher, H., & Applegate, J. (1984). Organizing communication behavior: The role of schemas. In R. Bostrom (Ed.), *Communication yearbook 8* (pp. 310-329). Beverly Hills, CA: Sage.

Sypher, B., Applegate, J., & Sypher, H. (1985). Culture and communication in organizational contexts. In W. Gudykunst, L. Stewart, & S. Ting-Toomey (Eds.), *Communication, culture, and organizational processes* (pp. 13-29). Beverly Hills, CA: Sage.

Tardy, C. (1992). Assessing the functions of supportive messages: Experimental studies of social support. *Communication Research, 19*, 175-192.

Trujillo, N. (1992). Interpreting (the work and talk of) baseball: Perspectives on ballpark culture. *Western Journal of Communication, 56*, 350-371.

Waltman, P. (1989, November). *Working toward a processural definition of social support*. Paper presented at the annual convention of the Speech Communication Association, San Francisco, CA.

Wheeler, L., & Nezlek, J. (1977). Sex differences in social participation. *Journal of Personality and Social Psychology, 35*, 742-754.

Zimmermann, S., & Applegate, J. (1992). Person-centered comforting in the hospice interdisciplinary team. *Communication Research, 19,* 240-263.

Zimmermann, S., Seibert, J., Billings, D., & Hougland, J. (1990). God's line is never busy: An analysis of symbolic discourse in two Southern Appalachian denominations. *Sociological Analysis, 51*, 297-306.

4

Counteracting Task-Induced Stress

Studies of Instrumental and Emotional Support in Problem-Solving Contexts

CHARLES H. TARDY

Clear trends characterize social support research. After establishing links between social support and positive physical, psychological, and relational outcomes (Cohen & Syme, 1985; Cohen & Wills, 1985; Krantz, Grunberg, & Baum, 1985), studies appear to be taking two new directions. Some investigations examine the mechanisms by which support produces positive physical and mental states. For example, Cohen (1988) proposed three general models to describe the paths by which social support affects health. Researchers have examined the relationship between social support and measures of cardiovascular reactivity while speaking (Tardy, Thompson, & Allen, 1989) and coronary occlusions (Seeman & Syme, 1987). Studies assessing the manifestation of support in relationships (e.g., Barbee, Gulley, & Cunningham, 1990; Barrera & Baca, 1990; Burleson, 1984; Cutrona, Cohen, & Igram, 1990; Duck, 1990) reflect a second direction evident in research. Hobfoll and Stokes (1988), for example, suggest that attention should be focused on "the actual building of supportive ties, seeking and obtaining aid, and behavioral, cognitive, and

AUTHOR'S NOTE: Study 1 was reported at the Iowa Conference on Personal Relationships, Iowa City, IA (May 31–June 2, 1987). Study 2 was reported at the Annual Convention of the Southern Communication Association, San Antonio, TX (April 9–12, 1992).

emotional reactions to that aid, as well as thoughts, emotions, and behaviors that mediate such reactions" (p. 497-498). This chapter reports a series of studies designed to assess reactions to supportive messages.

Factors Influencing Support Attempts

Many cognitive, emotional, social, and situational factors influence reactions to support attempts (Sarason, Pierce, & Sarason, 1990). Three stand out: the nature of the problem precipitating the support, the type of support provided, and the relationship between the recipient and provider of support. A goal of research should be to identify how people can provide support to alleviate distress (Gottlieb, 1983, 1988). This chapter focuses on a combination of these factors that have been neglected by most social support research: the type of aid given by nonintimates in response to stress-inducing tasks.

PROBLEMS PRECIPITATING SUPPORT ATTEMPTS

Research has frequently examined the provision, or lack thereof, of social support in response to stressful events. Numerous studies have examined support provided to people who became unemployed (Gore, 1978), bereaved (Walker, MacBride, & Vachon, 1977), depressed (Notarius & Herrick, 1988), etc. Few studies focus on stresses caused by specific task, work, or problem-solving events. Moreover, studies generally examine the effects of support on physical and mental health and not the manifestation of support and the attendant reception by the distressed person. This chapter reports studies on the efficacy of support provided to people undertaking a stressful task.

TYPES OF SOCIAL SUPPORT

Often social support is assumed to refer to the provision of aid which reflects concern for a person's emotional reactions to an event. However, several other types of support have been identified and studied (Cohen & McKay, 1984; Gottlieb, 1978). For example, House (1981; House & Kahn, 1985) recognizes instrumental, informational and appraisal in addition to emotional support. More recently Cutrona, Suhr, and MacFarlane (1990) identified five types of support but suggested that all could be reduced to two primary functions, problem solving and emotional adjustment. Studies demonstrate the utility of some of these distinctions among types of social support. For example, Cohen and Hoberman (1983) observed that self-esteem and appraisal support moderated the effects of stress on symptomatology but that tangible and belonging support did not. In an evaluation study of a smoking cessation program, Cohen, Mermelstein, Kamarck, and Hoberman (1985) found that appraisal support facilitated quitting. The studies reported in the current chapter assess the relative effectiveness of emotional and instrumental support provided to facilitate problem-solving performance.

RELATIONSHIP BETWEEN PROVIDER
AND RECIPIENT OF SUPPORT

As with the types of support, research has frequently focused on only the provision of support in close relationships. This focus is problematic for several reasons. People in distress do not always receive the social support they expect from friends, family and other intimates (Coyne, Wortman, & Lehman, 1988; Wortman & Lehman, 1985). People also receive support from nonintimate relationships (Cowen, 1982; Parks, 1982). Weak ties, as Adelman, Parks, and Albrecht (1987) note, "help compensate during times of crisis when our closer relationships are disrupted, are accessible to those with lower levels of communication skill, and can liberate us when our circle of intimate relationships proves too confining" (p. 129). Because acquaintances are much more numerous than close friends (Freeman & Thompson, 1989), these might be frequent sources of social support. This chapter, then, examines support provided by nonintimates.

Research on Task-Induced Support by Nonintimates

Several studies examined the effects of social support in problem-solving contexts. Costanza, Derlega, and Winstead's (1988) experiment indicated that people who talked about a stressful task, guiding a tarantula's movement through a maze, with friends prior to the task were no less anxious than those who waited alone. Only subjects who talked with their friends about an irrelevant topic evidenced lower anxiety scores. This study demonstrated that the type of support provided affects the distress experienced by subjects. Several other studies (Lindner, Sarason, & Sarason, 1988; Sarason, 1981; Sarason & Sarason, 1986) demonstrate that supportive messages improve subjects' performance on problem solving tasks. For example, in Sarason and Sarason's (1986) experiment, some subjects received supportive comments from the investigator while others did not, before performing a moderately stressful anagram task. Subjects in the support conditions completed more correct anagrams and reported less difficulty concentrating on the task than subjects in the control condition. In addition, an interaction effect indicated the experimentally provided support improved the performance of subjects who had lower but not higher than average levels of perceived social support as measured by Sarason, Levine, Basham and Sarason's (1983) Social Support Questionnaire (SSQ). Subjects with social support, either provided by the experimenter or by the support network, concentrated more on the cognitive task and, therefore, performed better.

The Sarason and Sarason (1986) study yielded some important conclusions and questions. It indicated that supportive messages spoken in the context of a nonintimate relationship, in contrast to naturally occurring close personal relationships, can improve subjects' performance on a problem-solving task. However, the Sarason and Sarason (1986) study leaves unanswered many important questions concerning the process by which messages provide support. The chapter reports a series of studies designed to specify the characteristics of a supportive message from a nonintimate source that improves subject performance on problem-solving tasks.

STUDY 1: EFFECTS OF INSTRUMENTAL AND EMOTIONAL SUPPORT ON TASK PERFORMANCE

Study 1 (Tardy, 1992) addressed two problems. The improved performance observed in Sarason's studies could be attributable to the message spoken by the support provider or to nonverbal experimenter-expectancy demands (Miller & Turnbull, 1986; Rosenthal & Rosnow, 1984). The provider of support may implicitly tell some subjects they are expected to perform better and others worse. So the first goal of this study was to replicate the findings of Sarason using an experimental procedure which removes these alternative explanations. The second issue addressed in this study was the characteristics of the message which improved subject performance. Sarason and Sarason's (1986) experimental manipulation included both instrumental support (offering to assist the subject) and emotional support (indicating interest in or concern for the subject's performance). Were the effects of their experiment due to a combination of support types? Or, may the effects be attributed to one or the other, or equally to both? Instrumental support probably most directly affected performance because an offer of practical assistance, even if unexercised, can help subjects perform a task. Glass and Singer (1972) discovered that subjects performed better on cognitive tasks when told they could turn off a stress inducing buzzer, even though subjects did not exercise that option. Another reason for expecting instrumental support to be more effective is because emotional support from a nonintimate might be seen as insincere.

One hundred and forty-eight undergraduate students completed a questionnaire containing the written directions operationalizing the experimental induction of social support (see Tardy, 1992), the stressful anagram task used by Sarason and Sarason (1986), and self-report measures, which are discussed elsewhere (Tardy, 1992) but not here. Subjects were randomly assigned to an instrumental, emotional, combination, or no support conditions.

The subjects ($M = 4.07$) receiving no support completed significantly fewer anagrams than the subjects ($M = 6.00$) receiving some form of support ($F(1,148) = 4.07$; $p < .05$; $\eta^2 = .03$). A 2×2 analysis of variance with emotional support and instrumental support as the independent variable revealed a significant interaction ($F(1,148) = 4.79$; $p < .05$; $\eta^2 = .03$). A multiple range test using Duncan's procedure revealed that subjects receiving instrumental support completed significantly more anagrams than subjects in the no-support control group.

The results of Study 1 support the conclusion of Sarason and Sarason (1986) that a brief supportive message can improve subjects' performance on a cognitive task. Since Sarason and Sarason's (1986) study was replicated with the use of written messages, the results indicate that the verbal content of the message affects performance. Though nonverbal communication may accentuate the supportive message, a positive effect may be obtained with words alone. These data further indicate that instrumental support produces the greatest gain in performance, a pattern which is consistent with the conclusion of Cohen, Mermelstein, Kamarck, and Hoberman (1985) who hypothesized that the deleterious consequences of stress will be buffered by the type of support content most directly related to the stressful event. In the present study the experimenter's offer to provide assistance, i.e., instrumental support, might be seen by subjects as more relevant to their problem-solving task than the statements encouraging the subject's efforts, i.e., emotional support. Perhaps emotional support is less influential when it comes from a nonintimate than from an intimate source. Hobfoll and Stokes suggest "attempts by nonintimate others may provide some replacement for losses but are unlikely to provide the underlying feelings of attachment, caring, and love that intimate support engenders" (1988, p. 517).

Study 1 did not examine the support recipient's appraisal of the supportive message or its source because Sarason and Sarason (1986) observed that a message comparable to those used in the present study affected behavior. Additionally neither this study or the prior one by Sarason and Sarason (1986) specified perceptions as intervening or explanatory variables. The support message might be received and processed with little conscious awareness. To assess this assumption, Study 2 focused on subjects' perceptions of messages which attempt to provide support.

STUDY 2: PERCEPTIONS OF EMOTIONAL AND INSTRUMENTAL SUPPORT MESSAGES

Study 2 (Tardy, 1992) examined subjects' evaluations of the instrumental and emotional support messages used in Study 1. In two recent publications, Cutrona and her colleagues (Cutrona, Cohen, & Igram, 1990; Cutrona, Suhr, & MacFarlane, 1990) attempted to conceptually explicate and empirically assess the process by which people assess supportive messages. Though noting that perceptions of support are the result of long- term, repetitive interactive patterns, these studies recognize that specific instances of support provision must be studied in order to understand the process by which people come to believe support is available. Cutrona, Suhr, and MacFarlane (1990) analyzed the content of role-played helping interactions of dyads and subsequently had participants as well as independent observers rate the supportiveness of these conversations. Cutrona, Cohen, and Igram (1990) examined subjects' perceptions of support provided in written scenarios describing conversations between a helper and a person who had recently learned of a parent's serious injury from an automobile accident. Emotional support was rated as more helpful than instrumental support, though subjects also rated as more helpful support that was consistent with the recipient's preference, regardless of whether it was emotional or instrumental support. In the context of a different distressful event, other types of support could be perceived as more helpful. When compared to the injury of a close relative, a problem-solving task should be seen as a less emotionally arousing stressor and as a situation in which practical assistance would be more efficacious.

Ninety-two undergraduate students completed questionnaires containing written descriptions of the experimental protocol used in Study 1. The scenario depicted a student participating in a psychology experiment involving a stressful cognitive task. In response to the students' distress, the experimenter gave no support, emotional support, instrumental support, or both, all messages being identical to the ones used in Study 1. Following the description of the conversation, the booklet contained questions asking students to rate the message's instrumental support, emotional support, and perceived effectiveness. To differentiate the independent and dependent variables in this report, the former will be labeled as provided and the latter as perceived support.

A 2 × 2 ANOVA revealed only a significant main effect for provided instrumental support ($F(1,88) = 42.92$; $p < .001$; $\eta^2 = .33$). The messages providing instrumental support ($M = 7.8$) were seen by subjects as being more helpful and providing more assistance than messages without instrumental support ($M = 4.1$). However, the second analysis with perceived emotional support as the dependent variable detected no significant main effect for provided emotional support. Unexpectedly, the ANOVA revealed a significant main effect for provided instrumental support ($F(1,88) = 64.82$; $p < .001$; $\eta^2 = .42$) and a significant interaction between provided instrumental and emotional support ($F(1,88) = 13.19$; $p < .001$; $\eta^2 = .14$). Examination of the combined group means indicated that messages providing instrumental support were perceived as more emotionally supportive than messages without instrumental support. An additional comparison among all four group means using Tukey's honestly significant differences procedure indicated that subjects rated the emotional support, the instrumental support, and the combined instrumental and emotional support messages, as more emotionally supportive than the no support message. Unexpectedly, the means for the instrumental and the combined support messages were also significantly greater than the mean for emotional support. These findings indicate that subjects perceived the instrumental support message as not only providing more help and assistance but also as indicating more concern and sensitivity.

A 2 × 2 (instrumental by emotional support) ANOVA revealed a significant 2-way interaction for the effectiveness variable ($F(1,88) = 4.81$; $p < .05$; $\eta^2 = .05$). Subjects rated the emotional support, instrumental support, and combined emotional and instrumental support messages as more effective than the no support message. The three types of support messages, however, did not differ significantly from each other.

Subjects perceived the instrumental support messages as providing more assistance and help than the other messages, thus validating the operationalization of this variable. However, the emotional support message was not seen as more sensitive or concerned than the instrumental support messages. In fact, the opposite was observed. The messages containing instrumental support were rated by subjects as being more sensitive and concerned than the emotional support message. The dependent measures and/or the independent variable may not adequately assess or embody emotional support. Though the scales possess face validity future research should perhaps employ a broader range of descriptors to assess emotional support. Likewise, future research might use messages that embody more attempts to affect the recipient emotionally. However, assuming that the measures do in fact assess emotional support, the findings indicate that such appeals may not be as effective as more tangible offers of assistance. Observers may perceive the need for assistance to be paramount in this problem-solving situation and see the offer of help to be more sensitive and to indicate more concern than merely offering encouragement or expressing good will.

Though the offer of help was rated by observers as more helpful and considerate, instrumental support was not rated as more supportive than the message offering encouragement or the combination message. Subjects perceived all three messages as more effective than the no support message.

STUDY 3: PRODUCTION OF SUPPORTIVE MESSAGES

Studies 1 and 2 were designed primarily to validate and extend the generalizations initially offered in the Sarason and Sarason (1986) study. This goal necessitated using their support message. However, extending this research further requires more attention to the messages that purportedly provide support. Study 2 noted that ostensibly instrumental messages also are perceived to be emotionally supportive and that ostensibly emotional support messages are not perceived to be sensitive and concerned.

Several methodological explanations might be offered for these findings. The messages used in these studies may not be good examples of the broader class or strategy which they represent. Or, the scales used to assess their emotional and instrumental supportiveness may not be valid. In order to assess the first of these possibilities, a third study was conducted. The goal of this study was to generate a range of instrumental and emotional support messages which would be appropriate in a situation where stress is induced by a problem-solving task.

Method. Twenty-six undergraduate students completed a questionnaire which asked them what should be said by the experimenter in the scenario used in Study 2, which was based on the protocol used in Study 1. Students were asked to tell what the experimenter should say in order to make the distressed student (a) "feel better—less distressed about her inability to solve the problems and more confident of her problem-solving skills," (b) "know that she can rely on him for help—that if she has a problem understanding or solving the problems, that he can assist her," or (c) both.

Results. Subjects produced 50 separate suggestions as to what the experimenter could say in order to achieve these goals. I classified these into two groups: (a) those that addressed the student's emotional reactions to the task ($n = 26$); (b) those that provided assistance to the student ($n = 24$). Examination of these two sets indicated that the messages used in Study 1 and Study 2 were clearly not the only ones that provide emotional and instrumental support. Table 4.1 contains a representative sample of the subject responses.

Discussion. Two observations based on the classification of these statements are noteworthy. First, students generally produced messages consistent with the goals given to them. Second, some students produced responses that served the goal other than the one given to them. That is, some students produced messages which were both emotionally and instrumentally supportive, even though they had been asked to suggest what should be said to achieve only one of these goals.

Though this study demonstrates that many different messages can embody the instrumental and emotional support goals, it does not address the relative efficacy of each. Consequently another study was conducted to replicate Study 2 with these new messages.

TABLE 4.1 Representative Support Messages Composed by Subjects

Emotional Support Messages

Chris, I couldn't help noticing the difficulty you were having in completing the problems. There is nothing to be worried about. I said most college students were able to complete the task but there are other students who have come in here with very bright minds and have not been able to finish. It could have been nerves or maybe they just don't work well under pressure, but I can assure you, that it's nothing that can't be overcome.

Relax. It's only an experiment, your grade is not affected by this.

Calm down Chris. Relax and take your time. You can do it Chris.

Instrumental Support Messages

If you get stuck on a group, then go to the next group, do not get fixated on one set for long if you can't make any progress. Pace yourself and try to solve the easy ones first, you have plenty of time left.

Dr. Jones should show her the simple solution to the problem, step by step. Then give her another problem to solve.

STUDY 4: PERCEPTIONS OF INSTRUMENTAL
AND EMOTIONAL SUPPORT MESSAGES

In order to assess the generality and validity of the conclusions of Study 2, another experiment was conducted. The first two studies are limited by the messages that represented the two types of social support. To see if other messages yield the same conclusions, a study must assess subject perceptions of these alternatives. Specifically, Study 2 concluded that instrumental and emotional support messages were perceived as similarly effective. Also, instrumental support was seen as more sensitive than was the purportedly emotional support messages. If Study 2 is replicated, strong support is given to its conclusions. If not, other message characteristics must account for the findings. Also, only two items were used in the scales measuring the perceptions of support. In this study, new 4-item scales were composed based on the work of House (House, 1981; House & Kahn, 1985) and Cutrona, Suhr, and MacFarlane (1990).

Method. Forty-eight college student subjects responded to a questionnaire similar in design to the one used in Study 2. Subjects completed perception measures after reading a depiction of the distressed-student and the experimenter's message. The support messages were derived

TABLE 4.2 Instantiations of Support Messages in Study 4

No Support Messages

1. You have 10 minutes to finish this part of the experiment.

2. You have several more problems to finish.

3. You have a few minutes left to solve some of your unfinished problems.

Emotional Support Messages

1. Many people do not solve all of the problems. You might be the kind of person who does better with other problems.

2. Not everybody finds these to be easy. No matter how you do on these problems there will be some other students who do worse and some who do better.

3. Some very intelligent people have difficulty solving these problems. People who don't do well on one type of task might do well on another.

Instrumental Support Messages

1. One strategy for solving the problems is to arrange the letters into prefixes and suffixes and then add the rest of the letters to create a word.

2. Pace yourself and try to solve the easy problems first. You have plenty of time left to solve some more of the difficult problems.

3. I can answer questions about solving these problems if you have any. If there is anything I can do to help, I suggest you ask me and I probably can help you.

from the ones produced by subjects in Study 3 (see Table 4.2). A series of 4 scales assessed subjects' perceptions of instrumental support (assistance, aid, advice, guidance), emotional support (concern, reassurance, encouragement, sympathy), and effectiveness (supportive, helpful, better, effectiveness). Unlike Study 2, students read and rated three different examples of the experimenter's message. Consequently a $2 \times 2 \times 3$ (emotional support by instrumental support by replication) design was used with two between- and one within- subject factors.

Results. Scales created for the three dependent variables for each of the three replications yielded coefficient *alphas* ranging from .83 to .93. For the measure of perceived instrumental support, these figures are much higher than the .63 *alpha* obtained for the two-item scale in Study 2. A $2 \times 2 \times 3$ analysis of variance was conducted for each of the three dependent variables. In each case, the replications factor yielded a significant main effect but no significant interactions for all three dependent variables: perceived instrumental support $(F(2,88) = 24.59;$ $p < .001; \eta^2 = .36)$, perceived emotional support $(F(2,88) = 42.65; p <$ $.001; \eta^2 = .49)$, and perceived effectiveness $(F(2,88) = 28.12; p < .001;$ $\eta^2 = .39)$. Examination of the means for the variables indicated that each subsequent message was rated more favorably on each of the three dependent measures. Since this main effect has no theoretical importance and none of the interactions which might have been methodologically important proved significant, no other reference will be made to this variable.

For the perceived instrumental support dependent variable there was a significant main effect for the instrumental support message independent variable $(F(1,44) = 13.94; p < .001; \eta^2 = .24)$ and a significant instrumental by emotional support interaction $(F(1,44) = 4.74; p < .05; \eta^2 = .10)$. Examination of the means (see Table 4.3) indicated, as expected, the subjects perceived the instrumental support messages to be more helpful than messages without instrumental support. Tukey's honestly significant difference procedure was used to interpret the interaction. Results indicated that the two messages containing instrumental support were rated significantly higher than the message without instrumental support. The message containing emotional support was not significantly different from any of the other three messages. Consequently, the data generally support the representational validity of the instrumental support messages.

For the perceived emotional support variable, main effects for both instrumental $(F(1,44) = 4.88; p < .05; \eta^2 = .10)$ and emotional $(F(1,44) = 6.48; p < .02; \eta^2 = .13)$ support, as well as the interaction $(F(1,44) = 9.16;$ $p < .01; \eta^2 = .17)$ proved significant. Examination of the means indicates that the messages containing emotional support are perceived as more concerned than the messages without support; and that the messages containing instrumental support were perceived as more concerned than the messages without this form of support. Follow-up tests for the interaction revealed that all support messages were rated significantly higher than the message without support, but that the three did not differ. Like Study 2, the data suggest that subjects perceive messages that offer assistance to be as sensitive and concerned as messages directly focusing on the person's emotional distress.

The third ANOVA used perceived effectiveness as the dependent variable. Again, all three effects were significant: main effect for instrumental

TABLE 4.3 Means and Standard Deviations for Perceived Emotional Support, Instrumental Support, and Effectiveness Variables

Support Condition	Perceived Emotional Support	Perceived Instrumental Support	Perceived Effective
No Support	9.72[a,b,c]	9.28[a,b]	9.83[a,b,c]
	(4.62)	(3.98)	(3.03)
Emotional Support	16.17[a]	12.75	17.75[a]
	(3.66)	(4.28)	(4.37)
Instrumental Support	15.78[b]	16.14[a]	18.53[b]
	(4.50)	(4.40)	(3.70)
Emotional and Instrumental Support	15.22[c]	14.56[b]	15.69[c]
	(3.05)	(3.35)	(3.68)

NOTE: Groups with common superscripts differ significantly, $p < .05$.

support ($F(1,44) = 9.53$; $p < .01$; $\eta^2 = .18$), main effect for emotional support ($F(1,44) = 5.59$; $p < .05$; $\eta^2 = .11$), and the interaction effect ($F(1,44) = 24.99$; $p < .001$; $\eta^2 = .36$). Means for the main effects indicated that messages lacking emotional support are perceived as less effective than those with emotional support and that messages lacking instrumental support are perceived as less effective than those with instrumental support. Follow-up tests for the interaction indicated that all three support messages were rated as significantly more efficacious than the message without support, but that the differences among the three support messages were not significant. This pattern is identical to the one obtained in Study 2.

Discussion. Study 4 replicated most of the findings of Study 2. In both experiments, the instrumental support message was perceived to be at least as sensitive as the emotional support message. Also, the two studies both observed that instrumental, emotional, and combined support messages were perceived to be equivalent and to be more effective than the nonsupport message in responding to a person's distress. Unlike Study 2, Study 4 concluded that emotional support messages were not perceived as less concerned or sensitive than instrumental support messages. In sum, these studies suggest that subjects discriminate between the assistance provided by the different messages but do not differentiate among the messages in terms of perceived sensitivity or effectiveness.

Conclusion

Three experimental studies using twelve different instrumental and emotional support messages suggest several conclusions. First, none of the studies demonstrated a significant difference in the effectiveness, or perceived effectiveness, between emotional and instrumental support messages. In every case, subjects perceived any type of support to be efficacious. Second, two experiments concluded that subjects perceive that some messages provide more aid, assistance, advice, and guidance than others. However, these instrumental support messages were also seen as more concerned, encouraging, etc., than the messages without instrumental support. Hence it appears that any attempt to support a distressed subject will be perceived to be providing what prior researchers refer to as emotional support. Third, one but not both perception experiments found that subjects distinguished between emotional and nonemotional messages in terms of their indications of concern, encouragement, etc. Since this second experiment utilized more messages than the first, its conclusions should be given more credence.

These studies demonstrate that people experiencing distress from a problem-solving task are sensitive and responsive to messages. Statements that offer assistance, indicate concern, give advice, etc., improve subject performance and/or are evaluated positively while neutral, descriptive statements do not produce positive outcomes. These results suggest the importance of making rather minor, noninvolving, and virtually costless efforts.

All three experimental studies conclusively demonstrate that people who are nonintimates of the recipient can provide support efficaciously. Supportive messages from people who are relative strangers result in improved performance and ratings of perceived helpfulness. Supportive messages were not only perceived as effective, but also as indicating concern and giving encouragement. Hence the provision of even emotional support is not limited to close personal relationships. No doubt there are limitations and restraints on the opportunity to provide this type of support outside of intimate relations. These data, however, demonstrate that within the confines of limited contact between nonintimates in a role relationship, instrumental and emotional messages can provide support (see also Costanza, Derlega, & Winstead, 1988; Winstead, Derlega, Lewis, Sanchez-Hucles, & Clarke, 1992).

The limitations and implications of these studies suggest directions for further research. Only three factors affecting subject reactions to support were considered in these experiments. The effects of other factors also deserve attention. Cutrona, Cohen, and Igram's (1990) analog study of support provided to people whose mother had been seriously injured in an automobile accident demonstrated that subjects' preferred mode of support affected reactions to provided support. A study might assess the importance of preferences in mediating the effects of instrumental and emotional support on problem-solving performance. Perhaps other subject-specific characteristics can be identified that interact with the type of support provided to affect behavior. The utility of various types of support provided by other sources or in other contexts remains to be discovered. Perhaps support will have different effects when provided by close relations (cf. Costanza, Derlega, & Winstead, 1988; Cutrona, Cohen, & Igram, 1990). Research might also focus on the interaction among factors. For example, studies might compare the relative efficacy of support types in intimate and nonintimate relations or in task-oriented and social-oriented situations. Systematic attention to issues such as these will increase our understanding of how and when social support produces positive outcomes.

References

Adelman, M. B., Parks, M. R., & Albrecht, T. L. (1987). Beyond close relationships: Support in weak ties. In T. L. Albrecht & M. B. Adelman (Eds.), *Communicating social support* (pp. 126-125). Newbury Park, CA: Sage.

Barbee, A. P., Gulley, M. R., & Cunningham, M. R. (1990). Support seeking in personal relationships. *Journal of Social and Personal Relationships, 7*, 531-540.

Barrera, M., & Baca, L. M. (1990). Recipient reactions to social support: Contributions of enacted support, conflicted support and network orientation. *Journal of Social and Personal Relationships, 7*, 541-552.

Burleson, B. R. (1984). Comforting communication. In H. E. Sypher & J. L. Applegate (Eds.), *Communication by children and adults: Social cognitive and strategic processes* (pp. 63-104). Beverly Hills, CA: Sage.

Cohen, S. (1988). Psychological models of the role of social support in the etiology of physical disease. *Health Psychology, 7*, 269-297.

Cohen, S., & Hoberman, H. (1983). Positive events and social supports as buffers of life change stress. *Journal of Applied Psychology, 13*, 99-125.

Cohen, S., Mermelstein, R., Kamarck, T., & Hoberman, H. N. (1985). Measuring the functional components of social support. In I. Sarason & B. Sarason (Eds.), *Social support: Theory, research and applications* (pp. 73-94). Dordrecht, The Netherlands: Martinus Nijhoff.

Cohen, S., & McKay, G. (1984). Social support, stress and the buffering hypothesis: A theoretical analysis. In A. Baum, S. E. Taylor, & J. E. Singer (Eds.), *Handbook of psychology and health. Vol. 4: Social psychological aspects of health* (pp. 253-267). Hillsdale, NJ: Lawrence Erlbaum.

Cohen, S., & Syme, S. L. (1985). *Social support and health*. Orlando, FL: Academic Press.

Cohen, S., & Wills, T. A. (1985). Stress, social support, and the buffering hypothesis. *Psychological Bulletin, 98*, 310-357.

Costanza, R. S., Derlega, V. J., & Winstead, B. A. (1988). Positive and negative forms of social support: Effects of conversational topics on coping with stress among same-sex friends. *Journal of Experimental Social Psychology, 24*, 183-193.

Cowen, E. L. (1982). Help is where you find it. *American Psychologist, 37*, 385-395.

Coyne, J. A., Wortman, C. B., & Lehman, D. (1988). The other side of support: Emotional overinvolvement and miscarried helping. In B. H. Gottlieb (Ed.), *Marshaling social support: Formats, processes and effects* (pp. 305-330). Newbury Park, CA: Sage.

Cutrona, C. E., Cohen, B. B., & Igram, S. (1990). Contextual determinants of the perceived supportiveness of helping behaviors. *Journal of Social and Personal Relationships, 7*, 553-562.

Cutrona, C. E., Suhr, J. A., & MacFarlane, R. (1990). Interpersonal transactions and the psychological sense of support. In S. Duck (Ed.), *Personal relationships and social support* (pp. 30-45). London: Sage.

Duck, S. (Ed.). (1990). *Personal relationships and social support*. London: Sage.

Freeman, L. C., & Thompson, C. R. (1989). Estimating acquaintanceship volume. In M. Kochen (Ed.), *The small world* (pp. 147-158). Norwood, NJ: Ablex.

Glass, D. C., & Singer, J. E. (1972). *Urban stress: Experiments on noise and social stressors*. New York: Academic Press.

Gore, S. (1978). The effect of social support in moderating the health consequences of unemployment. *Journal of Health and Social Behavior, 19*, 157-165.

Gottlieb, B. H. (1978). The development and application of a classification scheme of informal helping behaviours. *Canadian Journal of Behavioral Science, 10*, 105-115.

Gottlieb, B. H. (1983). *Social support strategies*. Beverly Hills, CA: Sage.

Gottlieb, B. H. (Ed.). (1988). *Marshaling social support: Formats, processes, and effects*. Newbury Park, CA: Sage.

Hobfoll, S. E., & Stokes, J.P. (1988). The processes and mechanics of social support. In S. Duck (Ed.), *Handbook of personal relationships: Theory, research & interventions* (pp. 497-517). Chichester, UK: John Wiley.

House, J. S. (1981). *Work stress and social support*. Reading, MA: Addison-Wesley.

House, J. S., & Kahn, R. L. (1985). Measures and concepts of social support. In S. Cohen & S. L. Syme (Eds.), *Social support and health* (pp. 83-108). Orlando, FL: Academic Press.

Krantz, D. S., Grunberg, N. E., & Baum, A. (1985). Health psychology. *Annual Review of Psychology, 36*, 349-383.

Lindner, K. C., Sarason, I. G., & Sarason, B. R. (1988). Assessed life stress and experimentally provided social support. In C. D. Spielberger & I. G. Sarason (Eds.), *Stress and anxiety: Vol. 11* (pp. 231-240). Washington, DC: Hemisphere.

Miller, D. T., & Turnbull, W. (1986). Expectancies and interpersonal processes. *Annual Review of Psychology, 37*, 233-256.

Notarius, C. I., & Herrick, L. R. (1988). Listener response strategies to a distressed other. *Journal of Social & Personal Relationships, 5*, 97-108.

Parks, M. (1982). Ideology in interpersonal communication: Off the couch and into the world. *Communication Yearbook, 5*, 79-108.

Rosenthal, R., & Rosnow, R. (1984). *Essential of behavioral research: Methods and data analysis.* New York: McGraw Hill.

Sarason, I. G. (1981). Test anxiety, stress, and social support. *Journal of Personality, 49*, 101-114.

Sarason, I. G., Levine, H. M., Basham, R. B., & Sarason, B. R. (1983). Assessing social support: The Social Support Questionnaire. *Journal of Personality and Social Psychology, 44*, 127-344.

Sarason, I. G., Pierce, G. R., & Sarason, B. R. (1990). Social support and interactional processes: A triadic hypothesis. *Journal of Social and Personal Relationships, 7*, 495-506.

Sarason, I. G., & Sarason, B. R. (1986). Experimentally provided social support. *Journal of Personality and Social Psychology, 50*, 1222-1225.

Seeman, T. E., & Syme, S. L. (1987). Social networks and coronary artery disease: A comparison of structure and function of social relations as predictors of disease. *Psychosomatic Medicine, 49*, 341-354.

Tardy, C. H. (1992). Assessing the functions of social support: Experimental studies of social support. *Communication Research, 19*, 175-192.

Tardy, C. H., Thompson, W. R., & Allen, M. R. (1989). Cardiovascular responses during speech: Does social support mediate the effects of talking on blood pressure? *Journal of Language and Social Psychology, 8*, 271-285.

Walker, K. N., MacBride, A., & Vachon, M. L. S. (1977). Social support networks and the crisis of bereavement. *Social Science and Medicine, 11*, 35-41.

Winstead, B. A., Derlega, V. J., Lewis, R. J., Sanchez-Hucles, J., & Clarke, E. (1992). Friendship, social interaction, and coping with stress. *Communication Research, 19*, 193-211.

Wortman, C. B., & Lehman, D. R. (1985). Reactions to victims of life crises: Support attempts that fail. In I. G. Sarason & B. R. Sarason (Eds.), *Social support: Theory, research and applications* (pp. 463-489). Dordrecht, The Netherlands: Martinus Nijhoff.

PART II

Characteristics of Supportive Interactions

5

Relationship-Specific Social Support

Toward a Model for the Analysis of Supportive Interactions

IRWIN G. SARASON

BARBARA R. SARASON

GREGORY R. PIERCE

This chapter presents an interactional-cognitive view of social support that deals with the roles played by situational, intrapersonal, and interpersonal factors in social relationships. We review several types of evidence (e.g., observational, experimental, and clinical data) that require a broadened perspective of social support, one that goes beyond the demonstration of social support-health correlations and deals with questions concerning the nature of support and the support process. We review in particular the contributions of both global (general, aggregate) support and relationship-specific support (support from particular persons) to the prediction of adjustment. One of our conclusions is that, since support is a product of the individual's history of social experiences, intensive study is needed of the behavioral and cognitive events that take place in interpersonal relationships.

An Interactional-Cognitive Perspective

THE GENERAL FRAMEWORK

Increasingly, research on personality and social psychology has focused attention on the multidimensional nature of persons and situations. It is by now almost self-evident that personal characteristics, covert events, and environmental stimulation interact with each other. For example, a red light is a powerful stimulus and usually is a dominant influence on the automobile driver's behavior. However, there are exceptions. Being upset or inebriated can drastically alter the usual response to a red light. Some psychotic people at times seem almost conventional in certain aspects of their interactions with others and at other times or under different circumstances seem virtually oblivious to external stimulation, failing to respond to questions, requests, and social advances.

The reality of human behavior is that it is modified by both environmental events and the stimulation people supply for themselves in the form of preoccupations, expectations, and interpretations of what is going on in the environment. Much of the individual's world is made up of social situations as they are cognitively represented (Magnusson, 1990; Sarason, 1977). An especially important feature of social attitudes and behavior is the context of interpersonal relationships in which they come to the fore. We believe that more attention needs to be paid to what actually goes on and what is perceived by participants to go on in settings that, at least potentially, can provide opportunities for social support.

Achieving this requires an analysis of both the objective and subjective events involved in the supportive process. What behaviors are intended by the provider to be supportive? Which of the provider's behaviors are used by the recipient in making attributions about the support he or she receives from the provider? What other factors influence the recipient's appraisals of the supportive interaction? What happens when one person tries to help another? Advances in theories of social support will come from attempts to understand the meaning of the association between the presence of another person (e.g., a loved one), on the one hand, and behavior and well-being, on the other.

Situational, Intrapersonal, and
Interpersonal Processes

Conceptualization of social support requires specification of the situations in which support either occurs or does not occur, assessment of how the individual interprets provided support, and determination of the relationship between the provider and recipient. In turn, this requires analysis of the interactive roles of the situational, intrapersonal, and interpersonal contexts of social transactions (Pierce, Sarason, & Sarason, 1990).

SITUATIONAL CONTEXT

The situational context includes, not only the events to which response is required, but also the social setting that includes the behavior of the support provider. The situational event might range from minor to major and from simple to complex. The impact of losing a job is likely to be complex because it involves several factors (how much money is in the bank account of the person who loses a job; whether the job loss resulted from poor performance, product phaseout, or company move; and the current state of the job market). While the aspect of the situational context that has received most attention from researchers concerns its stress-arousing features, a broader perspective of situations is needed. A person's sense of social support is shaped by positive day-to-day experiences, as well as by traumatic ones.

INTRAPERSONAL CONTEXT

The intrapersonal context refers to a person's unique stable patterns of perceiving self, important others, as well as relational expectations in general. Bowlby's (1980) attachment theory has influenced discussions of the intrapersonal context because it emphasizes the role of working or cognitive models in the formation of an individual's expectations, appraisals, and responses to the potentially supportive behavior of others, as well as to the provision of social support to others (Sarason, Sarason, & Pierce, 1990). These personal models consist of representations of self, important others, and the nature of relationships and are related to self-esteem, feelings of self-worth, and the perception of being loved, valued, and cared for by others. Stable personal models of what can be expected from people in general and from specific others lead to distinctive interpretations of others' behavior and interact with situational and social processes. One aspect of these models is a person's *sense of support*, personal beliefs about the forthcomingness of others (Sarason et al., 1991).

INTERPERSONAL CONTEXT

If social support involved only person and situational factors, we would merely be dealing with an extension of the interactional perspective as traditionally defined in personality and social psychology. However, in addition to attending to situations and the characteristics people bring to them, the study of social support also calls for attention to interpersonal relationships. The interpersonal context includes the distinctive qualitative (for example, support, conflict) and quantitative (for example, network size, density) features of specific relationships. In all likelihood, several features of specific relationships influence the impact of social support on health and well-being. These features include interpersonal conflict, the sensitivity with which one participant responds to the support needs of the other participant, and the structure of their interpersonal connections. We see interpersonal relationships as mediating the impact of specific supportive or nonsupportive behaviors. For example, there is evidence that the impact of social support is reduced strongly by the presence of conflict in particular relationships (Coyne & DeLongis, 1986; Zavislak & Sarason, 1992). Support received in the context of conflictive relationships may lead to feelings of indebtedness and ambivalence in the recipient and increase rather than decrease stress (Pierce, Sarason, & Sarason, 1992). An important aspect of the interpersonal context is the extent to which a support provider is aware of and sensitive to the needs of the recipient. In some circumstances, support in the form of empathic listening may be more effective than an offer of material aid.

Supportive efforts may be successful under certain conditions but not others. The success of the efforts depends upon the nature of the relationship between the provider and the recipient. Dakof and Taylor (1990) found that the effectiveness of supportive interventions depends upon their context, with particular actions being perceived to be helpful from some but not other network members. These researchers suggest that future investigations of social support would benefit from identifying the source as well as the type of support. The recipient, the provider, and the critical elements of their relationship need to be studied in an effort to better understand the give and take involved in social support processes. Mallinckrodt (1991) found that the outcomes of counseling sessions are related both to clients' current appraisals of their social support and their recollections of the support parents provided to them during childhood. This suggests that past support as retained in memory combines with current perceptions of support in influencing the working alliance between a client and a counselor. The complexity of the process of social support is reflected in Mallinckrodt's finding that the events of counseling are influenced particularly by clients' recollections of the supportiveness of their fathers. While he assessed present and past support only for clients, it would be interesting also to examine the client-counselor working alliance as a product of the counselor's sense of present and past support.

The Nature of Social Support

We see the sense of support as a product of interpersonal relationships and the meanings people attach to them. Although most social support indices reflect individuals' beliefs about the forthcomingness of the social environment, there actually are three general types of social support measures: (a) *network measures* that focus on the individual's report of social integration into a group and the interconnectedness of those within that group; (b) *measures of received support* that focus on what a person actually receives or reports to have received; and (c) *measures of perceived support* that focus on support the person believes to be available if he or she should need it.

A FOCUS ON PERCEIVED SUPPORT

While each of these types of support has been related to various dependent measures, perceived support measures have fairly consistently yielded the strongest positive association between support scores and health outcomes (Antonucci & Israel, 1986; Blazer, 1982; Wethington & Kessler, 1986). These findings regarding perceived support mesh with and are reinforced by the current emphasis on cognitive appraisal and the influence of cognitive or working models on behavior. They also fit with the conceptualizations offered by Cobb (1976) and Cassel (1976) referred to earlier which helped form the basis for the rapid expansion in social support research. Cobb hypothesized that social support's major role is to convey information to the individual that others care about and value him or her. Support is experienced not so much from what is done, but from how what is done is interpreted. The interpretation will, we think, be heavily influenced by the nature of the relationship between provider and recipient. Cassel emphasized the feedback function in social support because he believed that conveying to the recipient caring and positive regard was more responsible for the positive effect produced than was any specific behavior.

Some measures of perceived support assess availability of help and caring; others assess satisfaction. The Social Support Questionnaire combines both aspects of support in one instrument (Sarason, Levine, Basham, & Sarason, 1983). Interestingly, availability of support and satisfaction with what is available are not highly correlated (Henderson, Byrne, & Duncan-Jones, 1981; Sarason, Shearin, Pierce, & Sarason, 1987). Two research groups studying the Social Support Questionnaire have found that the Availability and Satisfaction scales represented separate dimensions (McCormick, Siegert, & Walkey, 1987; Sarason, Sarason, Shearin, & Pierce, 1987). Over many studies we have found the correlation between the SSQ Availability and Satisfaction scales over a number of populations to be only moderate (.30-.40). There are some indications that Availability may be more closely related to social skills, whereas Satisfaction is more closely related to personality characteristics such as the degree of neuroticism (Sarason, Sarason, Hacker, & Basham, 1985).

THE FUNCTIONS OF PERCEIVED SUPPORT

There are differences among researchers in the extent to which emphasis is given to viewing social support in terms of various functions (e.g., instrumental support, companionship) and assessing the availability of each component. Some researchers prefer to look at social support from a general factor point of view, for example, the sense of support. The functional approach to perceived social support measurement has often been linked to the buffering hypothesis, the idea that social support is a protective factor that becomes important when an individual experiences stress. The basis for the functional approach is the belief that for support to be maximally effective, the support available or provided must match the need created by the stress (Weiss, 1974; Cohen & Wills, 1985). Although the factor structure of some functional measures has been verified across independent samples, a problem with many existing instruments measuring the functions of social support is that the scales representing the different functions are highly correlated. For this reason, a number of researchers have expressed dissatisfaction with the functional approach as currently operationalized (House & Kahn, 1985; Orth-Gomer & Unden, 1987; B. Sarason et al., 1987; Stokes, 1983). Scales measuring different supportive functions often have intercorrelations as high as the subscale reliabilities, thus indicating that the subscales are not measuring distinct constructs.

THE STABILITY OF PERCEIVED SUPPORT

Because perceived support remains quite stable over time, even during periods of developmental transition, it has been suggested that perceived support might well be considered to be a personality variable (Lakey & Cassady, 1990; Sarason, Sarason, & Shearin, 1986). In this light, the stability of perceptions of support availability and a propensity to interpret others' behavior as supportive reflect the sense of support. This sense is a consequence of personality development and experience over the life span. If perceived support is an aspect of personality, it would not be surprising to find perceptions of support to be related to other aspects, such as self-image and beliefs about how others perceive the individual. We have found that SSQ Availability and Satisfaction scores are related to neuroticism, intraversion-extraversion, and loneliness (Sarason et al., 1983) and to self-described social skills (Sarason et al., 1985). These correlations are higher for Satisfaction. People who differ in social support scores also describe themselves differently in several respects, e.g., those high in social support have a more positive self-image than do those who are low (Sarason, Pierce, Shearin, Sarason, Waltz, & Poppe, 1991).

The correlates of perceived social support include a belief in one's interpersonal skills, feelings of self-efficacy leading to adaptive behavior under stress, low levels of anxiety, positive self-image, positive expectations about interactions with others, and a benign view of other people. All of these characteristics are consistent with the picture of people high in perceived social support as having a strong sense of acceptance, an important aspect of which is the person's belief that he or she is valued, not for superficial characteristics or performance, but as someone inde-

pendently worthy of this status without contingency. The sense of acceptance may be regarded as an inherent stable personality characteristic that
contributes to the perception of social support separately from what the
environment actually offers at any particular time.

ASSESSING PERCEIVED SUPPORT

Because we believe that the interpersonal contexts of social interactions
can add significantly to the variance accounted for by situational and
intrapersonal factors, in our research we have emphasized the interpersonal context in which supportive behavior and personal coping efforts
take place. Before describing some of the research that has grown out of
our interactional-cognitive model of social support, we shall describe the
two key instruments in several studies. These instruments measure global
or general support and relationship-based support.

Perceptions of social support are distinct from the observable features
of supportive transactions. The events that lead Person A to feel supported
might have no effect—or even a negative effect—on Person B. We believe
that people have a global or general sense of perceived support, somewhat
analogous to Spearman's g factor of intelligence. Aggregating perceptions
of support across many interactions contributes to an individual's sense
of the forthcomingness of the social environment. A person high in global
perceived support might seem to be something of a social optimist, i.e.,
the person believes the social environment can generally be counted upon
to provide help and support when it is needed. Contrasting with global
support is relationship-specific support, the support a person perceives to
be available from a particular significant person such as mother, father,
spouse, or best friend. If relationship-specific perceptions of support are
not merely reflections of global support, we would expect measures of
them to add to the variance accounted for by global measures.

MEASURING GENERAL PERCEPTIONS OF SUPPORT

We think of the Social Support Questionnaire (SSQ) (I. Sarason et al.,
1983) and the 6-item short form of the SSQ (I. Sarason et al., 1987), as
global measures that reflect the individual's multiple relationships and
feelings of being loved and cared about by others. A person with a high
Satisfaction score on the SSQ is satisfied not just with his or her relation-

ship with mother, father, or spouse, but with the totality of significant relationships in her or his life.

MEASURING RELATIONSHIP-SPECIFIC
PERCEPTIONS OF SUPPORT

The Quality of Relationships Inventory (QRI) was developed to assess perceived availability of support in specific relationships (e.g., "To what extent can you turn to this person for advice about problems?") (Pierce, 1990; Pierce, Sarason, & Sarason, 1988, 1991). The QRI can be used to assess any relationship in a person's life (for example, mother, father, spouse). Items were also developed to assess two other dimensions of specific relationships: the extent to which the relationship is perceived as being positive, important, and secure (e.g., "How significant is this relationship in your life?"), and the extent to which the relationship is a source of conflict and ambivalence (e.g., "How often does this person make you feel angry?"). A total of 25 items assess these three aspects of specific relationships.

ARE RELATIONSHIP-SPECIFIC PERCEPTIONS OF
SUPPORT DISTINCT FROM GENERAL PERCEPTIONS?

Research on social support suggests that people have a set of general expectations and attributions about social relationships that reflect their ideas about how approachable and forthcoming people within the social environment are likely to be. This aggregate may be what measures of perceived social support are tapping. For example, the Social Support Questionnaire seems to be assessing people's beliefs about whether others, in general, are likely to provide assistance and emotional support when needed (Sarason et al., 1987).

In addition to these generalized beliefs concerning social support, people also develop expectations and attributions about the availability of support in specific significant relationships. These specific expectations and attributions may not simply be instances that contribute to general perceptions of available support. For example, a person who generally sees the social environment as far from benign and forthcoming, might still have some specific relationships marked by warmth, caring, and reciprocity. While general and relationship-specific expectations for social support may be related, they reflect different facets of perceived support.

Global and relationship-based perceptions of support may each play an important and unique role in personal adjustment. Pierce, Sarason, and Sarason (1991) have investigated these possibilities by relating measures of both global and relationship-based expectations to personal adjustment.

Two measures were used to assess the quality of past and current relationships. In addition to using the QRI to measure current relationships, these researchers also administered the Parental Bonding Instrument (PBI), a retrospective measure of the quality of early parental relationships (before age 16) (Parker, 1983). General perceptions of available social support were assessed with two instruments: the Social Support Questionnaire (SSQ), and the Social Provision Scale (SPS), a measure of global perceived availability of social support (Cutrona & Russell, 1990). College students' scores on the UCLA Loneliness Scale (Russell, Peplau, & Cutrona, 1980) were used as a reflection of personal adjustment.

Factor analysis confirmed that the QRI is composed of three separate dimensions which we have labeled support, depth, and conflict. Items that load on the *support* dimension appear to measure the extent to which the individual can rely on the other person (e.g., mother, father) for assistance in a variety of situations. Items that load strongly on the *depth* dimension appear to assess the extent to which the individual believes the people in the relationship to be committed to it and positively value it. Items that load on the *conflict* dimension reflect the extent to which the individual experiences angry, ambivalent feelings regarding the other person.

For college students, while perceptions of support from mother and father were strongly related, the correlations between support from parents and friends were relatively low. It would seem that while people's perceptions of specific relationships within a category, such as parents, may be interrelated and their perceptions of a specific relationship may be distinct from their perceptions of other specific relationships.

We have found that perceptions of available support from specific relationships add to the prediction of loneliness after accounting for the contribution made by global perceived available support measured by two quite different measures of perceived social support (SSQ, SPS). The fact that the QRI scales predicted loneliness after partialing out variance associated with general perceptions of available support emphasizes the independent link between relationship-specific perceptions of available support and loneliness. While global perceptions of support may well reflect a personality characteristic or generalized cognitive model, the QRI seems to be assessing characteristics specific to particular relationships. For many research purposes, the QRI might provide a convenient method for quantifying specific properties of personal relationships. We need to know more about the links between personality characteristics and personal relationships (both global and specific). Research is needed, not only to explore the processes which shape the distinctiveness of specific interpersonal relationships, but also to investigate the mechanisms by which both aspects of perceived support might influence each other. Global perceptions and relationship-based perceptions of support might impact personal adjustment through different pathways. If so, theories of social support will be needed to specify the pertinent pathways.

Aseron, Sarason, and Sarason (1992) also investigated the associations of global and relationship-based support with personal adjustment. However, in addition to loneliness, they used a number of other adjustment indices: e.g., self-esteem, anxiety, and depression. Aseron et al. were particularly interested in the relationships between romantic partners. They found that after accounting for the contributions of global perceptions of support (SSQ) and (QRI) from support from mother, father, and same-sex best friend, support associated with romantic partners made a significant independent contribution to the prediction of adjustment.

Grissett and Norvell (1992) investigated the roles of general perceived and relationship-specific social support in a clinical population and found a number of significant differences between the social networks of bulimic and non-eating-disordered women. Bulimic women not only perceived less support in their social environments but also more conflict and ambivalence in specific significant relationships. These negatively-toned close relationships were very strongly associated with the severity of bulimic symptoms. Grissett and Norvell's findings show for a clinical population that relationship-specific measures of support provide information beyond that provided by general measures of support and conflict perceived.

An additional demonstration of the predictive value of relationship-specific assessment has been provided by Sarason, Pierce, Bannerman, and Sarason (1993) who investigated how parents' assessments of their children's positive and negative characteristics are related to each child's general and relationship-specific perceptions of social support. These researchers showed that family environments can be conceptualized in terms of the specific relationships within the family, for example, the association between relationship-quality and response is much stronger for fathers than for mothers. Interestingly, while mothers whose children saw their relationships as either conflictual or not conflictual cooperated equally often as participants in the study, fathers with whom children perceived conflict were less likely to cooperate. Generally, parents' descriptions of their children's positive and negative characteristics were more strongly related to their children's perceptions of the supportiveness of their parental relationships than to the children's general perceptions of the supportiveness of the social network of their peers.

Emphasizing the Relationship-Specific Component of Perceived Support

The interactional-cognitive perspective focuses attention on the need to study behavior in the context of situational, intrapersonal, and interpersonal factors. From this perspective, the sense of support, whether global or relationship-specific, is the product of the person's social interactions with particular individuals in a variety of situations that lead to the development of cognitive models pertinent to social interaction. These models, in turn, exert an impact on what social behavior will occur in particular types of situations and the evaluations made of the situations and behavior in them. The parent-child relationship provides an opportunity to study the impact on social behavior of personality processes and situational contexts among individuals with a long-shared history of experiences. Parents and their children during the course of their relationships are likely to have developed highly specific theories about their nature (Jacobson, 1990; Pierce et al., 1991). These include expectations about the other person's responsiveness toward, acceptance of, and sensitivity to one's needs. Social behavior and expectations concerning specific others are likely to influence each other. Someone who anticipates that another person will be supportive is more likely to interact with that person so as to elicit support.

Our research on social support in the context of specific relationships (for example, family members, friends, and strangers) (Pierce, Sarason, & Sarason, 1991; Pierce, Sarason, & Sarason, 1992; Sarason et al., 1991) has been directed toward providing a groundwork for a theory of relationship-specific support. The need for a framework that encompasses both person and situation variables, including relational factors, is illustrated by a basic question: Under what circumstances will a person get or perceive that he or she has received social support? One important determinant will be whether the person seeks social support, for example, when a particular challenge exceeds the person's perceived ability to cope without another person's help. Attempts to elicit support depend not only on whether people believe they need it, but also on their perceptions of the availability of particular kinds of relationships from which to seek it. People are unlikely to request support from someone whom they anticipate will not give it or from someone whom they think is likely to make them feel guilty about their request.

An additional issue concerns how the recipient interprets the behavior of the provider. Pierce, Sarason, and Sarason (1992) demonstrated that recipients' perceptions of the meaning of a specific behavior is a function of their perceptions of their relationship with the provider. When supportive behavior occurs, its perception as well as its effects may be overwhelmed by the conflict existing in the recipient-support giver relationship (see also, Coyne & DeLongis, 1986). Potential providers also have cognitions and emotions related to the relationship that undoubtedly will influence whether they provide support (Gottlieb, 1992). Potential providers may perceive a person's need for support as a function of situational demands or an estimate of the individual's coping repertory (Dunkel-Schetter & Bennett, 1990). Even if a need for support is perceived, people may be more likely to provide support to others they care about deeply than to those toward whom they feel neutral or ambivalent.

A relationship-specific approach to social support directs attention to what goes on—both cognitively and behaviorally—when people interact with each other. Our current work is concerned with what happens when people interact with each other, what they think about, and the situation which provides the focus for the interaction. Because parent-child relationships are so important for college students, both developmentally and contemporaneously, we are studying what happens when parents and children come together. Because personality and relationship variables may play different roles in different situations, we are investigating parent-child dyads in different kinds of situations. The two we have studied most are one in which the child is called upon to prepare to perform a task while the parent serves as a helper and one in which parent(s) and child discuss a conflict in their lives. Videotaped recordings of these interactions are then rated by observers.

A Focus on Parent-Adult Child Relationships

Examples of our approach to relationship-specific support are two studies of college students and their parents (Sarason, Pierce, & Sarason,

1992). In the first, students and parents were asked to work together to help prepare a speech to be given by the student. Observers made ratings of the extent to which the student and parent worked together in a supportive manner and seemed aware of each others' needs and the meaning of the others' communications. In the second study, students and their mothers were asked to discuss a current source of conflict in their relationship. Observers' rated the extent to which the student and mother discussed the conflict in a supportive manner and displayed warmth and sensitivity toward each other. In both studies the ratings reflected observers' judgments about the meaning the students' and parents' behaviors had for each other. The ratings focused on behaviors of theoretical interest in understanding the social support process: mutual support, sensitivity to and awareness of the other's communications and expressions of warmth directed to the other person. In each study, students and parents separately completed packets of questionnaires assessing several personality characteristics and their expectations of their own and other relationships at least a week prior to the laboratory session.

For the speech task, students' self-reported perceptions of the quality of their relationship with the participating parent were more strongly related to observers' ratings of the interaction than were students' perceptions of other specific relationships. The results were consistent with the hypothesis that adult children's perceptions of their parental relationships are to a large degree veridical in the sense that the kinds of social behavior exhibited by the parents in the laboratory might, over substantial periods of time, be expected to foster the expectations reported by the students. Although the observers' ratings were significantly related to general perceptions of social support (SSQ), the results were stronger for students' perceptions of the participating parent (QRI). In general, self-reports of both students' and parents' personality characteristics were less consistently related than were their assessments of their relationships and observers' ratings.

In the study in which student and mother discussed a current conflict, we found that their perceptions of their relationship with each other were more strongly related to observers' ratings of the videotaped interactions than were students' and mothers' perceptions of other relationships. Compared with other students, students who reported high levels of support and depth and a low level of conflict with their mothers, had interactions with their mothers that were described by observers as supportive and in which both student and mother were rated as warm and sensitive to each others' needs. We again found that students' and mothers' self-reported personality characteristics were less strongly and consistently related to the observers' ratings than were their perceptions of their joint relationship. Neither students' nor mothers' tendencies to describe themselves in a socially desirable manner was strongly related to the observers' ratings.

Both studies showed substantial associations between parents' and children's perceptions of their relationship, on the one hand, and observers' ratings of the videotaped interactions. For the mother-child conflict discussion, students' retrospective reports of early maternal overprotectiveness were strongly related to the observers' ratings of the quality of the videotaped interactions. For the speech preparation task, students' reports of early maternal warmth and caring were strongly related to the observers' ratings. Future research is needed to investigate family relationships in the context of multiple social situations in order to gain a more complete understanding of the relationship between family members and their behavior in specific types of situations. Put another way, we need studies in which multiple features of family members' self-reports and observable properties of their interactions are obtained for theoretically relevant situations.

The two studies described demonstrate the feasibility of this line of inquiry. Additional supporting evidence has been provided in a study carried out by Pierce, Sarason, Sarason, and Gilmore (1992) in which observer ratings were made of videotaped interactions of married couples. They found that spouses who reported a high level of satisfaction and support in the marital relationship were seen by independent observers as having a "good" marriage, one in which the marriage partners enjoyed each other and were affectionate and friendly. They also found that wives who reported high levels of depression had interactions with their husbands that were rated as indicating less enjoyment and affection and greater disagreement about the quality of their relationship.

EXPERIMENTAL STUDIES

Most research on social support has been correlational, involving associations between self-report indices, clinical outcomes, and, to a lesser extent, behavioral observations. A needed line of research involves laboratory studies in which the effects of supportive manipulations on behavior are recorded under standard conditions. Ultimately, this type of study could have important implications for clinical situations because self-help groups, individual psychotherapy, and group psychotherapy involve supportive processes. Our work suggests that the effectiveness of support depends on the context in which it is provided, the nature of the situation being confronted, and the relationship between supporter and recipient. Analogue studies of support provision conducted in laboratory situations might provide valuable clues to practical applications.

An example of what can be learned in laboratory research are our studies of the effects of manipulations intended to provide support (Sarason & Sarason, 1986; Lindner, Sarason, & Sarason, 1988). An experimenter's offer of help, if needed, to students who are about to work on problem-solving tasks defined the manipulation. The experimenter told the subjects that she would be available to them throughout their work and would answer any questions that might come up. Although no subject requested help, those who reported low satisfaction with their overall social support performed significantly better after receiving the supportive communication than a comparable low support satisfaction group that did not receive this communication. The performance of low satisfaction subjects who were given this intervention did not differ from the performance of subjects high in satisfaction, while the supportive condition did not raise the performance of those high in satisfaction, compared with that of an untreated high satisfaction group. Thus there was an interaction attributable to the manipulation: support was helpful only for subjects whose satisfaction with social support was low.

In another experimental investigation, Kamarck, Manuck, and Jennings (1990) investigated the effects of a nonevaluative social interaction on cardiovascular responses to psychological challenge. In one condition, a friend accompanied a college student who participated in two laboratory tasks. In the other condition, the subject came to the laboratory unaccompanied. Subjects who were accompanied by a friend showed reduced heart rate reactivity to both tasks relative to the alone condition. The result suggested that interpersonal support reduces cardiovascular responsiveness.

There is a need for intensive study of operationally defined supportive interventions and their effects. In addition to obtaining answers to questions concerning whether particular interventions are effective under controlled conditions, increased understanding of the process by which supportive interventions have positive effects is needed. Both psychological and physiological processes may play important roles in the support process. Empirical investigation of the support process will require attention to (a) the nature of interventions intended to be supportive, (b) the behavioral outcome the interventions are designed to influence, and (c) the effects of the intervention on self and social perception, physiological responsiveness, and relational attributions.

Toward the
Specification of Support Processes

We have come a long way from an interest simply in possible associations between social support and health and adjustment indices. We now realize that definitions of social support are not obvious or standard and that the many measures that have been developed to assess it probably have different correlates. Perceptions of support availability rather than support receipt seem generally to yield the strongest associations with health and adjustment criteria. We now realize that people have both global perceptions of social support and perceptions specific to particular relationships. Given the several examples presented here of the independent predictive contributions made by relationship-specific measures of support over and beyond the contributions of global social support, we believe that more attention must be paid to the relative importance of global and relationship-specific perceptions. All the clues available now point to relationship-specific perceptions providing information beyond what is provided by global measures.

Might relationship-specific support be a more powerful predictor of health and adjustment than global support? While we do not yet have the answer to this question, available evidence suggests that this might be the case, at least in certain instances. In any event, this issue requires careful inquiry. An illustration of evidence pertinent to this issue is Coyne and Smith's (1991) study of couples coping with a husband's myocardial infarction. Wives' ability to help their husbands cope with a heart attack depended on the character of the infarction, the couple's interactions with medical personnel, and the quality of their marital relationship. In a study of recovery from coronary artery surgery, King, Reis, Porter, and Norsen (1993) found that patients' perceptions of general esteem support was the only type of support that consistently accounted for a unique share of the relationship between social support and surgery outcome. These researchers concluded that this positive influence of general esteem support was probably due to the high-esteem person's feeling valued, loved, and competent. Future research on social support, whether defined globally or based on particular relationships, will need to take account of possible interactions with other individual difference and pertinent environmental or situational variables.

With hindsight we now see the need for a greater variety of research approaches to social support than has characterized work in the field to date. Experimental and observational studies, as well as longitudinal and clinical outcome studies all have much to contribute to our understanding of social support as a perception of the individual and as a process. A better appreciation of the social support process is likely to provide insights into the provision of social support both in clinical situations and in everyday life.

What are the elements of supportive processes? In coding parent-child interactions, we were able to identify three primary ingredients of personal relationships: the degree to which dyads show (a) cooperation, (b) sensitivity to each other's needs and (c) warmth. No doubt there are other important ingredients of personal relationships and this likelihood provides yet additional impetus for studying social support in the context of observable interactions. Coyne and DeLongis (1986) found that inappropriate, poorly timed or over-solicitous support from a spouse proves to be stressful for chronically-ill patients. Revenson and Majerovitz (1990) studied interactions between rheumatoid arthritis patients and their spouses and found that, while spouses are important sources of support for the patients, the amount and quality of extrafamilial support available to the spouses influences how supportive they are able to be toward the patients. Both specific relational support and general perceptions of support seem to play roles in clinical status and personal adjustment outcomes.

Analyzing the social support process will require not only identification of the individual's cognitions about the forthcomingness of the social environment and of personally significant individuals, but also of events that take place at the interface between the individual in need of support and a potential provider. The importance of determining the independent contributions to clinical and adjustment outcomes of various types of support (either general support or support from particular others) is suggested by studies of emotional support provided by a companion while women were undergoing labor and delivery. Kennell, Klaus, McGrath, Robertson, and Hinkley (1991) found that the presence of a supportive companion (another woman) had a significant positive effect on clinical outcomes. The companion met the study participant for the first time after hospital admission. Each companion stayed at her assigned patient's bedside from admission through delivery, soothing and touching the patient and giving encouragement. In addition, she explained to the patient what was occurring during labor and what was likely to happen next. The provision of social support had a number of effects including fewer caesarian sections being necessary in the supported as contrasted with the control group. The supported group also had significantly fewer forceps deliveries than did the control group and fewer infants born to mothers in the supported group required a prolonged hospital stay. Bertsch, Nagashima-Whalen, Dykeman, Kennell, and McGrath (1990) found significant differences in clinical outcomes when either male partners of obstetrical patients or female companions (who were strangers) were present during the delivery. The female companions touched the laboring women much more than the male partners. Male partners chose to be present for less time during labor and to be close to the mother less often than the female companions.

Further study is needed on the most active ingredients of the supportive process in these types of situations. Answers are needed to such questions as "Does the positive influence of a supportive companion reflect specific physiological changes in the recipient?" "Does this happen because maternal anxiety is reduced and uterine contractions and uterine blood flow are facilitated?" A companion's constant presence, physical touch, reassurance, explanations, and anticipatory guidance all probably play roles and may contribute to the laboring woman feeling safer and calmer and needing less obstetrical intervention for labor to proceed smoothly.

Conclusion

Perceived social support is not an isolated perception that comes into play only when individuals are confronted by a stressful situation that demands coping behavior. It is part of a constellation of cognitions that derive from a history of social interactions and accounts for differences in interpretations of situations, the motives of others, and beliefs about what others are "really like." Attention to this wide range of social phenomena related to the construct of perceived social support may contribute to a better understanding of both the events of everyday life and clinical conditions.

References

Antonucci, T. C., & Israel, B. A. (1986). Veridicality of social support: A comparison of principal and network members' responses. *Journal of Consulting and Clinical Psychology, 54*, 432-437.

Aseron, R. G., Sarason, I. G., & Sarason, B. R. (1992). *Social support and conflict: Global and relationship-specific aspects.* Paper presented at the Annual Meeting of the American Psychological Association, Washington, D.C.

Bertsch, T. D., Nagashima-Whalen, L., Dykeman, S., Kennell, J. H., & McGrath, S. (1990). Labor support by first-time fathers: Direct observations. *Journal of Psychosomatic Obstetric Gynecology, 11,* 251-260.

Blazer, D. (1982). Social support and mortality in an elderly community population. *American Journal of Epidemiology, 115,* 684-694.

Bowlby, J. (1980). *Attachment and loss: Vol. 3. Loss: sadness and depression.* New York: Basic Books.

Cassel, J. (1976). The contribution of the social environment to host resistance. *American Journal of Epidemiology, 104,* 107-123.

Cobb, S. (1976). Social support as a moderator of life stress. *Psychosomatic Medicine, 38,* 300-314.

Cohen, S., & Wills, T. A. (1985). Stress, social support, and the buffering hypothesis. *Psychological Bulletin, 98,* 310-357.

Coyne, J. C., & DeLongis, A. (1986). Going beyond social support: The role of social relationships in adaptation. *Journal of Consulting and Clinical Psychology, 54,* 454-460.

Coyne, J. C., & Smith, D. A. F. (1991). Couples coping with a myocardial infarction: A contextual perspective on wives' distress. *Journal of Personality and Social Psychology, 61,* 404-412.

Cutrona, C. E., & Russell, D. W. (1990). Type of social support and specific stress: Toward a theory of optimal matching. In B. R. Sarason, I. G. Sarason, & G. R. Pierce (Eds.), *Social support: An interactional view* (pp. 319-366). New York: John Wiley.

Dakof, G. A., & Taylor, S. E. (1990). Victims' perspective of social support: What is helpful to whom? *Journal of Personality and Social Psychology, 58,* 80-89.

Dunkel-Schetter, C., & Bennett, T. L. (1990). Differentiating the cognitive and behavioral aspects of social support. In B. R. Sarason, I. G. Sarason, & G. R. Pierce (Eds.), *Social support: An interactional view* (pp. 267-296). New York: John Wiley.

Gottlieb, B. H. (1992). Quandaries in translating support concepts to intervention. In H. O. F. Veiel & U. Baumann (Eds.), *The meaning and measurement of social support* (pp. 293-309)). NY: Hemisphere.

Grissett, N. I., & Norvell, N. K. (1992). Perceived social support, social skills, and quality of relationships in bulimic women. *Journal of Consulting and Clinical Psychology, 60,* 293-299.

Henderson, S., Byrne, D. G., & Duncan-Jones, P. (1981). *Neurosis and the social environment.* New York: Academic Press.

House, J. S., & Kahn, R. L. (1985). Measures and concepts of social support. In S. Cohen & S. L. Syme (Eds.), *Social support and health* (pp. 83-108). Orlando, FL: Academic Press.

Jacobson, D. (1990). Stress and support in stepfamily formation: The cultural context of social support. In B. R. Sarason, I. G. Sarason, & G. R. Pierce (Eds.), *Social support: An interactional view* (pp. 199-218). New York: John Wiley.

Kamarck, T. W., Manuck, S. B., & Jennings, J. R. (1990). Social support reduces cardiovascular reactivity to psychological challenge: A laboratory model. *Psychosomatic Medicine, 52,* 42-58.

Kennell, J., Klaus, M., McGrath, S., Robertson, S., & Hinkley, C. (1991). Continuous emotional support during labor in a U. S. hospital: A randomized controlled trial. *Journal of American Medical Association, 265,* 2197-2201.

King, K. B., Reis, H. T., Porter, L. A., & Norsen, L. H. (1993). Social support and long-term recovery from coronary artery surgery: Effects on patients and spouses. *Health Psychology, 12,* 56-63.

Lakey, B., & Cassady, P. G. (1990). Cognitive processes in perceived social support. *Journal of Personality and Social Psychology, 59*, 337-343.

Lindner, K. C., Sarason, I. G., & Sarason, B. R. (1988). Assessed life stress and experimentally provided social support. In C. D. Spielberger & I. G. Sarason (Eds.), *Stress and anxiety* (vol. 11, pp. 231-240). Washington, DC: Hemisphere.

Magnusson, D. (1990). Personality development from an interactional perspective. In L. A. Pervin (Ed.), *Handbook of personality theory and research* (pp. 193-222). New York: Guilford.

Mallinckrodt, B. (1991). Clients' representations of childhood emotional bonds with parents, social support, and formation of the working alliance. *Journal of Counseling Psychology, 4*, 401-409.

McCormick, I. A., Siegert, R. J., & Walkey, F. H. (1987). Dimensions of social support: A factorial confirmation. *American Journal of Community Psychology, 15*, 73-77.

Orth-Gomer, K., & Unden, A. L. (1987). The measurement of social support in population surveys. *Social Science and Medicine, 24*, 83-94.

Parker, G. (1983). *Parental overprotection: A risk factor in psychosocial development.* New York: Grune & Stratton.

Pierce, G. R. (1990). *Predicting perceptions of social support: An experimental study of behavioral, personality, relationship and situational variables.* Unpublished doctoral dissertation, University of Washington.

Pierce, G. R., Sarason, B. R., & Sarason, I. G. (1990). Integrating social support perspectives: Working models, personal relationships, and situational factors. In S. Duck & R. C. Silver (Eds.), *Personal relationships and social support* (pp. 173-189). Newbury Park, CA: Sage.

Pierce, G. R., Sarason, B. R., & Sarason, I. G. (1992). General and specific support expectations and stress as predictors of perceived supportiveness: An experimental study. *Journal of Personality and Social Psychology, 63*, 297-307.

Pierce, G. R., Sarason, B. R., Sarason, I. G., & Gilmore, K. (1992). Perceived and objective reality in marital interaction. Unpublished manuscript, Hamilton College, Clinton, NY.

Pierce, G. R., Sarason, I. G., & Sarason, B. R. (1991). General and relationship-based perceptions of social support: Are two constructs better than one? *Journal of Personality and Social Psychology, 61*, 1028-1039.

Pierce, G. R., Sarason, I. G., & Sarason, B. R. (1988). *Quality of relationships and social support as personality characteristics.* Paper presented at the annual meeting of the American Psychological Association, Atlanta, GA.

Revenson, T. A., & Majerovitz, D. (1990). Spouses' support provision to chronically ill patients. *Journal of Social and Personal Relationships, 7*, 575-586.

Russell, D., Peplau, L. A., & Cutrona, C. E. (1980). The revised UCLA Loneliness Scale: Concurrent and discriminant validity evidence. *Journal of Personality and Social Psychology, 39*, 472-480.

Sarason, B. R., Pierce, G. R., Bannerman, A., & Sarason, I. G. (1993). Investigating the antecedents of perceived social support: Parents' views of and behavior toward their children. *Journal of Personality and Social Psychology, 65*, 107-1085.

Sarason, B. R., Pierce, G. R., & Sarason, I. G. (1992). *Parent-child interactions.* Unpublished manuscript, University of Washington, Seattle.

Sarason, B. R., Pierce, G. R., Shearin, E. N., Sarason, I. G., Waltz, J. A., & Poppe, L. (1991). Perceived social support and working models of self and actual others. *Journal of Personality and Social Psychology, 60*, 273-287.

Sarason, B. R., Sarason, I. G., Hacker, T. A., & Basham, R. B. (1985). Concomitants of social support: Social skills, physical attractiveness, and gender. *Journal of Personality and Social Psychology, 49*, 469-480.

Sarason, B. R., Sarason, I. G., & Pierce, G. R. (1990). *Social support: An interactional view.* New York: John Wiley.

Sarason, B. R., Shearin, E. N., Pierce, G. R., & Sarason, I. G. (1987). Interrelationships among social support measures: Theoretical and practical implications. *Journal of Personality and Social Psychology, 52*, 813-832.

Sarason, I. G. (1977). The growth of interactional psychology. In D. Magnusson & N. S. Endler (Eds.), *Personality at the crossroads: Current issues in interactional psychology* (pp. 261-272). Hillsdale, NJ: Lawrence Erlbaum.

Sarason, I. G., Levine, H. M., Basham, R. B., & Sarason, B. R. (1983). Assessing social support: The Social Support Questionnaire. *Journal of Personality and Social Psychology, 44*, 127-139.

Sarason, I. G., & Sarason, B. R. (1986). Experimentally provided social support. *Journal of Personality and Social Psychology, 50*, 1222-1225.

Sarason, I. G., Sarason, B. R., & Shearin, E. N. (1986). Social support as an individual difference variable: Its stability, origins, and relational aspects. *Journal of Personality and Social Psychology, 50*, 845-855.

Sarason, I. G., Sarason, B. R., Shearin, E. N., & Pierce, G. R. (1987). A brief measure of social support: Practical and theoretical implications. *Journal of Social and Personal Relationships, 4*, 497-510.

Stokes, J. P. (1983). Predicting satisfaction with social support from social network structure. *American Journal of Community Psychology, 11*, 141-152.

Weiss, R. S. (1974). The provisions of social relationships. In Z. Rubin (Ed.), *Doing unto others* (pp. 17-26). Englewood Cliffs, NJ: Prentice Hall.

Wethington, E., & Kessler, R. D. (1986). Perceived support, received support, and adjustment to stressful life events. *Journal of Health and Social Behavior, 27*, 78-89.

Zavislak, N. M., & Sarason, B. R. (1992). *Predicting parent-child relationships: Influence of marital conflict and family behavior.* Paper presented at the Annual Meeting of the American Psychological Association, Washington, DC.

6

Social Support Communication
in the Context of Marriage

An Analysis of
Couples' Supportive Interactions

CAROLYN E. CUTRONA

JULIE A. SUHR

. . . for better, for worse, for richer, for poorer, in sickness and in health . . .

Traditional marriage vows remind couples that they will encounter adversity and stress during the course of their lives together. Husbands and wives are expected to provide each other with comfort, encouragement, advice, and assistance in times of misfortune. The spouse is frequently the first person from whom support is sought during crises (Blood & Wolfe, 1960; Burke & Weir, 1977), and evidence suggests that support from other sources cannot compensate for a lack of intimate or marital support. Brown and Harris (1978) found that a confiding relationship with a parent, sister, or friend did not compensate for the lack of a confiding relationship with one's spouse in preventing depressive reactions to negative life events. Among parents who had lost a child, there was no association between social support and well-being beyond the contribution of spousal support (Lieberman, 1982). Spousal social support has been associated with a variety of positive outcomes, including adaptation to parenthood, adjustment following myocardial infarction, lower vulnerability to depression, and compliance with medical regimens among heart transplant patients (Brown & Harris, 1978; Mermelstein, Lichtenstein, & McIntyre, 1983; Rogers, 1987; Waltz, 1986; Wandersman, Wandersman, & Kahn, 1980).

Although the potential value of support from an intimate partner in times of trouble has been well-documented, very little is known about the *process* through which partners communicate support to one another. The lack of attention to the processes underlying marital social support has precluded understanding of the mechanisms through which supportive intimate relationships promote adaptive coping with stress (Gottlieb, 1985). The study of marital social support processes requires an understanding of the interpersonal context in which it occurs. Two aspects of marital relationships that affect the exchange of help-intended communications will be considered in this chapter: interdependence and assertion of personal control.

According to a number of theorists, marital relationships are characterized by ongoing efforts to strike a balance between interdependence and autonomy (Bochner, 1984; Bowen, 1961; Minuchin, 1974). Ideally, couples maintain connectedness and cohesion, but keep clear boundaries between them (Bowen, 1961; Minuchin, 1974; Olson, 1981). Efforts to assert and maintain individual control must be balanced against the risk of losing intimacy and closeness. In the context of stressful life events, those in ongoing close relationships must make choices between dependence and independence in how they choose to deal with and the extent to which they involve their partner in their problems. Similarly, partners of persons facing stressful events must be sensitive to issues of dominance and control. Doing too much for their partner may be interpreted as domineering or "taking over"; whereas doing too little may be perceived as lack of concern or interest. Reciprocity in the exchange of assistance is also important (Antonnuci & Jackson, 1990). For example, Fisher and colleagues found that aid will be rejected or the helper derogated if the recipient expects to feel indebted or unable to repay the helper (Fisher, Nadler, & Witcher-Alagna, 1982). Although the need for immediate reciprocity may be less in intimate ("communal") relationships (Clark & Mills, 1979), one-sided support provision over long periods of time is likely to be demoralizing to both provider and recipient (Shumaker & Brownell, 1984).

Thus both interdependence and maintenance of personal autonomy or control are important contextual considerations in the study of social support in married couples. Members of a couple are affected by stressors that impact upon their partner, and by their partner's success in coping with stress (Gottlieb, 1985). However, each individual must safeguard a sense of personal control, which can be threatened in both the role of helper (when the type of help desired by one's spouse conflicts with personal needs) and in the role of support recipient (when excessive dependence threatens a valued self-image or leads to a sense of indebtedness) (Shumaker & Brownell, 1984).

FAILED MARITAL SUPPORT

Intimate partners are not always successful in their support efforts. For example, Turk, Kerns, and Rudy (1984) found that spousal support predicted poorer outcomes for low back pain patients. Among cardiac patients, poorer adjustment was associated with spousal over-protectiveness (Coyne, Ellard, & Smith, 1990). One possible explanation for the failure of certain studies to find positive effects for social support is that the type of support provided was not appropriate for the type of stress, or for the relationship context in which support was sought. Different stressful events pose different challenges, and lead to different psychological needs (Lazarus & Folkman, 1984). These needs may be shaped both by the nature of the stress and by the nature of the relationship between the stress victim and the support provider. For example, emotional support was preferred over tangible support in the context of a close relationship; but the two kinds of support were valued equally in the context of a casual relationship in a study by Cutrona, Cohen, & Igram (1990).

We are in the process of developing an optimal matching model of stress and social support (Cutrona, 1990; Cutrona & Russell, 1990). Originally, the model focused solely on characteristics of the stress as determinants of the most beneficial type of social support (Cutrona, 1990; Cutrona & Russell, 1990). More recently, we have come to believe that characteristics of the relationship between the stress victim and the support provider must be considered as well (Cutrona & Suhr, 1992). The original optimal matching model and our more recent critique of the model will be described below.

THE OPTIMAL MATCHING MODEL OF
STRESS AND SOCIAL SUPPORT

Components of Social Support

Although a variety of terms are used, researchers in the area have converged on five major categories of social support: informational, tangible, emotional, esteem, and social network support (Cobb, 1979; Kahn, 1979; Schaefer, Coyne, & Lazarus, 1981; Weiss, 1974). We have divided these support types into two broad categories: action-facilitating support and nurturant support (Cutrona, 1990; Cutrona & Russell, 1990). The kinds of messages communicated in each category will be briefly discussed, followed by a description of the kinds of stressful circumstances in which we have hypothesized each to be maximally beneficial.

Action-facilitating support is intended to assist the stressed individual to solve or eliminate the problem that is causing his or her distress. We include both informational support and tangible aid in this category. Information includes advice ("I think you should tell your supervisor"); factual input ("If you don't treat the infection quickly, it will get worse"); and feedback on actions ("You shouldn't have told her so bluntly"). Tangible aid includes offers to provide needed goods (e.g., money, food, books) and services (e.g., baby-sitting, transportation, typing).

Nurturant support encompasses efforts to comfort or console, without direct efforts to solve the problem causing the stress. Emotional support and network support fall into this category. Emotional support includes expressions of caring ("I love you"); concern ("Are you feeling better?"); empathy ("You must have been really hurt by his coldness"); and sympathy ("I'm so sorry you're ill"). Network support entails a sense of belonging among people with similar interests and concerns ("We'd like you to join our support group").

A final component, esteem support, may serve either an action-facilitating or nurturant function. Esteem support refers to expressions of regard for one's skills and abilities ("I know you'll do a good job") and/or for one's value as a person ("Losing your job doesn't mean you're worthless"). Reassuring a person of his or her competence may foster self-efficacy, which is associated with greater persistence and less discouragement in goal-directed behaviors (Bandura, 1977). Reassuring a person of his or her intrinsic worth may lessen the intensity of negative emotions engendered by stressful events, especially those involving failure or blame.

Matching Type of Support to Stress

In the original optimal matching model of stress and social support (Cutrona, 1990; Cutrona & Russell, 1990), the controllability of the stressful event or situation was of prime importance in determining the type of social support that would be optimally beneficial to the stress victim. Specifically, we proposed that in the context of *controllable* events (i.e., situations in which something can be done to prevent, eliminate, or diminish the source of stress), action-facilitating support would be optimally beneficial. In the context of *uncontrollable* events, we hypothesized that nurturant support (emotional support and network support) would be optimally beneficial, in that these supportive acts serve to diminish the intensity of negative emotions engendered by the stress. These predictions were modeled closely after Lazarus and Folkman (1984) regarding optimal coping activities following controllable versus uncontrollable stressors. As stated above, we believe that esteem support may serve an action-facilitating function in some circumstances. However, it may also serve an emotion-moderating function in the context of uncontrollable events.

In the original optimal matching model, we failed to consider a key question, i.e., controllable by whom? Support-intended communications involve at least two people, the stress victim and the support provider. The stressor may be controllable or uncontrollable by either. Furthermore there may be contextual constraints on the exercise of control by one or both participants. As described above, in the context of an ongoing close relationship, both provider and recipient must balance interdependence versus personal autonomy. For example, the wife may be a computer expert, and her husband a computer-phobic graduate student. If he is struggling with programming difficulties, the source of his distress may be readily eliminated by his wife, by virtue of her expertise. However, if the wife offers too much help, the husband may feel overly dependent or indebted. The wife may similarly feel uncomfortable, perhaps believing that he *should* have learned the needed skills earlier, or fearing that his pride will suffer from her intervention. In recognition of these issues, further tests of the optimal matching model in the context of the marital relationship were undertaken. Two studies will be described in this chapter, both of which assessed the controllability of current stressful life events by both members of the couple. Of central interest was the extent to which predictions derived from the optimal matching model of stress and social support would hold in the context of an ongoing, interdependent relationship such as marriage.

METHODOLOGICAL ISSUES

Virtually all prior research on marital social support has relied exclusively on self-report assessments of frequency and quality of help-intended behaviors. Evidence suggests that self-reports of partner behavior are relatively inaccurate. In one study, spouses agreed on fewer than 50% of the behaviors that occurred on a particular day (Wills, Weiss, & Patterson, 1974). Unhappily married couples are especially unreliable observers of events in their marriages (Christensen & Nies, 1980; Elwood & Jacobson, 1982). Although partners are more accurate when the target behavior is concrete, easily defined, and stable, they are very inaccurate when the target is abstract, subtle, or interactional (Sillars & Scott, 1983). Furthermore research suggests that the personality of the support recipient affects responses to measures of perceived social support. For example, people who show a dispositional tendency to evaluate themselves and their experiences in a negative light were found to misperceive or underrate the support provided to them (Vinokur, Schul, & Caplan, 1987). A variety of personality characteristics predict responses to social support questionnaires, including extraversion, self-esteem, and neuroticism (Procidano & Heller, 1983; Sarason, Sarason, Hacker, & Basham, 1985; Sarason, Sarason, & Shearin, 1986). Thus there is a need for observational studies of dyadic interactions to clarify the actual behaviors that are perceived as supportive, and to assess the relative contribution of these behaviors and of personal and relationship characteristics to the perception of spousal supportiveness.

CURRENT STUDIES

In this chapter we will describe the results of two observational studies of social support communication among married couples. First, we provide descriptive information regarding the types of support-intended communications most frequently used by husbands and wives in our sample. Next, we explore determinants of the frequency of supportive behaviors individuals provide to their spouse. In the third section, we examine determinants of perceived spousal supportiveness, including relationship evaluations, recipient personality, and the actual support behaviors received. Finally, we test specific hypotheses regarding which types of social support are optimally beneficial in the context of stressful life events that vary in controllability by both the stress victim and his or her spouse. Results will be interpreted within the context of marriage as a relationship in which both partners strive for a balance between interdependence and autonomy.

Method

Subjects

Subjects were married couples who were recruited through a mailing to university family housing units. Screening criteria included fluency in English and willingness of both spouses to participate. At least one member of each couple was a student at the University of Iowa. Each couple was paid $25 for participating in the project.

Thirty couples, who ranged in age from 19 to 47 years ($M = 28.12$), and had been married for 1 to 11 years ($M = 3.14$) were recruited to participate in Study 1 (Suhr, 1990). Recruitment for Study 1 occurred in 1988 and 1989. For a more complete description of the methods and results of Study 1, see Cutrona and Suhr (1992) and Suhr and Cutrona (under review).

Recruitment procedures for Study 2 were identical. Twenty couples who ranged in age from 19 to 41 years ($M = 26.02$) and had been married from less than 1 to 17 years ($M = 3.50$) were recruited in 1991 and 1992. The basic observational procedures used in Studies 1 and 2 were identical. The two studies differed in some of the self-report measures administered, as described below. In addition, a small number of minor changes were made in the observational social support coding system between Studies 1 and 2.

Procedure

Participants came to the laboratory with their spouse, where they were first asked to complete a set of questionnaires that assessed marital adjustment (Dyadic Adjustment Scale; Spanier, 1976), perceived social support from spouse (Social Provisions Scale–Spouse Version; Cutrona & Russell, 1987), neuroticism and extraversion (Eysenck Personality Inventory; Eysenck & Eysenck, 1964) and depressive symptoms (Beck Depression Inventory; Beck, Ward, Mendelson, Mock, & Erbaugh, 1961). They were randomly assigned to take the role of stress discloser or support provider in the first interaction. The person assigned to the stress discloser role was instructed to think of an "important stressor" in his or her current life. After briefly describing the stressor to the experimenter to increase its salience, the stress discloser was asked to discuss the stressful situation with his or her spouse. The individual assigned to the support provider role was told to respond naturally and spontaneously. The couple was situated in a comfortable room equipped with a videotape camera, and given 10 minutes to interact. After 10 minutes, the support recipient was asked to complete a 3-item measure of satisfaction with the interaction (*alpha* = .74) and a 20-item measure of perceived interaction supportiveness (*alpha* = .87). In Study 2, the support recipient was also asked to complete a brief measure of depressive mood (Depression Adjective Checklist (DACL); Lubin, 1981) after the interaction. The entire procedure was then repeated, with the spouses reversing roles.

It was of interest to determine whether personal perceptions or more objective assessments of event controllability would be more influential in determining the kinds of support behaviors that would be optimally beneficial. Thus, two different procedures were used to assess the controllability of stressful events in Studies 1 and 2. In Study 1, research assistants rated the events using the 7-item controllability subscale of the Stress Dimensions Scale (Swanson, 1990; *alpha* = .86; interrater reliability = .75). In Study 2, each member of the couple rated the extent to which he or she could exert control over the event using the same Stress Dimensions Scale (Swanson, 1990; *alpha* = .90).

In both studies, frequency of support behaviors was assessed using the Social Support Behavior Code (SSBC; Suhr, 1990). The SSBC is described in detail elsewhere (Cutrona, Suhr, & MacFarlane, 1990; Cutrona & Suhr, 1992). In brief, the SSBC was designed to assess the frequency of occurrence of 23 individual support-intended communication behaviors that fall into five categories: informational support (providing information about the stress itself or how to deal with it); tangible aid (providing or offering to provide goods or services needed in the stressful situation); emotional support (communicating love, concern, or empathy); social network support (communicating belonging to a group of persons with similar interests or concerns); and esteem support (communicating respect and confidence in abilities). Items for the code were developed by surveying descriptions of support behaviors in the literature and existing behaviorally-focused social support questionnaires, and through questionnaires administered to married couples in which they were asked to describe specific behaviors that they would like to receive from their spouse following stressful events (Suhr, 1990). All but one of the coded behaviors is verbal; the single nonverbal code is physical affection (e.g., touching, holding hands). In addition to the support behavior codes, frequency of negative or undermining behaviors is also recorded (e.g., criticism, sarcasm, disagreement). A total frequency score is computed for each of the five support categories, negative behaviors, and an overall support frequency score (sum of five support category frequencies). Mean interrater reliability across behavior codes is .77 (intraclass correlation; $p < .001$). Validity for the code is evidenced by significant correlations between total number of support behaviors coded and subjective observer ratings of interaction supportiveness ($r = .71$ to .79; Cutrona et al., 1990). The code was revised slightly between Studies 1 and 2. Table 6.1 contains the most recent version of the code, which was employed in Study 2. Brief code definitions are listed in Table 6.1.

Results

Because the coding systems and measures were slightly different in Studies 1 and 2, we decided not to combine data from the two studies. Unless explicitly stated otherwise, data reported below were derived from Study 1.

Frequency of Support Behaviors Provided

As reported previously (Suhr & Cutrona , 1992), marital partners most frequently offered each other informational support. Ninety-seven percent of the participants offered some kind of advice or factual input at least once. Emotional and esteem support were also offered relatively frequently, and by a large proportion of husbands and wives. Tangible support was offered approximately twice per interaction, although a third of the subjects did not engage in this behavior at all. Finally, network support was offered relatively rarely. Two thirds of the subjects engaged in at least one negative behavior during the interaction. Thus it is clear that couples use a wide range of support strategies in attempting to assist one another, but seem to rely most heavily on advice and factual input. Surprisingly, there were no significant mean differences between husbands and wives in the number of support behaviors they provided in any category. Table 6.2 provides a summary of these results.

TABLE 6.1 Social Support Behavior Code: Brief Summary of
Coded Behaviors

Informational Support

> Suggestion/Advice (offer ideas, suggesting actions)
> Situation Appraisal (reassess the situation)
> Teaching (teach how to do something or teach facts)

Emotional Support

> Relationship (express closeness or togetherness)
> Physical Affection (hug, kiss, hand hold, touch)
> Confidentiality (promise not to tell others)
> Sympathy (express sorrow and regret for situation)
> Understanding/Empathy ("I understand," self-disclose)
> Prayer (pray with person)
> Express concern (inquire after well-being)
> Reassurance (nonspecific comfort)

Esteem Support

> Compliment (emphasize abilities, say positive things)
> Validation (agree with and take other's side)
> Relief of Blame (say it's not other's fault)

Tangible Aid

> Loan (offer money or material object)
> Direct Task (offer to do something related to problem)
> Indirect Task (offer to do something not related)
> Active Participation (offer to join in reducing stress)
> Willingness (express willingness to help anytime)
> Comply with request (agree to do something after stressed person requests it)

Social Network Support

> Presence (offer to spend time with person, be there)
> Access (offer to provide access to new companions)
> Companions (others who have been through same)

Negative Behaviors

> Interrupt (change subject or interrupt other)
> Complain (talk about own problems)
> Criticism (negative comments about other or blaming)
> Isolation (will not help other, will not discuss it)
> Disagree/Disapprove (does not agree with other)

TABLE 6.2 Descriptive Statistics for Study Variables

Frequency of Support Behaviors	M	SD	Range	No. of Users
Information	7.07	3.86	0-16	58
Emotional	4.58	3.92	0-18	54
Esteem	4.23	3.38	0-11	54
Tangible	1.75	1.67	0-6	40
Social Network	.30	.50	0-2	17
Total	17.93	9.36	3-45	60

PREDICTORS OF SUPPORT BEHAVIORS PROVIDED TO SPOUSE

Personality, Mood, and Marital Satisfaction

As reported in Suhr and Cutrona (under review), we conducted analyses to determine the extent to which participants' marital satisfaction, personal characteristics (extraversion and neuroticism), and level of depressive symptoms predicted the number of support behaviors they provided to their spouse when in the role of support provider. As shown in Table 6.3, results differed somewhat for husbands and wives. Among women, marital satisfaction, depressive mood, and extraversion all were significant predictors of the number of support behaviors they offered to their husbands during the 10-minute interaction. Women who were satisfied with their marriages provided more support behaviors than those who were not satisfied. Extraverted women also provided higher levels of support than did introverted women. Women with high levels of depressive symptoms provided less support to their husbands. Perceived social support from husband closely approached significance ($p < .10$). Neuroticism was unrelated to support behaviors provided.

Among husbands, only marital satisfaction predicted the number of support behaviors they provided to their wives. Men who were more satisfied with their marriages provided a greater number of support behaviors during the 10-minute interaction. Neither extraversion, neuroticism, depression, or perceived spousal social support among husbands significantly predicted the frequency of support behaviors they supplied to their wives.

TABLE 6.3 Correlations Between Personal and Relationship Variables and Number of Support Behaviors Provided

Variables	Support Behavior Provided
Wives	
Depression	−.52**
Extraversion	.47**
Neuroticism	−.17
Marital Satisfaction	.45**
Perceived Spousal Social Support	.36
Husbands	
Depression	−.01
Extraversion	.15
Neuroticism	.16
Marital Satisfaction	.33*
Perceived Spousal Social Support	.21

NOTE: N = 30 males and 30 females.
$*p < .05; **p < .01$

Reciprocity of Support Behavior

In Study 2, we pursued the question of whether the number of support behaviors individuals received from their partner in the first interaction affected the number of support behaviors they gave to their partners in the second support interaction, i.e., whether reciprocity of support was characteristic of married couples. For these analyses, we selected the 20 individuals who received support in the first interaction and provided support in the second. Correlations were computed between frequency of support received and given. Total number of support behaviors received in the first interaction correlated significantly with number of support behaviors given to the spouse in the second interaction (r (18) = .64, $p <$ .001). Among the five support types, only emotional support showed statistically significant reciprocity. Persons who received high levels of emotional support from their partner in the first interaction gave high levels of emotional support to their partner in the second interaction (r (18) =.62, $p < .01$). A marginally significant correlation was found between frequency of negative behaviors received and given (r (18) = .38, $p < .10$). Thus, in addition to marital satisfaction and personality, recent support experiences appear to influence the amount of support that spouses provide to one another, although this pattern was only significant for emotional support.

Characteristics of Stressful Events

According to the optimal matching model, different kinds of social support are useful following different kinds of stressful events. We wondered whether support providers spontaneously provide different kinds of support depending on event characteristics. We were especially interested in whether event controllability would affect the types of support spouses provide to one another. Using data from Study 1, correlations were computed between controllability of stressful events (both by stress victim and by spouse) and frequency of each type of support behavior provided. Controllability ratings were made by research assistants rather than by the participants. As reported previously (Cutrona & Suhr, 1992), a significant correlation was found between the extent to which the event was controllable by the stress victim and the number of information support behaviors provided by his or her spouse. No other correlation attained significance. Thus partners appeared to respond to the controllability dimension spontaneously. When the stressor was objectively controllable, spouses spontaneously offered high rates of advice and information. When the stressor was objectively less controllable, they offered lower rates of advice and information.

In Study 2, we examined the extent to which victim and spouse *self-ratings* of stress controllability predicted the number of support behaviors of different types spontaneously offered by the support provider. A single correlation attained significance. The more control the victim felt he or she had over the stressful event, the more esteem support was provided by his or her spouse (r (38) = .33, p < .05). This result suggests that when people believe that they can do something to eliminate the source of their stress, their partners respond with encouragement and reinforcement of capabilities and skill. This may have the beneficial effect of bolstering the victim's self-efficacy, and fostering greater persistence in pursuing his or her goals (Bandura, 1977).

Determinants of Perceived Controllability

It is unfortunate that we did not obtain both observer and self-ratings of event controllability in either Study 1 or Study 2. Thus it is difficult to explain the discrepancy between findings obtained when control was rated from different perspectives. We do not know the extent to which observers and participants would converge in their controllability assessments.

We conducted an exploratory analysis using the data from Study 2 to examine determinants of participant controllability assessments. Personality (neuroticism and extraversion), depressive mood, marital satisfaction, and perceived social support from spouse were all tested as predictors of the extent to which stress victims believed they could control the consequences of the stressful events they reported. Significant correlations were found with both marital satisfaction (r (38) = .47, $p < .05$) and perceived social support from spouse (r (38) = .32, $p < .05$). Persons who were satisfied with their marriages and felt that their spouses were highly supportive evaluated their stressful events as more controllable than did those low in marital satisfaction and perceived spouse supportiveness. Thus perceptions of controllability appear to be influenced by the quality of the marital relationship. This is consistent with Lazarus and Folkman's (1984) concept of secondary appraisal. After a stress is confronted, people assess the resources they can bring to bear in coping with the stress. Our data suggest that people in high quality supportive marriages appraise negative events in a more benign manner because of the resources accessible to them through their marriage.

DETERMINANTS OF PERCEIVED SOCIAL SUPPORT

Personality, Mood, and Relationship Quality

In Study 1, a series of analyses was conducted to determine the extent to which marital satisfaction, personality, mood, and number of support behaviors received predicted ratings of partner supportiveness during the 10-minute interactions (Suhr & Cutrona, under review). As shown in Table 6.4, predictors of partner supportiveness were different for husbands and wives. Among women, the only predictor of supportiveness ratings was the number of support behaviors they received from their husbands during the 10-minute interaction (r (28) = .62, $p < .01$). When all four predictors were entered into a regression equation predicting supportiveness ratings, frequency of support behaviors retained its sig-

TABLE 6.4 Correlations Between Personal and Relationship Variables, Number of Support Behaviors Received, and Perceived Supportiveness of Interaction

Variables	Support Behavior Provided
Wives	
Depression	−.23
Extraversion	.29
Neuroticism	−.01
Marital Satisfaction	.21
Perceived Spousal Social Support	.31
Support Behavior Received	.62***
Husbands	
Depression	−.52**
Extraversion	−.11
Neuroticism	−.28
Marital Satisfaction	.59***
Perceived Spousal Social Support	.64***
Support Behavior Received	.30

NOTE: N = 30 males and 30 females.
$*p < .05; **p < .01; ***p < .001$

nificance (i.e., controlling for the effects of all other variables). Among men, depression and marital satisfaction were both significant predictors of supportiveness ratings. Men who scored higher on depressive symptoms rated their wives as less supportive (r (28) = -.52, $p < .01$). Men who scored high on marital satisfaction rated their wives as more supportive (r (28) = .59, $p < .01$). When all four predictors were entered into a regression equation predicting supportiveness ratings, both depression and marital satisfaction retained their significance (i.e., controlling for the effects of all other variables, including number of support behaviors received). Thus wives' perceptions of their husband's supportiveness during the 10-minute interactions were influenced primarily by the actual behaviors of their husband. By contrast, husbands' perceptions of their wives' supportiveness during the interactions were influenced primarily by their own mood and degree of happiness in the marriage. This gender difference was not predicted and is difficult to explain. Our results illustrate the complexity of processes that underlie perceptions of support in close relationships.

Characteristics of the Stress:
Tests of the Optimal Matching Model

Using data from Study 1, we tested specific predictions from the optimal matching model of stress and social support (Cutrona & Suhr, 1992). We hypothesized that in the context of controllable stressors, action-facilitating support (information and tangible aid) would be most predictive of interaction satisfaction. In the context of uncontrollable stressors, we hypothesized that nurturant support (emotional and network support) would be most predictive of interaction satisfaction. As reported previously (Cutrona & Suhr, 1992), two of the predicted interactions between controllability and support type attained significance in the prediction of interaction satisfaction. Both of these interactions involved information support. When the *spouse* was judged (by observers) to have a high degree of control over the event, information support positively predicted victim satisfaction. However, when the *victim* was judged to have a high degree of control over the stress, information support *negatively* predicted victim satisfaction with partner support. Thus informational input from one's husband or wife is welcome when that person has expertise or resources that are directly relevant to solving the problem. However, when the victim has the expertise or resources required to deal with the problem, advice from the partner is not welcome. The second major finding in this set of analyses was a significant main effect for emotional support. Regardless of event controllability by either partner, emotional support was associated with higher interaction satisfaction. These findings reflect the balance that marital partners strive to achieve between interdependence and autonomy. The closeness of emotional support was always welcome. However, attempts by the partner to give unneeded advice were met with displeasure.

In Study 2, participants themselves rated the controllability of events. Using this method, none of the interactions between type of support and self-ratings of event controllability attained significance. However, the main effect for emotional support once again attained significance. Across event types, the more emotional support participants received from their spouse, the more supportive they perceived him or her to be.

Because we realized that perceptions of controllability were influenced by relationship factors, we sought a more objective way to divide events into those that were high versus low in controllability by the participants. For this more objective categorization, we turned to the Stress Dimensions Scale (SDS; Swanson, 1990). The SDS asks subjects to rate the extent to which a stressful event affects each of four life domains: health, achievement, relationships, and assets. The life events discussed by participants fell into two broad categories: those that affected assets or achievement, and those that did not. Problems with school or work constituted almost all of the events that subjects said affected the asset and achievement domains. We reasoned that individuals would have relatively high control over their own work and school stressors, and that their spouse's control would be relatively low. We tested the hypothesis that advice from the spouse would be less desirable in the context of work/school stressors than in the context of other kinds of stressors. This hypothesis was confirmed. After disclosing a work or school stressor to their spouse, individuals reported a more depressed mood when their spouse gave frequent advice. When disclosing an event that did not involve work or school, individuals reported a less depressed mood when their spouse gave frequent advice.

Discussion

INTERDEPENDENCE AND AUTONOMY

We have argued that one key to understanding the process of social support among married couples is an appreciation of the tension between interdependence and personal autonomy (Bochner, 1983). Our findings support the importance of both interdependence and personal control. We found that the amount of support received by each individual was a function of the partner's dispositions, mood, and view of the relationship. Among men, those who are married to a nondepressed and extraverted spouse are likely to receive more support than those who are married to someone who is unhappy and introverted. Persons of both genders who encounter stressful events in their lives are more likely to receive support from their mate if he or she is satisfied with the marital relationship.

Interdependence is also evident in the way individuals *evaluate* their partner's attempts at providing support. Among men, regardless of the number of support behaviors they received from their wives, their ratings of interaction supportiveness reflected their level of marital satisfaction and perceptions of their wife's supportiveness *before* the interaction began. Thus it would be possible for a woman to provide exactly the "correct" or "optimal" kind and amount of support to her husband, but if he is

feeling dissatisfied with other aspects of the relationship, these acts may
go unappreciated and may fail to assist the man in coping with his current
problems. Among women, the converse appeared to be true. Unless the
husband provided a high rate of social support behaviors during the interaction, he was unlikely to receive a high supportiveness rating from his
wife. Neither prior evaluations of his supportiveness nor general marital
satisfaction were significant predictors of how positively his behavior was
rated.

Evaluations of stressful events were also affected by interpersonal
variables. Individuals' ratings of the control they were able to exert over
stressful events were strongly linked to both marital satisfaction and perceived spousal social support. Those in supportive and satisfying relationships felt capable of solving their own problems.

Evidence that marital partners strive not only for closeness, but also for
autonomy was clear in the results for information support. Husbands and
wives both welcomed emotional support, regardless of the type of stress
they were facing. However, their reactions to information support were
more variable. It appears that advice (the most frequent form of information support) was perceived as an effort by the spouse to assert control or
dominance (see Rogers & Farace, 1975). Although advice was appreciated
when the spouse had special expertise or resources relevant to dealing
with the stress, it was not evaluated positively when the individual himself or herself had the resources to cope independently. Individuals also
distinguished between life domains in their willingness to accept advice
from their spouse. When the target event occurred at work or school,
advice from the partner was not appreciated. This is consistent with prior
findings that marital support is less beneficial in the context of occupational problems, or other problems in which the spouse is not part of the
setting where the problem occurred (House, 1981; Pearlin & McCall,
1991).

Further insight into the reasons that emotional support and informational support are evaluated differently comes from Notarius and Herrick
(1988). They found that it was less taxing for support *providers* to offer
empathy and concern than to enter into problem-solving attempts. Notarius and Herrick hypothesized that support providers feel frustrated and
rejected when their suggestions are not accepted and their efforts to solve
the other's problem fail. By contrast, sympathetic listening involves no
expectation that the problem will be solved, and thus does not lead to
disappointment or anger in the provider. It is possible that the frustration
experienced by support providers who strive to solve the other's problem

is communicated to recipients, who sense the provider's displeasure, and react negatively to it. In those instances when the provider really does have expertise or resources needed to solve the problem, suggestions may meet with approval, and the provider's pleasure at having been helpful may be communicated to the recipient.

In conclusion, it is clear that many factors influence the occurrence and evaluation of support-intended behaviors in close relationships. Each partner's personality, mood, and satisfaction with the relationship affect the experience that the other will have when seeking support. Recent experiences with the partner also affect support transactions. Persons who have recently received support from their partner are more willing to provide high levels of support. The nature of the stress also affects the nature of helping transactions. Unless the partner has special expertise or resources relevant to eliminating the stressor, individuals prefer to solve their own problems. This is ironic, given the finding that advice is the most frequent type of support that couples give to each other. However, this assertion of independence is not complete; empathy, caring, and concern from the partner are virtually always welcome.

CURRENT STATUS OF THE
OPTIMAL MATCHING MODEL

Results of the two studies described above suggest the need for a significant overhaul of the original optimal matching model of stress and social support. Contrary to prediction, a single component of support, information or advice, was evaluated differently in the context of events that were high versus low in controllability. Furthermore different effects were found for events that were controllable by the stress victim versus those that were controllable by the spouse. Across all levels of controllability by victim and spouse, emotional support was positively correlated with perceived supportiveness. It appears that specific components of social support vary in the breadth of situations in which they engender the perception of support.

Another surprising finding was the failure of three support components (esteem support, network support, and tangible aid) to correlate with perceived support under conditions of high or low event controllability. Before concluding that these support behaviors are irrelevant to the perception of support, their utility must be examined in diverse samples. Subjects in both of our studies were relatively young and highly educated.

It may be that different support components would lead to the perception of support among elderly couples, or those with fewer resources or different needs than those in our sample.

A question that remains unanswered is whether people actually know what kinds of support benefit them the most. We do not know whether the perception that a behavior is supportive necessarily means that it contributes to the individual's well-being. Studies that tap both perceptions of support-intended behaviors and their consequences are needed to answer this question.

Taken together, results suggest that considerable work remains before we will uncover consistent patterns of optimal matches between stress and support type. Dimensions other than controllability should be investigated (e.g., severity, duration of consequences, life domain disrupted). A range of relationship types should also be systematically studied, including parent-child, friendship, and client-professional. For each relationship type, constraints, expectations, status differentials, and degree of interdependence should be considered in interpreting links between supportive communications and the perception of support. Personal dispositions of both participants should also be considered as determinants of the support that is offered and how it is interpreted. It appears that the optimal matching model was a significant over-simplification of a complex phenomenon. However, we hope that it will continue to serve a heuristic function as the complexities of support communications are uncovered in the future.

References

Antonucci, T., & Jackson, J. (1990). The role of reciprocity in social support. In B. Sarason, I. Sarason, & G. Pierce (Eds.), *Social support: An interactional view* (pp. 173-198). New York: John Wiley.

Bandura, A. (1977). Self-efficacy: Toward a unifying theory of behavioral change. *Psychological Review, 84*, 191-215.

Beck, A., Ward, C., Mendelson, M., Mock, J., & Erbaugh, J. (1961). An inventory for measuring depression. *Archives of General Psychiatry, 4*, 561-569.

Blood, R. D., & Wolfe, D. M. (1960). *Husbands and wives: The dynamics of married living.* Glencoe, IL: Free Press.

Bochner, A. (1984). The functions of human communication in interpersonal bonding. In C. C. Arnold & J. W. Bowers (Eds.), *Handbook of rhetorical and communication theory* (pp. 544-621). Boston, MA: Allyn & Bacon.

Bowen, M. (1961). Family psychotherapy. *American Journal of Orthopsychiatry, 31*, 40-60.

Brown, G. W., & Harris, T. (1978). *Social origins of depression.* London: Tavistock.

Burke, R. J., & Weir, T. (1977). Marital helping relationships: The moderators between stress and well being. *The Journal of Psychology, 95,* 121-130.

Christensen, A., & Nies, D. (1980). The Spouse Observation Checklist: Empirical analysis and critique. *American Journal of Family Therapy, 8,* 69-79.

Clark, M., & Mills, J. (1979). Interpersonal attraction in exchange and communal relationships. *Journal of Personality and Social Psychology, 37,* 12-24.

Cobb, S. (1979). Social support and health through the life course. In M. W. Riley (Ed.), *Aging from birth to death: Interdisciplinary perspectives* (pp. 93-106). Boulder, CO: Westview Press.

Coyne, J. C., Ellard, J. H., & Smith, D. A. F. (1990). Social support, interdependence, and the dilemmas of helping. In B. R. Sarason, I. G. Sarason, & G. R. Pierce (Eds.), *Social support: An interactional view.* New York: John Wiley.

Cutrona, C. E. (1990). Stress and social support—In search of optimal matching. *Journal of Social and Clinical Psychology, 9,* 3-14.

Cutrona, C. E., Cohen, B. B., & Igram, S. (1990). Contextual determinants of the perceived supportiveness of helping behaviors. *Journal of Social and Personal Relationships, 7,* 553-562.

Cutrona, C. E., & Russell, D. (1987). The provisions of social relationships and adaptation to stress. In W. H. Jones & D. Perlman (Eds.), *Advances in personal relationships* (vol. 1, pp. 37-67). Greenwich, CT: JAI.

Cutrona, C. E., & Russell, D. (1990). Type of social support and specific stress: Toward a theory of optimal matching. In I. G. Sarason, B. R. Sarason, & G. R. Pierce (Eds.), *Social Support: An interactional view* (pp. 319-366). New York: John Wiley.

Cutrona, C., & Suhr, J. (1992). Controllability of stressful events and satisfaction with spouse support behaviors. *Communication Research, 19,* 154-174.

Cutrona, C. E., Suhr, J. A., & MacFarlane, R. (1990). Interpersonal transactions and the psychological sense of support. In S. Duck & R. Silver (Eds.), *Personal relationships and social support* (pp. 30-45). London: Sage.

Elwood, R., & Jacobson, N. (1982). Spouses' agreement in reporting their behavioral interactions: A clinical replication. *Journal of Consulting and Clinical Psychology, 50,* 783-784.

Eysenck, H., & Eysenck (1964). *The manual of the Eysenck Personality Inventory.* London: University Press.

Fisher, J., Nadler, A., & Witcher-Alagna, S. (1982). Recipient reaction to aid. *Psychological Bulletin, 91,* 27-54.

Gottlieb, B. (1985). Social support and the study of personal relationships. *Journal of Social and Personal Relationships, 2,* 351-375.

House, J. S. (1981). *Work stress and social support.* Reading, MA: Addison-Wesley.

Kahn, R. L. (1979). Aging and social support. In M. W. Riley (Ed.), *Aging from birth to death: Interdisciplinary perspectives* (pp. 77-91). Boulder, CO: Westview Press.

Lazarus, R. S., & Folkman, S. (1984). Coping and adaptation. In W. D. Gentry (Ed.), *The handbook of behavioral medicine* (pp. 282-325). New York: Guilford.

Lieberman, M. A. (1982). The effects of social supports on response to stress. In L. Golberger & S. Breznitz (Eds.), *Handbook of stress: Theoretical and clinical aspects* (pp. 764-784). New York: Academic Press.

Lubin (1981). *Manual for the depression adjective check lists,* 1981 edition. San Diego, CA: Educational & Industrial Testing Service.

Mermelstein, R., Lichtenstein, E., & McIntyre, K. (1983). Partner support and relapse in smoking-cessation programs. *Journal of Consulting and Clinical Psychology, 51*, 465-466.

Minuchin, S. (1974). *Families and family therapy.* Cambridge, MA: Harvard University Press.

Notarius, C. I., & Herrick, L. R. (1988). Listener response strategies to a distressed other. *Journal of Personal and Social Relationships, 5*, 97-108.

Olson, D. H. (1981). Family typologies: Bridging family research and family therapy. In E. E. Filsinger & R. A. Lewis (Eds.), *Power in families* (pp. 3-14). New York: John Wiley.

Pearlin, L. I., & McCall, M. E. (1990). Occupational stress and social support: A description of microprocesses. In J. Eckenrode & S. Gore (Eds.), *Stress between work and family* (pp. 39-60). New York: Plenum Press.

Procidano, M., & Heller, K. (1983). Measures of perceived social support from friends and from family: Three validation studies. *American Journal of Community Psychology, 11*, 1-24.

Rogers, K. R. (1987). Nature of spousal supportive behaviors that influence heart transplant patient compliance. *Journal of Heart Transplant, 6*, 90-95.

Rogers, L. E., & Farace, R. V. (1975). Relational communication analysis: New measurement procedures. *Human Communication Research, 1*, 222-239.

Sarason, B., Sarason, I., Hacker, T., & Basham, R. (1985). Concomitants of social support: Social skills, physical attractiveness, and gender. *Journal of Personality and Social Psychology, 49*, 469-480.

Sarason, I., Sarason, B., & Shearin, E. (1986). Social support as an individual difference variable: Its stability, origins, and relational aspects. *Journal of Personality and Social Psychology, 50*, 1222-1225.

Schaefer, C., Coyne, J. C., & Lazarus, R. S. (1981). The health-related functions of social support. *Journal of Behavioral Medicine, 4*, 381-406.

Shumaker, S., & Brownell, A. (1984). Toward a theory of social support: Closing conceptual gaps. *Journal of Social Issues, 40*, 11-36.

Sillars, A., & Scott, M. (1983). Interpersonal perception between intimates: An integrative review. *Human Communication Research, 10*, 153-176.

Spanier, G. (1976). Measuring dyadic adjustment: New scales for assessing the quality of marriage and similar dyads. *Journal of Marriage and the Family, 38*, 15-28.

Suhr, J. A. (1990). *The development of the Social Support Behavior Code.* Unpublished master's thesis. University of Iowa, Iowa City.

Suhr, J., & Cutrona, C. (under review). Predictors of social support behavior and perceived supportiveness among married couples: An observational study.

Swanson, E. F. (1990). *Dimensions of stressful life events.* Unpublished master's thesis. University of Iowa, Iowa City.

Turk, D. C., Kerns, R. D., & Rudy, T. E. (1984). *Identifying the links between chronic illness and depression: Cognitive-behavioral mediators.* Paper presented at the 92nd Annual Convention of the American Psychological Association, Toronto, Canada.

Vinokur, A., Schul, Y., & Caplan, R. (1987). Determinants of perceived social support: Interpersonal transactions, personal outlook, and transient affective states. *Journal of Personality and Social Psychology, 53*, 1137-1145.

Waltz, M. (1986). Marital context and post-infarction quality of life: Is it social support or something more? *Social Science and Medicine, 22*, 791-805.

Wandersman, L., Wandersman, A., & Kahn, S. (1980). Social support in the transition to parenthood. *Journal of Community Psychology, 8,* 332-342.

Weiss, R. S. (1974). The provisions of social relationships. In Z. Rubin (Ed.), *Doing unto others* (pp. 17-26). Englewood Cliffs, NJ: Prentice Hall.

Wills, T., Weiss, R., & Patterson, G. (1974). A behavioral analysis of the determinants of marital satisfaction. *Journal of Consulting and Clinical Psychology, 42,* 802-811.

7

Friendship, Gender, and Social Support

Laboratory Studies of Supportive Interactions

VALERIAN J. DERLEGA

ANITA P. BARBEE

BARBARA A. WINSTEAD

There is considerable research demonstrating that an existing social relationship, such as a friendship, may help individuals to cope more effectively with a stressful event. Research indicates that friends may be helpful in coping with various life crises, such as losing one's spouse (Pennebaker & O'Heeron, 1984), facing retirement (Lowenthal & Haven, 1968), or living near the site of an accident at a nuclear power plant (Fleming, Baum, Gisriel, & Gatchel, 1982). However, relatively little research has been conducted on the types of social interactions that occur among friends when coping with stress. In particular, the impact of the gender of the support seeker and the support provider on the enactment of social support has not been systematically examined. We will offer an overall model of the social support process, indicating in particular how gender influences the interactions that occur between the support seeker and the support provider.

AUTHORS' NOTE: The preparation of this chapter was supported in part by a grant from the National Institute of Mental Health (1-R03-MH42002-01A2), Barbara A. Winstead, principal investigator.

There are widely held gender-linked stereotypes and expectations in North American culture about how males and females should behave. Generally men are expected to be task-oriented, valuing "being in charge" and exercising emotional control, whereas women are expected to be relationship-oriented, valuing emotional closeness and the disclosure of feelings (Maccoby, 1990, 1991; Tannen, 1990; Thompson & Pleck, 1987). We will suggest that gender-role expectations about appropriate behavior for men and women may influence how and when men and women seek, obtain, and enact "supportive" behaviors in stressful situations.

Our chapter relies on the social support activation model (Barbee, 1990; Barbee et al., 1993) to organize the discussion of the effects of gender on the social support process. This model will be useful in understanding the various steps in the activation of support giving and support receiving and in explaining how gender affects individuals' behaviors in the social support process.

Figure 7.1 presents a model of the social support activation process. The model begins with the assumption that the characteristics of the support seeker (including her or his gender) affects the experience of stress and who may need social support. Once a person is aware of and/or acknowledges a problem, then she or he must assess the nature and severity of the problem, one's personal responsibility for what happened, the likelihood of finding a solution on one's own, or if help is sought, from another person. Then the person must decide whether to seek support and select someone who might be able to provide assistance. Once the interactive support process has begun, the giver's response to the seeker will influence how the seeker proceeds and whether the seeker ultimately feels better or not. Behavioral strategies for gaining support may be either direct or indirect. Direct strategies might be verbal (e.g., asking for help) or nonverbal (e.g., crying). Indirect strategies might also be verbal (e.g., complaining or hinting about one's problems) or nonverbal (e.g., sulking or pouting).

Barbee (1990) uses the term interactive coping to refer to the behaviors enacted by the support provider and the support seeker when social support is, in fact, being enacted. Interactive coping behaviors are designed to control the emotions and cognitions associated with a stressful event, relying on the skills and resources of both the support provider and the help seeker. Interactive coping *giving* behaviors include: (a) *Support*: Emotion-focused approach behaviors designed to produce positive feelings in the help seeker and to convey a sense of being cared for and supported (e.g., giving affection or a hug, telling the support seeker about

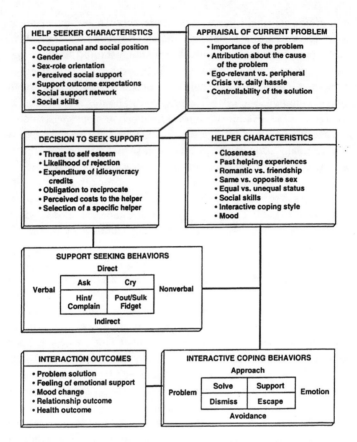

Figure 7.1. Model of Social Support Activation Variables

his or her positive qualities); (b) *Solve:* Problem-focused, approach behaviors designed to find an answer to the problem (e.g., offering suggestions); (c) *Escape:* Emotion-focused, avoidance behaviors designed to
discourage the display of negative feelings or to distract the support-
seeker (e.g., talking about something irrelevant); and (d) *Dismiss:* Problem-focused, avoidance behaviors designed to minimize the significance
of the problem (e.g., saying the problem is not serious).

The social support activation model is useful in guiding an examination
of how gender may operate at each phase of the social support process,
especially in problem appraisal, the decision to seek support, the choice

of a specific support provider, support seeking behaviors, and the enactment of support via interactive coping behaviors. However, given this volume's focus on the communication of social support, we will examine the impact of gender on whom support seekers solicit help from as well as on the behaviors that embody interactive assistance. We will report on our own research to illustrate what is known about these events. We will not describe in any detail the support seeker's behaviors, which are an inherent and important part of the process because of the focus of the research thus far.

Effects of Friendship and Gender Among Same-Sex and Opposite-Sex Friends on Stress Coping

Past research indicates that friendships in which one or both partners are female (female-female and male-female dyads) are often described as more intimate (Winstead, 1986). Female and male college students report being less lonely when they spend more time with female friends (Wheeler, Reis, & Nezlek, 1983) and they perceive their female friends, compared with male friends, as giving more emotional support (Hays & Oxley, 1986). If coping with stress is enhanced by emotionally supportive interactions (such as talking about one's feelings), female-female and male-female friends might be more successful in coping with stress than comparably paired strangers are, whereas male-male friends and strangers might not differ. This prediction assumes that the presence of a female in a pair of friends would be more likely to foster intimate behavior (*Support* in Barbee's interactive coping model) compared to the male-male pair.

On the other hand, if coping with stress is promoted by problem-focused (*Solve* in Barbee's model, such as giving information and advice) or distracting interactions (*Dismiss* or *Escape*), male-male and male-female pairs (regardless of level of relationship, because these interactions do not require emotional closeness) should be more successful in coping with stress than female-female pairs are. In a study in which topic of conversation was experimentally manipulated, Costanza, Derlega, and Winstead (1988) found that for female and male same-sex friends, talking about problem-solving or unrelated topics was more effective in reducing stress in anticipation of a frightening event (handling a spider).

To examine the impact of gender and friendship on coping, Winstead, Derlega, Lewis, Sanchez-Hucles, and Clarke (1992) randomly paired subjects with a same-sex or opposite-sex friend or stranger while waiting for stressful event (giving a speech). A series of analyses of covariance were conducted on self-report mood measures, including the anxiety, depression, and hostility scales of the MAACL Today Form (Zuckerman & Lubin, 1965) as well as for a fear of public speaking measure. There were no significant main effects on the mood measures for relationship (friend versus stranger) or subject gender. There was a significant relationship by gender match (same-sex versus opposite-sex dyads) interaction on the depression ratings, $F(1, 179) = 4.17, p = .04$. Additional tests indicated that depression scores did not differ in the friend ($M = 15.00$) versus the stranger ($M = 14.70$) conditions, $F(1, 121) < 1$, ns in the same-sex pairs, whereas depression scores were significantly lower in the friend ($M = 13.70$) versus stranger ($M = 15.52$) conditions in the opposite-sex pairs, $F(1, 161) = 4.21, p < .05$.

There was a significant three-way interaction of relationship by gender match by subject gender on subjects' confidence at Minute 1 of the extemporaneous speech, $F(1, 173) = 4.93, p = .03$. This interaction was primarily due to a trend ($F(1,29) = 3.64, p = .07$) for confidence ratings to be higher for females paired with a male friend ($M = 3.26$) than for females paired with a male stranger ($M = 2.61$), whereas there was no difference between females paired with a female friend ($M = 2.72$) and females paired with a female stranger ($M = 3.05$). There were no effects on the confidence ratings at Minute 1 for males as a function of relationship and partner gender.

For subjects' confidence at Minute 4 of the extemporaneous speech, there was a trend ($F(1, 172) = 3.68, p = .06$) toward an interaction between the relationship and the gender match variables. Friends ($M = 2.42$) and strangers ($M = 2.45$) were similar in confidence in same-sex pairs, but friends ($M = 3.00$) were more confident than strangers ($M = 2.36$) in opposite-sex pairs, $F(1, 57) = 4.57, p = 0.04$.

It might be expected that female-female and female-male friend pairs (friends and strangers) would use more emotion-focused talk and the male-male and female-male pairs would use more problem-solving and unrelated talk. The results of the talk categories were analyzed via 2(friend, stranger) × 3(male-male, male-female, female-female) analyses of variance. There were no effects on the problem-solving or unrelated-talk measures. But it was found that friends were more likely to engage in other-related talk ($M = 0.47$) than strangers ($M = 0.30$), $F(1, 76) = 10.81$, $p = 0.002$, whereas the amount of no talk was greater for strangers ($M = 0.19$) than for friends ($M = 0.03$), $F(1, 76) = 8.04, p = 0.006$.

There was a relationship by gender composition of the pair interaction on the disclosure of feelings measure, $F(2, 76) = 3.27$, $p = 0.04$. There were no differences among the different dyads for strangers. Friend dyads, however, did differ, $F(2, 33) = 4.83$, $p = 0.01$. Contrary to expectations, female friends were least likely to use emotion-focused talk ($M = 0.0$). Opposite-sex friends were most likely to use emotion-focused talk ($M = 0.09$); male friends were intermediate ($M = 0.04$).

Contrary to expectations, gender composition of the dyad did not affect problem-solving or unrelated talk. Among friends, female same-sex friends never used emotion-focused talk, although opposite-sex friends were more likely to use it than male same-sex friends.

The results of Winstead et al.'s (1992) study present a complex picture of the effects of gender and friendship in same-sex versus opposite-sex dyads. Subjects were less depressed after interacting with an opposite-sex friend compared to an opposite-sex stranger, whereas depression scores were unaffected by relationship in same-sex dyads. Also, subjects who had interacted with an opposite-sex friend were more confident during Minute 4 of their speech than were subjects who had interacted with an opposite-sex stranger. There were no differences between same-sex friends and strangers. Finally, females were more confident during Minute 1 of the extemporaneous speech after interacting with an opposite-sex friend than after interacting with an opposite-sex stranger; whereas there were no differences for females with same-sex friends or strangers. It could be that these effects result from a relative disadvantage of interacting with an opposite-sex stranger. The means, however, supported the interpretation that there is a positive benefit to interacting with an opposite-sex friend compared to opposite-sex strangers or same-sex friends or strangers.

Many studies on friendship (see, for reviews, Hays, 1988; Winstead, 1986) suggest that female friends are perceived by females and males as more emotionally supportive than male friends and that time spent with a female friend may be a buffer against loneliness (Wheeler et al., 1983). In Winstead et al.'s (1992) study there were no results to suggest special benefits from interacting with a female. In fact, for confidence while giving a speech (in Minute 1), scores for females paired with a male friend were better than those for any other group, indicating that in this situation females benefited from interacting with a male. For other measures (confidence at Minute 4 and the self-report measure of depression) females and males benefited more from opposite-sex friends. If females and males do bring different coping skills to an interaction, perhaps an opposite-sex friend complements one's own coping skills. On the other hand, opposite-sex strangers benefited least. Heterosexual anxiety aroused by interacting with an opposite-sex stranger may have interfered with coping.

Although the effects of friendship on the mood and behavioral coping measures are complex, friends were more likely to engage in behaviors that might be supportive. Friends were less likely than strangers to say nothing while waiting, and they were more likely to engage in talk about topics related to public speaking. Friends were also more likely than strangers to laugh and smile with one another. Although disclosure of feelings about the anticipated speech was generally low, female same-sex friends, unlike other groups, did none of this. This finding is contrary to previous research that suggests that female same-sex friends are especially likely to be emotionally supportive. There are at least two possible explanations for this finding: (a) females are believed and believe themselves to be emotionally supportive, but these self-and other-reports, based perhaps on gender stereotypes, do not, in fact, represent any actual sex differences in behavior; (b) talking about feelings, which were generally negative, is not what subjects mean when they describe themselves or others as emotionally supportive. In fact, although emotion-focused talk was the only talk category not to contribute to perceived social support in this research, emotion-focused approach behaviors (i.e., Support) were found to be successful in cheering up people in other research (Barbee, 1990; 1991).

Gender Effects on the
Support Seeker and the Support Provider

The results of Winstead et al.'s (1992) study do not allow one to distinguish between the behaviors enacted by a "support seeker" versus a "support provider." Both partners in the dyad anticipated going through a stressful situation. Hence behaviors enacted by the research participants in the separate roles of support provider and support seeker were inevitably blurred. In this section we will consider how gender influences individuals' behavior in the roles of support provider and support seeker. Three major questions might be asked: (a) Do individuals seek support from a female versus a male friend? (b) Does gender affect the interactive coping behaviors of the help provider as well as the help seeker? and (c) How does the gender of the help provider and help seeker influence the effectiveness of the support provided?

FROM WHOM DO MALES AND FEMALES
SEEK SOCIAL SUPPORT?

In general female friendships are more intimate and expressive, whereas male friendships are more instrumental and activity oriented. Also, males seem closer to and more satisfied with their friendships with females than with their friendships with males, and males tend to self-disclose more to their female friends than to male friends (Winstead, 1986).

On the other hand, there is evidence in the literature on helping behavior that males help more with task-oriented problems and females help more with relationship-oriented problems (Eagly & Crowley, 1986). If males are considered to be more competent in dealing with task-oriented problems and females are more competent with relationship-oriented problems, people generally may seek help from males for task problems and they may seek help from females for relationship problems. The effects of nature of the problem and gender of support seeker and support provider have been addressed by Barbee and her colleagues in a series of studies where the specific supportive behaviors, Support, Solve, Escape, and Dismiss (see beginning of chapter for definitions) are rated by subjects or trained observers.

Barbee, Gulley, and Cunningham (1990) examined how the gender of the potential support provider and the nature of the task influenced willingness to seek assistance. Males and female college students were asked to think about close friends who were of the same-sex and the opposite-sex and asked to indicate who they would prefer discussing a relationship or task-oriented problem. A 2(gender of subject) x 2(relationship versus task problem) × 2(same-sex versus opposite-sex friend) ANOVA was conducted on preferred friend for talking about problems. Contrary to what might be expected, both males and females preferred to talk to their same-sex friends ($M = 11.88$) rather than to their opposite-sex friends ($M = 10.53$) about both types of problems, $F(1, 201) = 57.96$, $p < 0.0001$. Nevertheless, the nature of the task did influence who the male and females selected as a support provider. Males preferred to talk with their male friends about the task ($M = 12.14$) rather than the relationship problem ($M = 11.22$), t(204) = 2.76, $p < 0.01$, and females also preferred to talk with their male friends about the task ($M = 11.10$) rather than the relationship problem ($M = 10.27$), $t(196) = 2.33$, $p < 0.02$.

The males and females in Barbee et al.'s (1990) study also had gender linked expectations about the kinds of supportive behaviors that their friends might provide. Males anticipated that their male friends would be more likely to use Dismiss behaviors in response to relationship ($M = 24.86$) as opposed to task problems ($M = 22.11$), $t(196) = 2.04$, $p < 0.05$. This finding may reflect male subjects' awareness of the discomfort their male friends experience in talking about relationship- rather than task-oriented problems.

Perhaps reflecting cultural stereotypes about women's expertise in coping with relationship problems, females expected their female friends to use more Solve ($M = 33.84$ versus $M = 32.36$, $t(196) = 1.51$, $p < 0.10$) and Support behaviors ($M = 45.52$ versus $M = 43.58$, $t(190) = 1.54$, $p < 0.10$) in response to relationship rather than task problems. Also, females expected their male friends, compared to female friends, to use more Dismiss behaviors ($M = 22.34$ versus $M = 19.84$) in response to both types of problems, $t(189) = 2.08$, $p < 0.05$, and more Escape behaviors ($M = 32.67$ versus $M = 29.97$) in response to relationship problems, $t(194) = 1.89$, $p < 0.06$.

EFFECTS OF GENDER ON PERCEPTIONS OF HELP SEEKING AND HELP GIVING

A study by Gulley, Barbee, and Cunningham (1992) provides evidence about subjects' reactions to being placed in the role of a support seeker or support provider when they *actually* had to cope with their own or a friend's problems. Males and females, assigned either to the role of a support seeker or support provider, gave impressions of their own and their partner's behavior immediately following a realistic supportive interaction.

Females, in the role of support seekers, reported receiving more Solve and Support behaviors than males perceived were given to them, $F(1, 111) = 6.25$, $p < 0.01$, and $F(1, 111) = 4.64$, $p < 0.04$, respectively (M's = 4.33 and 3.78 for females and males for Solve; and M's = 2.44 and 2.19 for females and males for Support). Support givers, however, perceived that they had given female support seekers more Dismiss and Escape behaviors than male support seekers, $F(1, 111) = 4.313$, $p < 0.04$, and $F(1, 111) = 4.198$, $p < 0.04$, respectively (M's = 2.05 and 1.78 for females and males for Dismiss; and M's = 1.76 and 1.55 for females and males for Escape). It is interesting that female support seekers perceived only the most positive forms of support, apparently ignoring the negative behaviors that support givers reported using toward female support seekers.

If males are uncomfortable dealing with stressful situations or prefer to contain their emotions, it might be expected that males would rely on support giving behaviors that minimize or avoid the problem. This idea was partially supported in that male helpers were perceived by their partners to employ more Dismiss behaviors ($M = 2.06$) than female helpers ($M = 1.78$), $F(1, 111) = 4.76$ $p < 0.03$. Male support providers, compared to female support providers, however, were also perceived to employ more Solve behaviors with family problems, $t(111) = 2.45$, $p < 0.02$, contrary to expectations about possible differences in helping orientations of males and females. Male, compared to female, support providers may have employed more Solve behaviors because they reported, on self-report measures, feeling more distress (M's = 2.59 versus 2.15), $F(1, 111) = 5.38$, $p < 0.05$, and sadness (M's = 3.68 versus 2.82), $F(1, 111) = 4.67$, $p < 0.03$, toward their partners.

A study conducted by Yankeelov, Barbee, Cunningham, and Druen (1991) provides additional data on the reactions of males and females in the role of support seekers and support providers. In particular this study provides additional support for the notion that males and females may be differentially successful in providing support based on the gender-linkage of the problem. This study was conducted among couples who were in dating relationships. In this laboratory study, one partner (the support seeker) received a negative mood induction designed to make her or him feel depressed. The person either watched a film clip depicting soldiers being killed (from the movie *Gallipoli*) and a mother having to give up her son or daughter to a Nazi soldier in a concentration camp (from the movie *Sophie's Choice*) or they were given results of a bogus test indicating that she or he was deficient in "mental dexterity." Next, the partners were allowed an opportunity to talk for five minutes so that the "support seeker" could explain his or her reactions to watching the film clip or to the test results. After the social interaction was completed, subjects were asked their reactions about the types of social interactions that occurred during their conversation and, in the case of the support seeker, how cheered up she or he felt after the conversation.

Yankeelov et al.'s (1991) study supports the idea that males may be more effective in the role of a support provider when their partner is confronting a traditionally masculine-type problem. Support seekers were asked if their partner did or said anything to try to cheer them up. Overall, female support seekers were more likely to view their opposite-sex partner as making more of a cheering up attempt (63%) than were male support seekers (45%), $z = 2.81$, $p < 0.0025$. However, this effect for males to be seen as making more effort to help, compared to females, occurred mainly in the test condition. In the test condition, male helpers were significantly more likely to be seen as providing a cheering up attempt (83%) than female helpers (53%), $z = 2.54$, $p < 0.05$. However, there was no significant difference between how the partners saw the male (43%) versus the female (37%) support providers in the movie condition, $z = 1.05$, *ns*. A related measure asked support seekers how successful was the cheering up attempt enacted by the support provider, based on responses to a seven-point scale. There was a significant interaction of the source of the support seeker's depression × gender of the support provider, $F(1, 107) = 6.93$, $p < 0.01$. In the test condition, male support providers ($M = 5.77$) were seen as more successful in their support attempts than were the female support providers ($M = 4.97$), $t(58) = 3.06$, $p < 0.002$. There was no difference between how support seekers saw their male and female partners in the movie condition on perceived effectiveness of support. It is important to remember that for both of these measures help seeker's ratings may reflect their own need for or resistance to cheering up and support as well as an appraisal of the partner's actual behaviors.

Support seekers were also asked about the specific types of behaviors used by the helpers during their 5-minute interaction. There was a trend for a gender of the support provider main effect, $F(1, 107) = 3.54$, $p < 0.06$. Male helpers ($M = 2.98$) were seen by their partners as providing more Support than the female helpers ($M = 2.69$). A two-way interaction of the source of the recipient's depression × gender of the helper was also found, $F(1, 107) = 12.66$, $p < 0.001$. In the test condition, male helpers ($M = 3.58$) were seen as using more Support than female helpers ($M = 2.73$), $t(58) = 3.38$, $p < 0.002$. There were no significant gender differences in the movie condition, $t(58) = 1.24$, *ns*. There was also a source of the support seeker's depression × gender of the helper interaction for Escape behavior, $F(1, 103) = 5.71$, $p < 0.02$. Female helpers ($M = 2.17$), compared to male helpers ($M = 1.74$), were viewed by their partners as using more Escape in the movie condition, $t(56) = 2.06$, $p < 0.05$. There were no effects involving the gender of the support seeker for the Solve and Dismiss behaviors.

When helpers were asked about their behavior during the social interaction, there was one effect for gender of helper. Male helpers reported using more Dismiss behavior than did female helpers, $F(1, 106) = 7.88$, $p < 0.006$.

In this study the interaction between the partners had been videotaped and subsequently coded for the frequency of Solve, Support, Dismiss, and

Escape behaviors used by the helper. These data provide a useful addition to the subjective reports about what happened during the social interaction. The total verbal behaviors enacted by the helper were divided into verbal Support, Solve, Dismiss, and Escape categories. There was a trend for a gender of the helper main effect for Support behavior, $F(1, 108) = 3.38$, $p < 0.07$. Male helpers ($M = 1.67$), compared to female helpers ($M = 1.19$), were rated by judges as providing more Support to their partner. For Dismiss behavior, there was a significant source of depression $\times$ gender of helper interaction, $F(1, 108) = 5.75$, $p < 0.02$. In the test condition, male helpers ($M = 3.18$) used more Dismiss behavior than did female helpers ($M = 1.44$), $t(58) = 2.45$, $p < 0.02$. There were no other effects involving the gender of the support provider and/or the support seeker on these cheering up behaviors.

Discussion

Females are generally believed to be better caretakers than males, to be more emotionally expressive and more interpersonally sensitive, and to be better providers of social support. When interactions involving social support occurred in the laboratory and were rated by the participants or trained observers, as in the studies reported here, gender differences did not fit well with the stereotypes and, in fact, for achievement-related stressors (giving an extemporaneous speech, being passed over for a promotion, handling a speeding ticket, dealing with problems at school, or being deficient in mental dexterity) males were perceived to be somewhat better than females in providing support, especially by their female friends or romantic partners. Even for relationship problems, females were not found to be superior to males as support providers in the laboratory situation.

Are males as good as or better support providers than females, despite the preponderance of self-report data to the contrary? Or is the laboratory situation not comparable to "real life?" Studying intimacy of self-disclosure, Reis, Senchak, and Solomon (1985) found that, while most studies report that females surpass males in intimacy of self-disclosure, in a videotaped interaction between same-sex best friends there were no gender differences in intimacy of self-disclosure. Self-reports require subjects to rely on their memories and an unspecified aggregation of events to rate how often or how much of certain behaviors or feelings they have displayed or experienced. Certainly, a helpful heuristic would be how much of the behavior or feeling someone of their gender is expected to display or experience. Similarly, when rating others, gender is a guide to estimating how that other behaved. In future research it is important to attempt to determine how much ratings of supportive behavior of self or other are influenced by subjects' gender stereotypes about giving and receiving support.

Global self-reports (as gathered in most questionnaire and survey research) are perhaps most likely to be affected by subjects' gender stereotypes. Several results reported in these laboratory studies, however, are also self-reports. The self-reports concern recently experienced events, but are nevertheless susceptible to gender-related biases. When subjects are exposed to stressors, i.e., asked to give a speech, talk about a problem, shown a sad movie, or given negative feedback about their mental dexterity, their own appraisal of the stressor in addition to their predispositions for seeking or accepting help will influence their ratings of partners who try to help them. As Gulley et al. (1992) found, while partners reported giving female support seekers more Dismiss and Escape behaviors than male support seekers, the females themselves reported that they were given more Solve and Support behaviors then did their male counterparts. Perhaps females are more willing to feel helped and/or males are resistant to feeling helped. Yankeelov et al. (1991) also found females giving their male partners higher ratings for helping than males gave to their female partners in the test condition. While there was a trend in this study for judges to rate male helpers as providing more Support than female helpers for both stress conditions, in the test condition male helpers were rated as displaying significantly more Dismiss behavior than female helpers. Clearly the perceptions of the receiver of support do not necessarily match those of the support provider or of objective judges. Understanding these differences and the role that gender plays in these differences is critical for a complete understanding of the complexities of social support.

Do males *not* talk intimately or behave supportively unless they are in a laboratory situation where they are asked to do so? It is true that there are demand characteristics in lab situations. Reis et al. (1985) concluded that, while there is no gender difference in capacity for intimate self-disclosure, males may choose, in everyday interactions, not to use it as often as females do. Similarly, while males may be capable of being as or more supportive than females, they may not choose to display this ability as often. Cues indicating that social support is needed or expected may also be less clear or embedded among other cues, making it more likely that males will miss them or more acceptable for them to ignore them. Similarly in marital therapy when husbands are asked to express feelings in response to problems, therapists note that wives sometimes say, "Well, he'll do this here, but he won't do it when we are at home" (Baucom, Sayers, & Sher, 1990; Markman & Kraft, 1989). In order to generalize from laboratory experiments on social support to naturally occurring social support, the connection between subjects' behaviors and experiences in laboratory situations and real life needs to be explored. One limitation of the laboratory situations is that it is time-limited. Supportive behaviors that make partners feel better or perform better in the moment may not be helpful with stress that occurs repeatedly or over a long period of time.

The studies do find some results consistent with those from other research. Barbee et al. (1990) found that both female and male subjects *expect* more Dismiss behavior from male friends than from female friends. In the Yankeelov et al. (1991) study, males were rated by judges as using more Dismiss behavior than females, but only in the test condition; although their romantic partners' ratings did not reflect this gender difference. These studies also indicate that males are more likely to be successful support providers when the stress is achievement-or task-oriented. The stressed subjects' expectations for a male helper in this situation, the male helper's greater ease with helping with this type of problem, and/or a match between males' helping style and the help needed with this type of problem may explain these results.

Bringing same-and cross-sex friends, romantic partners, or spouses into the laboratory and recording the social interactions in a stressful situation allows researchers to investigate the effects of gender, type of stress, and nature of social support on the stressed subjects' affective and behavioral outcomes. Despite the limitations of the laboratory setting, the direct observation of social support is crucial in advancing our understanding of this phenomenon. The studies reviewed here suggest that the type of stress, and possibly the gender-related expectations of support seeker and support provider will affect the behaviors and perceptions of the participants in a supportive interaction. The fact that support seeker, support provider, and objective observer may have different perceptions of supportive behaviors displayed in the interaction suggests that no one perspective is sufficient for understanding the social support episode.

A final thought: We have discussed at length behaviors enacted by helpers that might provide assistance. However, as emphasized by the social support activation model, the behaviors of both the support seeker and support provider must be included in an *interactive* model of coping. Future research needs to examine more closely the ways in which the support seeker activates support and how her or his specific support seeking behaviors influence the specific responses by the support provider and the subsequent tit-for-tat exchange that occurs between both individuals.

References

Barbee, A. P. (1990). Interactive coping: The cheering up process in close relationships. In S. Duck (Ed.), *Personal relationships and social support* (pp. 46-65). London: Sage.

Barbee, A. P. (1991, October). *The role of emotions and cognitions in the interactive coping process.* Paper presented at the Symposium on Interpersonal Causes of Emotions. Society of Experimental Social Psychologists, Columbus, OH.

Barbee, A. P., Cunningham, M. R., Winstead, B. A., Derlega, V. J., Gulley, M. R., Yankeelov, P. A., & Druen, P. B. (1993). Effects of gender role expectations on the social support process. *Journal of Social Issues, 49*(3), 175-190.

Barbee, A. P., Gulley, M. R., & Cunningham, M. R. (1990). Support seeking in close relationships. *Journal of Social and Personal Relationships, 7,* 531-540.

Baucom, D. H., Sayers, S. L., & Sher, T. G. (1990). Supplementing behavioral marital therapy with cognitive restructuring and emotional expression training: An outcome investigation. *Journal of Consulting and Clinical Psychology, 58,* 636-645.

Costanza, R. S., Derlega, V. J., & Winstead, B. A. (1988). Positive and negative forms of social support: Effects of conversational topics on coping with stress among same-sex friends. *Journal of Experimental Social Psychology, 23,* 182-193.

Eagly, A. H., & Crowley, M. (1986). Gender and helping behavior: A meta-analytic review of the social psychological literature. *Psychological Bulletin, 100,* 283-308.

Fleming, R., Baum, A., Gisriel, M. M., & Gatchel, R. J. (1982). Mediating influences of social support at Three Mile Island. *Journal of Human Stress, 8,* 14-22.

Gulley, M. R., Barbee, A. P., & Cunningham, M. R. (1992, August). *The effects of gender on the social support process.* Washington, DC: American Psychological Association.

Hays, R. B. (1988). Friendship. In S. W. Duck (Ed.), *Handbook of personal relationships* (pp. 391-408). Chichester, UK: John Wiley.

Hays, R. B., & Oxley, D. (1986). Social network development and functioning during a life transition. *Journal of Personality and Social Psychology, 50,* 305-313.

Lowenthal, M. F., & Haven, C. (1968). Interaction and adaptation: Intimacy as a critical variable. *American Sociological Review, 33,* 20-30.

Maccoby, E. E. (1990). Gender and relationships: A developmental account. *American Psychologist, 45,* 513-520.

Maccoby, E. E. (1991). Gender segregation in the workplace: Continuities and discontinuities from childhood to adulthood. In M. Frankenhauser, U. Lundberg, & M. Chesney (Eds.), *Women, work, and health* (pp. 3-16). New York: Plenum.

Markman, H. J., & Kraft, S. (1989). Men and women in marriage: Dealing with gender differences in marital therapy. *The Behavior Therapist, 12,* 51-56.

Pennebaker, J. W., & O'Heeron, R. C. (1984). Confiding in others and illness rates among spouses of suicide and accidental death victims. *Journal of Abnormal Psychology, 93,* 473-476.

Reis, H. T., Senchak, M., & Solomon, B. (1985). Sex differences in the intimacy of social interaction: Further examination of potential explanations. *Journal of Personality and Social Psychology, 48,* 1204-1217.

Tannen, D. (1990). *You just don't understand: Women and men in conversation.* New York: Ballantine.

Thompson, E. H., Jr., & Pleck, J. H. (1987). The structure of male role norms. In M. S. Kimmel (Ed.), *Changing men: New directions in research on men and masculinity* (pp. 25-36). Newbury Park, CA: Sage.

Wheeler, L., Reis, H., & Nezlek, J. (1983). Loneliness, social interaction, and sex roles. *Journal of Personality and Social Psychology, 45,* 943-953.

Winstead, B. A. (1986). Sex differences in same-sex friendships. In V. J. Derlega & B. A. Winstead (Eds.), *Friendship and social interaction* (pp. 81-99). New York: Springer-Verlag.

Winstead, B. A., Derlega, V. J., Lewis, R. J., Sanchez-Hucles, J., & Clarke, E. (1992). Friendship, social interaction, and coping with stress. *Communication Research, 19,* 193-211.

Yankeelov, P. A., Barbee, A. P., Cunningham, M. R., & Druen, P. (1991, May). *Interactive coping in romantic relationships.* Paper presented at the International Conference on Personal Relationships, Normal, IL.

Zuckerman, M., & Lubin, B. (1965). *Manual for the Multiple Affect Adjective Checklist.* San Diego, CA: Educational and Industrial Testing Service.

8

The Appraisal of Spousal Support by Women Facing Conflicts Between Work and Family

MARLA STEINBERG

BENJAMIN H. GOTTLIEB

The study of social support is undergoing a profound change. Historically support was conceptualized as a resource that some people had and others did not have. The dominant research questions revolved around two lines of inquiry both focusing on the determinants of support, one line assessing how the structural properties of the social network were associated with people's access to and receipt of support (e.g., Hirsch, 1980; Wellman, 1981), and the other assessing how various intrapersonal factors were related to these two aspects of support (e.g., Conn & Peterson, 1989; Dunkel-Schetter, Folkman, & Lazarus, 1987; Eckenrode, 1983; Fisher, Goff, Nadler, & Chinsky, 1988; Shinn, Lehman, & Wong, 1984; Shumaker & Brownell, 1984; Vaux, 1985).

Through in-depth interviews (Weiss, 1990), daily diaries (Cutrona, 1986), observational coding schemes (Cutrona, Suhr, & MacFarlane, 1990), and interaction records (Leatham & Duck, 1990; Reis, Wheeler, Kernis, Spiegel, & Nezlek, 1985), social psychologists and researchers in the field of communication are now presenting a more complex view of social support as a dynamic process, rather than as an individual attribute. It is a process that is subject to negotiation and influenced by a host of

AUTHORS' NOTE: This chapter is based on the first author's masters thesis. The second author gratefully acknowledges receipt of a Senior Research Fellowship from the Ontario Mental Health Foundation, which assisted with the completion of this chapter.

personal, situational, and relational factors. It is therefore most fruitfully examined from an interactional perspective that takes into account what the recipient and the provider bring to (e.g., their relational history and personal attributes) and make of their commerce. This new view of social support extends the focus of research beyond the determinants of support to more relationship oriented questions such as the significance of the support process for the conduct, meaning, and course of human relationships. In this sense the focus of the research is on how the supply and effective expression of support, or its absence, is at once shaped by personal, situational, and relational factors, and can also alter the ways people represent and conceive of themselves and their relationships.

In this chapter we bring an interactional perspective to bear on the support process that arises between married couples on those occasions when one of the partners experiences conflict between the demands of work and the demands of family life. Our particular objective is to identify the aspects of the interactional context that influence the wives' evaluations of their husbands' support, and thereby to enlarge our understanding of the personal, situational, and relational contingencies which influence the support process in this close relationship.

We begin by outlining four stages of the support process, reviewing what is presently known about the factors that bear on the expression and evaluation of support in each stage. Then we call on information gleaned from interviews with women facing work and family conflicts in order to identify aspects of their transactions with their husbands that bear on their appraisals of support. We present a classification scheme composed of 7 classes and 37 categories of behaviors and qualities that influence the wives' appraisals of support. Our discussion of the theoretical contributions of this scheme to the study of social support centers on the ways in which the meaning of support is conditioned not only by its practical and self-related consequences, but also by the messages it communicates about the functioning of relationships.

CONTINGENCIES DURING EACH
STAGE OF THE SUPPORT PROCESS

What are the implications of viewing support as an interactional process whose progress and outcomes are shaped by a variety of contingencies? One implication is that stages in the process can be discerned, each presenting the opportunity to identify corresponding interactional sequences that surround the issues germane to that stage. This analytic approach was developed and first used in Pearlin and McCall's (1990) study of employed men and women who were interviewed about issues surrounding the provision of support from their spouses for work related difficulties. The authors divided the support process into four stages, beginning with transactions surrounding the disclosure or recognition of the need for support, followed by the appraisal stage, when the donor makes several "key judgments" about the recipient's deservingness of support. The third stage involves transactions that influence the forms of support and the manner of their expression. The process culminates with the parties' evaluations of the impact or helpfulness of their exchanges. Using similar temporal frameworks, researchers have begun to examine the support process in the contexts of bereavement (Lehman, Ellard, & Wortman, 1986), and a child's chronic illness (Gottlieb & Wagner, 1991).

Two studies shed light on the social psychological and interpersonal issues arising in the first stage of the support process, when the need for support is revealed. Pearlin and McCall (1990) observed that job problems were not disclosed at all when an unhelpful response from the spouse was anticipated, which proved to be the case whenever the problems arose from an activity that the spouse did not approve of in the first place. In addition, they found that problems remained concealed from the spouse when he or she was implicated in their genesis or when he or she was expected to blame the other partner for needing support in the first place, or for failing to capitalize on the help received in the past. More generally, in their discussion of the process whereby support is initially activated, Eckenrode and Wethington (1990) have analyzed the costs and benefits of support that is spontaneously tendered versus support that is solicited, and have identified some of the circumstances under which each of these two avenues of mobilization occur. From these studies we learn that aspects of the precipitating event, including its genesis and legitimacy, as well as the success of past supportive efforts, influence whether or not support is sought and how it is conveyed.

Several studies have focused on the issues that are most salient for providers during the second and third stage of the support process, determining the likelihood and extent of their involvement. Many of the influences that surround the dynamics of disclosing a problem or need for support also influence the provision of support. For example, it has been found that the provision of support depends in part on the providers' sense of responsibility for the occurrence of the stressor (Coyne, Wortman, &

Lehman, 1988), their judgments of the recipient's responsibility for incurring the need for aid, and their own need to restore equity to the relationship (Fisher, Goff, Nadler, & Chinsky, 1988; Jung, 1988). Pearlin and McCall (1990) maintain that "the appraisal process . . . is fundamentally organized around a single issue, that of legitimization" (p. 48). If the donor does not believe the problem merits distress, that the degree of distress is exaggerated, or that the support provided in the past has not been used effectively, then support is likely to be withheld. Although these studies have contributed important information about the ways the provider construes the circumstances that may call for support, they do not reveal how these cognitions are played out in the process of negotiating support.

There is some evidence that in the third stage of the support process, the stage when the parties' transactions shape the forms of support that materialize, the recipient's ways of coping guide the provider's expression of support. For example, in recent research examining the interplay between the coping and the support process, Dunkel-Schetter, Folkman, and Lazarus (1987) found that support providers discerned whether and how to render assistance by observing the potential recipient's ways of coping. Coping by means of problem solving and positive reappraisal were both associated with the donation of support, whereas distancing was associated with the absence of support. Similarly, in a qualitative study of the ways parents coped with their children's chronic illness, Gottlieb and Wagner (1991) found that the mothers could gain support from their husbands only when they coped with their child's illness in ways that did not disrupt or threaten their husbands' ways of coping. Through a variety of communications, the husbands placed pressure on their wives to alter their coping to make it easier for the husbands to support their wives. In fact, many of the mothers were forced to feign ways of coping in order to appease and gain support from their husbands, adding to the burdens of caregiving which they shouldered.

Support providers are influenced not only by their observations of the other party's coping but by their own coping styles. In addition, they are guided by their beliefs about the types of support that are appropriate in given situations, and by the implicit theories they have about how coping should progress (Coyne et al., 1988; Heller, Swindle, & Dusenbury, 1986; Lehman et al., 1986; Shinn, Lehman, & Wong, 1984; Wortman & Lehman, 1985). What remains unresearched is whether these cognitions are manifested in the ways support is withheld, intensified, or withdrawn during this third stage of the process, as well as in the kinds and sequences of support that are expressed.

The final stage of the support process concerns the parties' evaluations of the effects of their transactions. Here, much more is known about the kinds of communications and deeds that are appraised as helpful and unhelpful, in terms of their value as coping assistance, than about the effects of support on relationships. Support has implications that extend beyond helping to deal with a stressful event. Supportive interactions can also alter the conduct of and sentiment toward the relationship. However, most of the research has concentrated on documenting the types of support that contribute to emotion- and problem-focused coping. For example, Dakof and Taylor (1990), Lehman et al. (1986), and Pearlin and McCall (1990) have found that unwanted or untimely advice, discouragement of open expression of feelings about being victimized or minimization of these feelings, pressure to make a more rapid recovery, and the use of automatic or scripted support are judged as impediments to the recipient's coping efforts.

Collectively, these studies have exposed a variety of personal, situational, and relational contingencies that influence each stage of the social support process. During the mobilization and appraisal stages, both would-be recipients and providers are influenced by their own sense of responsibility for the genesis of the stressor and their perceptions of its legitimacy as a basis for help-seeking. Relational history, particularly the success of past supportive efforts, and relational equity are also important in shaping the supportive transaction. Contingencies that influence the forms of support include the recipient's ways of coping and the provider's implicit theories of coping. During the final evaluation phase, researchers have examined how the forms and quantity of support influence its value as coping assistance, but they have not considered how they influence the character and course of personal relationships.

Our review of the numerous contingencies that affect the social support process does not, however, yield a coherent account of the factors that weigh most heavily in evaluations of the support that is expressed in a close relationship. With the exception of Pearlin and McCall's (1990) investigation, none of the studies we have cited has asked respondents to review their interactions in a close relationship and to identify the features that color their appraisals of support. There is reason to believe that the support communicated in close relationships, and in the marital relationship in particular, is more complicated and subject to a broader array of social psychological and situational contingencies than the more casual relationships that have been studied to date. This is because the partners have a shared history, a large stake in the relationship, and expectations of continued involvement with one another.

Moreover, while illuminating the stages of the support process, Pearlin and McCall's (1990) work does not address the broader relationship themes that underlie evaluations of support. We therefore planned a study which would provide an opportunity to elucidate the support process that unfolds between partners in a close relationship, and to restrict our focus to the contingencies affecting one of the partner's evaluations of support. We encouraged that partner to review all four stages of the support process and then to cite the reasons why certain aspects of the interaction were deemed to be supportive and others unsupportive. Our findings shed light on the interpersonal dynamics that are most salient to the recipient and that weigh more heavily in the appraisal of support and the relationship meanings it conveys.

Appraisals of Husbands' Support for Work-Family Conflicts

The study described in this chapter is based on intensive interviews with employed women in dual income marriages. The respondents began by citing episodes of conflict between their work and their family obligations, and then provided detailed descriptions of their husbands' involvement in responding to these conflicts. The women's evaluations of their spouses' responses were then solicited. The main focus of the interview was on the reasons for these evaluations since the study's primary purpose was to identify aspects of the interpersonal process that color its supportive meaning to the recipient.

There are several reasons why we believed our study's purposes would be achieved by interviewing employed, married mothers of preschool children. First, as Hochschild (1989), Crosby (1991), and Duffy, Mandell, and Pupo (1989) have observed in their compelling accounts of the day-to-day lives of employed mothers, episodes of conflict between the demands of work and family occur frequently, and therefore present multiple occasions for the mobilization of the spouse's support. Second, the physical labor and emotional drain entailed in simultaneously working inside and outside the home make the expression or absence of spousal support highly consequential for both the women's well-being and for the state of the relationship. Third, particularly when both spouses are employed, there are many complex influences on the division of labor in the home, and on the ways work and family demands are played out. We therefore anticipated that interviews probing evaluations of spousal support for work and family conflicts would elicit rich detail about the personal, situational, and relational contingencies operating during the support process.

Finally, our reading of the literature, which examines the role and effects of spousal support in the context of work-family interference, underscored the contribution that could be made by a qualitative study of the factors that influence the appraisal of support. Specifically, a number of investigations of the effects of spousal support on the health and well-being of employed women have reported contradictory findings (Baruch & Barnett, 1981, 1986; MacEwen & Barling, 1988; Ross & Mirowsky, 1988), but none of the studies gathered the kinds of qualitative data needed to explain the findings. Typically, conventional survey measures of actual or perceived support were used, thereby leaving obscure how the respondents' transactions with their spouses determined the beneficial or adverse effects of the spouse's support.

Nevertheless, the authors' speculations about the reasons for the adverse effects of spousal support spotlight several factors that may condition the wives' appraisals. Some authors have proposed that support could be detrimental if it threatens the wives' self-concept vis-à-vis their sex-role attitudes. When mothers who hold traditional sex-role attitudes relinquish child care tasks to their husbands, they may feel guilty or risk being ostracized by other like-minded family members (Baruch & Barnett, 1981; MacEwen & Barling, 1988; Yogev, 1982). In contrast, women who subscribe to an egalitarian ethic, but who fail to receive support that reinforces this ethic, may also be psychologically harmed (Hochschild, 1989). Sex-role attitudes may also influence men; a husband may be unwilling to provide support to his wife if it could be interpreted as sanctioning diminished domestic responsibilities for the wife (Hirsch & Rapkin, 1986). In general, the marital partners' expectations regarding the division of domestic labor may influence the way support is appraised.

Speculations about the effects of spousal support also center on aspects of the aid itself. The husband's support could actually add to the wife's burdens by leaving her with the less pleasant tasks or the tasks that must be completed every day, such as preparing dinner (Hochschild, 1989; Luxton, 1986). In addition, the support provided by the husbands may not address the type of work-family conflicts the women experience. These explanations suggest that the practical effect of the support on the wife may feature heavily in its psychological impact.

In sum, the purpose of this exploratory study is to identify the range of influences that affect the evaluation of supportive behavior in the context of work-family interference. We suggest that the way the support process unfolds— how support is mobilized, how it is provided, and its effects— not only colors its evaluation, but also conveys information about the partners' relationship, setting the stage for future commerce.

INTERVIEW STRUCTURE, CONTENT, AND RESPONDENTS

The first author conducted private interviews with 18 white, married, women who were recruited from three local child care centers. All the women were employed, as were their husbands, and all of them had at least one preschool age child in day care. The respondents ranged in age from 27 to 45 years, averaging 33.7 years, and had been married between 7 and 23 years, averaging 11.2 years. Seventeen of the women had two children and one woman had one child. The children were between the ages of 1 and 16 years. The average ages of the first born and second born children were 7.1 and 3.7 years, respectively. The women spent an average of 32.4 hours per week in paid employment. The average combined yearly family income was $58,000 (range = $35,000 to $86,000), of which the women earned an average of $21,000 per year.

Each interview was tape-recorded and began with the respondent describing a recent time "when things were happening in one domain that prevented you from either fulfilling a responsibility in the other domain or fulfilling a responsibility the way you usually like to." Once a work-family conflict was identified, the respondent was asked to describe her handling of the situation, and to indicate whether and how her husband had become involved.

We assumed that interactions may contain both helpful and unhelpful elements, as a function of the personal, relational, and situational contingencies affecting their expression during all four stages of the support process. However, in order to anchor the discussion of the factors that influenced the supportive meaning of the spouse's behaviors, the interviewee was asked to rate each of the husband's responses on a 7-point scale that ranged from "not helpful at all" to "very helpful." The ratings were used only to help the respondent reflect on the factors that added to and detracted from the supportive value of each of her husband's responses. These factors, which shaped the appraisals of support, constitute our main analytic focus.

Finally, in order to ensure that the interview tapped all the husbands' responses and interactions, even those not considered supportive, a specific question about unhelpful responses was included, followed by a request to explain the reasons for this appraisal. The interview schedule was then repeated for a second work-family conflict.

METHOD OF ANALYSIS

The goal of the qualitative analysis was to identify the contingencies affecting the respondents' appraisals of the supportive dimension of their husbands' involvement in the 35 episodes of work-family conflict. This was accomplished by extracting the reasons for their ratings of each of their husbands' responses from the interview transcripts. Within these narratives, 91 explanations were then identified, serving as the (scoring) units for the subsequent analysis. Whereas some women provided only one explanation for each evaluation, others furnished several. These units were then used as the basis for the development of a set of 37 categories, reflecting all the factors invoked in the women's appraisals of their husbands' support. In developing the category labels, we attempted to be faithful to the respondents' accounts by adopting their words and phrases whenever possible. Related categories were then grouped into classes according to the conceptual scheme that is alphabetically listed in Table 8.1. Once the initial classification scheme was established, the authors reviewed all interview excerpts, and, through discussion, agreed on the final organization and labeling of the categories and classes.

FINDINGS

The work-family conflicts reported by our respondents are similar to those documented in the work and family literature (cf. Anderson-Kulman & Paludi, 1986; Duffy et al., 1989; Hochschild, 1989). Chiefly, they stemmed from competing demands placed on the women by their children, their work, their domestic responsibilities, their husbands, and demands they placed on themselves. The most frequently reported episodes of work-family conflict involved breakdowns in routine child care arrangements and child care for sick children, problems in attending appointments as well as special events and activities involving children, and interestingly, occasions when husbands failed to help. These conflicts represent routine but nonetheless disruptive events that many working women experience.

When these conflicts occurred, the husbands' responses ranged from complete ignorance of and detachment from the conflict, to the provision of child care, and many other forms of coping assistance. Details regarding the husbands' responses appear in Steinberg (1990). The main focus here is on the factors affecting the wives' appraisals of these responses, which are described below and presented in Table 8.1.

The ways in which the husbands were first drawn into the episodes of conflict between work and family shaped the wives' judgments of their supportive value. Women devalued assistance that had to be solicited and praised support that was spontaneously tendered. In addition, the expectations the women brought to their interactions with their husbands also colored their evaluations. Their past experience in negotiating support, and their knowledge of how their spouse typically responded to and coped with different kinds of work, family, and personal demands conditioned these expectations.

The largest class of contingencies affecting the women's evaluations concerned the personal qualities and attitudes reflected by their husbands' responses. Six of the 14 categories in this class were invoked as explanations for positive evaluations of their spouses' responses, while the remaining eight negatively colored their evaluations. Support providers who were reliable, in the sense that they could be counted on to follow through on promises and intentions, were viewed more favorably. Understanding and objectivity were also valued qualities of support providers. The way support providers helped to resolve the conflict was also important; providers who were flexible and cooperative, and who showed a willingness to negotiate and to take an equal share of the responsibility for handling the problem, were perceived as more helpful. Responding in a manner that emulated the wife's handling of the problem also added to the value of support.

Some of the characteristics that shaped evaluations of husbands' responses as unhelpful were the polar opposites of these valued qualities. They involved inconsistency, a lack of understanding, and the spouse's failure to take equal responsibility for dealing with the conflict. Additional qualities and attitudes that contributed to unsupportive appraisals were that the husband shirked his responsibility, and showed either selfishness or self-protectiveness. The women also mentioned that the blunt or clumsy

TABLE 8.1 Factors Affecting the Appraisal of the Support Process

Class and Category	Examples
A. The way support was mobilized	
A1. Solicited/Spontaneously tendered	"So I guess its in the asking part, having to ask"
B. Recipient's Expectations	
B1. Met wife's expectations	"Because I was not expecting anything more from him"
C. Personal qualities and attitudes of provider	
C1. Reliable	"I always know I can always fall back on him"
C2. Flexible	"Because he is fairly flexible"
C3. Understanding	"He understands the strains and the pressures of what it is like to be at home"
C4. Recognition of equal responsibility for resolution	"We are a team rather than I'm subordinate to him"
C5. Willingness to negotiate	"We still had to negotiate back and forth"
C6. Objectivity	"He was one step more away from it so he could see things a little bit more, not as emotional"
C7. Inconsistent	"In that most of the time he is in tune with how to deal and understand me and then there are other times when he is very stubborn about things and can't see and that doesn't go over very well"
C8. Lack of understanding	"He didn't really understand all that I was dealing with"
C9. Shirks responsibility	"His first reaction was 'Well I can call mom she'll probably do it' and I didn't want that"
C10. Assigns responsibility for problem resolution	"He said that the problem was mine"
C11. Responds selfishly	"He was interested in having it all his own way, and I felt that was selfish"
C12. Responds self-protectively	"He had to deal with his own feelings and a certain defense mechanism probably kicks into play"
C13. Too blunt	"Sometimes his honesty can be quite blunt so that in meaning well sometimes it can come out blunt"
C14. Oblivious to need for help	"Just his whole attitude 'I never thought of it' "
D. The way support was provided	
D1. Emulates wife's handling of problems	"I was used to one way, he has his own ideas"
D2. With caring	"I guess because it was done very loving, and very caring"

TABLE 8.1 Factors Affecting the Appraisal of the Support Process

Class and Category	Examples
D3. Shows willing and cooperative attitude to providing support	"He did that willingly and I didn't have to beg him or ask him or anything"
D4. Too anonymous in style	"Because it was on a telephone, person to person would have been nicer"
E. Genesis of stress	
E1. Husband caused problem	"I felt he was the root cause of the problem"
E2. Equal responsibility for causing distress	"He realized we both got out of control and that we have to watch it in the future"
E3. Lays blame for stress	"Blames it on me, like it was my fault"
F. Quantity and form of support	
F1. Husband helped more than wife	"I don't do as much as he does"
F2. Husband helped as much as wife	"He is with the children every bit as much as I am"
F3. Husband helped less than wife desired	"There are still some things that I would like him to do"
F4. Deficient in form	"It was just an emotional type thing. The help wasn't that he rearranged his schedule and it wasn't that he completely ignored me and yelled that it is your responsibility, he just gave me a few encouraging words and that was it"
G. Supportive outcomes	
G1. Positive emotional impact	"The things he said made me feel much better"
G2. Reduced demands	"He cuts down on asking me so it doesn't put as much pressure on me"
G3. Enabled wife to pursue her own interests	"I would never have been able to do that if it hadn't been for him"
G4. Did not compound problem	"He did not make it any worse for me either"
G5. Resolved problem	"Because he gave me exactly what I should have done"
G6. Negative emotional impact	"So then he is making me feel guilty"
G7. Added to wife's demands	"They didn't clean up their mess"
G8. Produced emotional isolation	"It really annoys me when he says why should he worry when I worry enough for the both of us"
G9. Interfered with wife's goals	"It puts my progress for graduation back"
G10. Support did not entirely resolve problem	"Because he did talk to her and he does listen more to her and they tried to solve it but it didn't work out on Monday"

manner in which the husband attempted to resolve a conflict seriously undermined its supportive meaning. Men who appeared to be detached from their wives' conflicts or the feelings they engendered, and who were therefore oblivious to the need for support, were viewed as less helpful. Another factor emerging from the respondents' explanations for their support ratings concerned the genesis of the stressor. When the husband was perceived to be the cause of the conflict, or when he blamed his wife for its occurrence, his involvement was derogated. In contrast, when he acknowledged equal responsibility for causing the conflict or the distress it occasioned, his responses were likely to be viewed as supportive.

Only four of the categories touched on the quantity or type of support actually rendered by the spouse. Three of them concerned the relative quantity of help and support provided, and one concerned the fit between the type of support provided and the wives' needs or desires for support.

Finally, the outcomes of the interactions also affected the wives' appraisals. They reported an equal number of beneficial and adverse outcomes, the former encompassing positive emotional effects, reduced demands on the wife, and resolutions that enabled the respondents to pursue their own interests. Interactions that did not compound the problem were also rated more highly. The negative outcomes included unpleasant emotional effects, increased demands on the respondents, feelings of emotional isolation, frustration of their goals, and the inability to achieve a satisfactory resolution of the conflict itself.

Discussion

Our findings spotlight numerous factors that influence the supportive meaning of husbands' responses to the work-family conflicts that their wives experience. As we suggested earlier, the wives' accounts reveal that transactions occurring during each stage of the social support process affect its appraisal.

In the first stage of the support process, our respondents' evaluations were influenced by the ways in which their husbands' support was initially mobilized. Support that was provided spontaneously enhanced its rating while having to ask for support diminished its value. There are a number of reasons why support that is spontaneously tendered is more desirable and acceptable than support that must be solicited. First, it signals sensitivity to the recipient's needs (Eckenrode & Wethington, 1990). It confirms that the husband is attending to the relationship and living up to his responsibilities to share his partner's tasks as well as her emotional life. Conversely, support that must be solicited reflects less relationship synchrony and perhaps greater emotional detachment. Second, asking for support is seen as problematic because of its costs to the solicitor's self-esteem (Eckenrode & Wethington, 1990). It can arouse feelings of embarrassment, vulnerability, dependence on others, and indebtedness, and it requires an admission of one's own incompetence (Eckenrode & Wethington, 1990; Shinn, Lehman, & Wong, 1984). In this study the relationship implications of direct requests for support were of paramount importance. Respondents who had to ask for their husbands' assistance could not escape the inference that the principal responsibility for child care and domestic work falls upon the wife and mother. It also implies that the partners have different expectations for the division of the labor involved in raising a family, and perhaps different perceptions of the relationship.

Our respondents also spoke about the manner in which their husbands' support was conveyed, testifying to its relevance during the second and third stages of the social support process. Not surprisingly, interactions that facilitated management of the conflict without increasing the demands on the wife were deemed more supportive. For example, interactions that reflected a willing and cooperative attitude to providing support were viewed more positively, while interactions that involved arguing or obstructiveness negatively colored the wives' judgments. This is largely because prolonged struggles to gain support compounded the wife's problems and raised doubts about the mutuality of the marital relationship. A reliable husband does not add to problems once a resolution is achieved. Similarly, a husband who is willing to negotiate and is flexible also facilitates resolution. On the other hand, a husband who is inconsistent, lacks understanding, or shirks his responsibility aggravates his wife's problems, and is therefore viewed more negatively.

The forms and amount of support were additional contingencies that affected its appraisal during the third stage of the support process. In dealing with work-family conflicts, the women placed a greater premium on practical or instrumental assistance than on emotional support. This is not surprising given that the women estimated that an average of 70% of the child care and household tasks falls on them. In fact, in several instances, husbands provided emotional support, such as commiserating with their wives, when the wives wanted practical help.

In the final stage of the support process, which concerns evaluations of the effects of the transactions, there is abundant evidence that interactions that result in more favorable outcomes are more highly valued than interactions that produce adverse outcomes. Although this general proposition is hardly instructive, it is the range of outcomes that the respondents invoked that warrants attention. The outcomes of the interactions were evaluated in terms of their instrumental value in assisting coping with the conflict, their synchrony with the wife's ways of coping, their emotional impact on the wife, and their repercussions on the relationship and on other spheres of life in which the wife was involved.

For example, when the husbands resolved conflicts in a different way or less thoroughly than the wives wished, their responses were judged less supportive largely because they left the wives with two undesirable options: they could either lower their standards and accept the way their husbands had resolved the conflict, or they could reject their husbands' solution and face both the interpersonal tension such an action would produce, as well as the responsibility for resolving the conflict themselves. Moreover, a number of the respondents told the interviewer that they suspected that their husbands consciously or unconsciously provided substandard support in order to demonstrate their lack of skill at providing support, and to preclude further support requests.

RELATIONSHIP THEMES UNDERLYING
APPRAISALS OF SUPPORT

Based on their review of the literature on recipients' reactions to aid, Fisher, Nadler, and Whitcher-Alagna (1982) interpreted the dynamics underlying the appraisal of support in terms of a threat to self-esteem. They postulated that reactions to aid are determined by the self-related consequences of the aid; those aspects of the social-psychological context that enhance self-esteem make the aid more acceptable, while those that threaten self-esteem make the aid less acceptable. The authors maintain that a variety of situational conditions (donor characteristics, aid characteristics, and stressor characteristics) interact with recipient characteristics to determine whether help is primarily threatening or supportive.

Whereas selected findings of the present study could be interpreted in terms of this model, there is a competing framework that transcends this focus on the individual's self-esteem. The contingencies affecting our respondents' evaluations of their husbands' behavior can be viewed in terms of the meaning they convey about the present status of the relationship, and particularly about its equity and mutuality. For example, the ways in which the husbands' support was initially activated conveys information about the mutuality of the relationship. Wives who do not have to ask for help are more likely to conclude that their husbands are closely attuned to and recognize the legitimacy of their needs, and that the provision of emotional and practical support can be taken for granted in the relationship. In contrast, wives who have to request help may have to acknowledge to themselves that their husbands are either oblivious to their needs, fail to see their needs as legitimate, or loathe to share their tasks. Any of these admissions implies deficiencies in the intimacy and mutual responsiveness of the relationship. One can only speculate about the long-term demoralizing effect on the respondents of repeated disappointments of this sort, and what they portend for the future of the marriage.

The categories that concern the quantity of aid and the qualities of its provider also reflect equity considerations. Unfavorable ratings were assigned to interactions which revealed that the husbands helped less than the wives, and favorable ratings were assigned to occasions when the husbands' contributions matched or exceeded their spouses'. Interactions in which the husbands displayed qualities that facilitated resolution of the conflict without increasing the demands on their wives were similarly valued.

The personal qualities and attitudes that the husbands bring to their interaction with their wives, and the ways they furnish support also convey information about the status of the relationship. A spouse who is understanding, reliable, and flexible conveys that he is committed to meeting his partner's needs, and thereby contributes to the durability of the relationship. In Clark and Mills's (1979) terminology, he is acting in accordance with the norms that apply to a "communal relationship," chiefly a concern for his wife's welfare and for the welfare of the relationship. Yet our findings also reveal that some of the contingencies affecting the wives' support evaluations resemble the "rules" that operate in "exchange relationships." Briefly, Clark and Mills (1979) maintain that exchange relationships are characterized by the rule that each party will benefit the other relatively quickly, and in equal response to the benefit received from the other. Typically, these relationships have no expectation of mutually beneficial, long- term interactions, whereas communal relationships are marked by ongoing mutual commitment and responsiveness.

It is therefore particularly noteworthy that many of our respondents formed their evaluations of the supportiveness of their husbands' responses by carefully calculating the latter's relative contribution to resolving the work-family conflicts. One respondent described an elaborate accounting system that she had developed in an effort to obtain more help from her husband:

> We made a list of priority, high level basic jobs that have to be done. The home, shelter, washing the clothes, all that sort of stuff. We continued the list and on both sides we put my jobs and Tom's jobs. When we finished, not only was mine a lot longer, but 90% of the high priority jobs that were essential for our survival and had to be done almost every day or at least weekly were more heavily on my side. We then moved things to his side. It is almost like a mathematical balancing exercise that we did. Like bowling, moving things from one side of the ledger to the other.

This strict accounting of each spouse's relative contribution clearly reflects exchange rules being played out in the marriage, despite the fact that marriage is thought to be the prototypical communal relationship. Moreover, repeatedly having to ask for assistance from uncooperative husbands reveals more than the fact that the husband is not doing his share. It implies that he is not meeting his obligation to support the relationship. If the wife attaches importance to this dimension of the marriage, such an implication represents a serious threat to the woman's image of herself and her marriage.

The wives' concerns about issues of equity in the division of domestic labor are therefore critical determinants of their appraisals of spousal support. These concerns are likely to be magnified in dual income marriages because the routine nature of work-family conflicts presents numerous tests of the partners' commitment to mutual aid. When the couple is forced to make a strict audit of their relative contributions, it suggests that shared meanings regarding mutuality in the relationship have never been established or have broken down. In Clark and Mills's (1979) terms, communal relationships that operate in accordance with exchange rules have "disintegrated." However, explicit counting of benefits contributed and received can then either be a remedial means of restoring equity to the relationship, reminding the partners of their commitment to mutual responsiveness, or it can further harm the relationship by underscoring its obligatory, controlling, and asymmetrical characteristics.

It is important to underscore the fact that the respondents' concerns about equity issues touch on two dimensions: equity in the division of household labor, and equity in the exchange of support. On the latter score, it is evident that the women in this study had only modest expectations for support from their husbands. One woman stated that she was satisfied with the support she received "because I was not expecting anything more from him," while another stated that "I think he did the best he could, given the situation." In fact, positive appraisals were made even in instances when the only redeeming characteristic of an interaction was that it did not compound the wives' problems. Past interactions had no doubt moderated the respondents' expectations regarding the quality and extent of support they could gain from their husbands. By valuing interactions that meet such minimal standards, the respondents betray a measure of resignation to their husband's general unresponsiveness to their supportive needs. At the same time, their acceptance of such impoverished support insulates them from disappointment with whatever support is forthcoming.

Conclusion

The respondents' evaluations of their interactions with their spouses during episodes of conflict between work and family reveal that there are numerous contingencies that shape the supportive meaning and impact of behavior in close relationships. In addition to the three factors that have usually been included in studies examining recipients' evaluations of support, namely the form, source, and quantity of support, there is evidence that interactions gain or lose their supportive meaning on the basis of the ways support is elicited, the form and manner in which it is provided, and its effects on the recipient and on the conflict itself. Equally important, these transactions convey information about the status of the dyadic relationship and sow the seeds for future interactions. They carry messages about how the other party views the relationship, and thereby influence the ways in which the recipient views herself in the relationship. In this sense, relationships influence the nature and course of support, and support influences the nature and course of the relationship.

The seven classes of factors we have identified in this research are likely to be influential in determining appraisals of support in other close relationships. However, the 37 categories are probably more germane to the marital relationship and to the particular context of work and family conflicts we chose to study. It would be instructive to examine the support process that unfolds in other types of relationships and in different stressful contexts in order to identify the bases of support evaluations that are common to all personal relationships and those that apply exclusively to particular types of relationships. It would also be useful to investigate providers' perceptions of the support process, using methods of research, such as daily diaries, which can capture more detail on an ongoing basis. Such in-depth investigations of the interactions between relationship partners during each stage of the support process can only enrich our understanding of the interpersonal processes that influence the meaning and impact of support, as well as the conduct of close relationships.

References

Anderson-Kulman, R. E., & Paludi, M. A. (1986). Working mothers and the family context: Predicting positive coping. *Journal of Vocational Behavior, 28*, 241-253.

Baruch, G. K., & Barnett, R. C. (1981). Fathers' participation in the care of their preschool children. *Sex Roles, 7*(10), 1043-1055.

Baruch, G. K., & Barnett, R. C. (1986). Consequences of fathers' participation in family work: Parents' role-strain and well- being. *Journal of Personality and Social Psychology, 51*, 983-992.

Clark, M. S., & Mills, J. (1979). Interpersonal attraction in exchange and communal relationships. *Journal of Personality and Social Psychology, 37*, 12-24.

Conn, M. K., & Peterson, C. (1989). Social support: Seek and ye shall find. *Journal of Social and Personal Relationships, 6*, 345-358.

Coyne, J. C., Wortman, C. B., & Lehman, D. R. (1988). The other side of support. Emotional overinvolvement and miscarried helping. In B. H. Gottlieb (Ed.), *Marshaling social support* (pp. 305-330). Newbury Park, CA: Sage.

Crosby, F. J. (1991). *Juggling*. New York: The Free Press.

Cutrona, C. E. (1986). Behavioral manifestations of social support: A microanalytic investigation. *Journal of Personality and Social Psychology, 51*, 201-208.

Cutrona, C. E., Suhr, J. A., & MacFarlane, R. (1990). Interpersonal transactions and the psychological sense of support. In S. Duck & R. C. Cohen (Eds.), *Personal relationships and social support* (pp. 30-45). London: Sage.

Dakof, G. A., & Taylor, S. E. (1990). Victims' perceptions of social support: What is helpful from whom? *Journal of Personality and Social Psychology, 58*(1), 80-89.

Duffy, A., Mandell, N., & Pupo, N. (1989). *Few choices: Women, work and family*. Toronto, Canada: Garamond Press.

Dunkel-Schetter, C., Folkman, S., & Lazarus, R. S. (1987). Correlates of social support receipt. *Journal of Personality and Social Psychology, 53*(1), 71-80.

Eckenrode, J. (1983). The mobilization of social support: Some individual constraints. *American Journal of Community Psychology, 11*(5), 509-528.

Eckenrode, J., & Wethington, E. (1990). The process and outcome of mobilizing social support. In S. Duck (Ed., with R. C. Silver), *Personal relationships and social support* (pp. 83-103). London: Sage.

Fisher, J. D., Goff, B. A., Nadler, A., & Chinsky, J. M. (1988). Social psychological influences on help seeking and support from peers. In B. H. Gottlieb (Ed.), *Marshaling social support* (pp. 267-304). Newbury Park, CA: Sage.

Fisher, J. D., Nadler, A., & Whitcher-Alagna, S. (1982). Recipient reactions to aid. *Psychological Bulletin, 91*(1), 27-54.

Gottlieb, B. H., & Wagner, F. (1991). Stress and support processes in close relationships. In J. Eckenrode (Ed.), *The social context of coping* (pp. 165-188). New York: Plenum.

Heller, K., Swindle, R. W., Jr., & Dusenbury, L. (1986). Component social support processes: Comments and integration. *Journal of Consulting and Clinical Psychology, 54*(4), 466-470.

Hirsch, B. J. (1980). Natural support systems and coping with major life changes. *American Journal of Community Psychology, 8*, 159-172.

Hirsch, B. J., & Rapkin, B. D. (1986). Multiple roles, social networks, and women's well-being. *Journal of Personality and Social Psychology, 51*(6), 1237-1247.

Hochschild, A. (1989). *The second shift*. New York: Avon.

Jung, J. (1988). Social support providers: Why do they help? *Basic and Applied Social Psychology, 9*(3), 231-240.

Leatham, G., & Duck, S. (1990). Conversations with friends and the dynamics of social support. In S. Duck (Ed., with R. C. Silver), *Personal relationships and social support* (pp. 1- 29). London: Sage.

Lehman, D. R., Ellard, J. H., & Wortman, C. B. (1986). Social support for the bereaved: Recipients' and providers' perspectives on what is helpful. *Journal of Consulting and Clinical Psychology, 54*(4), 438-446.

Luxton, M. (1986). Two hands for the clock: Changing patterns in the gender division of labour. In M. Luxton & H. Rosenberg (Eds.), *Through the kitchen window: The politics of home and family* (pp. 17-36). Toronto, Canada: Garamond Press.

MacEwen, K. E., & Barling, J. (1988). Inter-role conflict, family support, and marital adjustment of employed mothers: A short term, longitudinal study. *Journal of Organizational Behavior, 9*, 241-250.

Pearlin, L. I., & McCall, M. E. (1990). Occupational stress and martial support: A description of microprocesses. In J. Eckenrode & S. Gore (Eds.), *Stress between work and family* (pp. 39-60). New York: Plenum.

Reis, H. T., Wheeler, L., Kernis, M. H., Spiegel, H., & Nezlek, J. (1985). On specificity in the impact of social participation on physical and psychological health. *Journal of Personality and Social Psychology, 48*, 456-471.

Ross, C. E., & Mirowsky, J. (1988). Child care and emotional adjustment to wives' employment. *Journal of Health and Social Behavior, 29*, 127-138.

Shinn, M., Lehman, S., & Wong, N. W. (1984). Social interaction and social support. *Journal of Social Issues, 40*(4), 55-76.

Shumaker, S. A., & Brownell, A. (1984). Toward a theory of social support: Closing conceptual gaps. *Journal of Social Issues, 40*(4), 11-36.

Steinberg, M. (1990). *Wives' perceptions of the support provided by spouses when work and family interfere.* Unpublished masters thesis, University of Guelph, Guelph, Ontario, Canada.

Vaux, A. (1985). Variations in social support associated with gender, ethnicity, and age. *Journal of Social Issues, 41*, 89-110.

Weiss, R. S. (1990). *Staying the course: The emotional and social lives of men who do well at work.* New York: Free Press.

Wellman, B. (1981). Applying network analysis to the study of support. In B. H. Gottlieb (Ed.), *Social networks and social support* (pp. 171-200). Beverly Hills, CA: Sage.

Wortman, C. B., & Lehman, D. R. (1985). Reactions to victims of life crises: Support attempts that fail. In I. G. Sarason & B. R. Sarason (Eds.), *Social support: Theory, research and applications* (pp. 464-489). Boston: Martinus Nijhoff.

Yogev, S. (1982). Are professional women overworked: Objective versus subjective perception of role loads. *Journal of Occupational Psychology, 55,* 165-169.

PART III

Characteristics of
Supportive Relationships

9

Everyday Communicative Contexts
for Social Support

MELANIE K. BARNES

STEVE DUCK

When people experience a crisis, however infrequently, however serious or acute, however soluble it ultimately turns out to be, they initially turn to those people with whom they have continuous relationships, rather than to people who are acknowledged experts in solving crises of the type that they are experiencing. While some previous research has focused on the qualities of the support that is enacted or is felt to be received, almost no research to date has looked at two key issues: (a) What are the everyday processes of continuous relationships that enable them to be places to which people turn in times of crisis? and (b) How are these processes conducted? In other words, what is it about the continuity of relationships that makes them safe havens (Leatham & Duck, 1990)? Some researchers have asked what are the mechanisms by which social support affects health and well being (Hobfoll, 1988), and others have asked what are the processes by which social support is delivered (Gottlieb, 1990). We believe that a key element of both questions is the ordinariness of mechanisms by which the basis of social support is sustained and provided. It is this that makes the first two questions become relevant. In this respect, we echo the remarks of Hays and Oxley (1986) that research should also look at the casual socializing of individuals rather than focusing only on the interactions that are directly and purposively supportive or crisis related. However, a research tradition stretching back to Malinowski

(1929) alerts us to the ways in which the daily behaviors of normal life construct and embody larger general principles, whether principles of cultural organization or, as we will claim here, organizational principles that lay the basis for specific management of crises.

Social support (which we define as those behaviors that, whether directly or indirectly, communicate to an individual that she or he is valued and cared for by others) emerges from the everyday behaviors that make up relationships. Everyday encounters thus provide background for any special forms of social support that are needed in a crisis. Furthermore whatever goes on in daily relational life and social support is an enhanced, not necessarily a completely special, set of behaviors fundamentally grounded in normal experience. Thus the routine experiencing of other people during the regular business of personal relationships provides persons with three things: (a) background knowledge and assessments of one another's likelihood of responding when help is required; (b) estimates of the likely capacity of those people to provide what is useful or needed; (c) the styles of interaction that provide a context for informal requests for help to be made both directly and indirectly.

We will first discuss how we believe everyday discourse helps to construct and embody personal relationships as dynamic structures within which social support functions. Next, we will examine how everyday talk operates in a supportive mode within on-going relationships. Then we will discuss this as a context for individuals' transitions from everyday talk to the "crisis" talk that has most often been the focus of research on social support. Finally, we will discuss some of the relational implications for social support and will consider support as part of the regular maintenance of relationships.

Everyday Talk in Relationships

No one who researches the social support or personal relationship fields really believes that the background communicative and relational structure and systems are not relevant to provision of social support in specific cases, but there has been relatively little close analysis of the precise relational background from which social support emerges. Still less have there been strong theoretical efforts that focus on everyday life as a background for the experience of crises. In fact, researchers have recently become more aware of the absence of careful study of the role of talk and conversation in the daily conduct of relationships as a whole (Baxter,

1992; Duck & Pond, 1989; Shotter, 1992) and especially in the study of social support (Leatham & Duck, 1990) and social networks (Duck, 1985; Morgan, 1990).

Researchers have explored variables such as attitude similarity, commitment, negotiation of roles, management of stress, coping, or delivery of everyday social support in relationships without attending to the exact nature of the talk through which such variables are effected in everyday life (but see Albrecht & Adelman, 1987a). Yet an emphasis on language and talk in everyday life "is centrally concerned with the ways in which sociopsychological constructs (attitudes, attributions, norms, identities) are constructed and reconstructed for individuals via interaction" (Giles & Coupland, 1991, p. xii). To this list of interpersonal constructs we would add all the mechanisms involved in the conjunction of the two areas of personal relationships and social support (Duck, with Silver, 1990; Sarason, Sarason, & Pierce, 1990).

Relationships are constructed for individuals during interaction (Duck & Pond, 1989), as are beliefs about partners and estimates of their value as resources. Likewise, Berger and Kellner (1964) who argued that marriage involved the social construction of reality for a couple and—a point that is often overlooked in the discussion of Berger and Kellner's article—such social construction of a "common objectivated reality" occurs *in and through everyday talk*. Thus routine daily activity is a perpetual process of "improvisation" that acts out our understanding of our culture and its relational forms. In this sense, relationships, whether "supportive" or not, are conversations and behaviors as much as they are abstract states of interdependence. It is also very important that research attends to the *enactment* of social constructs. A psychological understanding of major psychological variables does NOT represent them only as disembodied abstract constructs having no conversational implications. Concepts such as "identity management" or "self-disclosure" or "impression formation" or "perception of social support" or "support provision" all operate through daily talk, the very real interactional medium by which they are most often effected or deduced in real life. Talk cannot be relegated to a simple conduit for emotional expression, but is in essence a constructive mechanism through which persons enact their goals, influence others' beliefs, represent their vision of events, and reify the various abstract concepts listed above. Talk, especially everyday conversation between friends and acquaintances, does not simply function to convey social cognition, unreconstructed, from an individual's brain to the outside world, but is a complex process in itself that indexes and constructs the relationship (Giles & Coupland, 1991; Shotter, 1992). Talk is used in significant instrumental and indexical ways to achieve purposes in social interaction beyond the simple expression of psychological structures. People in relationship do a number of things through daily conversation that matter importantly for social support when that becomes necessary. They meet, they talk, they do things together in routine ways and in ordinary circumstances that "traffic in symbols" (Duck, 1994) that indicate the personal value of partners to each other and create expectancies about others' likely responses to requests or willingness to help if asked. Studies suggest that the mere existence of the daily routine encounters of friendship is enough to maintain the relationship and indeed is regarded by people in all manner of relationship types as a fundamental feature of relating (Duck, Rutt, Hurst & Strejc, 1991). One of the things that people do relatively INfrequently is to make direct emotional statements or direct statements of commitment or willingness to support. In social support research, however, the reverse picture is evident: Almost all research focuses on the direct marshaling of support and too little looks at the regular everyday background from which such requests arise (Gottlieb, 1990; Leatham & Duck, 1990).

In addition, relational partners seem to evaluate exchanges between themselves on a symbolic or generalized level rather than on a specific one (Bahktin, 1986; Shotter, 1992). Rather than assessing each transaction in terms of direct rewards and costs alone, individuals also form impressions and general ideas about the *meaning* of such exchanges—meanings that have effects on attitudes toward others and beliefs about relationships. Such deductions are effected all the time as people traffic in symbols, talk about everyday experience, other people and present circumstances or future plans, with the occasional foray into memory and past history of their relationship. While most of this activity is not direct but is symbolic and imprecise, it is nevertheless important. Such symbolic activity simultaneously communicates implicitly the value of each person to the other without direct billboarding of the commitment to or interest in the welfare of the other: These are left implicit in the symbolic content of the interactions. Also implicit and symbolized is the acknowledgment of the concerns of the other person and the problems or issues that confront them in minor ways each day. For example, it requires no great cognitive leap to recognize that friends very often talk to one another about the small concerns that bother each of them and the daily problems that each one faces (Duck et al., 1991). Clearly such discourse provides a context for any discussion or behavioral transactions about specific crises that may arise to cloud their lives. A third item symbolized by the daily routine interaction is the bond between the two persons. Daily discourse, by its regularity, its routineness and mundaneness confirms, reifies and refurbishes the existence of relationships (Duck et al., 1991). All these messages are conveyed by the fact of daily interaction and during the course of daily talk that reaffirms, without being capitalized and underlined, the essence of their relationship. Such normal everyday activity provides the transactional background for social support when it is needed to handle large crises. Also day-to-day experience offers situations where minor advice and consultation can occur without being made major features of the relationship.

We adopt the view that everyday talk creates and constructs a relationship rather than simply transmitting the cognitive contents of one brain to another, as if down a pipeline or conduit. Essentially, this view adopts a different conception of the nature of talk and hence of its role in social support, from that traditionally adopted by those who write as if "communication" were merely the simple exchange of messages between people (Berger, 1993; Duck & Pittman, in press). Because this latter (and, we believe, incorrect) conduit view of communication is widely held in psychology, too little attention has been paid to the functions that talk actually serves for people in real life beyond the transmission of facts from one mind to another (for example, to foster a favorable impression in the mind of the listener; to organize a relationship [e.g., to create a power and control structure]; to construct and validate a conjoint world view; to protect vulnerabilities, Bochner, 1984).

When two people "share joint activities" or "render social emotional care" or "provide practical service" to one another, talk is invariably a part of that whole process and stands in need of attention within the contextualizing effects of those other activities. Indeed it is hard to imagine social behavior without language and talk, even though some writers write as if communication, joint activity, support, and closeness are all conveniently separate actions. Nonetheless, while social behavior is enacted through talk, talk also serves to establish and continue various important backgrounds and contexts against which it becomes possible for persons to make requests, offer assistance and decline support.

Following Duck and Pond (1989), we note that everyday talk embodies relationships through rhetorical means, where overlap of meaning systems is an important consequence (Duck, 1994). Conversations of everyday life have symbolic force for creating, sustaining and manifesting relationships over and above any direct but incidental effects that they may have on the stylistic "shape" or character of the relationship. For example, Duck and Pond (1989) argue that, in their everyday talk, individuals deal with their relationship in symbolic ways that serve to enhance identification between the partners or awareness of similarity of meaning systems as well as projecting the future form of the relationship's continuation. Talk exerts such effects not only directly but also through its style, context, and a variety of other features (Duck & Barnes, 1992).

Thus while everyday talk has important defining characteristics for relationships in general, we believe that everyday talk also has significant implications for social support as it occurs within established relationships. The next section will discuss the ways in which routine conversations influence and affect interactants' perceptions of being supported. It also considers the link between everyday talk and the more intentional processes that are involved in the actual seeking and provision of specific types of support during crisis situations.

Everyday Talk in Social Support

Several researchers have discussed the multiple functions of communication (e.g., O'Keefe, 1988). However, most research has focused on the form of various functions in terms of achievement of known objectives, hence function is construed as "intent" or manifest functions (Merton, 1968). Manifest functions, according to Merton, are "those objective consequences contributing to the adjustment or adaptation of the system which are intended and recognized by participants in the system" (p. 105). Another perspective considers function as "result," for example, what outcomes occur as a function of a particular interaction or series of interactions, whether these results were planned or unplanned. Merton describes these consequences as latent functions, which he specifies as "neither intended nor recognized [by the participants]" (p. 105). Thus while everyday talk functions at both content and relational levels and has instrumental, interpersonal and relational objectives, we propose that everyday talk also implicitly performs six primary latent functions at a supportive level within relationships as presented in Table 9.1.

INFORMATION

First, everyday talk provides *information* and serves to shape people's perceptions about how others view the world (Berger & Bradac, 1982).

TABLE 9.1 Supportive Functions of Everyday Communication

Information	Provides background relational information about potential support providers
Detection	Provides baseline information about typical communication patterns such that, in the presence of unidentified stress, changes in patterns are detected
Ventilation	Provides an opportunity for ventilation regarding routine stressors to prevent escalation
Distraction	Provides distraction from the difficult situation
Perpetuation	Provides continuity in relationships, which increases support availability and greater ease in mobilization of support
Regulation	Provides regulation of face needs within relationships by reducing the severity of potentially embarrassing requests for help

Indeed, while people do engage in conversations regarding values, ideas, and personal beliefs, we suggest that talk about everyday situations also provides a background of information about the degree of similarity in individuals' interpretation of the world. Talk shapes and constructs the meaning systems of people and allows individuals to make assessments about the qualities of potential support providers. For example, a listener "hears" something about the way in which the speaker constructs a picture of adversity and the ways in which it should be faced in general. The speaker may, for example, seem to cast difficulties as externally controlled, or else may adopt a thoughtless or ego-defensive approach to the problem, or alternatively may imply a hidden ability to control and solve problems effectively.

This view notes that impression formation and information processing are not special behaviors. Individuals are regularly receiving and processing information and forming attributions regarding the daily events in their lives, even when the events are rather insubstantial. Most of this information is rapidly processed, in seemingly automatic fashion (Honeycutt, 1993), but nevertheless is stored in memory and is integrated into one's schemata, prototypes or working models of the partner. These internal working models are a means of providing valuable information about the relational context within which everyday "supportive communication" occurs. The regular, routine discourse provides a rich cognitive background against which the other interactions are perceived and evaluated. These interactions. taken collectively, are primary in leading to individual perceptions of the social supportiveness of others (cf. Sarason et al., 1990).

Over and above the specific content of disclosures made by one person to another, then, a speaker inevitably conveys a number of implications and extensions that could be relevant to a hearer's assessment of the value of that person during times of crisis in the future. For example, a person who appears to panic easily or to be unable to take a sensible view of a problem is implicitly conveying a sense of unreliability as a source of help in times of future distress. A person who cannot take charge of his or her own problems or who always blames others for difficulties is likely to be unhelpful as an adviser in times of one's own trouble—however closely one holds them in one's affections.

During discussions around the dinner table, or on coffee break, or while people are walking to and from the workplace, we suggest that people share information "extensively"—that is, in ways that carry implications beyond literal content. Even if unrelated to a stressor or seemingly relatively mundane or routine, such "extensive" comments may lead to interpretations such as "this person sees the world the same way I do," or "this person has a really diverse background and appears to be a creative problem solver," or "this person is a very good listener," or "this person has a unique way of making me laugh and feel good when I'm around him or her" or "this person seems to be very judgmental of others" or "this person is something of a busybody and gossips quite a bit." It is in everyday, routine situations that people acquire much important personal and relational information that can be molded into a developed sense of who would be there to offer "real" support to them in a difficult situation. Clearly such communications provide the basis for others to draw important inferences that will affect their own future behavior toward and reliance on others in times of need (Leatham & Duck, 1990).

Apart from direct assessments of such things derived from experience of the other, just as Berger and Bradac (1982) note in respect to information gathering generally, in the regular interaction of daily life one person may observe another person behaving in relation to third parties. For instance, one may observe an individual solving problems for others, offering advice, or generally structuring problems in ways broadly suggestive of competence or experience. Thus although the information contained in those encounters may not seem to be directly relevant to a particular present personal crisis, it may nevertheless provide important information upon which a person in crisis may rely when the time comes to ask for help for himself or herself. By focusing only on the encounters when help is presently needed, researchers would naturally miss out on this sort of informational context that everyday life conversations provide. The key is to see such conversations as dealing with a broader set of symbols than just the strict and immediate content.

DETECTION

Interaction in casual, routine conversations provides people with baseline information about individual styles of communicating. In this regard, individuals are able to *detect* variances in communicator style that may signal the presence of some difficulty, perhaps even before the verbal disclosure of a problem, for example, nonverbal cues to anxiety, mood swings, depressed stylistic behaviors, monotonous or absorbed self-focus. The relational knowledge that is obtained about another's general talkativeness or style of conversation provides general cues about the person's "standard operating procedure." Thus when there is significant deviation from the norm, the deviation may be a strong, albeit unverbalized, cue that there is some stress or change present. A close partner may notice such rate changes before a specific problem or crisis has ever been mentioned by the person. Eckenrode and Wethington (1990) suggest that because of the nature of everyday shared experiences, problems become more visible to interactants as individuals "detect early 'distress signals' which may generate the support that is needed to cope with stressors at an early stage or allow a person to acknowledge stressors unknown to his or her intimate which were threatening to self-esteem" (pp. 92-93). Thus everyday talk functions as a guide to and a revelation of differences in people's interaction styles.

VENTILATION

Because everyday talk allows *ventilation* of grumbles and complaints or frequently focuses on the regular hassles and disappointments that occur all too often in life, routine discourse functions to allow rapid processing of potentially threatening situations. Some research suggests that the everyday stresses are better predictors of mood and psychological well being than stress which results from major life events or chronic situations (e.g., Eckenrode, 1984). Discussion of these "normal" stresses in a casual manner, as well as direct ventilation of feelings of frustration or disappointment, provides individuals with the opportunity to defuse the emotional outcomes associated with the stressor. In this way, individuals receive informal support in dealing with a routine hazard before it cumulates with others to become major stressors. Ventilation of grumbles also provides chances for the listener to cheer up the speaker (Barbee, 1990) and so defuse the problem. Thus without it being acknowledged directly, the simple presence of the other as a listener when the person is ventilating could have important de-pressuring effects that lead to the person feeling less stressed—without the listener saying a word!

DISTRACTION

Additionally, because everyday talk may primarily be "talk for talk's sake" and NOT focus on any particular stressor, a fourth function of everyday communication is as *distraction* or distancing from existing stressors. Thus everyday talk can defuse stress even when the topic of conversation is not related to the stressor. For example, talk can offer the stressed person with the chance to provide nurturance to *others* (Weiss, 1974), that involves the stressed person in *giving* advice or helping an interlocutor out of personal difficulties. Also it leads to mental engagement with other sets of issues than the stress itself and so enhances the stressed person's sense of an ability to cope with problems while also defocusing the person from his or her own set of difficulties.

Our position contrasts somewhat with that of Barbee (1990) and Barbee, Gulley, and Cunningham (1990), who argue that behaviors such as talking about another topic or talking about something relevant to the helper are seen as "Escape" strategies—for the helper. By implication they suggest that because these strategies are not focusing on the issue that is relevant for the help-seeker, the escape strategies are NONsupportive. While Barbee and associates have focused on behaviors that are supposed to be occurring during "Supportive" interactions, we want to underscore the point that especially during regular interactions, *not* discussing a particular stressor may in fact be seen as supportive and as offering a respite from the situation.

However, in comparing explicit social support with general companionship, Rook (1990) observes that companionship activities, for example, simply spending time with one another and talking with one another, help people "transcend preoccupation with their own imagined or real inadequacies" (p. 228). In addition, Rook (1987) found that shared activities reduced the negative effects of minor life stresses more than overt forms of social support and she suggested that providing "social support" directly may cause the individual to focus more on the potentially unmanageable problems. In addition, engagement in talk unrelated to a stressor may lead to more positive, rather than negative affect, which may serve to alleviate part of the stress. Thus everyday activities and associated routine talk may serve to distract, at least temporarily, the person from his or her problem. Much everyday talk is essentially trivial, light, humorous, playful, and routine (Baxter, 1992; Duck et al., 1991). Thus, even if only temporarily, it is indeed supportive communication according to our earlier definition.

PERPETUATION

Everyday talk functions as a relationship *perpetuation* or maintenance strategy and serves as the grease that helps keep relationships' wheels moving, which in turn serves to sustain a person's sense of being supported. Because of the recollective and reconstructive feature of relationships, individuals are not required to "start at the beginning" with each interaction, but individuals have a knowledge history that brings continuity and cohesion to their lives (Honeycutt, 1993). Celebration of that history and its provision of a sense of comfort about the relationships as a haven of peace often occurs in the course of routine behaviors that sustain relationships (Dainton & Stafford, 1993). Married couples also routinely reported active use of such reminiscing and celebratory conversations when they felt that their relationship stood in hopes of benefiting from conscious maintenance work (Dindia & Baxter, 1987; Baxter & Dindia, 1990). By similar means, everyday talk functions to keep individuals aware of what may seem to be trivial, minute details, but that, when shared, are stored in memory and can be activated and processed in the event that the information becomes relevant, for example, in the presence of an actual stressor (Ross & Holmberg, 1992).

Thus a contextual background for more overt forms of support solicitation is formed through the sharing of the everyday experiences of people's lives through casual talk. Indeed it is now time for social support researchers to credit this provision of personal relationships, just as researchers have granted central importance to shared world views in the establishment and continuance of relationships (Byrne, 1971; Duck, 1994), and have emphasized the notion of such personality support as a provision of relationships (Weiss, 1974).

REGULATION

Finally, everyday discourse allows individuals to discuss minor events in a low-threat situation, without feeling as if they are actually having to deal with the problem or even to solicit or provide support. Thus everyday talk functions as a *regulation* mechanism for the face needs of the interactants (Tracy, Craig, Smith, & Spisak, 1984) and thereby reduces the risks associated with the dilemmas inherent in support seeking and provision (Albrecht & Adelman, 1987b; Fisher, Goff, Nadler, & Chinsky, 1988; Goldsmith, 1992). For example, the act of seeking support or asking for help presents the asker with face needs related to feelings of vulnerability, inadequacy, loss of autonomy, independence or control, and indebtedness (e.g., Tripathi, Caplan, & Naidu, 1986). Everyday, unfocused talk serves to buffer the person from direct addressing of such matters and allows the possibility of testing of the waters before a face-threatening issue is addressed directly. Similarly, Miell (1984) showed that persons who wished to self-disclose engage in some preliminary introduction of the topic before making the self-disclosure. Thus, for example, they would raise a topic in a general way, perhaps with a joking or slighting reference to it and would do so with increased vigilance about the partner's response to the topic. If the partner seemed comfortable with the topic then the would-be discloser returned to the issue after an acceptable gap in the conversation and at that point introduced the real self-disclosure with a greater confidence that the self-disclosure would be inoffensive to the partner and would not lead to rejection. In like manner, everyday talk offers a prologue to any scene that could exhibit any kind of direct dependence.

Another set of dilemmas exists for the support provider who must consider issues such as appearing intrusive or, on the other hand, appearing inadequate or insensitive if unable to provide the desired support (e.g., Chesler & Barbarin, 1984). General management of the processes of conversation thus serves to shield both the "support seeker" and the "support provider" by interpolating "stressless space" into conversations during which each can foreshadow and prepare a response to the face managing needs that will be presented by the declaration of a need for help. Therefore we suggest that within relationships, everyday communication serves to diminish the effects of face threatening acts involving the actual seeking or provision of support and, as a result, is thereby supportive.

Obviously everyday talk also has its limitations, for there are indeed times when individuals have specific needs for various forms of support, such as emotional, informational, tangible, or appraisal support. There will be situations where regular affiliation and simply being with other people may be necessary but are not perhaps sufficient in helping people cope with major life events. It is important for research to focus on these, but not to focus on them alone. Before scholars become too eager to explain the effects of such behavior they should first account for the much larger background and context for such effects that are evident in everyday social chitchat between friends and family members. The relative neglect of this important routine, casual (and occasionally even trivial) background for social support has obscured the range of influences that affect a person's willingness to request support, impressions of who would supply it, and the manner in which it is marshalled. A continuous background of relational communication makes up most of the human experience of the provisions of a relationship and the context of the relationship allows individuals the freedom to mobilize more specific types of support.

The Bridge Between Everyday Talk and "Supportive" Communication

Because this analysis is a new one and its proposal is unestablished, there is as yet no body of research that directly tests its claims. However, there are three types of research into other matters that can be woven together in our argument to illustrate its potential: the body of work on transactions of social support (e.g., Cutrona, Suhr, & MacFarlane, 1990); research on everyday conversation and its functions in relationships as a whole (e.g., Duck et al., 1991); and the investigation of request making in different types of relationships and the management of face (Tracy et al., 1984).

Cutrona, Suhr, and MacFarlane (1990) argue that social support occurs as a transactional process within relationships, and they found that elicitation strategies differed between married couples and college students. Marrieds reported significantly more direct requests for advice, tangible and emotional support from their spouses, while students reported indirect strategies to elicit support from their friends. This difference is also supported by Roloff, Janiszewski, McGrath, Burns, & Manrai (1988) who report that requests from intimates are less elaborate, perhaps because closer relationships have more obligations inherent in them and partners are simply expected to provide help when needed. This suggests that the method of asking for help may differ by type of relationship (Cutrona,

Cohen, & Igram, 1990) and perhaps by the type of stressor with which a person is faced (Eckenrode & Wethington, 1990). For example, the particular stressor may be one that has previously been discussed by the needy person during everyday talk with potential supporters (for example, a recurrent anxiety), and in that case the stressor is likely to be more readily evident to the other people in the network. As some researchers have noted (e.g., Eckenrode & Wethington, 1990), when a stressor is visible, support is frequently offered without having to be elicited and such unsolicited support is considered most satisfying and indicative of a smoothly running relationship. Our fundamental point is that stressors generally become "visible" primarily through the routine interactions of everyday discourse.

However, in some cases a stressor is not readily apparent to those in the network, and so despite the risks associated with support seeking (Goldsmith & Parks, 1990), support may still need to be mobilized. Indeed while routine ordinary conversations may serve to distract a person from his or her problems or may provide opportunities to ventilate feelings of fear or frustration, the stressor may be such that an individual must discuss the situation explicitly. In this case the person needs specific types of assistance, whether emotional, tangible, or in the form of advice or information. The point is not that everyday conversation has "failed" as a supportive mechanism, but that because of the type of situation within which a person finds her- or himself or because of the unpredictable nature of relationships and communication in general, other means of eliciting social support are enacted. This position is congruent with the findings of Conn and Peterson (1989) who showed a positive relationship between the reported seeking of social support and its perceived availability and suggested that support recipients are partly responsible for the support that they receive.

Thus in the wake of a particularly stressful event, individuals must consider those in the social network who would be the most appropriate or effective providers of support (which is determined in part by prior transactions, both everyday and overtly supportive ones), and the manner in which it is most appropriate and effective to garner support, while at the same time considering face needs.

FACE NEEDS

As Tracy et al. (1984) argue, request making is a potentially difficult situation requiring careful face management. Although the work of Tracy and associates focused on the discourse of request making in a compliance gaining setting, their work addresses the role of type of request (or situation generating the request) interacts with the nature of the relationship between the interactants to generate particular types of compliance-gaining strategy. These two factors (situation and relationship) are the two that are central to our discussion here also, so it is of great interest that Tracy et al. (1984) conclude that the "central way in which messages differed by situation and person appeared to be in their attention to face needs of the speaker and partner" (p. 533).

According to Brown and Levinson (1978), individuals have both positive and negative face needs and generally, "people cooperate (and assume each other's cooperation) in maintaining face in interaction, such cooperation being based on the mutual vulnerability of face" (p. 66). "Positive face" is the desire of individuals to be perceived as competent and desirable by others, while "negative face" concerns the desire that individuals be autonomous and unimpeded by others. Brown and Levinson's theory of politeness highlights the tension that results between individuals wanting to maintain a balance between not only their own positive and negative face needs, but also their partner's positive and negative face needs. Especially in the area of making requests, asking for assistance, and subsequently in offering advice or providing other types of support, much daily interaction is concerned with potentially face threatening acts.

Thus face needs are especially relevant in managing the risks of both requesting and offering social support. Those experiencing difficult situations, whether in the form of everyday hassles or severe crises or periods of acute or chronic stress, are presented with a dilemma regarding the manner in which they will maintain that delicate balance of protecting their face needs on the one hand, and the face needs of those in their social network. Those experiencing difficult situations may have a very real need for certain types of assistance but must also work at maintaining their positive face need to appear competent and attractive. Simultaneously they must maintain their negative face by not appearing overly indebted to anyone who offers assistance, whether emotionally or instrumentally. In addition, these same people are concerned about helping to maintain the other's face needs: the positive face need of appearing helpful, empathic and unselfish, and the negative face issue of not having to expend too much time, energy or resources to assist someone else to the extent that it is perceived as constraining by the provider.

Given these considerations, everyday conversation presents many types of communication that differ in style as well as content and the sequential nature of everyday conversations also allows a speaker to build up slowly to requests in a variety of manners. For example, Barbee et al. (1990); Barbee et al. (1993); Derlega, Barbee, and Winstead (this book); and Barnes (1992) have identified four styles of requests that could be embedded into everyday conversation in manners less encrusted with confronting formal requesting than has been studied in the past. These strategies include: Verbal Direct, Verbal Indirect, Nonverbal Direct and Nonverbal Indirect. Communicative behaviors in these categories were defined as follows: *Verbal Direct strategies* are those strategies in which a person directly verbalizes personal feelings or needs for support, for example, "just start talking about it," "verbally telling people face to face." *Verbal Indirect strategies* include hinting, talking about the problem but not directly asking for help, or telling a third party who is expected to relay the information back to the desired person, for example, "create a fictional friend and ask for advice for friend," and "not bluntly ask for help, but tell others how I am stressed." *Nonverbal Direct strategies* include crying, and specific, intentional paralinguistic cues such as facial expressions of "looking upset" or "looking as if they need help." *Nonverbal Indirect strategies* involve demonstrating a noticeable change in the person's "normal" behavioral state such that the individual demonstrates an increase or decrease in perceived baseline emotional states, for example, becoming moody, "following others around," and conversely, acting withdrawn, ignoring people, or being "quiet around people so they [would] help." The primary characteristics that distinguished between the Nonverbal Direct and Nonverbal Indirect strategies were the intentionality and overtness of the behaviors, with the more overt and obviously intentional behaviors being classified as Direct (Barnes, 1992).

The usefulness of such a fourfold typology is that it encompasses the general nature of explicitness and ambiguity which is fundamental in the facework framework and is also embedded in everyday talk. In addition, the modality of the message (verbal or nonverbal) is also relevant because nonverbal messages often are more ambiguous than verbal messages. In everyday conversations people routinely present their concerns, frustrations or anxieties using various types of strategies as a means of managing the face needs of those involved. Perhaps the reason why everyday discourse has heretofore been overlooked as a form of social support is that it is generally an indirect face-maintaining yet effective means of enabling people to feel supported.

Conclusion

It is necessary to consider more rigorously the import of everyday discourse, especially where this permits, by its nature, indirect strategies of support elicitation, when one is considering how individuals actually mobilize support. The trend has been to "jump in" at the mobilization point and disregard all that has happened before that time. What has happened between the participants prior to an actual crisis is just as important as what happens during the crisis. It provides a wealth of information about support availability and the manner in which support should be elicited. Further, the issue of face management explains why certain types of strategies are used in certain types of relationships and with certain types of situations.

We have suggested that in the routine business of daily relating, help is often provided unannounced or in ways that may not be recognized at the time, merely in the discourse that takes place about life in general and the concerns of the persons at the time. Thus two people may discuss a topic that concerns one of them, without any request for help being expressly made and without any offers of help being provided (Glidewell, Tucker, Todt, & Cox, 1982), yet the conversation itself may be instrumental in helping the person face up to and deal with the concern, primarily because of the way in which conversation shapes the person's view of it. Social support then, occurs in a variety of contexts, some of which may be in the direct or indirect marshalling and provision of support, some in strategic, as well as routine interactions, but also in general, everyday conversations. Our definition of social support is more loose than that of other scholars for we believe that social support is any set of behaviors that communicates to a person the knowledge that she or he is valued and cared for by others. Much of this knowledge is communicated through the processes of everyday talk.

References

Albrecht, T. L., & Adelman, M. B. (1987a). *Communicating social support.* Newbury Park, CA: Sage.

Albrecht, T. L., & Adelman, M. B. (1987b). Dilemmas of supportive communication. In T. L. Albrecht & M. B. Adelman (Eds.), *Communicating social support* (pp. 240-254). Newbury Park, CA: Sage.

Bahktin, M. (1986). *Speech genres and other late essays* (Vern W. McGee, trans.). Austin, TX: University of Texas Press.

Barbee, A. P. (1990). Interactive coping: The cheering-up process in close relationships. In S. W. Duck (Ed., with R. C. Silver), *Personal relationships and social support* (pp. 46-65). London: Sage.

Barbee, A. P., Cunningham, M. R., Winstead, B. A., Derlega, V. J., Gulley, M. R., Yankeelov, P. A., & Druen, P. B. (1993). Effects of gender role expectations on the social support process. *Journal of Social Issues, 49,* 175-190.

Barbee, A. P., Gulley, M. R., & Cunningham, M. R. (1990). Support seeking in personal relationships. *Journal of Social and Personal Relationships, 7,* 531-540.

Barnes, M. K. (1992, November). *"How do I tell you what I need?": A typology of support eliciting strategies.* Paper presented at the annual convention of the Speech Communication Association, Chicago, IL.

Baxter, L. A. (1992). Forms and functions of intimate play in personal relationships. *Human Communication Research, 18,* 336-363.

Baxter, L. A., & Dindia, K. (1990). Marital partners' perceptions of marital maintenance strategies. *Journal of Social and Personal Relationships, 7,* 187-208.

Berger, C. R. (1993). Goals plans and mutual understanding in personal relationships. In S. W. Duck (Ed.), *Understanding relationship processes 1: Individuals in relationships* (pp. 30-59). Newbury Park, CA: Sage.

Berger, C. R., & Bradac, J. (1982). *Language and social knowledge.* London: Arnold.

Berger, P., & Kellner, H. (1964). Marriage and the construction of reality: An exercise in the microsociology of knowledge. *Diogenes, 46,* 1-24.

Bochner, A. P. (1984). The functions of human communication in interpersonal bonding. In C. Arnold & J. Bowers (Eds.), *Handbook of rhetorical and communication theory* (pp. 544-621). Boston, MA: Allyn & Bacon.

Brown, P., & Levinson, S. (1978). Universals in language usage: Politeness phenomenon. In E. N. Goody (Ed.), *Questions and politeness: Strategies in social interaction* (pp. 56-395). Cambridge, UK: Cambridge University Press.

Byrne, D. (1971). *The attraction paradigm.* New York: Academic Press.

Chesler, M. A., & Barbarin, O. A. (1984). Dilemmas of providing help in a crisis: The role of friends with parents with cancer. *Journal of Social Issues, 41,* 47-63.

Conn, M. K., & Peterson, C. (1989). Social support: Seek and ye shall find. *Journal of Social and Personal Relationships, 6,* 345-358.

Cutrona, C. E., Cohen, B. B., & Igram, S. (1990). Contextual determinants of the perceived supportiveness of helping behaviors. *Journal of Social and Personal Relationships, 7,* 553-562.

Cutrona, C. E., Suhr, J. A., & MacFarlane, R. (1990). Interpersonal transactions and the psychological sense of support. In S. W. Duck (Ed., with R. C. Silver), *Personal relationships and social support* (pp. 30-45). London: Sage.

Dainton, M., & Stafford, L. (1993). Routine maintenance behaviors: A comparison of relationships type, partner similarity and sex differences. *Journal of Social and Personal Relationships, 10,* 255-271.

Dindia, K., & Baxter, L. A. (1987). Strategies for maintaining and repairing marital relationships. *Journal of Social and Personal Relationships, 4,* 143-158.

Duck, S. W. (1985). How to lose friends without influencing people. In M. E. Roloff & G. R. Miller (Eds.), *Interpersonal processes: New directions in communication research* (pp. 278-298). Newbury Park, CA: Sage.

Duck, S. W. (1994). *Meaningful relationships: Talking, sense, and relating.* Thousand Oaks, CA: Sage.

Duck, S. W. (Ed., with Silver, R. C.). (1990). *Personal relationships and social support.* London: Sage.

Duck, S. W., & Barnes, M. K. (1992). Disagreeing about agreement: Reconciling differences about similarity. *Communication Monographs, 59,* 199-208.

Duck, S. W., & Pittman, G. (in press). Social and personal relationships. In M. Knapp & G. R. Miller (Eds.), *Handbook of interpersonal communication* (2nd ed.). Thousand Oaks, CA: Sage.

Duck, S. W., & Pond, K. (1989). Friends, romans, countrymen, lend me your retrospective data: Rhetoric and reality in personal relationships. In C. Hendrick (Ed.), *Review of personality and social psychology, Vol. 10: Close relationships* (pp. 1-29). Newbury Park, CA: Sage.

Duck, S. W., Rutt, D. J., Hurst, M., & Strejc, H. (1991). Some evident truths about communication in everyday relationships: All communication is not created equal. *Human Communication Research, 18,* 228-267.

Eckenrode, J. (1984). Impact of chronic and acute stressors on daily reports of mood. *Journal of Personality and Social Psychology, 46,* 907-918.

Eckenrode, J., & Wethington, E. (1990). The process and outcome of mobilizing social support. In S. W. Duck (Ed., with R. C. Silver), *Personal relationships and social support* (pp. 83-103). London: Sage.

Fisher, J. D., Goff, B. A., Nadler, A., & Chinsky, J. M. (1988). Social psychological influences on help seeking and support from peers. In B. H. Gottlieb (Ed.), *Marshalling social support: Formats, processes, and effects* (pp. 267-304). Newbury Park, CA: Sage.

Giles, H., & Coupland, N. (1991). *Language in social context.* Milton Keynes, UK: Open University.

Glidewell, J. C., Tucker, S., Todt, M., & Cox, S. (1982). Professional support systems—The teaching profession. In A. Nadler, J. D. Fisher, & B. M. DePaulo (Eds.), *New directions in helping 3: Applied research in help-seeking and reactions to aid* (pp. 189-212). New York: Academic Press.

Goldsmith, D. (1992). Managing conflicting goals in supportive interaction: An integrative theoretical framework. *Communication Research, 19,* 264-286.

Goldsmith, D., & Parks, M. R. (1990). Communicative strategies for managing the risks of seeking social support. In S. W. Duck (Ed., with R. C. Silver), *Personal relationships and social support* (pp. 104-121). London: Sage.

Gottlieb, B. H. (1990). The contingent nature of social support. In J. Eckenrode (Ed.), *Social context of stress* (pp. 112-143). New York: Plenum.

Hays, R. B., & Oxley, D. (1986). Social network development and functioning during a life transition. *Journal of Personality and Social Psychology, 52,* 511-524.

Hobfoll, S. E. (1988). Overview of section on community and clinical. In S. W. Duck (Ed., with D. F. Hay, S. E. Hobfoll, W. Ickes, & B. Montgomery), *Handbook of personal relationships* (pp. 487-496). Chichester, UK: John Wiley.

Honeycutt, J. (1993). Memory structures for the rise and fall of personal relationships. In S. W. Duck (Ed.), *Understanding relationship processes 1: Individuals in relationships* (pp. 60-86). Newbury Park: Sage.

Leatham, G., & Duck, S. W. (1990). Conversations with friends and the dynamics of social support. In S. W. Duck (Ed., with R. C. Silver), *Personal relationships and social support* (pp. 1-29). London: Sage.

Malinowski, B. (1929). *The sexual life of savages*. New York: Harcourt Brace.
Merton, R. (1968). Manifest and latent functions: Toward the codification of functional analysis in sociology. *Social theory and structure*. New York: Free Press.
Miell, D. E. (1984). Cognitive and communicative strategies in developing relationships: Converging and diverging social environments. Unpublished doctoral dissertation thesis, University of Lancaster, UK.
Morgan, D. L. (1990). Combining the strengths of social networks, social support, and personal relationships. In S. W. Duck (Ed., with R. C. Silver), *Personal relationships and social support* (pp. 190-215). London: Sage.
O'Keefe, B. (1988). The logic of message design. *Communication Monographs, 55,* 80-103.
Roloff, M. E., Janiszewski, C. A., McGrath, M. A., Burns, C. S., & Manrai, L. A. (1988). Acquiring resources from intimates: When obligation substitutes for persuasion. *Human Communication Research, 14,* 364-396.
Rook, K. S. (1987). Social relationships as a source of companionship: Implications for older adults' psychological well-being. In B. R. Sarason, I. G. Sarason, & G. R. Pierce (Eds.), *Social support: A transactional view* (pp. 219-250). New York: John Wiley.
Rook, K. S. (1990). Parallels in the study of social support and social strain. *Journal of Social and Clinical Psychology 9,* 118-132.
Ross, M. D., & Holmberg, D. (1992). Are wives' memories for events in relationships more vivid than their husbands' memories? *Journal of Social and Personal Relationships, 9,* 585-604.
Sarason, B. R., Sarason, I. G., & Pierce, G. R. (Eds.) (1990). *Social support: A transactional view.* New York: John Wiley.
Shotter, J. (1992). What is a "personal" relationship? A rhetorical-responsive account of "unfinished business." In J. H. Harvey, T. L. Orbuch, & A. L. Weber (Eds.), *Attributions, accounts and close relationships* (pp. 19-39). New York: Springer-Verlag.
Tracy, K., Craig, R. T., Smith, M., & Spisak, F. (1984). The discourse of requests: Assessment of a compliance-gaining approach. *Human Communication Research, 10,* 513-538.
Tripathi, R. C., Caplan, R. D., & Naidu, R. K. (1986). Accepting advice: A modifier of social support's effect on well being. *Journal of Social and Personal Relationships, 3,* 213-228.
Weiss, R. S. (1974). The provisions of social relationships. In Z. Rubin (Ed.), *Doing unto others* (pp. 21-57). Didgery, NJ: Prentice Hall.

10

Unsupportive Relationships

Deficiencies in the Support-Giving Skills of the Lonely Person's Friends

WENDY SAMTER

Loneliness is typically defined as a lack of satisfying relationships: a discrepancy between ideal and perceived social resources (see Cutrona, 1982; Peplau & Perlman, 1982). Traditionally, research on loneliness has focused on identifying personality and communicative deficits that prevent the lonely person from initiating and maintaining satisfying relationships (see Bell & Daly, 1985; Chelune, Sultan, & Williams, 1980; Jones, Hobbs, & Hockenbury, 1982; Spitzberg & Canary, 1985). More recently, however, researchers (e.g., Jones & Moore, 1989; Stokes, 1985) have begun to investigate how features of the lonely person's social network influence subjective evaluations of loneliness. This work suggests that loneliness is associated with the perception that network members do not provide desired levels of social support.

Many forms of social support have been identified: Individuals may look to supportive others to extend access to information, goods, and services; to enhance control through tangible assistance; or to provide emotional acceptance and assurance (Albrecht, Adelman, & Associates, 1987; House, 1981). Several studies suggest that emotional assurance and acceptance is the type of social support lonely people perceive to be missing in their relationships with others (Jones & Moore, 1989; Sermat & Smyth, 1973). Loneliness has also been found to be related to the perception that network members do not engage in supportive behaviors (Stokes, 1985).

Most social support researchers have looked to objective characteristics of the lonely person's network (e.g., size and density) or skill deficiencies exhibited by the lonely person (e.g., perceptual biases) to explain why individuals do not feel supported in their relationships with others. However, the current chapter raises the possibility that the discrepancy between what lonely individuals want from their relationships and what they actually obtain may lie in the inability of *network members* to provide meaningful social support. In other words, lonely people may be dissatisfied with existing relationships because people with whom they form their relationships neither appreciate nor are skilled at forms of communication functional in providing emotional support and validation to others.

Interestingly, the personality and communicative characteristics that enable network members to engage in supportive forms of behavior have not been investigated in any detail. As noted earlier, most research on the relationship between social support and loneliness has examined either structural characteristics of the lonely person's network or deficiencies exhibited by the lonely person. The chapter begins with a review of this literature. Studies of the communicative correlates of young adult friendship are then summarized in an effort to identify particular forms of supportive communication that may be missing in the relationships of lonely students. A project examining the support-giving skills of the lonely person's peer contacts is presented. Data from this study provide some evidence that the social companions of lonely people neither recognize the importance of supportive communication nor are skilled at producing messages that attend to others' emotional and psychological needs.

Social Support and the Study of Loneliness

FRIENDSHIP, LONELINESS, AND SOCIAL SUPPORT AMONG YOUNG ADULTS

Young adults appear to be particularly susceptible to loneliness. In fact, several studies (e.g., Blau, 1973; Dyer, 1974; Rubenstein & Shaver, 1980) suggest an inverse relationship between age and loneliness, with college students—particularly college freshman—reporting the most loneliness of any group. This finding makes sense given that the transition from high school to college removes young adults from the emotional support of family, friends, and established routines. The task of constructing new relationships that will provide security and comfort is apparently quite difficult for many young adults. In one study of college freshmen (Cutrona, 1982), for example, almost 75% of the students surveyed reported feeling lonely during their first few weeks of college. As the year progressed, however, and new relationships developed, the number of students reporting loneliness significantly declined.

Interestingly, it was the development of new friendships that appeared to be most influential in preventing and/or overcoming loneliness. Cutrona (1982) found that students' satisfaction with current friendships was a better predictor of loneliness during freshman year than satisfaction with family or romantic relationships. Moreover, students who overcame loneliness by the end of freshman year did so because they developed new friendships, not because they initiated romances or maintained close ties with family members (also see Jones & Moore, 1989; Shaver, Furman, & Buhrmester, 1985). Thus, when discussing students who are lonely, the focus is frequently on students who have failed to develop satisfying friendships.

ACCOUNTS OF THE RELATIONSHIP
BETWEEN SOCIAL SUPPORT AND LONELINESS

Two accounts of the relationship between social support and loneliness have been offered. One account, referred to here as the "structural model," maintains that loneliness results from the amount of social support available to the individual. A second account, the "deficiency model," holds that loneliness occurs because the individual lacks skills enabling him or her to perceive, provide, and/or elicit social support.

The Structural Model

Some social support researchers have attempted to explain loneliness in terms of the social network to which the lonely person belongs. The assumption here is that structural features of networks such as size and density may vary as a function of loneliness; thus the amount and frequency of social support available to lonely persons may be less than that available to the nonlonely. Research conducted from the structural perspective has failed to yield a clear pattern of results.

For example, whereas some studies (e.g., Jones & Moore, 1989; Peplau & Perlman, 1982; Russell, Peplau, & Cutrona, 1980; Stokes, 1985) indicate that lonely students have fewer, less integrated social contacts than do nonlonely students, other studies (e.g., Cutrona, Russell & Peplau, 1979; Sisenwein, 1964) show that the lonely and nonlonely do not differ in terms of the size or density of their networks. Research investigating frequency of contact with network members has also yielded inconsistent findings (compare, e.g., Cutrona et al., 1979; Jones, 1981; Peplau & Perlman, 1982; Russell et al., 1980; Shaver et al., 1985).

Although structural characteristics of networks have not been found to vary consistently as a function of loneliness, one thing is clear amidst this array of mixed results: Loneliness is *not* synonymous with being alone. Lonely students have social networks, but whether these networks are smaller, less integrated, and/or less available for interaction is still uncertain.

The Deficiency Model

The deficiency account for the relationship between social support and loneliness has identified three types of deficits that may impact on the lonely person's ability to receive desired levels of social support: perceptual deficiencies (which may cause the lonely person not to recognize support when it is given), deficiencies in the provision of support to others (which may influence the lonely person's ability to form meaningful relationships that could provide support), and deficiencies in the ability to elicit support from others.

Several researchers have found that lonely students perceive and evaluate social encounters more negatively than nonlonely students. Indeed, lonely young adults tend to judge others harshly (Jones, Freemon, & Goswick, 1981), are pessimistic about social affirmation (Brennan & Auslander, 1979), and feel they have little control over social situations (Jones et al., 1981; Moore & Sermat, 1974; Solano, 1980). Such perceptual biases may lead lonely individuals to be skeptical about interaction in general, and thus overlook the positive nature of any particular interaction they encounter. This raises the possibility that lonely students may be involved in networks whose members provide adequate social support, but that such support is not recognized because of perceptual deficiencies on the part of the lonely individual.

Lonely people have also been found to possess several undesirable personality and communicative traits that may minimize the social support they provide to others. These personality and skill deficiencies may result in lonely individuals being unable to establish enduring relationships from which they can draw emotional support. Research indicates, for example, that students who experience loneliness tend to be shy, introverted, anxious, prone to depression, and reticent to engage in face-to-face conversation (e.g., Hojat, 1982; Jones et al., 1981; Richmond, 1984). Loneliness has also been linked to low levels of affiliation with others, less sociability, and the tendency to avoid expressing affection (Jones, 1982). Further, lonely people place less value on communication skills through which support is delivered (Samter & Burleson, 1990).

Albrecht et al. (1987) suggest that the act of seeking social support is often threatening because it challenges the individual's self esteem and sense of control, and because there is the recognition that it may incur costly effects on the relationship. While eliciting social support is thus challenging for most people, it may be especially difficult for lonely students. Young adults who are lonely tend to be passive and have difficulty asking questions of relational partners (see above). In many cases, eliciting social support requires active help-seeking behaviors (see Barbee, Gulley, & Cunningham, 1990)—behaviors lonely students may be unwilling or unable to perform. Also, research suggests that individuals are less likely to ask for support if they think providers will reject them, evaluate them negatively, like them less, or be unreceptive and judgmental toward their emotional displays (see Coates, Wortman, & Abbey, 1979; DePaulo, 1982; Silver & Wortman, 1980). Given their perceptual bent on the social world, lonely people may be particularly prone to these fears.

Summary and Implications

Although the structural and deficiency accounts have furthered our understanding of the relationship between social support and loneliness, they both suffer a significant limitation: Each assumes that members of the lonely person's network are capable of providing sensitive, effective, emotional support. In fact, it is possible that the locus of loneliness is not to be found either in structural features of networks or in the perceptual or behavioral skills of the lonely person, *but rather in the perceptual and behavioral skills of the lonely person's peer contacts.* In other words, one reason lonely students may be dissatisfied with existing friendships is because their friends neither orient to nor are skilled at forms of communication that provide support. In contrast, the nonlonely may have social companions whose attitudes and skills promote rather than detract from the goal of providing sensitive emotional support and assurance, and are thus more likely to be satisfied with the quality of companionship received from the people composing their friendship circle.

The project described subsequently hypothesizes that because supportive communication is the cornerstone of young adult friendship, individuals whose social companions lack attitudes and skills important to the support-giving process will experience poor peer relations and, therefore, greater loneliness than individuals whose social companions do not lack these attitudes and skills. Thus social acceptance and loneliness are investigated here in terms of the communicative characteristics of the friendship circle to which the individual belongs.

SUPPORT GIVING SKILLS
IN THE FRIENDSHIP RELATION

What conveys to another that he or she is being supported? That is, what specific attitudes and communication skills must one's friends exhibit in order for that individual to feel emotionally supported and, therefore, not lonely? Work investigating the communicative correlates of young adult friendship indicates that skills concerned with the management of affect play a key role in determining whether an individual is accepted by his or her peers. Three skills have been identified as particularly important correlates of acceptance and liking: comforting (defined as the ability to alleviate another's emotional distress), conflict management (defined as the ability to manage interpersonal disputes without threatening another's identity), and ego support (defined as the general ability to make others feel good about themselves). As the definitions suggest, each of these skills functions to provide some form of emotional acceptance and/or reassurance. Thus one reason why people with sophisticated comforting, conflict management, and ego support abilities may be liked by their peers is because they are seen as good sources of emotional support (see Samter & Burleson, 1990).

Research thus suggests that within adult friendship, affectively oriented forms of communication such as comforting, ego support, and conflict management allow partners to explore and validate themselves as well as their emotions. Interacting with "friends" who either do not appreciate such communication or who lack skills in these forms of communication may well be frustrating. In other words, lonely people may be dissatisfied with the support they receive from friends because individuals with whom they are friendly neither appreciate nor are skilled at the production of sensitive comforting, conflict management and ego support messages. Thus, in the project described here, comforting, conflict management, and ego support skills were targeted for study because they were believed to represent important types of message behaviors through which emotional support and reassurance are conveyed.[1]

A Study of the Support-Giving Attitudes and Skills of the Lonely Person's Social Companions[2]

PARTICIPANTS AND PROCEDURES

The design of the project called for the use of social systems whose members were sufficiently well acquainted with one another to make judgments about others' likability, social roles, and so forth. This made fraternities and sororities an especially attractive participant pool.[3] Eighty percent or more of the members living in two fraternities and two sororities participated in the study.

Participants completed several written and oral tasks including: (a) Burleson and Samter's (1990) Communication Functions Questionnaire (a measure of communication skill evaluations); (b) assessments of three support-giving skills (i.e., comforting, conflict management, and ego support skill; see Samter, 1989) as well as one instrumentally oriented communication skill (persuasive skill); (c) Russell et al.'s (1980) Revised UCLA Loneliness Scale (a measure of loneliness); and (d) two sociometric tasks (a peer nomination task and a peer rating task, both of which served as the basis for computing individual and group levels of peer acceptance).

IDENTIFICATION OF FRIENDSHIP CIRCLES

As part of the sociometric nomination task, participants were asked to nominate three people in the house whom he or she "most liked" and three people whom he or she "least liked." Because fellow house members constituted the largest and most obvious pool from which participants would draw friends, it was believed that relationships with "most liked others" would be the ones on which individuals judged the quality of their social lives. Thus a participant's friendship circle was defined as the three people whom that individual nominated as his or her most liked others. Indices reflecting the communicative attributes of members composing the friendship circle were derived by computing the mean of these three individuals' scores on various instruments.

Participants were also asked to rate, on a one-to-seven Likert scale, how much they liked each member of their respective housing communities. Together, the peer nomination data and the peer rating data served as the basis for identifying an individual's status within a given social system as well as the status of his/her primary companions. An individual's popularity was computed by summing the number of "most liked" nominations he or she received; an individual's rejection was computed by summing the number of "least liked" nominations he or she received; and an index reflecting the individual's overall likability within the social system was computed by taking the mean of the liking ratings he or she received. Indices reflecting the popularity and rejection of friendship circle were derived by computing the mean number of most liked and least liked nominations received by the three key social companions; the overall likability of the friendship circle was computed by taking the mean liking rating received by these individuals.

RESULTS AND DISCUSSION

Correlations were computed between indices of the individual's loneliness (i.e., his or her score on the UCLA Loneliness Scale) and peer acceptance (i.e., his or her popularity, rejection, and mean liking rating) and the friendship circle's social attributes, communication values, and communication skills. These correlations are presented in Table 10.1. To examine the effects of gender, within gender correlations were also computed and the correlations for males and females were compared with z-tests. Table 10.2 presents the results of this analysis.

Although the magnitudes of the correlations observed in the study were generally weak (see discussion below), there were several theoretically interesting and statistically significant findings. In general results suggested that (a) the lonely person's friendship circle is composed of others who suffer from poor peer relations and who are themselves lonely, (b)

TABLE 10.1 Correlations Between an Individual's Social Acceptance and Loneliness and the Friendship Circle's Social Acceptance, Loneliness, Communication Values, and Communication Skills

Friendship Circle Indices		Individual Items		
	Lonely	Positive Noms	Negative Noms	Liking Rating
Social Acceptance				
Positive Noms	−.04	.03	−.09	.21**
Negative Noms	−.03	.03	.32**	−.11
Liking Rating	−.14*	.03	−.28**	.39**
Loneliness	.15*	−.11	.09	−.25**
Communication Skill Evaluations				
Comforting Rank	−.15*	.05	.07	.10
Conflict Mgt Rank	−.02	.05	−.04	.05
Ego Support Rank	−.04	.12*	.18**	.01
Conversation Rank	.04	−.18**	−.06	−.17**
Persuasion Rank	.01	.10	−.09	.02
Comforting Rate	.08	.07	−.05	−.06
Conflict Mgt Rate	−.02	.06	−.08	−.03
Ego Support Rate	−.02	.01	−.13*	.03
Conversation Rate	−.05	.16**	−.05	.24**
Persuasion Rate	−.11	.04	−.09	.19**
Communication Skills				
Comforting Skill	.05	−.02	−.15*	−.07
Conflict Mgt Skill	.14*	.01	−.06	−.14*
Cel Ego Skill	.07	−.00	−.04	−.10
Enc Ego Skill	.17**	−.05	.06	−.16**
Persuasive Skill	.16**	−.01	.05	−.03

NOTE: *N*s range from 182 to 196
*$p < .05$; **$p < .01$

communicative characteristics of the lonely person's friendship circle differ from communicative characteristics of the nonlonely person's friendship circle, and (c) the relationship between features of the friendship circle and an individual's social acceptance and loneliness is somewhat influenced by gender.

TABLE 10.2 Gender Differences in Correlations Between an Individual's Social Acceptance and Loneliness and the Friendship Circle's Communication Values and Communication Skills

	Individual Items							
	Lonely		Positive Noms		Negative Noms		Liking Rating	
Friendship Circle Indices	M	F	M	F	M	F	M	F
Communication Skill Evaluations								
Comforting Rank	−.07	−.12	−.01	−.02	−.04[a]	.22*b	.06[a]	−.25**b
Conflict Mgt Rank	−.05	.07	.06	−.01	−.10	.01	.05	−.06
Ego Support Rank	−.12	.09	.18*	−.03	.19*	.13	−.13	.02
Conversation Rank	−.07	.03	−.18*	−.12	−.09	.00	−.09	−.08
Persuasion Rank	.01	−.06	.18*	.06	.02[a]	−.22*b	.05	.18*
Comforting Rate	.02	.02	.15	.09	.02	−.08	−.06	.18*
Conflict Mgt Rate	.08	−.14	.01	.18*	.02	−.16	−.17*a	.19*b
Ego Support Rate	.06 −	.11	.02	.06	−.06	−.19*	−.06[a]	.20*b
Conversation Rate	.04	−.03	.15	.14	−.04	−.09	.11	.22*
Persuasion Rate	−.01	−.06	−.10	.06	−.26**a	.02[b]	.09	.01
Communication Skills								
Comforting Skill	.07	−.11	.06	.06	.01[a]	−.31**b	.12	.14
Conflict Mgt Skill	.04	.10	.14	−.01	.06	−.16	−.04	.04
Cel Ego Skill	−.06	.05	.06	.04	−.07	.04	.15	−.06
Enc Ego Skill	.05	.16	.03	−.04	.09	.10	−.02	−.07
Persuasive Skill	−.03[a]	.27**b	.02	−.02	.08	.03	−.05	.04

NOTE: Ns = 99 for males and 97 for females. For each pair of correlations, entries with different superscripts significantly ($p < .05$) differ by the z-test for independent correlations. *$p < .05$; **$p < .01$

Relationships Between the Friendship Circle's Social Acceptance and Loneliness and an Individual's Social Acceptance and Loneliness

The strongest and most consistent relationships observed in the study were those between indices tapping the friendship circle's acceptance and loneliness and the level of acceptance and loneliness experienced by the individual. In general, these relationships reflect the truism that "birds of a feather flock together." For example, an individual's loneliness score was significantly correlated with the average loneliness score of his or her primary social companions, suggesting that feeling isolated was a shared phenomenon. An individual's social acceptance was also dependent, in part, on the extent to which members of his or her friendship circle were accepted within the larger peer group. People who were liked within fraternities and sororities came from friendship circles whose members received high mean liking ratings and low rejection scores. On the other hand, individuals who were rejected by fellow house members had social companions who received high numbers of disliked nominations and low mean liking ratings. This pattern indicates that lonely individuals were not accepted within the larger community and drew their friends from a pool of others who were not accepted. Thus the extent to which an individual's social companions experienced positive peer relationships (and subsequent satisfaction with those relationships) predicted the extent to which that individual also enjoyed positive peer relationships.

Relationships Between the Friendship
Circle's Communication Skill Evaluations
and an Individual's Social Acceptance and Loneliness

Burleson and Samter's CFQ was used to assess participants' communication skill evaluations. This instrument asks individuals to rate how important it is for same-sex friends to exhibit behaviors reflecting support giving skills (e.g., comforting, conflict management, and ego support), instrumentally oriented communication skills (e.g., persuasion), and conversational skill. The CFQ also asks subjects to rank order descriptions of these communication skills in terms of their overall importance to same-sex friendship. Average ratings and rankings assigned by the friendship circle were correlated with individual levels of acceptance and loneliness. There were few significant correlations, but those that were present indicated that the communication skills social companions valued in the friendship relation played a significant role in participants' levels of acceptance and loneliness. Participants who were liked by peers and/or satisfied with their relationships had social companions who placed a high premium on the comforting and conversational skills of friends. On the other hand, individuals who were disliked by peers and/or dissatisfied with their relationships had companions who devalued the importance of comforting and conversational skills in the friendship relation.

As Burleson and Samter (1990) argue, communication skill evaluations can be viewed as expressing fundamental conceptualizations of the friendship relation. The types of skills friendship circle members perceive to be important indicate something about how those individuals define friendship, what they see as key elements within friendship, and the standards they expect friends to uphold. Prior research suggests that the provision of emotional support is a key feature of adult friendship; moreover, it is presumably through sensitive conversations that such support is conveyed. Thus it makes sense that individuals whose social companions valued comforting and conversational skill were more accepted and more satisfied with their relationships than individuals whose companions did not value these support-giving abilities.

Positive evaluations of support-giving skills suggest that members of a social circle viewed both the provision of emotional acceptance and the activity of talk as key features of same-sex friendship. Social companions who valued these forms of communication saw friendship in a manner consistent with other young adults—namely, as a relationship rooted in and defined by talk centering on emotional support. However, social companions who did not value these skills may have seen friendship in a somewhat different way. Defining friendship in unusual and perhaps inappropriate ways may not have been appreciated by the larger peer group, and it was apparently not satisfying for individuals whose companions' skill evaluations reflected this tendency.

Some surprising findings were observed among the relationships between the friendship circle's communication skill evaluations and individuals' levels of acceptance and loneliness. Companions' rankings of ego support were positively related to an individual's positive and negative nominations ($r = .12$, $p < .05$, $r = .18$, $p < .01$, respectively); because a low ranking meant the skill was valued, these correlations indicate that individuals whose social companions valued ego support skill were more likely to reject (and less likely to be accepted) by their peers. Similarly, a positive correlation was observed between an individual's mean liking rating and his/her social companions' evaluation of persuasive skill ($r = .19$, $p < .01$); this suggests that the friendship circle's favorable evaluation of persuasion predicted the extent to which students were seen as generally likable within their respective housing communities. As will be discussed later, these two findings are largely attributable to gender differences in the relationship between companions' evaluations of communication skills and the relational quality an individual experiences.

Relationships Between the Friendship
Circle's Communication Skills and an
Individual's Social Acceptance and Loneliness

In the current study, communication skills were assessed by asking participants to respond to three hypothetical situations for each of the three support-giving skills (i.e., comforting, conflict management, and ego support skill). For example, one situation designed to elicit comforting messages asked participants how they would respond to a friend who had just been dropped by the person he or she had been seeing for a long time.

For each communication skill, responses to the hypothetical situations were content analyzed using hierarchically structured coding systems. The systems for coding conflict management and ego support were developed specifically for use in this study (see Samter, 1989). The systems for coding comforting and persuasive responses were adapted from other work; they were chosen because of extensive evidence documenting their reliability and validity (see Burleson, 1987).

Surprisingly, the support-giving communication skills of friendship circle members did not play a very significant role in the quality of relationships individuals experienced. In fact, results indicated that students whose friends exhibited relatively sophisticated conflict management and encouraging ego support abilities were *less* well liked and experienced *greater* loneliness than students whose friends were not skilled in these domains.

Other relationships observed between the friendship circle's communication skills and the individual's acceptance were, however, in the expected direction. For example, the friendship circle's comforting skill was inversely associated with the number of negative nominations individuals received ($r = -.15$, $p < .05$). This suggests that students rejected by the peer group were more likely to come from friendship circles whose members exhibited poor comforting skills than were students accepted by their peers.

Interestingly, a significant correlation was observed between friendship circle's persuasive ability and individual loneliness. This indicates that students whose social companions had fairly advanced persuasive abilities experienced more loneliness than students whose social companions were less skilled in this domain. As predicted, then, being friendly with people whose skills reflected an instrumental (as opposed to supportive) orientation to relationships was dissatisfying for students.

Gender Differences in the Relationship Between
the Friendship Circle's Communication Skills and
Values and an Individual's Social Acceptance and Loneliness

Compared to women, men place less emphasis on the intimacy, trust, reciprocity, and mutual support they receive from friends (see Winstead, 1986). Werking, Samter, and Burleson (1989) observed that although men and women both valued friends' affectively oriented communication skills, women placed even greater emphasis than men on the skills of comforting, conflict management, and ego support. Thus it seemed reasonable to examine whether friends' support-giving skills were more important to the quality of relationships women enjoyed (i.e., to their acceptance and loneliness) than to the quality of relationships men enjoyed.

As Table 10.2 indicated, several relationships observed between individual acceptance and loneliness and the values and skills of men's friendship circles were significantly different from relationships observed between individual acceptance and loneliness and the value and skills of women's friendship circles. For women, the friendship circle's evaluations of comforting and ego support skill were positively associated with peer acceptance. Relationships between the friendship circle's evaluations of these skills and peer liking were not observed for men. A similar pattern was reflected in the communication skills women's social companions actually exhibited. While a lack of comforting skill within the friendship circle predicted the number of disliked nominations women received, it was unrelated to the number of disliked nominations men received. Finally, positive evaluations of conflict management skill were inversely related to peer liking for men but positively associated with peer liking for women. Thus women appear to be largely responsible for the present results linking individual acceptance to the friendship circle's support-giving abilities.

In contrast, companions' evaluations of persuasion predicted relational success for men but spelled relational rejection for women. Men whose social companions did not perceive persuasion as an important skill for same-sex friends to possess were *less* well liked than men whose companions did attend to persuasion as a relevant feature of friendship. Women's evaluations of persuasive skill, however, demonstrated the opposite pattern. Given this pattern, it was not surprising to find that women whose social companions were skilled in the actual production of persuasive messages experienced loneliness; for men, however, loneliness was not predicted by the friendship circle's level of persuasive skill. These findings are consistent with studies suggesting that the worlds of male and female friendship may be somewhat different. Researchers (e.g., Aries & Johnson, 1983; Williams, 1985; Wright, 1982) investigating what young adults expect from and do with their friends have found that men typically organize their same-sex relationships around the sharing of activities; women, on the other hand, typically organize their same-sex relationships around the sharing of affect and support. Thus it makes sense that women's acceptance was predicted by being part of a social group that valued and was skilled at producing supportive messages, whereas men's acceptance was predicted by being part of a group that valued persuasion (a more instrumental or activity-based form of communication).

Summary and Conclusions

The project reported in this chapter was undertaken to examine whether the social and communicative attributes of an individual's friendship circle predict the extent to which that individual is accepted and, therefore, satisfied with the quality of companionship he or she receives. Because emotional support is a central feature of young adult friendship, it was believed that students would experience more loneliness when their companions neither appreciated nor were skilled in the production of support-giving messages. In general, this expectation was confirmed. Results indicated that the social ties lonely students do have are likely to be with others who are themselves lonely and rejected. Moreover, individuals with whom the lonely person is friendly appear to be relatively unconcerned with attending to others' psychological and emotional needs. There is some indication, then, that the communicative characteristics of an individual's friendship circle can be used to predict his or her levels of acceptance and loneliness.

Obviously, the project reported here has several significant limitations. Most notably, drawing participants from *social organizations* may have led to the exclusion of acutely lonely people in the current sample. However, the fact that statistically significant correlations did emerge is encouraging; the relationships observed here may actually underestimate those that actually exist in the general population. Subsequent studies examining how support giving features of the friendship circle influence individual loneliness and acceptance should utilize samples with a more representative range of loneliness scores.

In spite of this limitation, however, the data do suggest three broad implications for future work examining the relationship between social support and loneliness. First, the call for studies investigating what Jones and Moore (1989) term the "interpersonal correlates" of loneliness has largely fallen on deaf ears; little work has examined how qualitative features of the lonely person's social network influence subjective evaluations of loneliness. Results from the current project provide some evidence that the discrepancy between what lonely people want from their social relationships and what they actually obtain lies in the inability of network members to recognize and/or provide meaningful emotional support. Utilizing qualitative features of networks to predict an individual's social attributes appears, then, to be a viable approach to studying the relationship between social support and loneliness. Future work utilizing this approach should continue to examine not only what transpires between friends during supportive interactions, but how such interactions shape the relational quality of people's lives.

Comforting, conflict management, and conversational skills were particularly important forms of supportive communication for students in the current study. The companions of people who experienced loneliness did not recognize the importance of these forms of support in the friendship relation, nor were they skilled at producing messages that attended to others' psychological and emotional needs. This suggests that although lonely people may indeed perceive and respond more negatively to the social world than nonlonely people, they have good reason to do so.

Lonely people may have less to be happy about in their relationships with others—in particular, they may not receive the kind of support from their friends that reassures them of their worth, validates their identities, or helps them work through difficult emotional crises. It is not surprising, then, that loneliness coincides with rejection by the larger peer group. In the absence of sensitive emotional support from others, lonely people may be unable to work through stresses and disappointments which, in turn, may cause them to behave in ways that are unappreciated by their peers. In a very real way, then, it can be said that responses to the social world vary as a function of loneliness because *the nature of the social world varies as a function of loneliness.*

Finally, results from the present study suggest that the "friendships" lonely people do maintain may actually perpetuate the cycle of loneliness in which an individual gets caught. Most young adults not only believe emotional support is a key feature of friendship, but organize many of their interactions around the provision of emotional reassurance and support. This was not the case for lonely students—their companions were themselves rejected and lonely, failed to recognize the importance of attending to others' emotional needs, and were less able to produce messages through which support could be conveyed.

Thus lonely students not only maintained ties with others who, like themselves, experienced poor relational quality, but these ties were organized around conceptualizations and behaviors that departed from the norm. Although research (e.g., Cobb, 1976) indicates that some companionship is better than no companionship, being "friendly" with people whose ideas and behaviors reflect inappropriate assumptions about the nature of friendship may hinder the lonely person from developing skills that would ultimately allow him or her to establish relationships from which some satisfaction could be gained.

Given the pragmatic implications of these results, future studies should continue to explore how support giving features of social networks influence subjective impressions individuals form of their social relationships. Such work may well prove useful in further illuminating the causes and consequences of loneliness and in providing a foundation for constructing programs designed to help those who lack satisfying relationships.

Notes

1. It is important to note that the logic underlying this study does not preclude a "deficit model" of the relationship between social support and loneliness. It is recognized that individuals may contribute to their own loneliness by bringing to their relationships communicative attributes that prohibit them from providing emotional support to others and, thereby, from establishing successful peer relationships. However, it is suggested here that *in addition* to his or her own deficiencies, the lonely person may be part of a group of individuals who themselves are unliked and lonely and who lack attitudes and skills relevant to the support giving process. Put simply, lonely people may be friendly with others who are deficient in support giving forms of communication and, therefore, suffer from poor peer relations and subsequent feelings of loneliness.

2. Portions of this study were previously reported in Samter (1992).

3. In retrospect, the character of the subject sample used may have contributed to the surprising pattern of null results obtained in this study. The sociometric procedures employed in the current project required that participants be drawn from intact social systems. Fraternities and sororities were thus chosen because of their "closed" nature—a nature that ensured participants would be sufficiently well acquainted to make informed evaluations of one another. It is possible that the social nature of these organizations led to fewer cases of acute loneliness than would have been observed in the more general population of college students. Thus

the current sample may have had lower levels of loneliness as well as a truncated range of loneliness scores. Consistent with this interpretation, several researchers (e.g., Cutrona, 1982; Russell et al., 1980) have reported mean loneliness scores for their college samples ranging from 40 to 44; for the sample in this study, the mean loneliness score was 34.68 (*SD* = 7.57).

References

Albrecht, T. L., Adelman, M. B., & Associates. (1987). *Communicating social support.* Newbury Park, CA: Sage.

Aries, A., & Johnson, F. L. (1983). Close friendship in adulthood: Conversational content between same-sex friends. *Sex Roles, 9,* 1183-1196.

Barbee, A. P., Gulley, M. R., & Cunningham, M. R. (1990). Support seeking in personal relationships. *Journal of Social and Personal Relationships, 7,* 531-540.

Bell, R. A., & Daly, J. A. (1985). Some communicator correlates of loneliness. *The Southern Speech Communication Journal, 50,* 121-142.

Blau, Z. (1973). *Old age in a changing society.* New York: New Viewpoints.

Brennan, T., & Auslander, N. (1979). *Adolescent loneliness: An exploratory study of social and psychological pre-dispositions and theory.* Unpublished manuscript, Behavioral Research Institute, Boulder, CO.

Burleson, B. R. (1987). Cognitive complexity. In J. C. McCroskey & J. A. Daly (Eds.), *Personality and interpersonal communication* (pp. 305-349). Newbury Park, CA: Sage.

Burleson, B. R., & Samter, W. (1990). Effects of cognitive complexity on the perceived importance of communication skills in friends. *Communication Research, 17,* 165-182.

Chelune, G. J., Sultan, F. E., & Williams, C. L. (1980). Loneliness, self-disclosure, and interpersonal effectiveness. *Journal of Counseling Psychology, 27,* 462-486.

Coates, D., Wortman, C. B., & Abbey, A. (1979). Reactions to victims. In I. Frieze, D. Bar-Tel, & J. S. Carroll (Eds.), *New approaches to social problems* (pp. 21-58). San Francisco, CA: Jossey-Bass.

Cobb, S. (1976). Social support as a moderator of life stress. *Psychosomatic Medicine, 38,* 300-314.

Cutrona, C. E. (1982). Transitions to college: Loneliness and the process of social adjustment. In L. A. Peplau & D. Perlman (Eds.), *Loneliness: A sourcebook of current theory, research, and therapy* (pp. 291-309). New York: John Wiley.

Cutrona, C. E., Russell, D. W., & Peplau, L. A. (1979, August-September). *Loneliness and the process of social adjustment: A longitudinal study.* Paper presented at the meeting of the American Psychological Association, New York.

Damon, W. (1977). *The social world of the child.* San Francisco, CA: Jossey-Bass.

DePaulo, B. M. (1982). Social-psychological processes in informal help seeking. In T. A. Wills (Ed.), *Basic processes in helping relationships* (pp. 255-279). New York: Academic Press.

Dyer, B. M. (1974, Spring). Loneliness—There's no way to escape it. *Alpha Gamma Delta Quarterly,* pp. 2-5.

Hojat, M. (1982). Loneliness as a function of selected personality variables. *Journal of Clinical Psychology, 38,* 136-141.

House, J. S. (1981). *Work stress and social support.* Reading, MA: Addison-Wesley.

Jones, W. H. (1981). Loneliness and social contact. *Journal of Social Psychology, 113,* 295-296.

Jones, W. H. (1982). Loneliness and social behavior. In L. A. Peplau & D. Perlman (Eds.), *Loneliness: A sourcebook of current theory, research, and therapy* (pp. 238-252). New York: Wiley-Interscience.

Jones, W. H., Freemon, J. E., & Goswick, R. A. (1981). The persistence of loneliness: Self and other determinants. *Journal of Personality, 49,* 27-48.

Jones, W. H., Hobbs, S. A., & Hockenbury, D. (1982). Loneliness and social skills deficits. *Journal of Personality and Social Psychology, 42,* 682-689.

Jones, W. H., & Moore, T. L. (1989). Loneliness and social support. In M. Hojat & R. Crandall (Eds.), *Loneliness: Theory, research, and applications* (pp. 145-156). Newbury Park, CA: Sage.

Moore, J. A., & Sermat, V. (1974). Relationship between loneliness and interpersonal relationships. *Canadian Counselor, 8,* 84-89.

Peplau, L. A., & Perlman, D. (Eds.) (1982). *Loneliness: A sourcebook of current theory, research and therapy.* New York: Wiley-Interscience.

Richmond, V. P. (1984). Implications of quietness: Some facts and speculations. In J. A. Daly & J. C. McCroskey (Eds.), *Avoiding communicating* (pp. 145-156). Beverly Hills, CA: Sage.

Russell, D. W., Peplau, L. A., & Cutrona, C. E. (1980). The revised UCLA loneliness scale: Concurrent and discriminant validity evidence. *Journal of Personality and Social Psychology, 39,* 472-480.

Samter, W. (1989). *Communication skills predictive of interpersonal acceptance among college students in a group living situation: A sociometric study.* Unpublished doctoral dissertation, Purdue University, West Lafayette, IN.

Samter, W. (1992). Communicative characteristics of the lonely person's friendship circle. *Communication Research, 19,* 212-239.

Samter, W., & Burleson, B. (1990). Evaluations of communication skills as predictors of peer acceptance in a group living situation. *Communication Studies, 41,* 311-326.

Sermat, V., & Smyth, M. (1973). Content analysis of verbal communication in the development of a relationship: Conditions influencing self-disclosure. *Journal of Personality and Social Psychology, 26,* 332-346.

Shaver, P., Furman, W., & Buhrmester, D. (1985). Transition to college: Network changes, social skills, and loneliness. In S. W. Duck & D. Perlman (Eds.), *Understanding personal relationships: An interdisciplinary approach* (pp. 192-219). Beverly Hills, CA: Sage.

Silver, R., & Wortman, C. (1980). Coping with undesirable life events. In J. Garder & M. Seligman (Eds.), *Human helplessness: Theory and applications* (pp. 279-340). New York: Academic Press.

Sisenwein, R. (1964). *Loneliness and the individual as viewed by himself and others.* Unpublished doctoral dissertation, Columbia University.

Solano, C. H. (1980). Two measures of loneliness: A comparison. *Psychological Reports, 46,* 23-28.

Spitzberg, B. H., & Canary, D. J. (1985). Loneliness and relationally competent communication. *Journal of Social and Personal Relationships, 2,* 387-402.

Stokes, J. P. (1985). The relation of social network and individual difference variables to loneliness. *Journal of Personality and Social Psychology, 48,* 981-990.

Werking, K. J., Samter, W., & Burleson, B. R. (1989). *Gender differences in the perceived importance of communication skills in same-sex friends: Two studies.* Unpublished manuscript, Department of Communication, Purdue University, West Lafayette, IN.

Williams, D. G. (1985). Gender, masculinity-femininity, and emotional intimacy in same-sex friendship. *Sex Roles, 12,* 587-600.

Winstead, B. A. (1986). Sex differences in same-sex friendship. In V. J. Derlega & B. A. Winstead (Eds.), *Friendship and social interaction* (pp. 81-100). New York: Springer-Verlag.

Wright, P. H. (1982). Men's friendships, women's friendships and the alleged inferiority of the latter. *Sex Roles, 8,* 1-20.

Youniss, J. (1980). *Parents and peers in social development.* Chicago: University of Chicago Press.

11

Beyond the Ties That Bind

Exploring the "Meaning" of
Supportive Messages and Relationships

KATHERINE MILLER

EILEEN BERLIN RAY

Over the past two decades, communication scholars have devoted increasing attention to the study of social support. This research has generally taken either an individual- or network-level approach to the study of supportive communication and has spanned the interpersonal, organizational, and health communication contexts. At the individual, or micro level, social support researchers have examined the perceived reception or availability/accessibility of support and focused on support functions and sources. At the network, or macro level, characteristics of ongoing relationships of support networks have been emphasized.

Although these bodies of work add to our understanding of the role of communication in the support process, they suffer from several weaknesses (see Ray, 1993). First, at the individual level, research has emphasized the perception of support by recipients. What has not been considered is the specific messages that generate these perceptions. Second, at the network level, research has not considered shared meanings of supportive or unsupportive communication among network members and how these meanings may influence various outcomes.

This chapter addresses these weaknesses by focusing on the *meaning* of supportive communication. Specifically, it recommends two additional approaches for the study of social support. These techniques—memorable messages and semantic networks—add new conceptualizations and methods to the study and understanding of the role of communication in social support.

Current Approaches
to the Study of Social Support

STUDYING SOCIAL SUPPORT
AT THE INDIVIDUAL LEVEL

The majority of social support research has been conducted at the individual level of analysis, and typically the approach used is one that highlights the importance of perceptions of support on the part of the recipient. For example, Albrecht and Adelman (1987), in discussing the communication of social support, note that "meaning does not reside in the message exchanged but in the perceptual processes of each participant" (p. 21). Thus many researchers conclude that an action or interaction is not supportive unless it is understood as such, and thus, have concentrated efforts on the investigation of receiver perceptions.

Within this general category of research, however, there are widespread differences in research strategy. For example there is a large body of research that considers the *functions* that support can play in alleviating stress. This body of research began with the notion that different types of stress could be most effectively dealt with through different kinds of support (see, e.g., Cobb, 1976). In the last 15 years, extensive work has considered this notion of "matching" support to stress, and recently Cutrona and Russell (1990) have proposed a "theory of optimal matching" that provides an integration of previous work on support functions.

Other researchers studying perceived support at the individual level eschew functional approaches and propose that social support is better conceptualized as a general "sense of acceptance" (Sarason, Pierce, & Sarason, 1990, p. 109). These researchers note that operationalizations of support functions are often highly intercorrelated (Sarason, Shearin, Pierce, & Sarason, 1987) and further recognize that self-reports of perceived support are relatively consistent over time. Thus it is argued that individuals develop "working models" of social support in which "people who believe they have something positive to contribute to relationships are confident that others will find them to be desirable relationship partners" (Pierce, Sarason, & Sarason, 1990, p. 182).

Finally, other support researchers have differentiated among *sources* that are available to provide support for an individual. For example, occupational stress has been studied through a consideration of the different types of support received from supervisor and from coworkers. Others have considered the extent to which kin and non-kin sources of support may be differentially effective.

Thus at the individual level, we have concentrated on recipient *perceptions* of support, though distinctions are often made in terms of the function that support serves or the source from which support is received. One continuing shortcoming of this approach is that it is difficult to know what behaviors or messages lead individuals to the perception of support (at either a functional or general level).

To answer these complex questions, one recent move has been toward the investigation of support messages. For example, Cutrona and her colleagues (Cutrona & Suhr, 1992; Cutrona, Suhr, & MacFarlane, 1990) have conducted studies in which college students or married couples are asked to provide support in a stressful situation. Through these investigations, we are beginning to understand what support really looks and sounds like and what particular categories of messages lead to satisfaction with support interaction. However, this line of work still leaves questions unanswered, as the situations in which support is provided are at least partially contrived and the messages provided are coded by individuals outside of the support-provision situation. Thus to a large extent we still don't know what counts as support in "real life" stressful situations and for the "real life" recipients of the support.

STUDYING SOCIAL SUPPORT
AT THE NETWORK LEVEL

A second prevalent approach to the study of social support has roots in the sociological study of networks. The connection between social support and social networks perhaps began with Cassel's (1974) epidemiological work investigating the relationship between the social environment and vulnerability to disease. Gottlieb (1981) sums up this work, noting, "Cassel's main legacy rests on the two lines of ecological inquiry he spurred: inquiries devoted to analyzing how people's interactions with the social environment conspire to augment their vulnerability to illness and disease, and how social forces can be mobilized in these situations for the sake of health protection" (p. 23).

Since this early work, theorists and researchers have been attracted to the notion of social support networks. The underlying assumption has been that network relationships provide the infrastructure in which social support can be provided. Gottlieb (1985) has categorized this work as the "mezzolevel of analysis" in which the focus is on the structure and supportive functions of relationships within a social network.

It should be noted, however, that the social network concept has been applied with varying levels of exactitude. Hall and Wellman (1985) have argued that many researchers embracing the support network concept have done so only at a metaphorical level and have "ignored the battery of available concepts and methods" (p. 33). There has also been considerable variance in research techniques among those who *do* use network techniques.

Regardless of the intricacy of research technique, however, network approaches to social support have several weaknesses. First, researchers have found consistently low correlations between characteristics of social networks and individuals' *perceptions* of support (Cutrona, 1986; Sandler & Barrera, 1984; Vaux & Harrison, 1985). Given the widespread acknowledgment of the primacy of perceived support in the prediction of positive social and health outcomes, this finding is troubling. As Pierce, Sarason, and Sarason (1990) note, "this conclusion suggests the need to incorporate the assessment of qualitative, as well as quantitative, aspects of personal relationships" (p. 176).

In a related vein, network approaches to support rarely acknowledge the possible *dysfunctions* of network participation and network relationships. There is little doubt that not all relationships are positive ones, and it is unreasonable to assume that all network ties are equally supportive (Ward, Sherman, & LaGory, 1984).

In sum, then, the network perspective has provided us with a means to look at the structured milieu in which support can be enacted. However, it is clear that a concentration on the mere "existence" of network structure tells us very little about how individuals interpret the web of relationships in which they interact. Further, unless we know more about the meaning imbued in these relationships, it is impossible to make inferences about which relationships have the potential for providing meaningful support.

Meaning and Social Support

The preceding sections of this chapter have reviewed two dominant approaches to the study of social support: the individual-level investigation of perceived support and the network-level investigation of social support structures. Neither of these approaches has yet fully excavated the notion of "meaning" in the context of social support. For example, at the individual level, we know that perceptions of emotional support can be helpful in dealing with stressful life events. However, we know little about what particular messages are interpreted as meaningful support, and even less about the influence of contextual and individual factors on the interpretation process. Similarly, at the network level, we know that some relationships lead to the perception that meaningful support is available and some do not. However, we know little about the interpretive process through which some network linkages are perceived as meaningful support conduits and others are not.

In the next two sections of this chapter, we propose two approaches to the study of social support that have thus far been underutilized. These approaches make the notion of *meaning* central to research.

THE INDIVIDUAL LEVEL: MEMORABLE SUPPORT MESSAGES

As noted earlier, most researchers who study social support at the individual level concentrate their efforts on recipient *perceptions* of support, be those perceptions of received support, available support, or a generalized sense of acceptance. At this point, however, theorists and researchers are still exploring the antecedents of perceptions of support.

Cutrona and her colleagues have turned their attention to actual support interaction, positing that "certain *regularities* or *recurring interaction patterns* can be identified that characterize relationships from which individuals derive a psychological sense of support" (Cutrona, Suhr, & MacFarlane, 1990, p. 31, emphasis in original). A somewhat different tack is taken by Sarason et al. (1990), who advocate a reconceptualization of perceived support as a "sense of acceptance" that is developed through early life relationships. "[E]arly primary relationships lead an individual to develop a sense of acceptance that reflects the extent to which the individual believes that he or she is loved, valued, and accepted by significant others" (Sarason et al., 1990, p. 119).

Thus two attempts made so far to explain perceptions of support are somewhat at odds with each other. Sarason, et al. take the "long view" in considering the impact of early life events on the formation of a stable sense of acceptance. Cutrona and her colleagues take the "short view" by considering actual behavioral manifestations of support in interactions (though they acknowledge that multiple supportive interactions are necessary for the development of support perceptions). Both of these approaches have great promise for explaining the process through which support perceptions are created.

However, it is likely that there is some middle ground that needs to be considered between the "long view" of early life relationships and the "short view" of specific support interactions. This "middle ground" lies not in childhood relationships or in day-to-day interaction, but in the consideration of messages that make a special impact on individuals—those messages that are remembered and lead people to believe that support has been provided and that there are people they can count on in the future should support again be needed.

Knapp, Stohl, and Reardon (1981) originated the use of the term "memorable message." In their exploratory study of messages remembered by a sample of students and parents, they found that most memorable messages were rule-oriented, cliché-like injunctions designed to solve a personal problem. Memorable messages tended to be offered at times of uncertainty, in private settings, by sources of higher status. Thus these researchers conceptualized memorable messages as verbal communications long-remembered by recipients, delivered at times of uncertainty in recipients' lives, and perceived by recipients as significantly influencing their lives.

Though Knapp et al. did not explicitly link the notion of memorable messages with social support, such a connection can be made on a number of levels. First, like social support, memorable messages are provided at times of uncertainty. As Knapp et al. (1981) note, "the message usually occurs at a time when the person is seeking help" (p. 40). Second, like social support, memorable messages can serve a variety of functions. "The subject matter concerns such personally important issues as one's self-concept, getting along with others, and performing effectively on the job" (Knapp et al., 1981, p. 40). Third, like social support, memorable messages constitute a base which can be drawn on later in times of stress. "Regardless of how they are constructed or recalled, an important part of the memorable nature of these messages is the perceived applicability of the verbalized formula to the person's current social and emotional needs" (Knapp et al., 1981, p. 36).

There have been several recent research efforts that have pointed to the importance of specific remembered messages in the perception of social support. The most well-developed of these research areas is the work by Dunkel-Schetter (1984) and Dakof and Taylor (1990). These researchers have considered the special support context experienced by victims of cancer, and built on the theoretical framework developed by Wortman and Dunkel-Schetter (1979, 1987). As Dunkel-Schetter (1984) notes, "the experience of cancer represents a paradoxical circumstance: Social support is potentially a strong resource for adjusting to cancer, yet reaction to the disease can interfere with support's provision" (p. 81). Within this context, Dunkel-Schetter (1984) and Dakof and Taylor (1990) investigated the specific types of behaviors and messages that were remembered as "helpful" and "unhelpful." These researchers found that different message sources were remembered as being particularly helpful in the provision of particular kinds of support. For example, Dakof and Taylor (1990) note that "intimate others are clearly most valued for the esteem/emotional support they provide . . . Cancer patients and physicians, however, are more valued for the information role they are able to serve" (p. 86).

This line of research has been helpful in pointing out the importance of "remembered" support, in emphasizing that actions intended as supportive can be viewed as both helpful and unhelpful, and in delineating the importance of message sources in social support provision. However, this research has still dealt with general *categories* of support rather than particular messages that are remembered as helpful or unhelpful.

One study that has considered the specifics of message content, context, and provision was performed by Lyles and Miller (1992). This study involved interviews with college students. The students were asked to recall "something someone had said that has had an important effect on their lives." Follow-up open-ended and closed-ended questions inquired about the context in which the message was delivered, the source, and the perceived supportiveness of the message when it was delivered and in retrospect.

Lyles and Miller (1992) found, not surprisingly, that memorable support messages were most often sent at times of stress and transition by higher status sources (usually parents, in this sample). This study, however, also considered the content of the memorable support messages through independent coding of the messages reported. Several interesting findings emerged. First, this study found that perceptions of support changed over time as cliché-like messages (e.g., "When life gives you a lemon, make lemonade") were proven true through experience. Second, this study found that messages perceived as the most supportive were those that bolstered self-esteem in a manner that was *unconditional* (e.g., "Whatever you do, we will back you up; whatever choices you make, we'll support them").

We are currently working on a further application of this approach in the study of memorable messages recalled by cancer survivors during the diagnosis, treatment, and recovery phases of their illness. There are several goals of this study. One is to examine the changing support needs of cancer patients as they move through the various phases of the cancer experience. A second goal is to examine specific messages that are perceived as particularly supportive or unsupportive. For example, though we know that communication of "acceptance" is critical, we know little about what friends, families, or health care professionals can *say* to communicate such acceptance. Thus we hope to gain finely-grained information about what messages are supportive and unsupportive (and from who these messages are received) as a cancer patient progresses through various illness phases.

THE NETWORK LEVEL:
SEMANTIC NETWORKS

Studies of social support networks rely almost exclusively on the investigation of relationships that are defined either in terms of a formal role (e.g., spouse, kin, friend, acquaintance, etc.) or in terms of interaction (e.g., amount of communication in a given week). Thus researchers often implicitly assume that relationships defined through role or through interaction are, indeed, supportive relationships. This implicit assumption is the basis of two additional points that must be reiterated about the network approach: (a) researchers have consistently found *low* levels of correspondence between network indicators of support and perceived support, and (b) researchers have typically ignored the impact of relational dysfunction (e.g., conflict, misunderstanding, relational de-escalation) on social support networks.

Given these problems in the network approach, it is important to find a way to build the notion of *meaning* into the study of support networks. Pierce et al. (1990) have labeled this as studying the "qualitative" as well as the "quantitative" aspects of social relationships. Wills (1985) has advocated a study of the supportive "functions" of relationships. Regardless of the labels used, however, what seems critical is to move away from a "conduit" metaphor for social support in which the mere existence of a link is assumed to provide access to social support. We must move, instead, to a consideration of the types of links most likely to serve as transmitters of support. We believe that one useful avenue for investigating the efficacy of various support conduits is through the study of semantic networks.

Monge and Eisenberg (1987) introduced the notion of "semantic network" to the study of organizational communication as a response to criticisms that the study of networks in the organizational context had traditionally ignored content, meaning, and interpretation. They proposed

> expanding the notion of network linkages to include not only the presence or intensity of interaction, but also the degree of understanding (do the communicators share a common symbol-referent system?) and agreement (do they agree in opinion on the topics being communicated about?). (p. 333)

Thus a semantic network consists not of linkages based on formal roles or interaction patterns, but linkages based on shared meaning and interpretation. Two people are "connected" in a semantic network not if they talk to each other or have a formal relational connection, but rather if they hold similar interpretations for important shared symbols. A "dense" semantic network is not one in which all network members talk to all others, but one in which there is a high degree of convergence among communicators about the content being communicated.

Monge and Eisenberg (1987) suggested the study of semantic networks in the organizational setting through a combination of content analytic and network analytic techniques.

> Individuals could be provided with key vocabulary, slogans, or stories, and asked to provide their interpretations; interpretations could be analyzed via content analysis, as could the degree of overlap of interpretations. Linkages would be defined in terms of degree of overlap or convergence of interpretations . . . We would call the resultant configuration a *semantic* network. (p. 333)

There are several arguments to support the importance of the study of semantic networks in the study of social support. First, a great deal of research has emphasized the importance of shared context in the provision of support. For example, Ray (1987) argues that support in the organizational context can be best provided by coworkers and supervisors because of shared understandings regarding the workplace. She notes:

> Talking about stress with people who share the same organizational context can provide a valuable coping mechanism (Albrecht & Adelman, 1984) and help to alter members' perceptions of potentially stressful events (McLean, 1985). They share common organizational referents that nonmembers do not, enabling a shared code a value system (Katz & Kahn, 1978). (p. 174)

A second argument for the importance of semantic networks in the study of social support stems from Burleson's (1990) recent application of the literature on comforting to the field of social support. Burleson argues, following past critiques of the network approach, that "relationships themselves are not directly supportive (or unsupportive)" (p. 66) but that "it is specific actions that one relational partner carries out on behalf of the other partner that provide support" (p. 66). Burleson goes on to argue that individuals who are effective in providing *comforting* messages will be perceived as most supportive.   .

Burleson defines comforting behaviors as "those messages having the goal of alleviating or lessening the emotional distresses experienced by others" (1990, p. 68). He discusses an extensive body of research that has demonstrated that individuals who have high levels of cognitive complexity produce messages that exhibit more concern for the recipient's feelings and perspective. Further, he considers research that has demonstrated the efficacy of these messages in relieving the distress of others.

The relevance of this area of research for the consideration of semantic networks is found in the emphasis it places on factors that influence the production of comforting messages. The work of Burleson and his colleagues emphasizes the importance of cognitive complexity in the production of sophisticated support messages. However, there are probably variables other than cognitive complexity that might predict the production of messages that exhibit concern for the recipient's feelings and perspective. One of these variables may well be the degree to which an individual indeed *shares* or *understands* that perspective. This notion of shared meaning and perspective is, of course, at the heart of the semantic network approach. Thus we would argue that individuals who are connected in a semantic network will have the ability to produce more effective support messages through their shared understanding of the recipient's situation.

Although the semantic networks concept is relatively new, there have been several applications that point to its possible importance in the investigation of meaning and interpretation in social situations. Eisenberg, Contractor, and Monge (1988) provided an initial investigation of semantic networks in the organizational context, and found that perceived convergence of meaning sometimes exceeded actual levels of convergence, and that the degree of perceived convergence (e.g., shared meaning) was positively correlated with organizational commitment.

In the social support context, we recently investigated the role of semantic networks in perceptions of social support among employees of a nursing home (Miller & Ray, 1992). This study was highly exploratory in nature, and data collection methods did not allow for a complete consideration of the role of semantic convergence in the social support process. However, this study of perceived support, stress, and organizational meaning within a nursing home suggests that the semantic network concept holds some promise for further investigation of social support.

Through an evaluation of employee meanings for key organizational concepts (respect, good working environment, and quality care), we found that employees formed "subcultures of meaning." For example, one group of individuals were *idealists* in that their meaning for the concept of respect revolved around the concepts inherent in the "Golden Rule." These individuals were characterized by the perception of low levels of coworker support and low levels of client depersonalization. In contrast, a group of *realists* interpreted the respect concept as meaning "self-respect." Though these individuals perceived higher levels of coworker support, they also exhibited higher levels of client depersonalization. Thus, even in this exploratory study, the meaning groups revealed through semantic network analysis exhibited differential patterns of perceived support. Clearly, a next step in this research would be to explore nature of support messages produced by individuals within these semantic groups.

Summary and Conclusions

In this chapter we have argued that traditional individual- and network-level approaches to the study of social support fail to fully embrace the importance of *meaning* within the social support process. We proposed two concepts developed within the field of communication—memorable messages and semantic networks—that should be useful for investigations of the meaning inherent in support messages and the importance of shared meaning within the infrastructure of relationships that provide support.

The concept of *memorable messages* highlights the fact that support messages live on in memory, and that recalled messages can provide both informational and emotional support and the assurance that there are others we can turn to in times of need. An initial investigation of memorable support messages (Lyles & Miller, 1992) suggests that perceptions of the supportiveness of messages change over time, that memorable support messages are received from predictable sources, and that supportive messages have identifiable content characteristics. Thus it appears that the investigation of memorable messages may hold great promise for the consideration of meaning within social support messages.

The semantic network approach also appears to hold promise. With the semantic network approach, we move from a consideration of meaning in messages to meaning within relationships. It seems natural to expect that social support can be best communicated among individuals who share interpretations of key symbols, and our initial investigation of support within a nursing home (Miller & Ray, 1992) would suggest that this is true.

In sum, we believe that it is only through a consideration of shared and remembered meaning that we can fully understand the process through which social support is provided and interpreted. The investigation of memorable messages at the micro level and semantic networks at the macro level will contribute to our understanding of these aspects of meaning. However, we should emphasize that no single theoretical or methodological approach will allow us to fully consider the importance of meaning in the support process. Rather, it is critical that we remain open to alternative means of conceptualizing and interpreting social support if we are to move to a level in which the "meaning" of support becomes clear.

References

Albrecht, T. L., & Adelman, M. B. (1984). Social support and life stress: New directions for communication research. *Human Communication Research, 11*, 3-32.

Albrecht, T. L., & Adelman, M. B. (1987). *Communicating social support.* Newbury Park, CA: Sage.

Burleson, B. R. (1990). Comforting as social support: Relational consequences of supportive behavior. In S. Duck (Ed., with R. Silver), *Personal relationships and social support* (pp. 66-82). London: Sage.

Cassel, J. (1976). The contribution of the environment to host resistance. *American Journal of Epidemiology, 104*, 107-123.

Cobb, S. (1976). Social support as a moderator of life stress. *Psychosomatic Medicine, 38*, 300-314.

Cutrona, C. E. (1986). Objective determinants of perceived social support. *Journal of Personality and Social Psychology, 50,* 349-355.

Cutrona, C. E., & Russell, D. W. (1990). Type of social support and specific stress: Toward a theory of optimal matching. In B. R. Sarason, I. G. Sarason, & G. R. Pierce (Eds.), *Social support: An interactional view* (pp. 319-366). New York: John Wiley.

Cutrona, C. E., & Suhr, J. A. (1992). Controllability of stressful events and satisfaction with spouse support behaviors. *Communication Research, 19,* 154-174.

Cutrona, C. E., Suhr, J. A., & MacFarlane, R. (1990). Interpersonal transactions and the psychological sense of support. In S. Duck (Ed., with R. Silver), *Personal relationships and social support* (pp. 30-45). London: Sage.

Dakof, G. A., & Taylor, S. E. (1990). Victims' perceptions of social support: What is helpful from whom? *Journal of Personality and Social Psychology, 58,* 80-89.

Dunkel-Schetter, C. (1984). Social support and cancer: Findings based on patient interviews and their implications. *Journal of Social Issues, 40,* 77-98.

Gottlieb, B. H. (Ed.) (1981). *Social networks and social support.* Beverly Hills, CA: Sage.

Gottlieb, B. H. (1985). Social support and the study of personal relationships. *Journal of Social and Personal Relationships, 2,* 351-375.

Hall, A., & Wellman, B. (1985). Social networks and social support. In S. Cohen & S. L. Syme (Eds.), *Social support and health* (23-41). Orlando, FL: Academic Press.

Katz, D., & Kahn, R. L. (1978). *The social psychology of organizations.* New York: John Wiley.

Knapp, M., Stohl, C., & Reardon, K. (1981). "Memorable" messages. *Journal of Communication, 31,* 27-41.

Lyles, J. S., & Miller, K. I. (1992). *Memorable messages as social support.* Paper presented at the annual meeting of the Speech Communication Association, Chicago.

McLean, A. A. (1985). *Work stress.* Reading, MA: Addison-Wesley.

Miller, K. I., & Ray, E. B. (1992). *Shared meaning and social support: A semantic networks approach.* Paper presented at the Sunbelt Social Networks Conference, San Diego, CA.

Monge, P. R., & Eisenberg, E. M. (1987). Emergent communication networks. In F. M. Jablin, L. L. Putnam, K. H. Roberts, & L. W. Porter (Eds.), *Handbook of organizational communication* (pp. 304-342). Newbury Park, CA: Sage.

Pierce, G. R., Sarason, B. R., & Sarason, I. G. (1990). Integrating social support perspectives: Working models, personal relationships and situational factors. In S. Duck (Ed., with R. Silver), *Personal relationships and social support* (pp. 173-189). London: Sage.

Ray, E. B. (1987). Supportive relationships and occupational stress in the workplace. In T. L. Albrecht & M. B. Adelman (Eds.), *Communicating social support* (pp. 172-191). Newbury Park, CA: Sage.

Ray, E. B. (1993). When the links become chains: Considering dysfunctions of supportive communication in the workplace. *Communication Monographs, 60,* 106-111.

Sandler, I. N., & Barrera, M., Jr. (1984). Toward a multimethod approach to assessing the effects of social support. *American Journal of Community Psychology, 12,* 37-52.

Sarason, B. R., Pierce, G. R., & Sarason, I. G. (1990). Social support: The sense of acceptance and the role of relationships. In B. R. Sarason, I. G. Sarason, & G. R. Pierce (Eds.), *Social support: An interactional view* (pp. 97-128). New York: John Wiley.

Sarason, B. R., Shearin, E. N., Pierce, G. R., & Sarason, I. G. (1987). Interrelations of social support measures: Theoretical and practical implications. *Journal of Personality and Social Psychology, 52,* 813-832.

Vaux, A., & Harrison, D. (1985). Support network characteristics associated with support satisfaction and perceived support. *American Journal of Community Psychology, 13*, 245-268.

Ward, R. A., Sherman, S. R., & LaGory, M. (1984). Subjective network assessments and subjective well-being. *Journal of Gerontology, 39*, 93-101.

Wills, T. A. (1985). Supportive functions of interpersonal relationships. In S. Cohen & S. L. Syme (Eds.), *Social support and health* (23-41). Orlando, FL: Academic Press.

Wortman, C. B., & Dunkel-Schetter, C. (1979). Interpersonal relationships and cancer. *Journal of Social Issues, 35*, 120-155.

Wortman, C. B., & Dunkel-Schetter, C. (1987). Conceptual and methodological issues in the study of social support. In A. Baum & J. Singer (Eds), *Handbook of psychology and health* (pp. 63-108). Hillsdale, NJ: Lawrence Erlbaum.

12

The Role of Relationship Characteristics in the Provision and Effectiveness of Supportive Messages Among Nursing Professionals

SANDRA METTS

PATRICIA GEIST

JULIE L. GRAY

The perceived availability of social support from others, both within and outside the work environment, has been identified as an important element in the ability of nurses to cope with the variety of stressful circumstances that characterize that occupation (Allanach, 1988; Cronin-Stubbs & Rooks, 1985; Jennings, 1990; Smythe, 1984). Most research on this topic views support "effectiveness" as the degree of correspondence between respondent perceptions of available support and global measures of emotional exhaustion, depression, or burnout. Little attention has been directed to features of the interactional context that might influence the dynamics of support attempts and their effectiveness in reducing stress.

An interactional level of analysis is an important alternative to traditional practices (Leatham & Duck, 1990). Certainly, the sense of being integrated in a supportive network is a critical component in the ability to cope with stress. However, the utility of assessing global perceptions of support is limited. Indeed, cautions expressed by Gottlieb (1985) toward the study of social support generally might also be expressed toward research conducted on social support in the nursing profession. He argues that the psychological perspective does not "gauge actual or experienced support that is expressed in ongoing social interactions" but rather taps into a "cognitive representation of the phenomenon whose correspondence with social reality is uncertain" (p. 356). It is imperative to begin systematic investigation of elements in the "social reality" that contribute to successful support attempts and subsequently to overall assessments of support availability.

The Relationship as a Context for Social Support

Current work indicates that the process of providing situated social support is exceedingly complicated and challenging. A theme increasingly evident in the literature is that the supportive interaction is a problematic episode characterized by several dilemmas (Albrecht & Adelman, 1987). The potential for negative consequences and relational strain are in direct proportion to the severity of the stress and complexity of the support needed. To seek support is to make oneself vulnerable to inept, ineffectual, and sometimes painful support attempts (La Gapia, 1990) and to possible loss of "face," reputation, or sense of competence (Goldsmith, 1992). To provide support is effortful; it requires understanding the problem and its severity, assessing the type of support that would be most appropriate, and the ability and motivation to construct the messages that accomplish the intention (Silver, Wortman, & Crofton, 1990). Most important, this must all be accomplished without inadvertent messages of resentment, or disregard for the integrity of the recipient (La Gapia, 1990). Ironically, even the best intended support efforts can be problematic. Witness, for example, gifts of money to a person who seems distressed over inadequate financial resources being perceived by the recipient as indications of his or her financial incompetence.

The study presented here is a first attempt to sort out the role of what we believe to be a fundamental component of the social reality that gives pattern and form to support episodes: the nature of the relationship between the provider and recipient. Specifically we assess both the type of support received and the effectiveness of these support attempts for work-related problems in two types of episodes: one in which the support is offered in a formal or professional relationship and one in which the support is offered in an informal or personal relationship. Furthermore, we assess relationship quality in both types of relationships and incorporate it as a variable into a larger model comparing predictors of support effectiveness in work and nonwork relationship episodes.

This approach treats relationship type and quality as antecedent variables with frequency and perceived effectiveness of the support attempt as the outcome variables. We recognize that this is not an orientation typically reflected in the literature. The more common perspective is to view interaction quality as having a summative effect on perceptions of the supportiveness in the relationship. This is illustrated in Cutrona, Suhr, and MacFarlane's (1990) argument that certain regularities in interaction patterns lead to an individual's perception of which relationships in his or her network are supportive.

Although it is certainly true that perceptions of relationship quality are derived from interpretations of interactions, it is also true that relationship categories (e.g., father or husband; supervisor or lover) and relationship quality create an interpretive framework within which messages are understood. In a particularly apt rendering of this mutual transformation, Bradac (1983) refers to language and relationships as "theoretical entities with mutual entailments." In marriage, for example, "hidden agendas" (e.g., beliefs that one's partner is seeking domination, or fears that one's partner does not feel love) lead individuals to "hear" neutral messages as consistent with the controlling agenda (Krokoff, 1990). In work relationships where personal knowledge of other is more limited, individuals use role-related knowledge to judge the presumed intent of a message (Bradac, 1983). Criticism from a supervisor, for example, is generally considered appropriate, whereas criticism from a coworker is not. In the latter instance, interpretation of the criticism is more complicated in that nonrole information must be inferred to explain the motivation for and intent of the criticism. If the affective quality of the relationship is generally supportive and positive, the criticism will probably be heard as constructive; if the affective quality is generally nonsupportive and suspicious, the criticism might be heard as competitive or antagonistic.

We assume that a similar logic operates during episodes involving social support attempts. Setting aside the question of effectiveness for a moment, we reason that contextual constraints being as they are, some types of support will occur more commonly at work than outside of work, at least in a relative sense. That is, in most work relationships personalized information is limited but professional knowledge is shared in common and physical/task needs are obvious. We would expect instrumental and informational support to be more common than other forms of support and to be more frequent at work than at home. Provisions of tangible support are easy for the recipient to observe and to reciprocate; they are a practical medium of exchange in noncommunal, equity-oriented relationships. For informal and personal relationships where work-related problems are not visible or immediate, but where personalized knowledge is greater, we would expect that more person-specific, and emotionally sophisticated support is likely to be offered for work-related problems. Thus, emotional/nurturant support should be more common than other forms of support and should be relatively more common in nonwork support episodes than work episodes.

Returning to the question of effectiveness, however, we do not believe that the relative frequency of support messages is an adequate measure of their effectiveness in reducing stress. In fact, the empirical literature addressing the issue of effectiveness is problematic. The prevailing designs tend to study relationship and type of support independently rather than together. Although both show a strong correlation with global measures of effectiveness (e.g., symptoms of occupational burnout), the relative contribution that types of support make to effectiveness for interactions occurring within each type of relationship is not clear. In addition, little attention has been given to the differences in affective quality of relationships that are aggregated because they are structurally or categorically similar. As Leatham and Duck (1990, p. 14) note, labels such as coworker, friend, or spouse "could very well be the most significant dimensions, but could also be misleading. It seems both an unlikely assumption and a naive one, akin to the one made by workers in personal relationships who have constantly assumed that the existence of a certain type of relationship is a sufficient condition for deducing its quality."

We review below several studies that have examined the effectiveness of various conceptualizations of social support among nursing professionals. Although none of these studies measures effectiveness as an outcome of a specific support episode, they do provide inferential evidence that some forms of supportive messages are more effective in reducing stress than others. Moreover, careful reading of these studies indicates that supportive actions are not isomorphic with relationship quality. Finally, we review those studies concerned with the relative effectiveness of support provided by work relationships compared to nonwork relationships.

TYPE OF SUPPORT AND EFFECTIVENESS

A consistent finding in the nursing literature is that the domain of support efforts known variously as nurturant support, emotional support, esteem support, affect support and the like are more highly correlated with burnout and its symptoms (chronic stress, depression, and exhaustion) than is the domain of support efforts known as tangible assistance, instrumental aid, and informational support. For example, Cronin-Stubbs and Rooks (1985) found that affect support (composed of expressing liking, admiration, respect, or love) predicted lower levels of burnout among critical care nurses in comparison to other types of support, including affirmation (recognition by others and evaluation of correctness of actions), and aid (assistance with money, objects, time, and information).

Norbeck (1985) combined the affect and affirmation scales into a single scale that she labeled emotional support. She correlated this scale along with the aid scale (labeled tangible support) and a "work support" scale with outcome measures of job stress, job dissatisfaction, and psychological symptoms. She found that although all were correlated with job stress and psychological symptoms, work support evidenced a particularly strong association (24.4% of the variance) with job stress. The items that comprise this scale are worth noting: "How much can you talk about your work with this person?" "How much does this person help you to relax or re-energize after work?" Although Norbeck labeled these items work support, we think a case could be made that this scale is more clearly a measure of relationship quality than it is a measure of a particular type of social support. It seems to reflect a degree of openness and comfort characteristic of a satisfying relationship. To the extent that this is true, Norbeck's study provides evidence that the quality of the relationship is an important element in the support process, either as a main effect or as a moderating variable.

Additional evidence that some measures of support may be tapping into relationship quality is found in a study of nursing staff perceptions of their superior's support effectiveness by Firth, McIntee, McKeown, and Britton (1986). Both a measure of esteem support called Personal Respect (e.g., "Does actually thank people for things they have done") and a measure of emotional support called Empathic Attention (e.g., "Interrupts others a great deal") were perceived to be important components of a superior's support effectiveness. In addition, Personal Respect was correlated with reduced role ambiguity and reduced exhaustion.

Of particular interest here, however, are three other scales in the original questionnaire. These three scales proved to be problematic in this study because they showed little or no agreement among the staff in terms of ratings of a targeted superior. These were Absence of Interpersonal Defensiveness (e.g., "Readily gets defensive when any criticism is implied" and "Avoids answering questions directly"), Absence of Indignation or

Impatience (e.g., "Takes offense at remarks made to them"), and Concern for Feelings ("Their concern for me is obvious"). In reference to the lack of agreement on these dimensions, Firth et al. (1986, p. 278) note that although some aspects of a charge nurse's behavior seem to be exhibited consistently across staff members and contexts, there are other aspects "which are either more specific to interactions with particular staff, or which are largely reflections of subordinates' own perceptions." This suggests that although training or social scripts enable superiors to demonstrate support-related behaviors that can be recognized as such by staff persons, the quality of the individual relationships remain very much a distinguishable feature of the support system. Whether this quality then affects the way supportive messages are "heard," and therefore their effectiveness in reducing stress or facilitating the coping process, is a question that motivated our research.

TYPE OF RELATIONSHIP AND EFFECTIVENESS

A second area of research on support effectiveness concerns the influence of type of relationship on perceived effectiveness of support attempts. Although there is a common tendency to assume that work relationships have a greater impact on effectiveness (when measured as burnout and related symptoms) than personal relationships, the association is not without qualification. In direct comparisons of both sources, some studies confirm the importance of work relationships, some find personal relationships to be more influential, and some find no significant difference (compare Boyle, Grap, Younger, & Thornby, 1991; Constable & Russell, 1986; Lees & Ellis, 1990).

Although these studies attest to the importance of work-related support, they may or may not be valid indicators of whether attempts to provide support at work for specific work-related problems or stressors is more effective than attempts to provide support for these same problems or stressors outside of work. Some researchers argue that support received in personal relationships is more beneficial than that received in work relationships, primarily because it tends to have greater breadth. Albrecht and Adelman (1987), for example, argue that "of the range of supporters available, it appears that those with whom we have the closest interpersonal ties are also those whom we depend on for the broadest scope of supportive interactions" (p. 36). Whether this claim is valid for work-related problems has not been adequately tested. Moreover, the very connectedness that facilitates the support function in close relationships may intensify the influence that negative relationship quality has in support effectiveness. Personal relationships become enmeshed and complex; efforts from conflicted or ambivalent relationships may not function as support at all, but as a source of stress. As Sarason, Pierce, and Sarason (1990, p. 117) characterize the dilemma: "the help or emotional support that comes from a conflict-filled relationship may exact a price high enough to vitiate its positive qualities" and extract an emotional price that the recipient doesn't want to pay.

In sum, we find the social support literature to be inconclusive for our purposes and in some ways quite muddled. It is difficult to determine the role of structural and interactional variables in the support process when support messages are confounded with relationship quality and when outcome measures of effectiveness are global perceptions of undifferentiated interactions. We are not the first to comment on the confusion in the social support area. Sarason et al. (1990) have noted the confusion over conceptualizations of support and Gottlieb (1985) has pointed to the limitations in current measures of support in psychological rather than transactional terms. Our intent therefore is not to voice criticism but begin systematic exploration of support episodes based on what can be reasonably abstracted from existing literature.

HYPOTHESES

With this in mind, we pose three hypotheses. First, we predict that the distribution of types of support offered to nursing professionals will be constrained by structural and relational factors associated with the type of relationship in which the support is offered. Specifically, work relationships should provide proportionately greater tangible assistance and nonwork relationships should provide proportionately greater emotional support.

Second, in terms of effectiveness, we make two predictions. We expect that emotional support will be perceived as more effective than other forms of support, regardless of relationship type. Although this is based primarily on findings from global measures, Cutrona and Suhr (1992) found that ratings of satisfaction with a particular conversation between married couples were positively correlated with the number of emotional support messages produced during the conversation. (Informational support was also correlated with satisfaction, but only when the recipient felt unable to control the event.) In addition, we also expect that the association between emotional support and effectiveness will be more sensitive to relationship quality in nonwork relationships than in work relationships.

A Study of Relationship Influences
on the Types and Effects of Social Support

PROCEDURES AND PARTICIPANTS

Questionnaires were mailed to 1,000 nurses randomly selected from lists provided by the California State Board of Registered Nurses and the Illinois State Nurses Association. One hundred and twenty-one question-naires were returned, for a return rate of approximately 12%. Of these, 6 were not usable because respondents indicated they had left the profession or retired. Of the 115 usable questionnaires, 112 were completed by females and 3 were completed by males.

INSTRUMENT

Embedded within a longer questionnaire were several questions concerned with a support episode recently experienced at work and a support episode recently experienced at home. Although social support was not formally defined, the cover letter contained the following description:

> By social support we mean the variety of efforts that people make to reduce others' stress. These might be in the form of physical assistance, such as taking on part of a chore without being asked, or covering for someone who is extremely busy. Another type of social support might be emotional support such as those occasions when someone lends a sympathetic ear to complaints or problems. Social support might even be in the form of informational or instrumental support, as when someone shows us how to do something that we would otherwise be left to struggle with on our own. Of course not all attempts at providing social support are equally effective; some meet our needs well, whereas some simply don't work, or even increase stress.

The only restrictions on the episode selected was that in both cases the problem or stressor stimulating the episode had to be work-related.

Following each of these descriptions were specific questions relating to the support episode. Among these were categories for designating the type of relationship between the provider and recipient (e.g., supervisor, co-worker or spouse, friend), and a seven-point scale for rating the effectiveness of the support attempt (1 = not at all effective to 7 = extremely effective). Respondents also rated the quality of the relationship they experienced with the provider of the support by responding to items from the Hirsch and Rapkin (1986) scale.

Although this scale was originally created to reflect the positive and negative quality of **interactions** that nurses might have with network members, we used it as a measure of relationship quality for two reasons. First, the items are reasonably read as indicators of how supportive or rejecting a relationship is perceived to be. For example, items such as "is sympathetic to my values and ideals about nursing," or "seems to know the right thing to say or do when I'm distressed" or "I feel particularly close to this person" are representative of scale items that are easily applied to overall supportive or rejecting tenor of a relationship.

Second, we used the Hirsch and Rapkin scale because it measures a characteristic of relational climate that is fairly comparable across relationship types. Although all relationships develop some level of affective quality, it is unlikely that the commonly used measures of affective dimensions such as closeness, intimacy, commitment, and satisfaction are experienced in the same way in work relationships as in personal relationships. On the other hand, a general sense of positive regard and acceptance (both for oneself as a person and for one's commitment to a profession) should be experienced in much the same way in both formal, role relationships and informal, personal relationships.

Consistent with Hirsch and colleagues (Hirsch, Engel-Levy, Du Bois, & Hardesty, 1990; Hirsch & Rapkin, 1986), a factor analysis of our data yielded four dimensions: "General Support," "General Rejection," "Profession (Work) Support," and "Profession (Work) Rejection." General Support was represented by such items as "This person seems to know the right thing to say or do when I'm distressed" and "I feel that this person really likes and cares about me." General Rejection was represented by such items as "Gets me really upset, annoyed, or irritated" and "Hurts my feelings." Profession Support was represented by such items as "Supports me when I am upset by a patient" and "Helps me to set priorities for balancing my job with my nonwork life." Profession Rejection was represented by such items as "Criticizes the way I do my job in a way that isn't helpful" and "Undermines my efforts to be the kind of nurse I really want to be."

EPISODE DESCRIPTIONS

The descriptions of support episodes inside and outside of work were coded for type of stress (and/or problem) and for type of support received. Adapting the themes commonly found in the literature to the events actually reported by respondents led to a parsimonious set of six categories: (a) working conditions (lack of resources and heavy workload); (b) organizational constraints; (c) patient needs (direct patient care and patient's family); (d) work relationships (coworkers, doctors, and supervisor/subordinate); (e) personal concerns; and (f) general/unspecified job stress.

Type of support was coded using the Social Support Behavior Codes as presented most recently by Cutrona and Suhr (1992, p. 161). There were two broad categories of support behaviors, Action-facilitating and Nurturant support, and five subcategories. Subcategories of Action-facilitating behaviors include: **informational support** (advice, factual input, and feedback on actions) and **tangible assistance** (providing needed goods and services). Subcategories of Nurturant behaviors include: **emotional support** (expressions of caring, concern, empathy, and sympathy), **network support** (sense of belonging among people with similar interests and concerns), and **esteem support** (expressions of regard for one's skills, abilities and intrinsic value).

All instances of support in the episodes described by respondents were recorded. However, repetitions of one specific behavior were counted only once. For example, "She listened to the whole story; I mean really listened to everything I said" was counted as one instance of "listening," although other manifestations of emotional support that might appear in the description were counted.

RESULTS AND DISCUSSION

Descriptive Data

The sample produced a total of 244 support messages for work relationships and 195 for nonwork relationships. Nineteen respondents could not recall an episode outside of work in which they were offered social support for a work-related problem.

As might be anticipated from previous research, emotional support was the most frequently mentioned support type across all episodes (36.7% of total). Less consistent with previous research was the fact that tangible assistance was the second most frequently mentioned form of support (26.4%) and informational support the third (19.6%). Esteem support, a consistently strong predictor of reduced stress and depression in the burnout literature accounted for only 13.7% of the support attempts for the combined sample. Network support was relatively rare, accounting for only 4% of the total and was therefore dropped from subsequent analyses.

Most support providers in the workplace were coworkers (64%) or supervisors (26%). A small number were administrators (2%) or other staff (6%). Most support providers outside of work were spouses and other romantic partners (69%) or friends (21%). Some providers were family members such as parents or children (6%) and a few were acquaintances (4%).

Hypothesis 1

Our first prediction was that the distribution of types of support would reflect the constraints and influences of the type of relationship in which the support was offered. That is, we expected work relationships to provide proportionately greater tangible assistance and nonwork relationships to provide proportionately greater emotional support. As Table 12.1 indicates, this is generally true. Tangible assistance is not only the largest proportion of support messages produced in the episodes for work relationships (.39), it is also a significantly larger proportion than that produced in nonwork relationships (.11). Likewise, emotional support accounts for almost half (.49) of all supportive actions in nonwork relationships and is a significantly greater proportion than is found in the work relationships (.27).

Less immediately interpretable is the relatively greater amount of informational support reported in nonwork relationships. This finding is consistent with Cutrona and Suhr's (1992) finding that informational support was the most common form evidenced in conversations of married couples. However, in our data, the problem motivating the support attempt was a work-related one; thus, we expected more informational support from coworkers and supervisors than from nonwork relational partners.

After looking at the distribution of specific support messages within the informational support category, we are able to speculate why informational support appeared so frequently in nonwork relationships. Two manifestations of informational support were especially prominent: (a) reassesses or redefines the situation, and (b) offers ideas and suggests

TABLE 12.1 Frequencies and Proportions of Support Messages Reported in Work and Nonwork Episodes

	Episode				
	Work		Nonwork		
Support Message	Freq.	Prop.	Freq.	Prop.	z^*
Information	39	.16	47	.24	$-2.05 > 1.96$
Tangible Assistance	95	.39	21	.11	$6.67 > 1.96$
Esteem	40	.16	20	.10	$1.82 < 1.96$
Network	5	.02	11	.06	$-2.11 > 1.96$
Emotional	65	.27	96	.49	$4.47 > 1.96$
Total	244	1.00	195	1.00	

*Test for significance of difference between two proportions

actions. When a work-related event, problem, or stressor is told to a spouse or friend who was not present during its occurrence, it is necessary to clarify and elaborate; in that process, the support provider has the opportunity to co-construct an interpretation of the event that is favorable to the distressed person. Moreover, to the extent that the informality of the nonwork relationship minimizes the face threat inherent in advice, spouses and friends might feel more free to give suggestions about work-related problems in spite of their comparatively lesser knowledge. Reciprocally, a coworker or supervisor may have less time and less need to co-construct details of stressful events. They may also hesitate to give explicit advice, despite their qualifications to do so. Explicit advice about a work-related matter may threaten one's professional face. Glidewell, Tucker, Todt, and Cox (1982) observed what may be a similar phenomenon among school teachers, who also avoided explicit advice, but provided constant support in the form of analogues, personal narratives, and other exemplars.

Hypothesis 2

Our concern with effectiveness was twofold. First, we wanted to determine whether the types of support offered most often in work and nonwork relationships are perceived by the recipient as the most effective. Based on the burnout literature, we speculated that even though tangible assistance might be more common in the workplace, emotional support would be considered most effective across both contexts.

TABLE 12.2 Comparison of Means for Effectiveness in Work and Nonwork Episodes

| Support Message | Episode | | t | p |
	Work	Nonwork		
Informational	5.48^a	5.31^a	0.89	.21
Tangible Assistance	6.10^b	5.87^{ab}	1.39	.14
Esteem	5.97^{ab}	6.18^b	-1.55	.11
Emotional	6.31^b	5.71^{ab}	3.03	.01

NOTE: Means with any subscript in common do not differ significantly at the .05 level.

As Table 12.2 indicates, our speculation was not supported. Paired *t*-tests revealed that, in fact, emotional support was significantly more effective when offered during a work episode than when offered outside of work. Moreover, a comparison of means within contexts revealed that for work relationships, emotional support was perceived to be more effective than informational support and esteem support, but not more effective than tangible support [$F(3,111) = 2.91$, $p < .04$]. For nonwork relationships, esteem support proved to be significantly more effective than all other forms of support and informational support proved to be significantly less effective than all other forms of support [$F(3,89) = 3.12$, $p < .02$].

To unpack these findings, we offer a profile of effectiveness that essentially confirms the dissociation between frequency and effectiveness. The profile reveals lower ratings of effectiveness for informational support across relationships (rather than the hypothesized higher ratings for emotional support). Apparently giving advice and reframing events is a common phenomenon, especially outside of work, but it does relatively little to relieve stress associated with the problem. The profile also suggests that both tangible and emotional support are effective at work, but that in nonwork episodes esteem support is comparatively more effective. The effectiveness of emotional support at work is consistent with predictions based on existing literature. The importance of tangible support from work relationships is not consistent with existing literature using burnout as a measure of effectiveness, though it is intuitively logical. McIntosh (1991) suggests that the effect of instrumental support may be indirect, in that "increased instrumental support may lead to less physical exertion, and less physical exertion may reduce emotional exhaustion or increase capacity for coping with it" (p. 215). We would argue also that measuring effectiveness at the level of the interaction detects a direct impact of tangible assistance on stress as well.

Finally, the profile here suggests that although esteem support and emotional support are both considered nurturant support, they may be qualitatively different. Within the nonwork context, esteem support was significantly more effective than other forms of support, including emotional. But it was not significantly more effective in nonwork than in work episodes. This suggests that the effect of attempts to confirm a person's sense of worth and validate his or her competence is not affected by relationship factors to the degree that attempts to provide emotional support is.

Several reasons for the lower effectiveness ratings for emotional support in nonwork episodes (compared to work relationships) can be offered. Structural factors, for example, might include the fact that work peers are present when many of the problems arise and are therefore able to provide emotional support almost immediately. If immediacy contributes to effectiveness ratings, this might contribute to the higher ratings at work. A slightly different explanation may be that the more difficult problems to remediate are the ones that get carried home—precisely because they were not relieved at work. Thus attempts to provide emotional support for resistant problems will necessarily be less obviously effective at the episode level. Examination of the proportion of stressors discussed in both types of relationships revealed that 43% of the stressors motivating the support episodes outside of work were personal concerns or unspecified job stress. In both cases, focused support messages are difficult to construct and therefore are perhaps less likely to receive high ratings on effectiveness.

Another line of explanation is not structural or circumstantial, but relational. That is, it may be the case that nonwork relationships are more varied affectively and represent both very effective emotional support attempts and very ineffective emotional support attempts. Interestingly, it is not the case that any particular type of personal relationship offers more effective support than any other, because there was no significant difference in effectiveness ratings across categories of nonwork relationships $[F (4,86) = 2.01, p > .10]$. However, comparison of the quality measures (general support, general rejection, profession support and profession rejection) indicates that spouses were perceived to be significantly higher in general rejection than any other category of personal relationship (2.33 compared to friends, 1.52, and family, 1.59).

TABLE 12.3 Simultaneous Regression Analyses Predicting Effectiveness of Support Messages Received in Work Episodes

Variable	Beta	R^2	Overall F	P
Tangible Assistance	.33***	.22	5.06	.000
General Support	.30**			
Emotion	.24*			
General Rejection	−.19			
Professional Rejection	−.18			
Esteem	.18			
Professional Support	.11			
Information	.15			

* = p < .05; ** = p < .01; *** = p < .001

Hypothesis 3

This speaks to the relevance of our second effectiveness question: To what extent is the contribution of relationship quality to effectiveness greater in nonwork compared to work relationships? Based on the greater degree of shared knowledge and potential enmeshment in personal relationships relative to role relationships, we predicted that episodes emerging from nonwork relationships would reveal a more complex pattern of associations among type of support, relationship quality, and perceived effectiveness.

Stepwise multiple regressions for each context separately indicates support for this prediction. In those episodes occurring at the workplace, three elements predicted effectiveness of support attempts: tangible assistance, general supportiveness in the relationship, and emotional support (see Table 12.3). This reflects a classically simple model for reducing stress at the interactional level: "Give me a little help, show acceptance for me in our interactions over time, and listen with empathy and confidentiality." For nonwork episodes, however, the picture is more complicated. Tangible assistance is relatively less important, but general supportiveness of the relationship and support for the nurse's professional commitment are predictors of effectiveness, followed by emotional and esteem support. Even professional rejection entered the nonwork equation, negatively predicting the effectiveness of support attempts (see Table 12.4).

TABLE 12.4 Simultaneous Regression Analyses Predicting Effectiveness of Support Messages Received in Nonwork Episodes

Variable	Beta	R^2	Overall F	P
General Support	.36**	.59	22.07	.000
Professional Support	.32**			
Emotion	.20**			
Esteem	.20**			
Tangible Assistance	.19*			
Professional Rejection	−.19*			
General Rejection	−.12			
Information	.09			

* = $p < .05$; ** = $p < .01$

Conclusion

Our findings suggest that aggregated and global measures of social support availability and effectiveness may be misleading. Emotional support is not uniformly effective in reducing stress, although informational support may be almost uniformly ineffective in reducing stress. Or, perhaps more accurately, informational support is one component in the support process that has a cognitive utility, but seems to be unrelated to the more affective domain of stress reduction. Moreover, esteem support appears to be akin to the sociological construct of face, particularly positive face (Brown & Levinson, 1987). To the extent that regard for one's positive face has the universal appeal that Brown and Levinson (1987) claim and to the extent that persons have more fully scripted plans for providing face support than emotional support, esteem support may be easier to give and appreciate. At the very least, the conceptual overlap between esteem support and positive face support should be explored.

Our data suggest that direct comparisons of work and nonwork relationships that do not also measure and control for relationship quality will probably continue to find work relationships more effective in reducing stress. There are few relational agendas to influence the provision and receipt of support.

We encourage reconceptualization of the relationship between event or problem, support attempts, and outcomes. Cutrona's work with the dimension of "controllability" as one feature that influences how support is received is promising. However, it may place undue emphasis on the event, ignoring the relational context in which the event is being processed. We think a case could be made for viewing the very notion of controllability as something negotiated between provider and recipient, and thereby a product colored by the level of trust and support in the relationship.

References

Albrecht, T. L., & Adelman, M. B. (1987). Communicating social support: A theoretical perspective. In T. L. Albrecht & M. B. Adelman and Associates (Eds.), *Communicating social support* (pp. 18-39). Newbury Park, CA: Sage.

Allanach, E. J. (1988). Perceived supportive behaviors and nursing occupational stress: An evolution of consciousness. *Advances in Nursing Science, 10,* 73-82.

Boyle, A., Grap, M. J., Younger, J., & Thornby, D. (1991). Personality hardiness, ways of coping, social support and burnout in critical care nurses. *Journal of Advanced Nursing, 6,* 850-857.

Bradac, J. J. (1983). The language of lovers, flowers, and friends: Communicating in social and personal relationships. *Journal of Language and Social Psychology, 2,* 141-162.

Brown, P., & Levinson, S. (1987). *Politeness: Some universals in language usage.* Cambridge, UK: Cambridge University Press.

Browner, C. H. (1987). Job stress and health: The role of social support at work. *Research in Nursing and Health, 10,* 93-100.

Caroselli-Karinja, M. F., & Drozd Zboray, S. (1986). The impaired nurse. *Journal of Psychosocial Nursing and Mental Health Services, 24*(6), 14-19.

Constable, J. F., & Russell, D. W. (1986). The effect of social support and the work environment upon burnout among nurses. *Journal of Human Stress, 12,* 20-26.

Cronin-Stubbs, D., & Rooks, C. A. (1985). The stress, social support, and burnout of critical care nurses: The results of research. *Heart & Lung, 14,* 31-39.

Cutrona, C. E., & Suhr, J. A. (1992). Controllability of stressful events and satisfaction with spouse supportive behaviors. *Communication Research, 19,* 154-174.

Cutrona, C. E., Suhr, J. A., & MacFarlane, R. (1990). Interpersonal transactions and the psychological sense of support. In S. Duck (Ed., with R. Silver), *Personal relationships and social support* (pp. 30-45). London: Sage.

Everly, G. S., & Falcione, R. L. (1976). Perceived dimensions of job satisfaction for staff registered nurses. *Nursing Research, 25,* 346-348.

Feutz, S. A. (1991). The new look in nursing documentation. *Nursing, 91, 21*(8), 54-55.

Firth, H., McIntee, J., McKeown, P., & Britton, P. (1986). Interpersonal support amongst nurses at work. *Journal of Advanced Nursing, 11,* 273-282.

Friedman, E. (1990). Nursing: New power, old problems. *Journal of the American Medical Association, 264,* 2977-2982.

Galarowicz, L. R. (1991). Six steps for keeping your spirit strong. *Nursing, 91, 21*(1), 94-102.

Glidewell, J.C., Tucker, S., Todt, M., & Cox, S. (1982). Professional support systems: The teaching profession. In A. Nadler, J. D. Fisher, & B. M. DePaulo (Eds.), *Applied research in help-seeking and reactions to aid* (pp. 189-212). New York: Academic Press.

Goldsmith, D. (1992). Managing conflicting goals in supportive interaction: An integrative theoretical framework. *Communication Research, 19,* 264-286.

Gottlieb, B. H. (1985). Social support and study of personal relationship. *Journal of Social and Personal Relationships, 2,* 351-375.

Hirsch, B. J., Engel-Levy, A., Du Bois, D. L., and Hardesty, P. H. (1990). The role of social environments in social support. In B. R. Sarason, I. G. Sarason, & G. R. Pierce (Eds.), *Social support: An interactional view* (pp. 367-393). New York: John Wiley.

Hirsch, B. J., & Rapkin, B. D. (1986). Social networks and adult social identities: Profiles and correlates of support and rejection. *American Journal of Community Psychology, 14,* 395-411.

Jennings, B. M. (1990). Stress, locus of control, social support, and psychological symptoms among head nurses. *Research in Nursing and Health, 13,* 393-401.

Kalisch, B. J., & Kalisch, P. A. (1982). An analysis of the sources of physician-nurse conflict. In J. Muff (Ed.), *Socialization, sexism, and stereotyping: Women's issues in nursing* (pp. 221-233). Prospect Heights, IL: Waveland.

Krokoff, L. J. (1990). Hidden agendas in marriage: Affective and longitudinal dimensions. *Communication Reports, 17,* 483-499.

La Gapia, J. J. (1990). The negative effects of informal support systems. In S. Duck (Ed., with R. Silver), *Personal relationships and social support* (pp. 122-139). London: Sage.

Leatham, G., & Duck, S. (1990). Conversations with friends and the dynamics of social support. In S. Duck (Ed., with R. Silver), *Personal relationships and social support* (pp. 1-29). London: Sage.

Lees, S., & Ellis, N. (1990). The design of a stress-management programme for nursing personnel. *Journal of Advanced Nursing, 15,* 946-961.

McAbee, R. (1991). Occupational stress and burnout in the nursing profession: A model for prevention. *AAOHN Journal, 39,* 568-575.

McIntosh, N. (1991). Identification and investigation of properties of social support. *Journal of Organizational Behavior, 12,* 201-217.

Norbeck, J. (1985). Types and sources of social support for managing job stress in critical care nursing. *Nursing Research, 34,* 225-230.

Pierce, G. R., Sarason, B.R., & Sarason, I.G. (1990). Integrating social support perspectives: Working models, personal relationships, and situational factors. In S. Duck (Ed.), *Personal relationships and social support* (pp. 173-189). London: Sage.

Sarason, B. R., Pierce, G. R., & Sarason, I. G. (1990). Social Support: The sense of acceptance and the role of relationships. In B. R. Sarason, I. G. Sarason, & G. R. Pierce (Eds.), *Social support: An interactional view* (pp. 97-128). New York: John Wiley.

Sarason, B. R., Sarason, I. G., & Pierce, G. R. (1990). Traditional views of social support and their impact on assessment. In B. R. Sarason, I. G. Sarason, & G. R. Pierce (Eds.), *Social support: An interactional view* (pp. 9-25). New York: John Wiley.

Silver, R. C., Wortman, C. B., & Crofton, C. (1990). The role of coping in support provision: The self-presentational dilemma of victims of life crisis. In B. R. Sarason, I. G. Sarason, & G. R. Pierce (Eds.), *Social support: An interactional view* (pp. 397-419). New York: John Wiley.

Smythe, E. E. M. (1984). Developing social support: We're all in this together. In E. E. M. Smythe (Ed.), *Surviving nursing* (pp. 218-238). Menlo Park, CA: Addison-Wesley.

Steffen, S. M. (1980). Perception of stress: 1800 nurses tell their story. In K. E. Claus & J. T. Bailey (Eds.), *Living with stress and promoting well-being* (pp. 35-58). St. Louis, MO: C. V. Mosby.

13

The Quality of Relationships Inventory

Assessing the Interpersonal Context of Social Support

GREGORY R. PIERCE

The theoretical and empirical developments reported in this book attest to researchers' growing interest in the topic of social support. Investigators now appear to be in nearly unanimous agreement that social support, defined in a variety of ways, has important implications for physical and psychological health (House, Landis, & Umberson, 1988; Sarason, Sarason, & Pierce, 1990a). There is, however, considerably less agreement about the construct's conceptualization and appropriate procedures for assessing it (Sarason, Sarason, & Pierce, 1990b). Presentations of these issues often involve efforts to pit several competing perspectives against one another and the conclusion that one of the approaches is to be preferred above others. Still other viewpoints are offered without reference to any potential integration to be achieved between the approach being advocated and those taken by other researchers. My colleagues and I have proposed that the many different theoretical perspectives have merit but that investigation of their interrelationship might lead to important insights (Pierce, Sarason, & Sarason, 1990). Our own efforts have been directed toward (a) such an integration of these diverse theoretical

AUTHOR'S NOTE: I wish to thank Lauren C. Nagle, Barbara R. Sarason, Irwin G. Sarason, and Penny L. Yee for their helpful comments on an earlier draft of this chapter.

approaches and (b) development of psychometrically sound, valid measures of several features of the social support construct.

The purpose of this chapter is to describe an instrument we have developed, the Quality of Relationships Inventory (QRI), to assess the supportive and conflictual aspects of close relationships. The chapter has three parts. It begins with an overview of approaches taken to study the social support construct. Then the QRI and its psychometric properties and correlates are described. Finally, an interactional-cognitive model of social support (Pierce et al., 1990; Sarason, Pierce, & Sarason, 1990) is presented that incorporates recent findings based on the QRI. This model emphasizes the role of situational, intrapersonal, and interpersonal contexts in social support processes.

General Approaches
to the Social Support Construct

Conceptualizations of the social support construct, either as explicated by researchers or as appear implicit from the instruments used to assess the construct, focus on various levels of the individual and his or her social network. Some conceptualizations focus on a person's general perceptions of the social environment, for example, the extent to which global or specific social resources are available to the individual (Cutrona & Russell, 1987; Sarason, Levine, Basham, & Sarason, 1983). Researchers have noted that these general perceptions, while undoubtedly related to features of the respondent's social network, may also reflect properties of the respondent, such as his or her working models regarding the nature of close relationships (Procidano & Heller, 1983; Sarason, Sarason, & Shearin, 1986). Approaches that focus on global appraisals of the social environment (e.g, the perceived availability of emotional or instrumental support) share a common emphasis on qualitative features of the individual and his or her social milieu. Other perspectives emphasize quantitative properties of the social network, including its size, density (i.e., the interconnectedness of network members) and composition (e.g., the proportion of family members and friends) (Stokes, 1985; Vaux & Harrison, 1985).

Research generated from these perspectives suggests that social support can be viewed profitably as a general characteristic of one's social network. But what about the support inherent in personal relationships? Some research, although not driven by a particular theoretical formulation of the social support construct, reflects a relationship-based strategy. These studies focus on the contribution of a particular relationship (e.g., the marital relationship) to the physical or psychological well-being of one or both of the relationship participants. Studies have investigated the effects of a broad range of specific relationships, including those between marital partners (Coyne, Ellard, & Smith, 1990), caregivers and recipients (Coyne, Wortman, & Lehman, 1988), and older parents and their adult children (Rundall & Evashwich, 1982). One limitation to this single-relationship design is that it neglects the possible effects that other relationships might have on the functioning of the relationship under investigation, as well as impacts that the relationship being studied might have on other relationships in the participants' networks. Belsky and his colleagues (Gable, Belsky, & Crnic, 1992) have recently argued, for example, that the impact of parental relationships on children's personality development cannot be examined comprehensively without also examining the role of the marital relationship. This approach reflects a systems perspective in which the interdependent nature of close relationships is emphasized.

We have recently proposed an interactional-cognitive model of social support, one in which focus is placed on several specific relationships simultaneously (Pierce et al., 1990; Sarason et al., 1990). One reason that researchers have neglected incorporating several specific relationships into their investigations may be that most studies examining a specific relationship employ measures developed specifically for the particular relationship under investigation. Items are written that tap aspects of the relationship assumed to be pertinent to the hypotheses under investigation. These measures often incorporate items obtained from measures of aggregated or general support, or are not derived from a clear conceptualization of the social support construct. The instruments' relevance to relationship-specific features of social support is therefore unknown. An impediment to a broader, systems approach to research on social support is the lack of an instrument to tap dimensions pertinent to a wide range of relationships. This chapter describes a recently developed reliable, valid instrument with which to investigate the role of a variety of specific relationships in social support processes.

The Quality of Relationships Inventory:
Instrument Development

My colleagues and I have undertaken a program of research aimed at developing a measure of relationship-specific support (and other dimensions of close relationships pertinent to social support processes). The resulting instrument, the Quality of Relationships Inventory (QRI), has been used in a series of studies to investigate the role of relationship-specific perceptions in a variety of interpersonal contexts (Pierce, Sarason, & Sarason, 1991, 1992; Sarason, Pierce, & Sarason, 1992).

Development of the QRI has been guided by four goals: The instrument should (a) provide a convenient index of relationship qualities, (b) assess multiple aspects of relationships, (c) be appropriate for use with a broad range of relationships, and (d) be consistent with a theoretical framework accounting for the role of specific relationships in social support (and perhaps other) processes.

A CONVENIENT INDEX

We sought an instrument that could be used in a variety of contexts, including research, clinical, and other applied settings. This goal led us to focus on a self-report questionnaire rather than an interview strategy or other more time-consuming assessment procedures. Thus while several interview measures are currently available to assess features of close relationships (e.g., Henderson, Duncan-Jones, Byrne, & Scott, 1980), these instruments are not always practical to use in a wide range of settings in which time limitations are a critical factor. In contrast, the QRI contains 25 items that respondents rate using a 4-point scale regarding their perceptions of a specific relationship and takes approximately 4 minutes to complete.

A MULTIDIMENSIONAL APPROACH

Based on the interactional-cognitive model's emphasis on the multidimensional nature of close relationships, the QRI was constructed to measure three features of relationships: support, conflict, and depth. Relationship-specific support reflects the extent to which a relationship participant perceives the other person to be a source of assistance in a variety of situations. Relationship participants also have specific expectations regarding the amount of conflict they anticipate experiencing with a potential support provider. Evidence suggests that this aspect of relationships is quite distinct from support (Hirsch, 1979; Pierce et al., 1991). However, interpersonal conflict does appear to influence recipients' perceptions of supportive behavior received from others (Pierce, Sarason, & Sarason, 1992). Interpersonal depth reflects the perceived importance of the relationship, that is, the extent to which the relationship is believed to exert a significant impact on the person's life (Pierce et al., 1991). Although we have hypothesized that this aspect of close relationships is related to the perceived supportiveness of a relationship, it remains distinct.

APPROPRIATE FOR ASSESSING A
BROAD RANGE OF RELATIONSHIPS

There are a variety of measures available to assess relationship participants' perceptions of their close relationships. Unfortunately, many of these instruments were developed to assess qualities relevant only to a small number of relationships. The Dyadic Adjustment Scale (DAS) yields four subscales and a total score assessing spouses' perceptions of the quality of their marital relationship (Spanier, 1976). These scales, while of potential interest to social support researchers investigating marital relationships, are not necessarily pertinent to the assessment of other types of relationships (e.g., those between parents and their children or among peers). In order to address this limitation, the QRI was developed to provide scales that are applicable to a broad range of relationships (e.g., peers, family members, coworkers, romantic partners/spouses). The QRI in its present format, however, is not appropriate for use with very young children.

CONSISTENT WITH A THEORETICAL FRAMEWORK

Most social support instruments reported in the literature are only loosely based on a theoretical model of social support (Sarason et al., 1990a). These atheoretical and quite diverse measures have impeded efforts to integrate findings emerging from three decades of research. A few currently available social support instruments, such as the Social Provisions Scale (SPS) (Cutrona & Russell, 1987, 1990) and the Social Support Questionnaire (SSQ) (Sarason et al., 1983; Sarason, Sarason,

Shearin, & Pierce, 1987), have scales consistent with an explicit conceptualization of the social support construct. While these instruments have clearly led to important findings, they focus on general properties of the support network rather than on specific relationships. We therefore developed the QRI based on the interactional-cognitive model (Pierce et al., 1990; Sarason et al., 1990; see also Sarason, Sarason, & Pierce, Chapter 5), which distinguishes between general and relationship-specific perceptions of social support.

Assessing the Quality of Specific Relationships: The Quality of Relationships Inventory

PSYCHOMETRIC PROPERTIES

The current version of the QRI includes 25 items that assess the amount of support, conflict and depth in a broad range of close relationships (see Appendix 13.1; Pierce et al., 1991; Pierce, Sarason, Sarason, & Gilmore, 1992). In a cross-sectional study of college students, 94 male and 116 female undergraduates completed the QRI three times to assess their perceptions of their relationships with their mother, father and a best friend of the same sex (Pierce et al., 1991). The QRI items are rated on a 4-point scale, ranging from 1 = Not at all, to 4 = Very much. When factor analyzed, the QRI yielded three scales consistent with our conceptualization. Seven items loaded strongly on the first dimension, which was labeled support (e.g., "To what extent can you turn to this person for advice about problems?" and "To what extent can you count on this person to listen to you when you are angry?") The second dimension, labeled conflict, included 14 items, two of which were discarded because of overlap with the other dimensions. Items retained for the conflict scale included: "How often do you have to work hard to avoid conflict in this relationship?" and "How much does this person make you feel guilty?" The third scale, labeled depth, included the following items: "How significant is this relationship in your life?" and "How much do you depend on this person?" The factor structure for responses assessing students' relationships with their mother, father and best friend were highly similar, suggesting that this model is appropriate for a diverse range of close relationships.

Internal consistency for each of the scales was high, with Cronbach's alpha in the .80s and .90s. As was expected, the three scales were modestly to substantially intercorrelated, with the scales assessing support and depth correlating the most (average $r = .71$); the scales measuring support and conflict showed a substantially smaller association (average $r = -.31$). Despite the fact that the scales were correlated, both the support and conflict scales each contributed uniquely to the prediction of loneliness.

These results suggest that the QRI scales are consistent with our theoretical model of close relationships and have desirable psychometric properties. A growing body of research employing the QRI indicates that the QRI scales are valid, reliable measures of the quality of close relationships.

THE QUALITY OF RELATIONSHIPS INVENTORY: CONVERGENT AND DISCRIMINANT VALIDITY

The interactional-cognitive model emphasizes the need to distinguish between general and relationship-specific perceptions of support (as well as interpersonal conflict and depth). While a person's general working model concerning the social environment is likely to influence his or her social behavior with specific others, one relationship participant's general working model is not the sole operative factor in the development and maintenance of his or her relationship with another person. Instead, the other person's working model also contributes to ongoing interactions. The relationship that unfolds is a product of both persons' working models and their social interactions. Given the multidetermined nature of dyadic relationships, it seemed reasonable to hypothesize that perceptions of available support within specific relationships are distinct from general perceptions of available support.

In investigating the discriminant validity of the QRI scales, it was therefore important to demonstrate whether they assessed relationship-specific perceptions of support, conflict, and depth as opposed to general perceptions of the support network. Findings from two studies focusing on the development of the preliminary and current versions of the QRI are consistent with the hypothesis that relationship specific perceptions of support are distinct from general or global beliefs about support. In both studies, the correlations between the several QRI scales assessing perceptions of a particular relationship were much larger than were the correlations between QRI scales assessing perceptions of different relationships, suggesting that the perceptions tapped by the QRI scales are highly relationship specific and form a coherent, unique view of each relationship.

Hierarchical multiple regression analyses indicated that the contribution made by the QRI scales to the prediction of several measures of personal adjustment was in addition to the contribution made by measures of general perceived social support. This finding further suggests that personal adjustment, while certainly influenced by a person's general dispositions, is also partly determined by the impact of specific relationships, particularly the supportive and conflictual aspects of close relationships. In addition, these results buttress the conclusion that the QRI scales assess beliefs about the quality of a specific relationship, rather than a generalized appraisal of the social network.

STABILITY

The interactional-cognitive model suggests that perceptions of close relationships are relatively stable across time because they are influenced by the participants' general working model regarding the nature of supportive relationships. This does not mean that participants never behave in a way that violates the other person's expectations. Developmental transitions (e.g., becoming a parent) may lead to changes in the quality of close relationships. However, these relationship-specific expectations are based on a history of experiences and reflect a consistent pattern of social interactions between the two relationship participants. Once established, these expectations guide each participant's behavior, which further contributes to the stability of the interpersonal context. We therefore hypothesized that the QRI scales, when used to assess the quality of a longstanding relationship, would show considerable stability over time.

Evidence supporting this hypothesis comes from the Hamilton Longitudinal Study of Families (Pierce, Sarason, Sarason, Solky, & Nagle, 1992). This study was begun by recruiting 52 male and 85 female students at Hamilton College (located in upstate New York) and each of their parents, with 65% of the families still intact. These students and their parents have each completed a variety of questionnaires, including QRIs assessing the students' and parents' perceptions of their parent-adult child relationship, and the parents' perceptions of the quality of their marriage (with parents in non-intact families completing the QRI regarding their current spouse or partner, if applicable). This study, while in its initial stages, has already yielded intriguing findings. For example, 47 students were recontacted and agreed to complete QRIs assessing their perceptions of their relationships with their mother and father 4 months after completing the QRIs for these relationships during the first wave of testing. Results from this subsample indicate that the QRI scales have high test-retest reliability, with correlations between scores on each scale across the 4 month period ranging from .66 to .82, with an average correlation of .75. In fact, these test-retest correlations are close to the internal consistency estimates, indicating that nearly all of the reliable variance in the QRI scores is attributable to a stable conception of the relationship. Further research is needed to extend these findings to other categories of relationships (e.g., peers, coworkers, and other family members).

AN EXPERIMENTAL STUDY OF
THE QUALITY OF RELATIONSHIPS

The interactional-cognitive model suggests that the quality of the provider-recipient relationship (as well as situational and interpersonal variables) influences recipients' appraisals of support providers' behavior. Evidence supporting this hypothesis was obtained in a recent experimental study involving college students and their mothers (Pierce, Sarason, & Sarason, 1992). In this study 54 undergraduates and their mothers each completed a packet of questionnaires, including a QRI assessing their perceptions of the quality of their relationship and the SSQ as a measure of general perceived support. Approximately 2 weeks later, subjects and their mothers returned to the laboratory to participate in a structured interaction. Students and their mothers were told that the student was to prepare and give a speech arguing for the value of a college education. The experimenter explained that the researchers were interested in finding out about the student's views concerning college; the mother was therefore going to be taken to another room where she would be working on several other tasks. The experimenter added that because one aspect of the research project concerned the nature of parent-student interactions, the mother would have the opportunity to write and send two notes to the student before and after he or she gave the speech. The experimenter's instructions also included an experimental manipulation intended to induce either high or low stress to study the impact of the situational context on support appraisals.

The mother was then taken to another room where she was asked to copy in her own handwriting two standard notes. One of the notes was given by the experimenter to the student prior to giving his or her speech ("Don't worry—just say how you feel and what you think and you'll do just fine"); the other was given to the student after he or she had given the speech ("I liked your speech. That's a tricky topic to spend a whole lot of time on, and you covered it well"). The student rated the perceived supportiveness of each note immediately after receiving it. This procedure made it possible to examine the impact of situational (the stress manipulation), interpersonal (SSQ scores) and interpersonal (QRI scores) variables on students' appraisals of their mothers' supportive behaviors (the notes).

Regression analyses indicated that these three variables accounted for 14.83% and 40.93%, respectively, of the variance in students' perceptions of their mothers' two messages. Consistent with our hypothesis, unique effects were found for students' perceptions of support and conflict in the mother-student relationship (as assessed by the QRI). Compared with other students, those who described their maternal relationship as particularly supportive perceived their mother's prespeech and postspeech notes to convey more support (beta = .41 and .40, respectively, p's < .01). Students who reported relatively low levels of maternal conflict also described their mothers' postspeech note as especially supportive (beta = .32, p < .05). The effect for conflict on students' perceptions of the prespeech note was, however, contrary to our prediction: students who reported high levels of conflict in their maternal relationships perceived their mothers' notes as particularly supportive (beta = .35, p < .05). Other variables in the model were also influential. Students who were in the high stress condition rated their mothers' postspeech note as more supportive than did other students (beta = .23, p < .05); the stress manipulation appeared to have no impact on students' ratings of the prespeech notes. General perceived support as assessed by SSQ scores was related univariately (i.e., when the simple correlation was examined) to the students' perceptions of their mothers' prespeech note (r = .28, p < .05); this association, however, appeared to be accounted for by the link between SSQ and QRI scores when considered in the context of the multiple regression analyses.

These results underscore several important points. As we predicted, several facets of the support provider-recipient relationship influenced recipients' perceptions of the support provider's behavior. The relationship-specific beliefs about support and conflict each appeared to play an important role. In addition, the influence of relationship-specific perceptions of support and conflict were independent of the impact of general perceptions of support (which in this case appeared not to play a unique role). This latter finding suggests that general views of relationship participants may influence social behavior in close relationships through their impact on the development of the interpersonal context.

THE QUALITY OF RELATIONSHIPS INVENTORY AND SOCIAL INTERACTIONS

Findings from several behavioral observation studies of family interactions suggest that the QRI scales are consistently and strongly related to observers' ratings of family members' social behavior in a wide range of interactions (Pierce, Sarason, Sarason, & Gilmore, 1992; Sarason et al., 1992). Sarason et al. (1992) reported two observational studies in which college students participated with either their mother or father in a supportive interaction (Study 1) or participated with either their mother or father in an interaction emphasizing interpersonal conflict (Study 2). In Study 1, college students completed the preliminary version of the QRI, the SSQ, and several individual difference measures; approximately one week later, they and one of their parents participated in a speech task similar to the one employed in the Pierce, Sarason, and Sarason (1992) study, except that the parent remained in the room with the student during the speech preparation period and was allowed to provide assistance if the parent and the student desired it. Observers rated the videotaped interactions to assess the supportiveness of the student-parent dyad during the speech preparation [e.g., "If the student (or parent) had a personal problem, to what extent could he or she count on the parent (or student) to help solve it?"] and the degree of sensitivity displayed by the student or parent toward the other person [e.g., "To what extent was the student (or parent) sensitive to the parent's (student's) needs?"].

Students' QRI scores assessing the perceived depth of and conflict in their relationship with the participating parent were consistently and strongly related to the observers' ratings (average $r = .39$, and $r = -.37$, respectively). The students' QRI scores for the nonparticipating parent were more modestly related to the observers' ratings (average $r = .26$ for depth, and $r = -.24$ for conflict). Regression analyses indicated that these latter associations were accounted for by the correlations between students' perceptions of their relationships with the participating and nonparticipating parent. In general the students' personality characteristics were less strongly predictive of the observers' ratings, although reports of depressive symptomatology were consistently related to the students' and parents' social behavior. These results are consistent with our hypothesis that relationship-specific expectations, as assessed by QRI scores, stem from a history of shared experiences.

Observational studies involving the QRI have not been limited to parent-adult child relationships. We have also investigated the social behavior of spouses. In a recent study (Pierce, Sarason, Sarason, and Gilmore, 1992), college students and both of their parents participated in a series of interactions involving different combinations of family members. In one interaction, the parents were separated from the student and were asked to discuss "the ways in which having children have affected your lives individually, and your relationship with each other." Trained raters coded the videotaped marital interaction to assess the degree to which the couple's behavior indicated enjoyment, affection, problems in their marriage, and disagreement about the quality of their marriage. The wives' and husbands' QRI scores assessing support, conflict and depth in their relationship were highly predictive of the observers' ratings of their social behavior (average r_{wives}, QRI scores = .38, and $r_{husbands}$, QRI scores = .34, absolute values). These results buttress and extend the findings obtained with parent-adult child relationships and further indicate that objective features of relationship participants' social interactions are related to their perceptions regarding the amount of support, conflict and depth they experience in their relationships.

THE QUALITY OF RELATIONSHIPS INVENTORY AND SUPPORT SEEKING

Evidence also suggests that QRI scores are predictive of participants' behavioral intentions. In order to investigate this issue, Pierce and Williams (1992) developed 12 vignettes describing situations in which the subject might desire to seek social support. After reading each vignette, students were asked to rank order their desire to seek support from their mother, father, and best friend of the same sex. Results indicated that the QRI support scores for each relationship were consistent predictors of students' support seeking intentions from that specific relationship participant; QRI support scores for one potential support provider (e.g., their mother) did not, however, predict their intentions to seek support from other potential providers (e.g., their father or same sex best friend). Furthermore QRI support scores for a particular relationship proved to be good predictors of behavioral intentions across the diverse ranges of situations described in each of the vignettes.

THE QUALITY OF RELATIONSHIPS INVENTORY AND EARLY PARENTAL RELATIONSHIPS

Evidence from retrospective accounts of early childhood relationships suggests that QRI scores are related to perceptions of the quality of early parent-child relationships. In the Pierce et al. (1991) study, students also completed a retrospective measure of the quality of their early parental relationships prior to the age of 16, the Parental Bonding Instrument (Parker, Tupling, & Brown, 1979). The results indicated that students' perceptions of their current relationships with their parents were strongly linked to their perceptions of the quality of their childhood parental relationships. Students who perceived their mother and father to be highly supportive in adulthood described that parent as having been especially warm and caring ($r = .71$ and $r = .67$, respectively, both p's < .001), and not overprotective during childhood ($r = -.39$ and $r = -.29$, respectively, both p's < .001). Students who reported currently experiencing high levels of conflict with their mother and father perceived their early relationship with each parent to have been less supportive ($r = -.65$ and $r = -.49$, respectively, both p's < .001) and more overprotective ($r = .47$ and $r = .41$, respectively, both p's < .001). These results suggest a high degree of congruence between students' retrospective perceptions of their early parent-child relationships and their current perceptions of these relationships based on QRI responses (Pierce et al., 1991). These findings have been replicated in the Hamilton study described earlier (Pierce et al., 1992).

SUMMARY

The QRI was developed to assess three features of close relationships (i.e., support conflict, and depth) hypothesized to play an important role in social support processes. Accumulating evidence suggests that the QRI is a reliable, valid measure of these three aspects of close relationships. Studies attesting to the psychometric properties and validity of the QRI scales reflect a broad range of methodologies, including (a) cross-sectional, (b) longitudinal, (c) experimental, (d) observational, and (e) retrospective designs. As mentioned earlier in the chapter, our program of research reflects strong, mutual influences between instrument and theory development. Thus the QRI has been influenced by, and has served as an impetus for, our efforts to develop an interactional-cognitive model of social support. This theory, while emphasizing the role of qualitative features of close relationships, also acknowledges the important roles played by situational and intrapersonal factors in social support processes.

An Interactional-Cognitive Model of Social Support

The theoretical model of social support we have proposed calls attention to three classes of variables, including the (a) situational, (b) intrapersonal, and (c) interpersonal contexts in which supportive efforts occur (Pierce et al., 1990; Sarason et al., 1990). The term interactional does not refer simply to statistical interactions among these three sets of variables; instead, the term implies that social interactions occurring among network members, including but not restricted to those involving social support, are a primary determinant of social support processes. The term cognitive emphasizes our proposition that appraisal processes occurring in the context of social interactions also have important implications for social support processes. Objective properties of supportive exchanges are not assumed to be unimportant; however, interpretations that participants give to their social interactions also need to be considered.

Situational context. According to the interactional-cognitive model, the situational context includes features of the environment in which supportive interactions take place. Along with many other social support researchers, we have been interested in the role of stress, both in terms of its impact on the provision of support as well as the participants' appraisals of supportive behaviors (Cohen & Wills, 1985; Cutrona & Russell, 1987, 1990; Pierce et al., 1990, 1992; Sarason et al., 1990). Other features of the situation include the setting (e.g., work, social, or medical) in which potentially supportive interactions take place and the tasks (e.g., intellectual, social, or athletic) to which the participants' attention is directed. Recognition of the important role played by properties of the situation has led us to investigate supportive transactions in which participants' interactions are directed toward a wide range of interpersonal processes, including conflict and support.

Intrapersonal context. The intrapersonal context refers to the participants' general predispositions to engage in, respond to, and interpret social behavior in particular ways. We have adopted Bowlby's (1980) and other attachment theorists' notion of working models which reflect an individual's expectations regarding both the self and important others in that person's life. Working models are hypothesized to develop as a consequence of a history of experiences with important others in an individual's life, particularly those with one's parents. If John, in childhood, receives support that is consistent and responsive to his needs, he is likely to develop a working model of others, in general, as likely to provide support should he need it. On the other hand, if John only receives inconsistent support from his parents or they are unresponsive to his needs, he is likely to develop a working model of others as unwilling or unable to meet his needs. These working models are hypothesized to influence potential recipients' efforts to elicit support as well as their appraisals of support providers' behavior. We believe that general perceived social support measures such as the SSQ (Sarason et al., 1983; Sarason et al., 1987) and the SPS (Cutrona & Russell, 1987) tap this aspect of the social support construct.

Interpersonal context. The interpersonal context directs attention to the expectations participants develop regarding specific relationships in which potentially supportive interactions occur, including the extent to which the relationship is a source of support, conflict and depth. Supportive relationships are those in which individuals are sensitive to each other's needs; the participants are confident that they can count on the other person to provide support regardless of the specific needs engendered by the situation. One of the intriguing findings in recent social support research has been the observation that supportive relationships are not free from conflict (Hirsch, 1979; Pierce et al., 1991). Instead, both supportive and unsupportive relationships can be sources of distress, anger and ambivalence, a situation that may undermine supportive efforts. Relationship depth refers to the degree to which the relationship is secure and important to the participants. This aspect of relationships is hypothesized to be distinct from both support and conflict; participants can perceive the relationship as playing an important role in their lives without regarding the other person as a source of either social support or conflict. The QRI therefore was developed to assess each of these aspects of the interpersonal context.

We believe these three contexts, situational, intrapersonal, and interpersonal, need to be considered together when conceptualizing social support processes. For example, in some situational contexts, particular relationships (e.g., coworkers) may play an especially important role in the coping process. Qualitative features of these various relationships may be more or less important depending on the type of situation being confronted (Sarason et al., 1992). For instance, interpersonal conflict may be less important during a medical emergency, at least in the short term, because support providers' and recipients' attention may be more strongly directed toward the challenges posed by the situation, rather than to the long-term implications of indebtedness or reciprocity.

Having made the observation that each of these three contexts needs to be taken into account in research on social support, our research efforts have emphasized two issues. First, my colleagues and I have focused on understanding the role of the interpersonal context because of its relative neglect in the social support literature. Second, we believe efforts to answer questions regarding the impact of the interpersonal context, issues which lie at the heart of social support processes, have been hampered by a lack of psychometrically sound, theoretically based assessment devices with which to investigate the role of specific relationships. Therefore, we have developed the QRI, a brief self-report measure of the extent to which a relationship is characterized by support, conflict and depth. Results from several studies suggest that the QRI may provide a valuable means of investigating the role of the interpersonal context in social support processes.

Conclusion

Research on social support has proved remarkably fruitful in implicating features of the social environment in physical and psychological health. Still needed, however, are theories and appropriate instruments to investigate the processes by which these linkages arise. We believe that theory development can be facilitated by the availability of psychometrically reliable and valid measures of pertinent features of the social environment. Toward this end, we have developed the QRI and investigated its psychometric properties and correlates. Findings obtained with the QRI have led to substantial revisions in the interactional-cognitive model we have proposed; similarly, hypotheses derived from the model have greatly influenced our approach to instrument construction. We believe such an interplay between theory and assessment is a valuable component in any research program.

References

Bowlby, J. (1980). *Attachment and loss. 3. Loss: Sadness and depression.* New York: Basic Books.

Cohen, S., & Wills, T. A. (1985). Stress, social support, and the buffering hypothesis. *Psychological Bulletin, 98,* 310-357.

Coyne, J. C., Ellard, J. H., & Smith, D.A.F. (1990). Social support, interdependence, and the dilemmas of helping. In B. R. Sarason, I. G. Sarason, & G. R. Pierce (Eds.), *Social support: An interactional view* (pp. 129-149). New York: John Wiley.

Coyne, J. C., Wortman, C., & Lehman, D. (1988). The other side of support: Emotional overinvolvement and miscarried helping. In B. Gottlieb (Ed.), *Social support: Formats, processes, and effects* (pp. 305-330). Newbury Park, CA: Sage.

Cutrona, C. E., & Russell, D. (1987). The provisions of social relationships and adaptation to stress. In W. H. Jones & D. Perlman (Eds.), *Advances in personal relationships* (vol. 1, pp. 37-67). Greenwich, CT: JAI Press.

Cutrona, C. E., & Russell, D. (1990). Type of social support and specific stress: Toward a theory of optimal matching. In B. R. Sarason, I. G. Sarason, & G. R. Pierce (Eds.), *Social support: An interactional view* (pp. 319-366). New York: John Wiley.

Gable, S., Belsky, J., & Crnic, K. (1992). Marriage, parenting, and child development. *Journal of Family Psychology, 5,* 276-294.

Henderson, S., Duncan-Jones, P., Byrne, D. G., & Scott, R. (1980). Measuring social relationships: The Interview Schedule for Social Interactions. *Psychological Medicine, 10,* 723-734.

Hirsch, B. (1979). Psychological dimensions of social networks: A multimethod analysis. *American Journal of Community Psychology, 7,* 263-277.

House, J. S., Landis, K. R., & Umberson, D. (1988). Social relationships and health. *Science, 241,* 540-545.

Parker, G., Tupling, H., & Brown, L. B. (1979). A parental bonding instrument. *British Journal of Medical Psychology, 52,* 1-10.

Pierce, G. R., Sarason, I. G., & Sarason, B. R. (1990). Integrating social support perspectives: Working models, personal relationships, and situational factors. In S. Duck (Ed., with R. C. Silver), *Personal relationships and social support* (pp. 173-189). Newbury Park, CA: Sage.

Pierce, G. R., Sarason, I. G., & Sarason, B. R. (1991a). General and relationship-based perceptions of social support: Are two constructs better than one? *Journal of Personality and Social Psychology, 61,* 1028-1039.

Pierce, G. R., Sarason, B. R., & Sarason, I. G. (1991b). General and specific support expectations and stress as predictors of perceived supportiveness: An experimental study. *Journal of Personality and Social Psychology, 63,* 297-307.

Pierce, G. R., Sarason, B. R., & Sarason, I. G. (1992). General and specific support expectations and stress as predictors of perceived supportiveness: An experimental study. *Journal of Personality and Social Psychology, 63,* 297-307.

Pierce, G. R., Sarason, B. R., Sarason, I. G., & Gilmore, K. (1992). *Perceived and objective reality in marital interactions.* Unpublished manuscript, Hamilton College, Clinton, NY.

Pierce, G. R., Sarason, I. G., Sarason, B. R., Solky, J. A., & Nagle, L. C. (1992). *Assessing the interpersonal context of social support: The Quality of Relationships Inventory.* Manuscript submitted for publication.

Pierce, G. R., & Williams, G. E. (1993). *Predicting potential recipients' support seeking preferences from family members and friends.* Unpublished manuscript.

Procidano, M. E., & Heller, K. (1983). Measures of perceived social support from family and friends: Three validation studies. *American Journal of Community Psychology, 11,* 1-24.

Rundall, T., & Evashwich, C. (1982). Social networks and help-seeking among the elderly. *Research on Aging, 4,* 205-226.

Sarason, B. R., Pierce, G. R., & Sarason, I. G. (1992). *Personality, relationship, and task-related factors in parent-child interactions: Two observational studies.* Manuscript submitted for publication.

Sarason, B. R., Sarason, I. G., & Pierce, G. R. (1990a). *Social support: An interactional view.* New York: John Wiley.

Sarason, B. R., Sarason, I. G., & Pierce, G. R. (1990b). Traditional views of social support and their impact on assessment. In B. R. Sarason, I. G. Sarason, & G. R. Pierce (Eds.), *Social support: An interactional view* (pp. 9-25). New York: John Wiley.

Sarason, I. G., Levine, H. M., Basham, R. B., & Sarason, B. R. (1983). Assessing social support: The Social Support Questionnaire. *Journal of Personality and Social Psychology, 44,* 127-139.

Sarason, I. G., Pierce, G. R., & Sarason, B. R. (1990). Social support and interactional processes: A triadic hypothesis. *Journal of Social and Personal Relationships, 7,* 495-506.

Sarason, I. G., Sarason, B. R., & Pierce, G. R. (1992). Relationship specific social support. In T. Albrecht, I. G. Sarason, & B. Burleson (Eds.), *Supportive Interactions: Symbolic discourse and relationships.* Newbury Park, CA: Sage.

Sarason, I. G., Sarason, B. R., & Shearin, E. N. (1986). Social support as an individual difference variable: Its stability, origins, and relational aspects. *Journal of Personality and Social Psychology, 50,* 845-855.

Sarason, I. G., Sarason, B. R., Shearin, E. N., & Pierce, G. R. (1987). A brief measure of social support: Practical and theoretical implications. *Journal of Social and Personal Relationships, 4,* 497-510.

Spanier, G. B. (1976). Measuring dyadic adjustment: New scales for assessing the quality of marriage and similar dyads. *Journal of Marriage and the Family, 38,* 15-28.

Stokes, J. P. (1985). The relation of social network and individual difference variables to loneliness. *Journal of Personality and Social Psychology, 48,* 981-990.

Vaux, A., & Harrison, D. (1985). Support network characteristics associated with support satisfaction and perceived support. *American Journal of Community Psychology, 13,* 245-267.

Appendix 13.1

Quality of Relationships Inventory

Please use the scale below to answer the following questions regarding your relationship with _____.

1	2	3	4
Not at all	A little	Quite a bit	Very Much

1.[a]	To what extent could you turn to this person for advice about problems?	1 2 3 4
2.[b]	How often do you need to work hard to avoid conflict with this person?	1 2 3 4
3.[a]	To what extent could you count on this person for help with a problem?	1 2 3 4
4.[b]	How upset does this person sometimes make you feel?	1 2 3 4
5.[a]	To what extent can you count on this person to give you honest feedback, even if you might not want to hear it?	1 2 3 4
6.[b]	How much does this person make you feel guilty?	1 2 3 4
7.[b]	How much do you have to "give in" in this relationship?	1 2 3 4
8.[a]	To what extent can you count on this person to help you if a family member very close to you died?	1 2 3 4
9.[b]	How much does this person want you to change?	1 2 3 4
10.[c]	How positive a role does this person play in your life?	1 2 3 4

11.[c]	How significant is this relationship in your life?	1 2 2 4
12.[c]	How close will your relationship be with this person in 10 years?	1 2 3 4
13.[c]	How much would you miss this person if the two of you could not see or talk with each other for a month?	1 2 3 4
14.[b]	How critical of you is this person?	1 2 3 4
15.[a]	If you wanted to go out and do something this evening, how confident are you that this person would be willing to do something with you?	1 2 3 4
16.[c]	How responsible do you feel for this person's well-being?	1 2 3 4
17.[c]	How much do you depend on this person?	1 2 3 4
18.[a]	To what extent can you count on this person to listen to you when you are very angry at someone else?	1 2 3 4
19.[b]	How much would you like this person to change?	1 2 3 4
20.[b]	How angry does this person make you feel?	1 2 3 4
21.[b]	How much do you argue with this person?	1 2 3 4
22.[a]	To what extent can you really count on this person to distract you from your worries when you feel under stress?	1 2 3 4
23.[b]	How often does this person make you feel angry?	1 2 3 4
24.[b]	How often does this person try to control or influence your life?	1 2 3 4
25.[b]	How much more do you give than you get from this relationship?	1 2 3 4

[a] Item included in the Support scale.
[b] Item included in the Conflict scale.
[c] Item included in the Depth scale.

Epilogue

Social Support and Community

A Historical Account
of the Rescue Networks in Denmark

TERRANCE L. ALBRECHT

While most of the rest of the world was a silent witness to the genocide of six million innocent people, the Danes not only protested verbally and in writing but at great personal risk rescued thousands of the condemned Jews. (Abrahamsen, 1972, p. 161)

Audacity springing from coolness and realistic imagination guided by alert observation—these were the hallmarks of the Danish underground fighters. . . . The professor and the fisherman, the doctor and the taxi driver, the priest and the policeman—all understood each other without as much as saying a word. (Leni Yahil in Meltzer, 1988, p. 100)

We often refer to social support as the acts of concerned kindness or the messages of reassurance that people communicate to one another in a few types of personal and social relationships. Indeed, most of the authors contributing to this book have focused on supportive messages and interactions occurring in ordinary contexts, primarily among married couples,

friends, and coworkers (see, for example chapters on supportive interactions in marriage by Cutrona & Suhr and Steinberg & Gottlieb, the
nature of supportive versus unsupportive friendships by Samter and
features of coworkers' supportive messages as described by Zimmerman
& Applegate). However, supportive behavior can also extend to include
the truly extraordinary, heroic deeds of helping, such as providing refuge
from harm or safe passage for those in danger. These acts may be performed on behalf of a wide range of others, from intimates to strangers.
We are better able to define the quality of *community* when we talk about
the spontaneous help mobilized by close and distant ties (especially under
conditions of personal threat for doing so), as well as the supportive
messages communicated among friends and family through the more
routine ups and downs of life.

In this Epilogue I build on the previous sections of this book to describe
how the basic elements of social support are situated in the larger relational structures that encompass people's lives. Supportive messages,
interactions and relationships are manifestations of the overarching community in which they are embedded. Hence an important question for
current research is to explore how a community shapes, sustains, and
values supportive messages, interactions and relationships. An equally
important question is how supportive communication becomes, in turn, a
relational process that represents, enacts, and reinforces the values and
structures of the larger culture.

A central argument in this chapter is for the inclusion of historical, as
well as contemporary, data in the analysis of community support processes. Observations of historical events are useful for tempering current
perspectives on the characteristics of supportive networks and for developing explanations for the success of large scale support initiatives.
Tracing historical accounts of cultural patterns of behavior can provide
the basis for comparing generally nonsupportive communities (with dis-
cernible, large scale patterns of alienation, disinterest, and lawlessness)
to more supportive ones (with frequent, impromptu mobilization of aid to
persons in need). In short, juxtaposing such macro level comparisons of
intact historical case studies can unmask a unique and poignant understanding of the interplay between dense relational structures, the moral
imperative of social support, and cultural identity. Such comparisons
widen the boundaries of our knowledge about supportive communication,
promote understanding of supportive behavior as a cultural and systemic
phenomenon, and assist in framing the types of research questions that
should be addressed in the next generation of studies.

Support Networks and Community

It is at the level of community that supportive messages, interactions and relationships are woven into a constellation that forms the fabric of a society. For example, comforting messages (as elucidated by Burleson) are interpreted and perceived within different types of relationships with varied cognitive and behavioral patterns (see Sarason, Sarason & Pierce in this volume). The range of interpersonal contexts for supportive processes forms an aggregate level for the overall experience of social support in life.

Support in community is, in part, a function of a shared moral code, reinforced by networks of interaction and mutual influence. Just as we have delineated the empirical features of supportive versus unsupportive messages, interactions and relationships earlier in this volume, we can expand the unit of analysis of support to include variances in the moral codes that make some communities more supportive than others. Understanding the structural and communicative features of supportive relational networks is a first step toward explaining how people are able to coordinate their noble and heroic acts when undertaking social support on a large scale. We begin to ask such questions as: Who are the people who willingly risk their lives to befriend and help familiar and unfamiliar others? What are the conditions that facilitate major mobilization efforts of help and assistance? What motivates people to support friends, acquaintances, and even strangers, at great potential cost to themselves and their families?

The distribution of supportive ties and behavior throughout a network (defined as sets of overlapping dyadic linkages, see Albrecht & Adelman, 1987) influences the ways that the social architecture of life is qualitatively experienced and interpreted by community members. The perceived distribution of support can have a motivating effect necessary to prompt individuals to support others. It is also a lens through which people may interpret a sense of caring in others' actions toward them. The relative distribution of moral behavior throughout the network forms a holistic "stratosphere" of support, diminishing perceptions of loneliness, anomie, and alienation (Albrecht & Adelman, 1987; Warren, 1982). Equally important, supportive links among strong and weak ties can establish powerful relational systems. These are nonsummative in nature, fostering the requisite momentum to spur individuals and groups to prosocial behavior, even in the face of personal danger (illustrated in the case of the rescue networks in Denmark, described later in this chapter).

Individuals and dyads do not exist in a vacuum in a community; they are inextricably tied through their overlapping connections to the larger social order. Network structures are outcomes of micro level "structuring" or interactive behaviors occurring in each dyadic relationship (Mehan, 1978). Community networks are iconic representations of the array of micro, repetitive interactions that occur among family members, friends, neighbors, acquaintances, and strangers. Communication networks are not based on the simple aggregation of dyadic relationships; rather, they are relatively integrated social webs characterized by *density*, or the degree of interconnection among a set of ties (computed as the ratio of actual relationship ties to theoretically possible relationship ties in the system). The network system, or analogously, the web of ties, enmesh individuals in relational spheres that can have helpful and harmful effects (Evans, Palsane, Lepore, & Martin, 1989; Garrison, 1978; Hoffman, 1975; Mitchell & Hodson, 1983).

The structural property of density is the reason that the larger network system can influence the internal dynamics of embedded relationships (Albrecht, in press; Parks, Stan & Eggert, 1983; Ridley & Avery, 1979). The data from community populations that have been studied the past fifteen years tell a story of the positive and negative outcomes of high interconnection among strong and weak ties (Albrecht & Adelman, 1987; Adelman, Parks, & Albrecht, 1987). The results of these studies have implications for understanding the motivations and behaviors of community members who help during crisis situations. The basic finding has been that individuals in low dense, heterogeneous network structures generally fare better on a variety of social-psychological indicators than those who do not (e.g., Evans et al., 1989). Network structures of relatively lower density are helpful to individuals for facilitating coping with stress and role transition, increasing perceived personal control, and opening up information paths for obtaining needed health and welfare referrals (e.g., Hirsch, 1980; Horowitz, 1977; McKinlay, 1973; McLanahan, Wedemyer, & Adelberg, 1981). Greater density in networks is helpful for reinforcing a sense of positive social identity, belongingness, and for obtaining tangible services (Hamburg & Killilea, 1979; Hammer, 1983).

Closely knit ties can be helpful without necessarily stunting one's needs for growth and new information. Integrated ties can offset feelings of anomie, especially in populations where lifestyles are mobile and temporary (see Parks, 1977). Dense ties also promote the psychological adjustment of those in post-trauma conditions (see Kadushin, 1982, for a discussion of the benefits of social density for the mental health of returning Vietnam combat veterans). Denser ties facilitate coping with particular types of job stress, including the uncertainty experienced from organizational change or human service work conducted in the field, outside normal organizational boundaries (see Albrecht, Irey, & Mundy, 1982; Ray, 1987; Szilagyi & Holland, 1980). Finally, networks of dense ties are more efficient for assimilating newcomers into formal organizations, by meeting their needs for information earlier in the entry process and reducing generalized uncertainty (Wilson, 1986).

In sum, observable, structural properties of community networks have been found to covary with an array of social and behavioral outcomes. These contemporary findings will be contrasted in the next section with the historical case study of prosocial behavior in Denmark.

Support and Rescue in Denmark

This Epilogue is an opportunity to affirm the import of historical data for building macro theories to drive contemporary studies of supportive communication. Historical accounts provoke questions about accepted explanations for what constitutes functional social structures (explanations often based exclusively on contemporary data). Studying a historical case is useful for analyzing retrospectively why people risk their lives to help those in distress (Paldiel, 1988) and how people coordinate their actions to accomplish tasks effectively and efficiently.

Appreciation of historical events of support or nonsupport can help us better understand current community initiatives to aid vulnerable, disenfranchised groups. Conclusions based on previous experiences are also relevant to developing macro-communication theories of socio-cultural exigencies. We can begin informed speculation on how communication patterns function to motivate collective action and protect the larger community from external threat.

THE DANISH RESCUE EFFORT

The story of the resistance movement in Denmark during World War II is a prototypical example of the powerful intersection of heroic organizing activity, social structure, and the patterns of communication that reinforce sustained acts of communal morality. Unlike most of Europe, Denmark (and Norway) provided unparalleled protection of the Jewish population during the period of Nazi oppression. The people who formed rescue networks in Denmark saved approximately 8,000 Jews from deportation to the death camps or the concentration camp at Theresienstadt (Petrow, 1974) during the Nazi occupation. While other resistance movements existed in countries such as Poland and France (notably the efforts led by Magda and Andre Trocme in the French village of Le Chambon, see Hallie, 1979), it was the widespread and fervently nationalistic resistance work of the Danes that distinguished their collective heroism and the magnitude of success of their efforts (Petrow, 1974).

Precipitating Events

On April 9, 1940, the Nazis invaded Denmark. According to Carr (1984), most Danes viewed passive resistance as their most realistic response to the Nazi occupation, given their extreme military disadvantage against the strength of the German *Wehrmacht*. Written accounts of what occurred in Denmark vary. The following is taken from the detailed description in Carr (1984, pp. 67-70).

The Nazi roundup of Danish Jews was planned to occur during one night, October 1-2, 1943. The Nazis arranged that 2,000 Jews in the interior regions of Denmark would be transported out of the country by train, and the 4,000 Jews living in Copenhagen would be sent to the concentration camps by ship. Georg Ferdinand Duckwitz was the shipping attache for the Nazis, a man who had served in the Danish capital since 1928 (Hilberg, 1985). Dr. Werner Best, the German envoy in Copenhagen, apparently informed Duckwitz of his October plan on September 11, 1943, and ordered him to estimate the shipping needs for the deportation operation (Carr, 1984). On September 25, Duckwitz flew to Stockholm, Sweden, to ask Swedish officials if they would take Jewish refugees in the future. The Swedes agreed to accept 8,000 Jews. Duckwitz also went to the headquarters of the Social Democratic Party at 22 Roemer Street in Copenhagen and informed the leader, Hans Hedtoft, that the deportation would begin in 24 hours. Hedtoft then contacted and tried to warn C. B. Henriques, the head of the Jewish community in Copenhagen. However, apparently Henriques did not believe the deportation would occur. Rabbi Marchus Melchior, the Chief Rabbinate of Copenhagen, warned his congregation assembled for Rosh Hashana services on the morning of September 29 that they should immediately go into hiding. (Friedman, 1978, reported that a relatively small number of Jews attended the services so few were apprised of the plan at that time.) This information spread among the Jews primarily through face to face contact, given that radio broadcasts were unavailable and use of telephones was dangerous.

The intended scale of the raid on October 1, 1943 generally failed. The Nazis found 202 Jews the first day and by November 1 the total was 472 (see Carr, 1984). While some have speculated that the worsening war situation in late 1943 was one reason that fewer German troops were sent for the roundup (Oliner & Oliner, 1988), the rescue was an undeniably heroic orchestration of courageous support and the only one of such proportions that occurred in Europe.

Anecdotal examples of support chronicled in the literature include the following:

• Rabbi Melchior called a Lutheran pastor, Hans Gildeby, who lived in Oerslev (60 miles from Copenhagen). Melchior asked him to take two of his children into hiding; Gildeby, however, insisted on sheltering the entire family. Melchior arranged with another pastor to hide the scriptures and other sacred objects from the synagogue. (Carr, 1984; Friedman, 1978)

• Ambulance driver Jorgen Knudsen had a reaction "typical" of other Danes. Because he was not personally acquainted with any Jews, his response was to find a phone booth and circle Jewish names in the phone directory. He began calling to warn each one, finding several frantic Jewish citizens without hiding places. He drove to their homes, picked them up in his "ambulance" and took them to Bispebjerg Hospital where he knew that Dr. K. H. Koester would hide them under assumed names as patients. (Carr, 1984, pp. 69-70)

• In hospitals all over Denmark, Jewish patients "recovered," and were discharged, only to be immediately readmitted under Gentile names. (Carr, 1984, p. 70)

• On October 2, 1943, the faculty and students at the University Copenhagen canceled all class meetings, "in view of the disasters which have overtaken our fellow citizens." (Abrahamsen, 1972, p. 160)

• German gunboats were stationed all along the water route yet the majority of Jews escaped in small groups in precarious fishing boats by sea (Friedman, 1978, p. 153). However, Denmark's relative proximity to Sweden increased the likelihood that those Jews who fled by boat across the sea would reach safety. (Baron, 1985/1986; Yahil, 1969)

Reasons For Rescue And Support

A conclusion from the review of the highly dispersed accounts (often in source material of limited accessibility) is that at least two structural and processural communicative factors contributed to the success of the Danish rescue: relational density and the fervency of a shared cultural and moral code.

The Jewish population had been well integrated into the national community (Mason, 1984) and hence were connected into dense relational networks with the general citizenry. The Jews were "completely integrated into the life of the country, having been granted full rights of citizenship in 1814" (Friedman, 1978, p. 149). F. Christmas Moller, former Minister of Industry in Denmark and Chairman, Danish Council of Great Britain, writing in 1943, noted:

> In democratic Denmark there has never been a Jewish question . . . in spheres of politics, science and commerce, Danish Jews, of whom in fact there were not very many, have done great work, which has been regarded primarily as the achievement of loyal Danish citizens. One of the most firmly embedded traits in Danish national character is that of treating all fellow-beings equally, the judgment of the next man being based entirely on his personal character and his worth as a human being. (1943, p. 1)

The successful rescue was partially due to the Jews' "high level of assimilation and to close personal ties with Danish gentiles" (Oliner & Oliner, 1988; p. 17). Ethnic prejudice is usually a "group attitude" shared by members of a well connected social group who castigate the characteristics of an out group (van Dijk, 1987). There were few such distinctions among the Danes. The close social and personal relationships among neighbors and friends predisposed Danish bystanders to actively assist their Jewish neighbors and friends who were threatened (as opposed to most Europeans who remained either inactive bystanders or became Nazi collaborators, Mason, 1984; Oliner, 1984). Interaction with Jews in childhood also led to significant differences between those who helped and supported and those who did not (Grossman, 1984), presumably because early contact minimizes the development of prejudice.

In addition, central concepts in the moral code shared by the Danes reflected a sense of equality, honor and the impetus for helping others. As Abrahamsen (1972) described:

> This nation had developed over the centuries what the Danes call "livskunst," i.e., the art of living, a society where people cared about one

another, where respect for individual and religious differences, self-reliance, cooperation, and good humor had become hallmarks of a civilized nation. These moral, intellectual, and ethical attitudes made the Danes say: "the Jews are our fellow-citizens and fellow-human beings; we shall not give them up for slaughter." And they did not. That's why the Danes became the real victors in Europe. They did not lose their souls. (pp. 161-162)

Such moral codes reinforced cognitive and behavioral patterns that reflected community values and loyalty that was fiercely anti-Nazi. The underground press that existed for 3 years of the occupation prior to the deportation plan was one significant way the code was integrated into the network of the resistance.

THE MOUNTAIN PEOPLE

The supportive actions of the Danes stand in stark contrast to the nonsupportive actions of citizens in other countries in Europe and indeed other societies. The integrated networks and values of the Danes is quite different from the description of the Ik, a group of African tribespeople, given by anthropologist Colin Turnbull (1972). "Loveless," "hostile" and "dehumanized," when Turnbull observed them, the Ik were a once prosperous people whose social structure had deteriorated to scattered bands of isolated families. Each family was internally disconnected also, with members showing little respect or care for one another's needs and exploiting the old and the young. The culture of the Ik, unlike the culture of the Danes, was destined to succumb to entropy given the only thread of connection among the Ik was self-interest. They were, in Turnbull's terms, a society of "individuals," and thus highly distrustful and devious toward members of their own group. He noted that the language of the Ik retained vestiges of terms reflecting goodness toward others, terms communicated in previous generations but infrequently invoked at the time of his observation and fieldwork.

Lessons and Perspectives

Support giving must begin to be studied not only as random, limited acts (e.g., observed on a short term basis among a few individuals [such as the hospice workers observed by Zimmerman & Applegate] or manipulated under experimental conditions [as achieved by Tardy]), but approached more globally and systematically as behavior that is best understood against a cultural tapestry. Supportive interactions may occur as relatively isolated acts of kindness or caring, but they are also often linked to larger community and cultural variations reflected in network patterns, language and morality.

Previous theoretical work has identified the central functions of social support as facilitating personal control and uncertainty reduction (Albrecht, Adelman, & Associates, 1987). This framework, based on cross sectional data and the observation of micro level relational patterns, has been limited and incomplete. History pushes us further to engage multiple levels of analysis in our explanation of supportive acts. One conclusion that might be drawn from the brief historical analysis presented here is that macro structures of highly integrated individuals are more likely to help. This may be based on the expediency with which support can be mobilized. In short, studies of social support need to look at messages and interactions cast against the larger system. A macro view gives a background understanding of the activity that sets initial conditions for the impulse to support, the social costs of support, and the social costs of nonsupportive behavior and relationships.

We also see the historic and heroic actions of the Danes differently cast against the present evolution of theories of social support. The "heroism" of the Danes as members of a large and integrated community can be deconstructed and reinterpreted through the interplay of communication structure, cultural codes and cognition. This is relevant to the developing empirical link between sociative structures and patterns of thought (Albrecht, in press). Contemporary research relevant to explaining what happened in Denmark has shown that prosocial moral reasoning is linked to political attitudes (Eisenberg-Berg, 1976). These are attitudes tied to social structures in which systems of discourse reflect and reinforce how people think about morality and how they then judge their experiences as calls for moral action.

Undertaking a cultural-historical analysis of support involves a triangulation of archival, testimonial and interview data, assembled to represent the network structures and values of the particular system in question. A retrospective investigation, such as my own undertaking of the experience in Denmark, can have the following characteristics:

• A thick description of the system by triangulating archival and oral testimonies of first person accounts as well as second generation interviews to recreate a network structure.

- Reciprocated ties (independent corroboration of links among people). Oliner and Oliner (1988) wrote that the successful rescue was partially due to the high level of connection and the close personal relationships that Danish Jews had with Danish Gentiles. Had Jews previously helped the Gentiles before the invasion? Was there a history of reciprocated helping among Jews and Gentiles in the cities and rural communities? On the basis of contemporary network findings, the key research question is: Are threat and risk best tolerated in strong, multiplex, dense, reciprocated network ties?

- Documentation of evidence is needed to support the claim that moral behavior was the negentropic force in the otherwise dense system—that the moral imperative of support was acted out because of the dense relationships reinforced by a language code (e.g., *livskunst*). The central hypothesis is that macro structures of highly integrated individuals are more likely to spawn instances of coordinated help giving—because of the expediency with which support can be mobilized. The central question to ask throughout the analysis is: What are the determinants of a collective mind such that individuals are willing to act independently and in concert together, knowing that the risk of social action can yield righteous outcomes?

In sum, the prototype of Denmark, and in contrast, the Ik, is a basis for how we think about the moral imperative of supportive communication networks in contemporary communities. The archival and testimonial data of historical events is evidence for the central role of communication in the practice of supporting and helping others and shapes a future agenda for groundbreaking conceptual work.

References

Abrahamsen, S. (1972). The rescue of Denmark's Jews. *American-Scandinavian Review, 60,* 157-164.

Adelman, M. B., Parks, M. R., & Albrecht, T. L. (1987). Beyond close relationships: Support in weak ties. In T. L. Albrecht, M. B. Adelman, & Associates, *Communicating social support* (pp. 126-147). Newbury Park, CA: Sage.

Albrecht, T. L. (in press). Patterns of sociation and cognitive structure. In G. Philipsen & T. Albrecht (Eds.), *Contemporary communication theory.* Albany, NY: SUNY Albany Press.

Albrecht, T. L, & Adelman, M. B. (1987). Communication networks as structures of social support. In T. L. Albrecht, M. B. Adelman, & Associates, *Communicating social support* (pp. 40-63). Newbury Park, CA: Sage.

Albrecht, T. L., Adelman, M. B., & Associates (1987). *Communicating social support.* Newbury Park, CA: Sage.

Albrecht, T. L., Irey, K. V., & Mundy, A. (1982). Integration in a communication network as a mediator of stress. *Social Work, 27,* 229-234.

Baron, L. (1985/1986). The Holocaust and human decency: A review of research on the rescue of Jews in Nazi occupied Europe. *Humboldt Journal of Social Relations, 13,* 237-251.

Carr, J. J. (1984). *Christian heroes of the Holocaust: The righteous Gentiles.* South Plainfield, NJ: Bridge Publishing.

Eisenberg-Berg, N. (1976). The relation of political attitudes to constraint-oriented and prosocial moral reasoning. *Developmental Psychology, 12,* 552-553.

Evans, G. W., Palsane, M. N., Lepore, S. J., & Martin, J. (1989). Residential density and psychological health: The mediating effects of social support. *Journal of Personality and Social Psychology, 57,* 994-999.

Friedman, P. (1978). *Their brothers' keepers.* New York: Holocaust Library.

Garrison, V. (1978). Support systems of schizophrenic and nonschizophrenic Puerto Rican migrant women in New York City. *Schizophrenia Bulletin, 4,* 561-596.

Grossman, F. G. (1984). A psychological study of Gentiles who saved the lives of Jews during the Holocaust. In I. W. Charny (Ed.), *Toward the understanding and prevention of genocide: Proceedings of the International Conference on the Holocaust and Genocide* (pp. 202-216). Boulder, CO: Westview Press.

Hallie, P. P. (1979). *Lest innocent blood be shed: The story of the village of Le Chambon and how goodness happened there.* New York: Harper & Row.

Hamburg, B. A., & Killilea, M. (1979). Relation of social support, stress, illness and use of health services. *In healthy people: The Surgeon General's report on health promotion and disease prevention.* Washington, DC: U. S. Department of Health, Education and Welfare, Public Health Service.

Hammer, M. (1983). "Core" and "extended" social networks in relation to health and illness. *Social Science and Medicine, 17,* 405-414.

Hilberg, R. (1985). *The destruction of the European Jews.* New York: Holmes & Meier.

Hirsch, B. J. (1980). Natural support systems and coping with major life changes. *American Journal of Community Psychology, 8,* 159-172.

Hoffman, L. (1975). "Enmeshment" and the too richly cross-joined system. *Family Process, 14,* 457-468.

Horowitz, A. (1977). Social networks and pathways to psychiatric treatment. *Social Forces, 56,* 86-105.

Kadushin, C. (1982). Social density and mental health. In P. V. Marsden & N. Lin (Eds.), *Social structure and network analysis* (pp. 147-158). Beverly Hills, CA: Sage.

Mason, H. L. (1984). Testing human bonds within nations: Jews in the occupied Netherlands. *Political Science Quarterly, 99,* 315-343.

McKinlay, J. B. (1973). Social networks, lay consultation and help seeking behavior. *Social Forces, 51,* 275-292.

McLanahan, S. S., Wedemyer, N. V., & Adelberg, T. (1981). Network structure, social support, and psychological well being in the single parent family. *Journal of Marriage and the Family, 43,* 601-612.

Mehan, H. (1978). Structuring school structure. *Harvard Educational Review,* 48, 32-64.

Meltzer, M. (1988). *Rescue: The story of how Gentiles saved Jews in the Holocaust.* New York: Harper Trophy.

Mitchell, R. E., & Hodson, C. A. (1983). Coping with domestic violence: Social support and psychological health among battered women. *American Journal of Community Psychology, 11*, 629-654.

Moller, F. C. (1943, November). The Jews in Denmark. *The Jewish Bulletin, 27*, 1-2.

Oliner, S. P. (1984). The unsung heroes in Nazi occupied Europe: The antidote for evil. *Nationalities Papers, 12*, 129-136.

Oliner, S. P., & Oliner, P. M. (1988). *The altruistic personality.* New York: Free Press.

Paldiel, M. (1988). The altruism of the righteous Gentiles. *Holocaust and Genocide Studies, 3*, 187-196.

Parks, M. R. (1977). Anomia and close friendship communication networks. *Human Communication Research, 4*, 48-57.

Parks, M. R., Stan, C. M., & Eggert, L. L. (1983). Romantic involvement and social network involvement. *Social Psychology Quarterly, 46*, 116-131.

Petrow, R. (1974). *The bitter years: The invasion and occupation of Denmark and Norway April 1940 - May 1945.* New York: William Morrow.

Ray, E. B. (1987). Supportive relationships and occupational stress in the workplace. In T. Albrecht, M. Adelman & Associates, *Communicating social support* (pp. 172-191). Newbury Park, CA: Sage.

Ridley, C. A., & Avery, A. W. (1979). Social network influence on the dyadic relationship. In R. L. Burgess & T. L. Huston (Eds.), *Social exchange in developing relationships* (pp. 223-246). New York: Academic Press.

Szilagy, A. D., & Holland, W. E. (1980). Changes in social density: Relationships with functional interaction and perceptions of job characteristics, role stress and work satisfaction. *Journal of Applied Psychology, 65*, 28-33.

Turnbull, C. M. (1972). *The mountain people.* New York: Simon & Schuster.

van Dijk, T. A. (1987). *Communicating racism: Ethnic prejudice in thought and talk.* Newbury Park, CA: Sage.

Warren, D. I. (1982). Using helping networks: A key social bond of urbanites. In D. Biegel & A. J. Naparstek (Eds.), *Community support systems and mental health* (pp. 5-20). New York: Springer.

Wilson, C. E. (1986). *The influence of communication network involvement on socialization in organizations.* Unpublished doctoral dissertation, University of Washington, Seattle.

Yahil, L. (1969). *Rescue of the Danish Jewry: Test of a democracy.* Philadelphia, PA: Jewish Publication Society.

Index

About the Authors

Terrance L. Albrecht is Professor and Chairperson of the Department of Communication, and Professor of Management, University of South Florida. She holds a PhD and MA in Human Communication and a master's degree in Labor and Industrial Relations (Michigan State University). Author of more than 60 publications, research reports, and convention papers, she is senior author of the book, *Communicating Social Support* (with M. Adelman and Associates, Sage, 1987), and was senior editor of the special issue of *Communication Research* on communication and social support (April, 1992, Vol. 19) on which this book is based. She is currently writing a forthcoming text, *Communication in Organizations: A Relational Perspective* (with B. Bach) and co-editing *Developing Theories of Communication* (with G. Philipsen). She has conducted and supervised field research projects on communication networks, social support, and innovation processes in 30 organizations across the country.

James L. Applegate is Chair and Professor in the Department of Communication at the University of Kentucky. He was a University Fellow and received his doctorate from the University of Illinois in 1978. His doctoral dissertation examining reasons for differences in the communication abilities of children and adults received the Golden Anniversary Award from the Speech Communication Association of America as one of the three outstanding communication dissertation completed in America that year.

Since coming to the University of Kentucky, he has authored more than 50 articles, book chapters, and research reports examining factors affecting individual development of communication ability with special emphasis on social cognitive and cultural antecedents. He has been invited to present his research at national and international meetings throughout the United States and in England, Canada, and Mexico. He co-edited the book *Communication by Children and Adults* and is currently writing another book examining current research on communication competence. Applegate recently served as President of the Southern States Communication Association. He has chaired his research division in the Speech Communication Association and serves on the editorial boards of a number of journals, including the *Quarterly Journal of Speech*, *Southern Communication Journal*, and the *International Journal of Personal Construct Psychology*.

Anita P. Barbee received the 1989 International Network on Personal Relationships Dissertation Award for her experimental studies on interactive coping processes in close relationships. Trained as a social psychologist at the University of Georgia, she is now a Research Scientist conducting training evaluation and assessment research in the area of child and family welfare. Her affiliation is with the Kent School of Social Work at the University of Louisville in Kentucky. She continues to publish in the areas of social support, personal relationships, and the effects of gender on perceptions of attractiveness in collaboration with Michael R. Cunningham. Barbee is on the editorial boards of the *Journal of Social and Personal Relationships*, *Motivation and Emotion*, and *Journal of Social Behavior and Personality*.

Melanie K. Barnes is a doctoral candidate in the Department of Communication Studies at the University of Iowa. Her primary research interests concern how communication constructs and creates meaning systems for individuals in relationships, and she has been conducting a research program regarding how individuals convey social support during both routine and crisis situations. She has examined the role of confiding during grief and loss experiences, and is co-author of a chapter entitled "Held Captive by Their Memories" (in press), which examines individuals' reluctance to accept the ending of close personal relationships. She has also published in the areas of interpersonal attraction and social perception. Barnes received an MS in Speech Communication and a BS in Mass Communication at Illinois State University.

Brant R. Burleson is a Professor in the Department of Communication, Purdue University, West Lafayette, Indiana. He received his PhD from the University of Illinois at Urbana-Champaign in 1982. His research interests center on functional communication skills, especially prosocial communication skills such as comforting, and ways in which these skills facilitate interpersonal relationships. He has conducted studies of communication skill development during childhood and adolescence, the contributions of social-cognitive and personality factors to the development and use of communication skills, the effects of parental communication practices on skill development by children, and the effects of different communication skills on social relationships. His recent research has focused on how interpersonal skills contribute to the initiation and maintenance of intimate relationships, especially how similarities in people's communication skills affect interpersonal attraction and relationship development. His research has appeared in several edited volumes and journals. He currently is editor for *Communication Yearbook*, a Sage publication sponsored by the International Communication Association.

Carolyn E. Cutrona is a Professor of Psychology at Iowa State University in Ames, Iowa, where she recently moved after 12 years at the University of Iowa. She splits her time between the Department of Psychology and the Center for Family Research in Rural Mental Health. She received her PhD in clinical psychology at UCLA in 1981. Her interests are in the areas of social support and depression. She has conducted research on the protective effects of social support against depression and on the protective effects of social support in a variety of stressed populations, including pregnant adolescents, caregivers of Alzheimer's patients, and spouses of cancer patients. She has published a number of papers and chapters on determinants of perceived social support, using a range of methods (daily diary, observation, informant reports). With Julie Suhr, she has developed an observational method for assessing social support behaviors in dyadic interactions. Her most recent work focuses on social support in the context of marriage, and she is in the process of writing a book on that topic. Cutrona is an Associate Editor for the *Journal of Personality and Social Psychology*.

Valerian J. Derlega is Professor of Psychology at Old Dominion University. His research interests include self-disclosure, personal relationships, sex roles, and the impact of the HIV diagnosis on social support. He is on the editorial boards for the *Journal of Social and Personal Relationships*,

Journal of Social and Clinical Psychology, and *Journal of Nonverbal Behavior.* He has co-edited *Self-Disclosure: Theory, Research, and Therapy* and *Personality: Contemporary Theory and Research* and recently co-authored two books, *Psychotherapy as a Personal Relationship* and *Self-Disclosure.*

Steve Duck is Daniel and Amy Starch Research Professor of Interpersonal Communication at the University of Iowa, holding appointments in the Department of Psychology and the Department of Communication Studies. He is also the founder and Editor of the *Journal of Social and Personal Relationships* and the founder of INPR (International Network on Personal Relationships), the professional society for the relationships field, which has more than 1,000 members. He has written or edited 27 books and numerous articles on relationships.

Patricia Geist received her PhD in Communication from Purdue University in 1985. She is an Associate Professor in the School of Communication at San Diego State University where she teaches organizational communication, health communication, and naturalistic research methods. Her research interests focus on negotiating ideology, control, and identity in organizations, predominantly in the health care professions. Her recent book, *Negotiating the Crisis: DRGs and the Transformation of Hospitals* (with Monica Hardesty), examines communication among nurses, physicians, and hospital administrators as they negotiate a controversial change in hospital policy and structure. Her work also appears in a variety of journals as well as in edited volumes.

Daena J. Goldsmith is Assistant Professor of Speech Communication at the University of Illinois, Urbana-Champaign. Her research on facework and supportive communication is part of a broader research program examining the influence of culture in interpersonal communication. She has contributed articles to *Communication Research, Communication Education,* and *Research on Language and Social Interaction.*

Benjamin H. Gottlieb is a Professor in the Department of Psychology at the University of Guelph and a Senior Research Fellow of the Ontario Mental Health Foundation. He has written extensively on the subject of social support, authoring *Social Support Strategies: Guidelines for Mental Health Practice.* He is presently conducting several studies that examine coping in the context of chronic stress, including a study of people providing care to a family member with dementia and employees who are trying to balance their work and family responsibilities.

Julie L. Gray is a Graduate Teaching Assistant and master's student in the School of Communication at San Diego State University, scheduled to complete her degree in 1994. Her research interests lie in the field of organizational communication, exploring diverse issues such as the organizational aspects of support groups, and organizational socialization. She has presented her work at the Western States Communication Association Convention in Albuquerque, New Mexico, as well as at the Speech Communication Association Conventions in 1992 and 1993. She has also co-authored (with Patricia Geist) a chapter on women's experiences with miscarriage to appear in the book *Women's Words, Woman's World*, edited by Linda Perry and Patricia Geist.

Sandra Metts received her PhD in Communication Research from the University of Iowa in 1983. She is a professor in the Department of Communication at Illinois State University where she teaches interpersonal communication, intercultural communication, language, and research methods. Her research interests focus on the management of problematic social and relational episodes including embarrassment, relationship disengagement, deception, relational transgressions, and sexual communication. Recent books include *Self-Disclosure* (with Val Derlega, Sandra Petronio, and Stephen Margulis) and *Facework* (with William Cupach). Her work also appears in a variety of journals as well as in edited volumes.

Katherine Miller is Associate Professor in the Department of Communication at Arizona State University. She received her PhD from the University of Southern California in 1985. Her research focuses on communication processes that cause burnout among human service workers and the communication processes that help human service workers cope with burnout. She is currently investigating communication and the provision of services among agencies working with the homeless and the development of empathy among medical students. She is the current editor of *Management Communication Quarterly*. Her research has been published in outlets including *Communication Monographs, Human Communication Research, Health Communication, Academy of Management Journal, Communication Research*, and *Journal of Applied Communication Research*.

Gregory R. Pierce is Assistant Professor of Psychology at Hamilton College. A graduate of the University of Washington (BS in Psychology; MS and PhD in Personality Psychology), he has published nearly two dozen papers on experimental, observational, and longitudinal studies of social support. His work concerns support and conflict in close relationships, especially within families, with research focusing on supportive processes in family and peer relationships in both laboratory and applied (e.g., athletic, academic) situations. He is actively involved in the development of assessment techniques to quantify the quality of family and peer relationships; in addition to the Quality of Relationships Inventory, he and his colleagues, Irwin and Barbara Sarason, have also developed the Parental Punishment Inventory and the Self-Concept Questionnaire. He is currently conducting the Hamilton Longitudinal Study of Families, an investigation of the role of family relationships in adolescent adjustment, and is a member of the Center for Cognitive Studies at Hamilton College.

Eileen Berlin Ray is Associate Professor in the Department of Communication at Cleveland State University. She received her PhD from the University of Washington in 1981. Her research focuses on examining the role of supportive communication as a mediator of job stress and burnout among human service workers. Her current work also includes investigating semantic networks and memorable supportive and unsupportive messages among survivors of sexual assault and assessing the efficacy of rape education programs on college campuses. She is the editor of *Case Studies in Health Communication* and co-editor of *Communication and Health: Systems and Applications*, has published in many outlets, and is the author of numerous book chapters. She serves on the editorial boards of *Human Communication Research*, *Communication Monographs*, *Management Communication Quarterly*, *Health Communication*, *Journal of Applied Communication Research*, and *Communication Studies*.

Wendy Samter is an Assistant Professor in the Department of Communication at the University of Delaware. She received her PhD from Purdue University. Her research has examined the communicative correlates of young adult friendship, qualitative feature of a lonely person's social network, and communication skill similarity as a predictor of close friendship. Her most recent work has appeared in *Communication Research*, *Communication Studies*, *Human Communication Research*, and *Southern Communication Journal*.

Barbara R. Sarason is Research Professor of Psychology at the University of Washington. She does research on the role of social support in social interaction, the support perceptions of family members, and cultural factors that influence these perceptions. Much of her research involves the study of social interaction under controlled conditions.

Irwin G. Sarason is Professor of Psychology at the University of Washington. His research concerns the assessment of social support, its correlates, and the role it plays in behavior. He is interested in social support as an element in stress coping and in personal development.

Marla Steinberg is a doctoral candidate in social psychology at York University in Toronto, Canada. The chapter in this book is based on her thesis research for the MA degree she received from the University of Guelph. Her main research interests concern the use of psychological knowledge in the public policy process, feminist research methods, and alternative epistemologies. Steinberg's dissertation extends her research in the work-family area. It is a phenomenological study of the meanings that work-family coping arrangements convey for personal and marital functioning.

Julie A. Suhr is currently a psychology intern in the Brown University Psychology Consortium. She is completing her PhD in Clinical Psychology at the University of Iowa in Iowa City. Her current research interests are in neuropsychology, particularly executive functioning and problem-solving deficits in psychiatric and neurological disorders. In collaboration with Carolyn Cutrona, she has published several papers in the area of social support.

Charles H. Tardy, a Professor of Speech Communication at the University of Southern Mississippi, obtained his PhD from the University of Iowa. His research on interpersonal communication focuses on social support, physiological responses to speech, and self-disclosure. He edited *A Handbook for the Study of Human Communication* and has published in *American Behavioral Scientist*, *Communication Monographs*, *Communication Research*, *Human Communication Research*, and other communication and social science journals.

Barbara A. Winstead is a Professor of Psychology at Old Dominion University. Her research interests include the characteristics of social interactions (e.g., friendship and gender composition of dyads) that alleviate stress and the influence of gender on clinical diagnoses and treatment. She is an advisory editor for *Contemporary Psychology*, and she has co-edited two books, *Friendship and Social Interaction* and *Personality: Contemporary Theory and Research*. She is also a co-author of the recently published book, *Psychotherapy as a Personal Relationship*.

Stephanie Zimmermann is Assistant Professor of Communication Studies at San Jose State University. She received her PhD from the University of Kentucky in 1989. Her research interests include social cognition and communication in interdisciplinary health care terms, storytelling in religious organizations, communication competence in the selection interview, and health care organizations' change and adaptation strategies. Her research has been published in *Journalism Quarterly*, *Communication Research*, and *Sociological Analysis*.